Saddle the Pale Horse

Saddle the Pale Horse

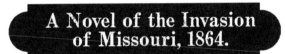

A Novel of the Invasion of Missouri, 1864.

With an extensive collection of photographs,
maps and the facts behind the story.

Darryl W. Levings

Kansas City Star Books
Kansas City, Missouri

Saddle the Pale Horse: A Novel of the Invasion of Missouri, 1864
by Darryl W. Levings
Designer: Kelly Ludwig

First edition, first printing
ISBN: 978-1-61169-019-4
Library of Congress Control Number: 2011938185

Published by Kansas City Star Books
1729 Grand Blvd.
Kansas City, Missouri, USA 64108
All rights reserved
Copyright © 2011 Darryl W. Levings

Printed in the United States of America by Walsworth Publishing Co.,
Marceline, MO

To order copies, call StarInfo at (816) 234-4636 and say "Operator" or order
online at www. TheKansasCityStore.com

Cover: Teenage guerrilla Riley Crawford of Missouri. Courtesy of the
collection of Emory A. Cantey, Jr., quantrillsguerrillas.com

Contents

Prologue

"And I looked, and behold a pale horse: and his name that sat on him was Death, and Hell followed with him."

— Revelation 6:8

ее∂е∂е∂е∂

THE TOMB OF ULYSSES S. GRANT in New York's Riverside Park focuses the gaze of the admirer, the tourist, the Civil War buff, the schoolchild upon the darkly gleaming sarcophagus of the long-dead hero.

Almost unnoticeable off in the corners are a pair of architectural afterthoughts, tiny rooms in which old flags, once proudly carried in battle, now sag from their staffs. Painted on the walls above are maps showing battlegrounds, many of them Grant's, others strode by other Union commanders. The map on the east side shows Chancellorsville, Cold Harbor and Appomattox. The map nearer the Hudson River on the west charts New Orleans, Shiloh and Vicksburg. All are pieces of our national DNA.

It is the second map, the western one, that suffers the grievous oversight.

The young artist Dean Fausett, put to work in 1937 by the Public Works Administration, lettered in a good share of lesser-known killing grounds on those maps. Inside the borders of Missouri his brush painted Wilson's Creek, Lexington, Carthage, New Madrid, Island 10, Belmont and Ironton. But look to where the Missouri River bends to the east, and it is blank. No words denote the Battle of Westport.

Ironton is there. The southeast town marked just the opening volleys of the Battle of Fort Davidson, one of the three major clashes of Major General Sterling Price's 1864 invasion and certainly the bloodiest day in Missouri history. But it's only there because Grant was there in 1861, on the day word came of his promotion to brigadier general. To the south in Tennessee and Mississippi, of course, the brush gets busier, but nothing past 1862 is painted on Missouri. Perhaps no one told Fausett about the four-day running fight that climaxed at Westport or about Mine Creek, the largest clash of cavalry west of the Mississippi, which followed 48 hours later in Kansas. But then, Fausett's map finds no room for that state at all.

Westport, the climactic day of the fight on the banks of the Blue River and Brush Creek, has been called the "Gettysburg of the West" by generations of historians in the Kansas City area. It was not. No chance of winning or losing the war or even forcing a settlement existed in the Trans-Mississippi after the surrender of Vicksburg. Missouri's star was sewn on the Confederate flag, but Union possession of the state had not been in doubt for two years. Gettysburg left more than 40,000 dead, wounded, missing or captured. At Westport, the toll was not a tenth of that.

But blood spilt is no true measure of struggle. The soldiers in the Missouri fight exhibited the same iron that clashed on the better-known fields. By the time the armies met on the bloody Sabbath of October 23, 1864, most Missourians and Kansans had been tempered by more than three years of fire. On either side of the Westport battle lines, in fact, were men so hard that today they would fit easily in the dock of a war crimes trial.

At the same time, thousands under the Union flag were untrained Kansas militiamen — escaped slaves among them — called out just weeks earlier to defend their homes. Thousands more were green southern boys who joined Major General Sterling Price and his Confederate force looking for adventure.

In the bickering ranks of generals were West Pointers, professional soldiers, but there were also lawyers, doctors, hatters and hemp-growers. Among the raiders were a couple of the South's most dashing cavaliers, saddled by a commander past his prime.

Muddy roads led them all to Westport, not Gettysburg. Surely Fausett, spreading his earthy colors in the quiet of the giant mausoleum in New York City, erred by omitting their place of destiny.

e/ɔe/ɔe/ɔe/ɔe/ɔ

Around 40,000 soldiers, militia, recruits and guerrillas were in the Kansas City region on October 22 and 23, 1864, easily making it the largest body *gathered* for battle west of the Mississippi. Two-thirds probably breathed burnt gunpowder in 10 hours of ferocious fighting on the second day.

This is not in the same league as the Army of the Potomac's struggles with the Army of Northern Virginia. The combatants at Westport, however, did outnumber those at this nation's earlier battles of New Orleans in 1815 or Saratoga in 1777. Compared with more modern times, about the same number of men, Japanese and American, faced each other on Guadalcanal in the first month of that struggle.

Best estimates of Sterling Price's three Confederate divisions number 12,000 as they neared the Kansas border. Price's so-called Army of Missouri had suffered in charging the heavy guns of Fort Davidson at Pilot Knob, but its losses had been far more than made up — in numbers, at least — by thousands of new recruits, mostly unarmed. The guerrilla band led by George Todd may have added a hundred more.

In his freshly coined Army of the Border, Union Major General Samuel Curtis commanded a mix of 3,000 seasoned cavalry and several thousand raw Kansas militia. Major General Alfred Pleasonton brought 4,000 more troopers to the fray. And always near was Major General A. J. "Whiskey" Smith's infantry of around 9,000.

How many paid the butcher's bill at Westport? The fatalities are only vaguely recorded, which perhaps contributes to the battle's junior status. Interestingly, the one-day affairs at Fort Davidson and Mine Creek, which acted as bookends for the Lexington-through-Westport fight, both generated better documented but perhaps smaller casualty lists.

When the curious of Westport and Kansas City wandered the battlefield in the aftermath, few bothered to count the dead. The best account we have is from a Dr. W. Booth Smith, who, according to the *Daily Times* of Leavenworth, arrived about two hours after the fight: "He thought he'd seen about 100 bodies, though no correct estimate could be formed, as they were strewn and scattered along the blood-stained track of the enemy's route and retreat, lay buried in hollows and ravines, or concealed in the brush and timber." His observation would not have included the row of dead cavalrymen at Byram's Ford on the Big Blue River that morning or the victims of the vicious Mockbee farm fight the day before. Nor would it have counted the casualties incurred in two different running fights through the Little Blue River on one side of Independence to the Blue River on the other.

In *Action Before Westport*, Howard Monnett estimated that 3,500 were killed or severely wounded over the three days of action through Jackson County. But Fred L. Lee, in his *Gettysburg of the West, the Battle of Westport,* puts the number much lower, around 800. Whatever the battlefield sums, later deaths from blood loss, infections and tetanus or pneumonia and dysentery certainly deepened the toll.

⋐⋑⋐⋑⋐⋑⋐⋑⋐⋑⋐⋑

Unlike on eastern battlefields, men who raised their hands in surrender in Missouri and Kansas often got a bullet in their heads in reply. This was war on the Border, all the way down to the knife, and, as they said then, a bit more to the hilt.

Before those terrible three days around Gettysburg, life in that Pennsylvania town was normal. What was too often the normal in the regions around Kansas City was this visit by Kansas troops to a farm south of Westport, as described by Margaret Hays:

"Their was 95 came to our house surrounded it. Demanded my husband. I told them I had not saw him but once in nearly two months (he had been at home a little while the day before and called a few moments that morning) They then gave me thirty minutes to take out what I wanted in the house. I went to carrying out things that I needed worse. Some of the men helped me and Mary as I was a little excited and not very well. They went to the barn which was a very large fine one and filled with oats, corn, hay, set it on fire. Then came and Set fire to the rest of my outhouses, even my new hen house as it was a very fine one.

"Then next the house. Ordered me to take my Children out of the house. I then beged them to spare my house for the Sake of my little Children as it was cold and I thought they had destroyed enough to be satisfied but all to no purpose. They went to the upper rooms. Set fire to ever corner, then set fire above and below on the portico and on the porch. I lost a great many things in the house, my beadsteads, one Bureau, some two or three carpets on the floors, my press with what dishes I had been using. I had all of my finest dishes burried. I never went to the Sellar to get anything out. They feared I would try to put out the fire and let the well buckets in the well, set the well house on fire. They left me with the little Children a setting by the few things left me. They took all my bead clothing and everthing else they could carry off…"

In the larger sense, the Battle of Westport, of Jackson County, of the Border, of all Missouri and eastern Kansas had been going on at least 1,289 days. Historians often note that Missouri provided the stage for 1,162 battles and skirmishes. Kansas was good for dozens more. A day's worth of blood in those fights at their worst would only make a drop at Antietam or Cold Harbor, yet on either side of the border it was a seemingly unending trickle, bleeding white thousands of square miles.

At Gettysburg, just one civilian was struck by a stray ball. In Missouri and Kansas, civilians very often *were* the targets. Death got delivered daily in small vicious drabs by killers wearing embroidered guerrilla shirts, but also Federal blue. Men were slain at their weddings, burned in their homes, executed in front of their children. The family horse trotted down the lane to the home place with an emptied saddle, and men caught out on the roads got their throats opened. Neutrality was not an option, and revenge and retribution always lurked in this dark corner of the war to restore our Union.

No one has summed it up better than Bowen Kerrihard: "The Civil War came early to Missouri and Kansas, stayed late, and was characterized at all times by unremitting and unparalleled brutality. More than anywhere else, it was truly a civil war."

The events in Charleston Harbor on April 12, 1861, in the vernacular of the time "opened the ball." If so, "Bloody Kansas" from 1854 to 1858 provided the warm-up act. The cross-border grudges left behind ripened into nearly indiscriminate killing.

Missouri's war was the most complex of the whole conflict. The countryside with its agrarian aristocracy contrasted with St. Louis, which had its industrial ties to the north and a large immigrant population. Although slavery was the taproot of the conflict, Missourians had fewer slaves per capita than any slave state except Delaware. Those in bondage were found in just about every county, but clustered largely in the counties along the big rivers, places dominated by landowners born in Virginia and Kentucky.

"In that day for a man to speak out openly and proclaim himself an enemy of Negro slavery was simply to proclaim himself a madman," Mark Twain would write. "For he was blaspheming against the holiest thing known to a Missourian, and could *not* be in his right mind."

An extra dollop of paranoia was caused by the state's geography. Illinois and Iowa to the east and the north were free states. Statehood for Kansas not only threatened to hem in the slave trade, but promised another wide path to freedom for black runaways. And unlike Illinois or Iowa, where the plight of the African-American was as often as not met with indifference, many Kansas leaders brimmed with fervent abolitionism.

President Lincoln was cognizant of the snarl of politics and property represented by Missouri's slaves (valued at $44 million overall in 1860 by the state auditor), as well as those in Kentucky and Maryland when his Emancipation Proclamation exempted them in late 1862. The African-American was not officially freed in Missouri until January 1865, after Lincoln safely won re-election, and the war neared its end.

The southerners' demand for state sovereignty in the face of the powers of the Washington government was heard just as loudly in Missouri. Perhaps nowhere, in fact, did the call against "Northern aggression" ring as loudly in the early months of the war as in Missouri. While its governor professed neutrality, Federal authorities saw duplicity and quickly chased him out of the state. The state's elected officials found "temporary" quarters in Marshall, Texas, as occupation troops from northern states poured into Missouri, prompting resentment even from pro-Union men.

In trying to deal with the insolvable complexities and unending violence of Missouri, Federal authorities resembled a man crashing down a dark staircase, never getting a footing and making misstep after misstep. They ordered every able-bodied man to join the Enrolled Missouri Militia — in effect forcing southerners to wear the blue and take up arms against friend and kin. As a result, many sons of southern families took to the brush or finally resolved to join the Confederate army in Arkansas. The Federals, including fellow Missourians in their ranks, adopted a no-quarter-given policy to guerrillas and got the same served back to them. Ultimately, frustrated and angry about the enemy's easy movement among the population and landscape, the Union officers took harsh action — at first jailing and banishing the women of the guerrillas, then emptying a large swath of the countryside — each time swelling the bushwhackers' ranks.

The other great motivator for a Missourian to pick up the rifle was the devil next door, the Kansan. Organized as jayhawkers, Red Legs or U. S. cavalry regiments, the result usually looked the same, homesteads and hate smoking behind.

The backdrop of murderous feelings many Kansans had for Missourians and vice versa is difficult to fathom today. Before the war, Charles B. Stearns, a Kansas abolitionist who was considered something of a pacifist, wrote: "When I deal with men made in God's image, I will never shoot them; but these proslavery Missourians are demons from the bottomless pit and may be shot with impunity." To which John Stringfellow, a Missourian who crossed the river to edit the *Squatter Sovereign,* might have replied: "If murder and assassination is the programme of the day, we are in favor of filling the bill. Let not the knives of the Pro-slavery men be sheathed while there is one Abolitionist in the territory…. Let our motto be written in blood upon our flag: "Death to all Yankees and Traitors in Kansas."

Once Lincoln was elected, murder and assassination *did* become the programme of the day. Before the inauguration, the diminutive Kansas doctor Charles Jennison was hanging pro-slavery men. The firing upon Sumter gave local southerners the signal to empty the U. S. Army Arsenal at Liberty, Missouri, eight days later. When the St. Louis steamer *Sam Gaty* landed April 18 at the Leavenworth wharf, townspeople hauled out their cannon, "Old Kickapoo," to force the packet to remove the Confederate flag it flew. On April 30, a drunken mob raged through Kansas City looking for Union men to pummel. On May 10, dozens of St. Louis civilians were gunned down in street riots provoked by Federal actions; a few days later St. Joseph's City Council banned flying the U. S. flag.

By June 13, 1861, Fort Leavenworth soldiers under Captain W. E. Prince had exchanged bullets with secessionists drilling and drinking at Rock Creek in what is now southwest Independence, Missouri. The next month, Jennison was ordering seven more unfortunates to dig their own graves in Cass County, Missouri. And the little fight outside Carthage July 5 between troops loyal to Governor Claiborne Jackson and those commanded by Union Colonel Franz Sigel left a couple dozen dead.

All this occurred *before* the first major battle, Bull Run, fought July 21 at Manassas, Virginia.

Unlike in New York or Georgia, thousands of Missouri civilians were forced to choose sides, often fatally. Even the "right" side, no matter how peacefully pursued, could run counter to the sentiments of your neighbors, or more dangerously, the heavily-armed combatants who came galloping down your lane. Whether they were Southern "secesh" or Union "milish," too often the question was whether they would just ride off with the livestock in the pen or gun down the owner on the porch. In almost all seasons, men dangled from trees like rotting fruit.

"They tried to make my uncle Harrison an informer, but he wouldn't do it. He was only a boy. They tried to hang him, time and again they tried it, 'stretching his neck,' they called it, but he didn't say anything. I think he would have died before he'd said anything. He's the one I'm named after, and I'm happy to say that there were people … who said I took after him." Those words were written by Harry S Truman, about Federal intelligence-gathering against the terrorism of the time.

Year after year, the strife stalked the citizenry of all but the largest communities in western Missouri and eastern Kansas. Massachusetts or North Carolina both had towns named Lawrence, but no marauders swept through them intent on killing every man and boy big enough to pull a trigger. Many rank William Clarke Quantrill's 1863 raid on Lawrence as the Civil War's worst atrocity, where nearly 200 were shot down or burned in their homes. But such fortune was hardly confined to Kansans.

A year later, Leavenworth's *Daily Times* crowed: "We have reports brought in by reliable parties to the effect that our forces destroyed Camden Point (Mo.) on Wednesday night. Yesterday morning they burnt Platte City, from which the guerrillas had fled…A report is also current that New Market had been burned by our troops. If true it is good evidence that the Colorado and Kansas boys are making short work of the various rebel nests in that section."

The vengeance that followed Lawrence, when angry Kansans again roamed into Missouri looking for the "demon" Quantrill, is not generally known. Their officers would report more than 100 bushwhackers killed. Several rebels, lacking good horseflesh or judgment, *were* flushed out and shot on the spot. But many were innocents, such as John S. Cave and his neighbors near Lone Jack, who were obeying General Thomas Ewing's Order 11 to leave their farms. As they loaded their wagons with belongings and children, cavalry troopers of the Ninth Kansas appeared. Cave and five other men, apparently all noncombatants aged 17 to 75, were taken away and shot.

If 100 "guerrillas" were "mustered out," it did little to hamper Quantrill and his band, who had the nerve and numbers weeks later to leave 88 dead outside a small Union fort in Kansas on their way south to Texas. Nor did it dent the bushwhackers' depredations in spring 1864. Their bands had refilled with a crop of angry new men, rootless and revenge-seeking after the mass exile forced upon their families.

So the score was "evened" again and again, with the lives of civilians making up a good share of the tallies.

In September 1864, General Egbert Brown wrote a superior how a young Holden man who had guided Union patrols had been murdered by bushwhackers. "Last night four citizens, known as rebel sympathizers, or, as they call themselves, 'Southern men,' were killed by an some unknown persons in uniform … in retaliation.…"

Way ahead of Sherman's smoking "war is hell" march across Georgia, blackened chimneys called "Jennison tombstones" marked what was left of Missouri homesteads torched by men wearing blue. The war was not even a year old when a passing Ohio soldier noted: "Butler clearly deserted. Buildings, principal ones burned down. Harrisonville also nearly desolate."

That observation was made two years *before* Ewing — Sherman's step-brother — decided to create the final firebreak between the two states. His Order No. 11 decisively cooled the border, but again the cost was borne largely by the noncombatants of four Missouri counties, given 15 days to evacuate and lose nearly all they owned. Such a tactic would not be seen again in this country until the relocation of Japanese-Americans in World War II.

In a time when a nation was tearing itself apart, no state felt the pain more than Missouri— a place where men who would be named the "Butcher of Palmyra" or "Bloody Bill" held sway, where hanging and firing squads metastasized into scalping and beheading. While many today point across the state line at the jayhawkers for these grim events, the truth is that Missourians quite energetically killed more of their fellow Missourians — not just in the hollows and over the prairies of their home state, but on the killing fields outside Vicksburg, Mississippi or Franklin, Tennessee — than the Kansans could have even imagined in their most violent dreams. What other state has to admit that?

e/ɔe/ɔe/ɔe/ɔe/ɔ

One more difference between the Gettysburg of the East and the so-called one of the West: Perhaps a thousand books have been dedicated to the former, less than a dozen to Westport. As this volume is added to the smaller pile, it must be understood that it is intended foremost as a history even though written in fictional style. I did not wish to track over the more traditional histories of this period and this place, but hoped to offer the modern reader a different, story-telling path toward the truth of what happened on the border 150 years ago. Events are seen through the eyes of actual characters, "heroes" resurrected from the pages of the past: raiders and defenders, bushwhackers and jayhawkers, and a few more.

A clue to the tale: Everyone with a surname in this history is an actual figure. Their historical footprints may be faint, but they were real. Those few with only a single name are my creations to help carry the dialogue or chain of events.

Facts and occurrences in this tale are as accurate as I could make possible. In telling the history as they created it or remembered it, obviously, no one knows exactly what the characters were thinking. Many of the actors' actual words, however, are borrowed from letters, orders, diaries and memoirs.

Some liberties were taken, especially with a main character, young Riley Crawford, who skips across history's pages hardly a handful of times. Where was he exactly in late October of '64? Rolls of guerrillas list him as one of George Todd's band, but we know that the year before his revenge-seeking mother literally gave him — at age 15 — to Quantrill. A description by a woman at Lawrence seems to put Crawford at the bloody raid. An oft-told guerrilla tale has him at the Baxter Springs massacre later in 1863. Did he participate the next fall in the bloodbath at Centralia with Anderson and Todd? "Membership in such bands could be fluid: A man might belong to one outfit for a while and, then, for any number of reasons, shift to another," according to Edward E. Leslie's *The Devil Knows How to Ride.*

If Riley Crawford were still alive in October 1864, he would have had a choice: Ride to battle near Independence with the doomed Todd or continue bushwhacking with Anderson, who also had only days to live. While all of Crawford's dialogue is imaginary, the stories he tells come from the record and bushwhacker lore.

Hard choices had to be made about the "heroes" to enlist and whose accounts to accept. Many of those I employ had deeper foundations in our history, requiring less of the mortar of author's imagination between the hard stones of fact. The generals and lesser officers often left their marks in a wealth of official orders, as well as memoirs, telegrams, letters and biographical works, certainly more than the typical soldier. Take this sparse diary entry covering the Big Blue River fight of October 23 by Private Taylor Bray: "We started at 6 a.m. Marched 3 or 4 miles. Firing commenced at 10 a.m. Hard fight at big bloo. Our brigade took the front." So a healthy portion of more loquacious army brass is found here, sprinkled with observations of those who watched history march by.

Even with the more documented recountings, the fog of war arises and knots of contradiction cannot be untangled. Did Federal officers nearly mutiny in the Gillis House on battle's eve? How did Frank James get that scar? Whose body was that outside the Wornall home after the Westport battle? The stories were sorted to find the best grounded in research, but when faced with competing memories, I often chose the more entertaining.

I have tried to reach two audiences, first the reader who might be less grounded in the Civil War and its particular condition in Missouri and Kansas. While *Saddle the Pale Horse* could not fail being an action story, it is grounded in fascinating fact and follows engaging characters. For the many Civil War aficionados, I have tried to weave my research in different patterns and fresh interpretations of some of the old stories. Behind the narrative are stacked copious footnotes in the hope they will entertain and inform the old hand as well as the freshly enlisted enthusiast in this critical part of our history.

I can only thank the authors who followed Sterling Price's doomed campaign ahead of me.

This story begins just after the former Missouri governor brings his Confederate army back into his home state from Arkansas.

I

Homecoming

"Twenty-seven months ago tomorrow I left the state of Missouri, an exile and a refugee. Today I enter it with an Army which God grant may be a victorious one and relieve this downtrodden state."

— Confederate Major William McPheeters

e/e/e/e/e/e/e/e

South of Poplar Bluff

Butler County, southeast Missouri

STRETCHED OUT ON THE BORROWED BED, the general finger-combed his side-whiskers. The old habit of vanity helped him gather his thoughts.

From outside came a rustle, someone trying to be quiet in the dark. In the slow waking, the little noises beyond the window were comforting. The fat man's army was coming to life, throwing off blankets, breaking sticks to resurrect campfires, hawking and spitting into the struggling embers. It meant dawn wasn't far off. He heard a soldier moan: "Whoever said Missouri rocks would be softer than the Arkansas variety has spoken falsely."

The general heard the chuckles outside and joined in, his eyes still closed.

Well, maybe the rocks weren't *that* hard, but yes, Missouri could be a right uncomfortable place for a Confederate soldier these days. The general intended to fix that, but right now the room was chilly, and he was putting off abandoning his featherbed.

Soon, his aide would knock. Shifting his great bulk, the general tried to remember which side of the bed hid the chamber pot. The pressure on his bladder was superseded by a sharp twinge in his hip. He grimaced. Just getting north to the Missouri border had been a long haul, more than 300 miles from southwest Arkansas, and he was feeling it. Ride with the ambulance again, or have them saddle up old Bucephalus?

So went Major General Sterling Price's first awakening in his home state since 1861. In Missouri, there was a saying about how the state had five seasons — spring, summer, fall, Price's Raid and winter — yet the old governor had not made a foray north in those three years. Tried to invade Missouri in '62, but before he could even get out of Arkansas, he had run into a tough Iowa general named Samuel Curtis. The raids of '63 were led by younger men, iron-assed cavalry commanders, and even they had escaped by the skin of their teeth.

Now it was Price's turn again, and this time it was not a quick raid. It was an invasion, a chance to redeem Missouri. He was leading 12,000 men. Even if a third of his soldiers had no weapons to speak of, it still represented the largest Confederate army seen in Missouri in more than three years of war.

With it, he intended to sack St. Louis, one of the North's largest cities, where they sewed shoes, stacked flour sacks and floated ironclads. Full of the foreigners who were trying to steal his state away, it also was a giant Federal supply center, and one that was lightly guarded.

That part of the plan most excited Lieutenant General E. Kirby Smith,

Price's superior as commander of the Trans Mississippi, the Confederacy on the river's west side. "Make St. Louis the objective of your movement…," said Smith's order, issued August 4, 1864 — Price had shouted that idea for years, but who listened? — "…which if rapidly made, will put you in possession of that place, its supplies, and military stores, and which will do more toward rallying Missouri to your standard than the possession of any other point."

Almost as an afterthought Smith said that, failing to take St. Louis, Price should head to Kansas and strip it of livestock and military supplies as he withdrew. It showed that Smith's mind mostly was on bringing home supplies for the winter and new blood for the ever-dwindling Confederate army. "Remember that our great want is men," Smith had said.

Price's "great want" was Missouri. Some few had flocked to the banner already, but the richest recruiting ground was up around the Missouri River. Price was glad to see every eager young man, but would be happier if more arrived with decent weapons. Some didn't even have horses.

Not all the faces were even eager. On the way through northern Arkansas, Brigadier General Joseph Orville Shelby, known to all as "Jo," rounded up perhaps 3,000 deserters, many at gunpoint. Most were assigned to the other two division commanders, James Fagan and John Marmaduke, both major generals.

In Price's opinion, Kirby Smith thought small — but then none of his superiors in the army had his vision. Once St. Louis was taken, Price knew, the long-suffering southerners in Missouri would rise up, armed with the weapons that Price figured on capturing. After that would come Jefferson City, the capital. The pretenders would be driven out like the moneychangers from the Temple, and he could stick Tom Reynolds in the governor's office and get him out of his hair.

Reynolds, at least, grasped the significance of the invasion. In July, he had written to Price: "Our affairs in the eastern half of our Confederacy are in a critical condition. Major Cabell writes me that the President and Secretary of War are impatient for an advance into Missouri."

Price had replied, "I have confidence of the happiest results," and noted that delay was dangerous.

The general knew that Kirby Smith had not wanted him for this expedition, but he'd had no choice, had he? Who else had the popularity in the state? When the war began, Price had been the only choice to lead the Missouri State Guard, raised in the first weeks of the hostilities to resist intruders, the Federals.

Jefferson Davis didn't care much for Price, either. The feeling was mutual. It stemmed in part from Missourians' efforts to walk an impossible tightrope of neutrality at the beginning of the conflict. Right after Fort Sumter fell, Governor Claiborne Jackson showed his hand by denouncing Lincoln's call for 75,000 troops. He called it "illegal, unconstitutional and revolutionary; in its object inhuman & diabolical. Not one man will Missouri furnish to carry on any such holy crusade against her southern sisters."

Yet Jackson, no matter how fervent a secessionist, was hamstrung by a state convention that voted overwhelmingly against breaking away from the Union and by the growing Federal control of St. Louis. Early on, the governor talked of neutrality, and that permanently affected his relations with Davis. Nor did the president in Richmond ever forget how General Price was one of the votes *against* secession at the state convention.

Lincoln's strongest allies in St. Louis, Union Army firebrand Nathaniel Lyon and Congressman Frank Blair believed, correctly, that Jackson and Price were trying to blow smoke in their eyes by talking of neutrality while buying time until southern munitions could reach the state. On June 11, 1861, Lyon listened for hours to proposals by Jackson and Price, did not like what he heard, stood and proclaimed war. Price had been taken aback by the wild-eyed Lyon, who had hissed: "Rather than concede to the State of Missouri for one single instant the right to dictate to my government in any matter however important. I would see you, and you, and you, and you, and every man, woman and child in the State, dead and buried!"

But it was Lyon who was dead now, was it not? Killed in a battle Price had won south of Springfield in '61.

Now, as Price's invasion of Missouri began, the general was aware of his doubters. He recognized that the Yankees, once sent packing across the Mississippi, would come swarming back, their ranks fed by the foreigners who filled the slums of the northern cities. But that would mean whole Yankee corps, even armies, would be diverted back west, draining men away from Sherman and the other Federal generals. Washington, if not Richmond, appreciated Missouri's importance. Even if Price were forced back south, it would take the Federals months to accomplish it. And Abraham Lincoln did not have months. It was only weeks now until their elections.

Lincoln was riding high now with the capture of Atlanta. But Grant was stuck in the Virginia trenches, the Red River campaign in Louisiana had been a Federal disaster, and a good many in the North were tired of their president. If Missouri slipped from his grasp, if the people rose up, the tyrant Lincoln would be humiliated. If Price rode through the streets of St. Louis — he would definitely ride Bucephalus on that occasion — a howl would erupt in the East. God knew that Americans, both sides, were weary of this war.

That was the key to toppling Lincoln: The bold stroke! If the tyrant lost to the Democratic candidate, Major General George McClellan, those in the North wanting the conflict ended would be in power, would let the South go in peace.

This was a wildly optimistic scenario, but many southerners clung to it in the darkening days of 1864. First, not all of Lincoln's opponents were "Peace Democrats" — the most defeatist of whom were called Copperheads — who would forgo Union victory and let the South go. Many, including McClellan, disagreed with the Democratic platform and would pursue the war.

Wood smoke teased Price's nostrils. The woman of the house chosen as camp headquarters was frying ham. Outside, skillets and coffee pots rattled amid his escort company, one of Shelby's. Price wasn't sure what was boiling in them. The Union blockade had made coffee beans a precious commodity in the South. Confederates had to have their brew, however, so into the pot went various substitutes: toasted acorns, beets, wheat, barley, rye, okra seeds, asparagus tops, potatoes, sweet potatoes, field peas, chicory — recommended with browned turnips — or even the all-purpose corn meal, roasted.

His army had not found much yet in the foraging. This part of Missouri was always poor country. And now not a lot left after so many years of war. Always hogs loose in the timber, of course, if you were quick with the trigger. Some corn in the fields, some fruit in the orchards.

But coffee and flour and Springfield rifles lay just ahead, waiting to be plucked in the wake of fleeing Federals. Everything was going well. All of the columns had avoided the Yankee forces across Arkansas and had gathered just as planned. The many Missourians in the invasion force seemed to step a little quicker back on their own soil.

Heaving himself up from bed— uunnhh, that hip! — Price realized the decision was made. Bucephalus need not earn his oats today. Price knew he was getting quite stout, probably nigh to 300 pounds. And at 54, it was getting harder to stay long in the saddle. Fifty-four? He knit his white eyebrows, trying to place the date. He bawled the question through the door at Lauchlan MacLean, his adjutant. Why it was the 20th, he heard. So, yes, it was his birthday. He was fifty-five.

And Missouri would be his birthday gift.

SEPTEMBER 21

Camp Gamble
St. Louis

THE TOE OF HIS LEFT BOOT did not clear the end of the wickedly warped plank, and the Federal captain sprawled onto the crude camp sidewalk.

"Hell and blazes!" Levi Utt barked as a sergeant helped him up and handed him his hat. Utt quietly thanked the sergeant and straightened his coat.

Inside the tent a man chuckled, "Sounds like ol' Timber Toes is here."

Angry, Utt proceeded through the canvas flaps. He realized his boot sole was now partly ripped off. That made him even angrier.

"Brace!" the sergeant roared. The three men already were on their feet. Now they stiffened to various interpretations of attention.

"Privates Tefft, Thompson and Newman, sir!"

The Seventh Kansas Volunteer Cavalry officer did not need to be told who they were.

"You men did not make roll call again. The sergeant here considers you to be malingerers. I'm inclined to agree." A glance at Tefft told Utt he might be wrong in his case. The young fellow was having trouble standing still.

"Tefft, what is your story?"

"Sir, I'd be mighty obliged if I could head for the jakes right now."

Utt heard the urgency, nodded and hoped the private made it.

"Keep an eye on him, sergeant. Get him to the infirmary tent if he isn't better by tomorrow."

Whatever it was, it was going around. Sanders, his second-in-command of A Company, was down with fever, which was why Utt had to conduct this morning's distasteful duty. The captain turned to Thompson, a hard case.

"Thompson, I hear you've got a bad back."

"Yes, sir. It's hurting me something awful, I just can't...."

"This is the same bad back that kept you with the other coffee coolers, out of the fight in Coffeyville and Tupelo?"

"Yes, sir, it's just ..."

"The same back that was in pretty good shape a couple weeks ago when you were arrested for drunkenness and fighting? Sergeant, what cure do we have for an 'old soldier' with a bad back?"

"Well, sir, I always recommend the stick."

"Excellent suggestion."

Having to carry the "stick," a good-sized log, for three hours at a time would be just the thing. By the third hour he'd be begging for mercy. Utt was sure it had been Thompson who referred to him as "Timber toes." Not that most of the men didn't behind his back, but he'd heard a sneer in Thompson's tone.

Utt, having lost his foot charging a rebel battery in Alabama, wasn't taking sneers from a goddamned shirker. A shell had landed in the earth directly under Utt's feet and blew him up into the air, according to one regiment account, "tearing off his left leg at the ankle... The men of Co. A took hold of the captain and attempted to draw him out of the fire into the ditch but the agony was so great that he begged them to leave him alone."

Utt was left behind, and the Confederates let him stay at a hotel in Tuscumbia, Alabama, where the local girls reportedly brought him strawberries and cream. Later, when he had rejoined his unit, he supposedly repaid the ladies by getting them passes through the lines to buy goods not obtainable in the South.

Now Captain Utt stood before the third trooper, Newman. It was clear from his weaving that Newman suffered from too much drink.

"Another rough night, private? Sergeant, let's help Newman sober up. We have a barrel for him to wear, do we not?"

All in all, nothing unusual for the morning routine.

Most of the Seventh was fit and getting refitted. The regiment had been in Memphis, ready for more brawling with Bedford Forrest or whatever reb was still wandering around Tennessee or Mississippi, when it was called to St. Louis. Price really was coming north — the rumors apparently were right, for once — and Ol' Rosy wanted somebody to hold his hand.

"Old Rosy" was the soldiers' nickname for Major General William Rosecrans, commander of the Department of Missouri. Headquartered in St. Louis, he'd had his ears to the ground, all right. Price began marching from southern Arkansas on August 30, and less than three weeks later, Rosy had the Seventh unloading in St. Louis with some other seasoned cavalry and infantry. With 10 new regiments of 30-day men, mostly from Illinois, Rosecrans was sleeping better.

"That is all, sergeant," Levi Utt said. He stepped out of the tent into the morning sun and returned to the makeshift officers' quarters to change footwear and tighten the straps holding his prosthetic to his ankle. He wondered if he could wheedle new boots from the quartermaster. The man acted like everything in his wagons once belonged to his sainted mother.

Utt decided to join two other captains, Pitts and Moorhouse. There was a second lieutenant, too, a fellow named Wildey whom Utt hardly knew.

The cook, Moses, a former contraband and long with the regiment, had a cup of coffee in front of Utt before he settled in his chair.

"Mornin,' Levi," said Pitts. "How is Sanders?"

"Still down," Utt said, "but he's done puking, I believe." Pitts had been a lieutenant in Utt's A Company until promoted to take over D Company. B. C. Sanders had taken his position. Utt much preferred Pitts, missed his sense of humor.

"Physician, heal thyself," Pitts said. He was referring to Sanders' pre-war profession. "At least it's not the smallpox like last time we were here."

"Amen to that, Brother Pitts."

Utt got busy putting sorghum on some still-warm biscuits.

"Moses, these biscuits are lighter than a drunkard's promise!" His mouth was full as he shouted the compliment to the cook.

"What do you hear about Price?" asked Captain Moorhouse.

"No more than you. He's got Shelby out in front. Some of the Indiana boys down at Jefferson Barracks have been told they'll be taking the cars on Monday. Somewhere south of here."

"Maybe Rosy can catch us a ride, too," said Moorhouse.

"Rosecrans couldn't catch a cold," Pitts said.

Although Rosecrans' care for his soldiers was appreciated in the ranks, General-in-Chief Ulysses S. Grant thought him slow and unaggressive. St. Louis was nearly as far away as Grant could get Rosecrans transferred.

"Well, he ain't no Sheridan, that's for sure," Moorhouse agreed. The newspapers were full of tales of how Little Phil had just whipped Jubal Early at Winchester, Virginia, after Early's raid had nearly reached the streets of Washington D. C.

"No Jennison, neither," Utt said, holding out his coffee cup as a signal to the cook to refill it.

"Amen to that, Brother Levi."

Moorhouse laughed. "Well, we'd have better horses if Jennison was still in command."

"Out of Missouri, by Jennison," Pitts recited. Jennison was renowned for making off with Missouri horses.

Lieutenant Wildey had only enlisted earlier in the year, so he had not been with them during their jayhawking days on the Border with Charles "Doc" Jennison. But he knew the stories.

Jennison, who had been raiding Missouri for months with the Mound City Sharp's Rifle Guards, had formed the First Kansas regiment in Leavenworth. It was an attempt to make the jayhawkers conform to military standards and regulations. The Kansans got new uniforms but did not shed their attitudes. As their new colonel, Jennison made their position clear: "All pro-slavery supporters in the border counties in Missouri shall promptly surrender all arms and belongings, and shall forfeit all property. Those who do not shall be considered traitors and slain, their property seized, houses burned. In no case will anyone be spared."

With a thousand men in the now-renamed Seventh Kansas Cavalry and the borrowed authority of the Federal government, Doc Jennison terrified the Border counties and began grabbing anything not nailed down — slaves, livestock, silver, furniture, whatever. Jennison joked of growing "stoop-shouldered carrying plunder out of Missouri," all in the name of patriotism.

A correspondent for *The New York Times* was with Jennison and his second in command, Daniel Read Anthony, during operations across the farm country south of Kansas City. He lamented the villainy of the southerners who left a Unionist family near Pleasant Hill only "a half wagon load of furniture, and four milch cows, out of some eighty head of stock." He approved, however, of how Anthony secured for the "government" 470 head of cattle and 32 wagons, undoubtedly from the farms of supposedly southern sympathizers.

"Most of the wealthy men in this place are of secession productivities, and many of them are active, though secret agents of the rebels," the article continued. "The Colonel (Jennison) sent to request their attendance at headquarters… They were then set at fatigue duty, such as hauling hay, corn, wood and water, chopping wood, etc. Among the individuals thus set to work were doctors, lawyers and judges…."

The visits of the Seventh to Independence were memorable as well, according to Captain Henry Palmer. On their return, he said, "They marched through Kansas City nearly all dressed in women's clothes, old bonnets and outlandish hats on their heads …"

In Harrisonville, the Kansans found the place nearly picked clean, except for some Good Books stored at the American Bible Society. Almost out of habit, they stole them. Such behavior led George Caleb Bingham, the Missouri artist and then state official, to remark: "A little blue cloth and a few brass buttons neither make a soldier nor unmake a thief."

The jayhawkers' treatment of Missourians appalled Union generals, who realized pro-Union slaveholders were being driven into the arms of the Confederacy or the bushwhackers. The jayhawkers wore the Union uniform, Major General Henry Halleck complained to War Secretary Edwin Stanton in March 1862, but "their principal occupation for the last six months seems to have been the stealing of negroes, the robbery of houses, and the burning of barns, grain and forage. The evidence of their crimes is unquestionable. They have not heretofore been under my orders. I will now keep them out of Missouri, or have them shot."

When not made a general the next month, Jennison sulked and decided to leave the service. The little fellow should have kept his mouth shut and just gone off to play his beloved poker, but Jennison made a speech against "red tape" and his superiors. He ended up arrested for nearly inciting a mutiny — several boys of some of the worst companies did skedaddle — and Jennison got marched off under guard to St. Louis.

Abolitionist politicians raised a fuss and got Jennison released. Federal commanders, however, decided the best remedy for their headaches was to get the Seventh away from their infuriated neighbors, so it was shipped to Tennessee.

But now here the regiment was again, back in Missouri.

Utt looked from the business of wiping up his egg yellows with another biscuit to see Private Cody of H Company telling Moses in a rather uppity way that his captain wanted a pot of coffee taken over to his tent.

"Private," he called over. "Since when have you become Captain Walls' aide-de-camp?"

"Don't know, sir. I was just walking by his tent, and he grabbed me for this errand."

"Is that right?" Utt didn't know Private William Frederick Cody well, but what he knew he didn't like. He wondered whether Walls was really behind this coffee-fetching.

"Well, carry on, but don't be putting on airs with Moses, hear?" Utt ordered.

Pitts observed: "If Walls gets much lazier, he'll be having Cody pour it into his mouth."

"I'll bet the little bastard is making it up," Utt said. "I'm going to check with Walls later."

"Don't be too tough on Cody," Wildey suggested. "His family's had a hard time. Folks are dead, old man was stabbed in the lung by a slaver back in the '50s. Cody's new, but damn good with a team. Been driving freight since he was a sprat."

"Heard he was a pony rider," Moorhouse added.

"Well, I heard he was worthless saloon tough and horse thief," Utt responded. "And I know he's a liar."

Uninterested in the story of a teamster, Pitts steered the conversation back toward whether Rosecrans would just keep them in the city as his personal bodyguard.

"Oh, we're going to see action, I'm sure of it," Utt informed his messmates, popping the last of a third biscuit into his mouth.

"I can feel my left toes tingling. That's always a sure sign."

SEPTEMBER 22

Near Patterson
Wayne County, southeast Missouri

"Hey, there, nigger, what you got in that skillet?"

Billy Hunter looked up from poking the edges of the eggs sizzling in the bacon grease. A raggedy white fellow was approaching. He did not know him, but the man looked mean — hungry mean.

Hunter was not overly concerned. First, he had a knife in his boot. Second, he had a good portion of Marse Jo's brigade in the neighborhood.

"Got the gen'l's eggs, suh."

That was a bit of lie. Hunter planned to eat what was in the skillet himself, but he had other stolen eggs that he would fix up for his master later, if he could get him to sit down long enough to eat them.

"What gen'l be that? Who you?"

"Be Gen'l Jo Shelby. I his man."

"Shebby? Them his boys riding round here?"

"Yassah, we coming home to Missouri."

"That right?"

The white man looked around, thinking. He had a shotgun, in much better repair than his clothes.

Hunter measured the yards. First, he'd fling the hot skillet and grease toward his face and go for him, if it came to that.

The white man had made up his mind. He stepped toward the little fire.

"Good to hear. Thinking of pitching in with him. Been about to go to Arkansas when heard you all was comin' up. Thot to save a trip. Ya'll took yore time."

Hunter relaxed a little. At least he wasn't no Union bushwhacker, it seemed. The idea of rushing a scattergun hadn't particularly appealed.

"We're here, tho'. Sit down and hand me that bag. Got some bread, if you a mind to have a bite."

A thin smile sneaked through the white man's rusty beard.

"Believe I might." He laid the double-barreled in the grass and squatted, the stress on one knee of his pants ripping wider a hole there.

Hunter took a piece of bread and stabbed into a yoke, mashing it down to soak up yellow and white, left it there a moment more to heat some and then handed it, dripping, to the white man. It disappeared between bad teeth.

"Oh, that hit the spot."

The man watched as Hunter took a smaller piece, dipped and ate it himself, to let the fellow know what was what. Hunter was used to eating after white folk, but better ones than this vagabond. So they'd take turns. He made sure the pieces that went to the fellow were clearly bigger than his own.

"Say yore Shebby's man?" His losing of the "L" in saying the name irritated Hunter, who did not let it show.

"Been his man since Kentucky. His folks done bought me for him when I was 11, no, maybe I was 12. He just a tad then, too. Been taking care of him eber since."

"An' yo're seeing to him now, too, out in the fighting?"

"Where he go, I go."

Hunter had been with Jo Shelby when he had gone to Transylvania College and when he moved to Missouri to start up his hemp business in Waverly. He kept Shelby's clothes, cooked for him, saddled his horse, carried his heavy sword and carefully loaded his Navy Colt revolver, his "maybe." Right now, Marse Jo's "maybe" was over with the horse grazing several yards away.

He had left the column to forage a bit, and got lucky in finding a hidden coop. Some farm wife was going to be disappointed this morning. He had accidentally cracked a couple of eggs and decided not to waste them, but cook them on the spot.

Another big piece of bread went into the second yoke and then quickly into the maw of his guest. This time the man actually chewed a second or two. The fellow was pretty thin. Hunter wondered why he wasn't seeing some of the division around. The boys had been thick as flies not a half hour before.

"Been thinking of joining Hildebran' but never can ketch him. Neither can the Yankees. Maybe I should pick up with you fellers 'stead."

Hunter knew who Hildebrand was, felt he was a low brand of trash. For sure, this fellow would fit in better with him than with Marse Jo. But Hunter was polite. Even without the presence of the shotgun, he was inclined that way.

"Well, you got a horse? Because this here is a fast-moving bunch. We way out in front of Ol' Pap."

"No, not now, but know where I could get one. A place over that way." But he did not look over that way. His eyes had flitted at Hunter's mount.

"Well, better be no plow horse. You hear how we got up to Wav'ley last year?"

"Somethin' bout it. Long raid."

"Yes, it were."

"You were riding with Shebby then?"

"What I been tellin' you?"

This might have sounded a little uppity, but it was accompanied with a third piece of bread, with the crusty bits of over-cooked egg white on top. If no offense was taken, certainly the bread was.

"I with him at Elkhorn, at Oak Hills, Lexington, Helena …all them fights."

"So you ever shot?"

"No sah, been lucky in that way. I what you call a high private in the rear ranks most times. Been knocked with a skillet or a piece of fence rail and run over by horses and shot at, but I never shot."

The man got off his haunches and lay down on his side, all relaxed like, with a hand holding up his head. The other hand was jammed into a coat pocket, and Hunter tensed. A brown bottle came out to be unstoppered and sipped from. It was not offered, but right then Hunter wasn't interested in liquor, anyway. Needed to stay sharp. He slid the empty and smoking skillet off the embers.

"So what was Elkhorn like? Heard genr'ls died like flies there?"

"Ol' Pap got winged, but not Marse Jo. But he got hit at Helena. In his right wrist. I was trying to lead him off the field and he kept arguing with me. He tole me I had better go and attend to my own business. I tole him my business was to attend to him. The fightnest man you ever saw. Why boss, I can't hardly stop him from fighting long enough to get a cup of coffee down him. Brave as ba'r."

"You got coffee?"

The man squinted at him, the wheels a-turning again.

"Nah, haven't seen none fer months. But I was about to tell you about Elkhorn Tavern.

"I got cut off from Marse Jo and the country was full of dem blue coats. I nearly always carried Marse Jo's saber and his big Navy pistol. I had on my regimentals, too. A long grey coat Marse Jo bought for me. I didn't want to lose that big saber, and I couldn't hide it under my coat. I scouted them corn fields for days."

The fellow tipped up the bottle again. Hunter grabbed some leaves to wipe out the skillet.

"One day I saw a regiment of blue coats crossing a ridge and I made up my mind to surrender, 'cause I was just starved out. I deployed into the big road and the blue coats rode up on me. And who do you spec' it was?"

Hunter laughed. "Billy Quantrill! Half of his men was wearing blue coats. I was safe, and they took me back to the command. Such shooting and hollering you never heard when they saw me coming into camp. Marse Jo jumped up and and cussed me and yelled 'Thah's my nigger! Bless God, dah's my nigger!'

"Mars Jo always would cuss me. You know if he don't cuss anybody, he don't like 'em. That's a sure sign, yes 'tis."

He was laying it on pretty thick now, could see the other man digesting all this along with the bread and eggs. This boy, the white man must be thinking, was somebody special. Maybe robbing or killing him might bring more trouble than the other poor folks he'd probably met up with. Maybe, he'll just let it be, Hunter thought to himself. Maybe.

There's just always that "maybe," ain't there?

"See, Marse Jo's particular 'bout his eatin.'" He picked up the heavy pan and began putting it into his sack. "Other darkies didn't know how to cook for him; I always done his ....'"

Hunter abruptly smiled toward the empty road behind the fellow, who alertly craned his neck to see who it was. His hand snaked toward the shotgun, but Hunter was quicker. Springing across the campfire, he swung the iron skillet full into the white man's rising head as hard as he could. The rim split the scalp line wide open. The man grunted, his shoulders collapsed into the grass. His eyes rolled back up into his sockets.

Hunter considered slamming him again, but it wasn't necessary. He pulled the 10-gauge away from the twitching fingers and flung it into some nearby brush. Picking up fresh leaves, he wiped blood off the skillet.

Just like the Colt, Billy Hunter's frying pan was always handy when you needed a "maybe."

II

Partisan rangers

"Mother I am wicked enough some times to wish I was a man, I need not tell you what I would do if I was one."

— Margaret Hays, 1864

cɔeɔeɔeɔeɔ

SEPTEMBER 23

In the brush
Howard County, central Missouri

THEY CALLED THEMSELVES THE PARTISAN RANGERS, guerrilla fighters for the Southern Cause. Bushwhackers was the more common term, used by the frustrated Federals when they weren't calling them devils, demons and every variety of murderers.

One of the more angel-faced devils, Riley Crawford, was sitting around one of the fires that warmed the mingled bands of George Todd, John Thrailkill and Dave Pool. In the moist woods just north of the Missouri River, a late September night held a wet chill that touched the bones. To ward it off, whiskey was being passed around, the best kind of skull-bust, the kind that earlier in the day had been taken off dead Yankees.

John McCorkle, one of the older men — although not many truly older men were found among the guerrillas — demanded one of the bottles. McCorkle's face was ominous in the changing shadows around the blaze.

"When I reckon I'm ready," Riley fired back at McCorkle, "and not a damned minute before."

McCorkle had been killing folks a lot longer than Riley, but the smooth-faced teenager felt smugly confident that the most menacing aspects of his friend were the growls coming from his stomach. Taking another swig mostly for effect, Riley swiped the arm of his coat over his lips — and then handed the bottle back the other way around the circle, to Buck James.

"You little snot-nose, I'm gonna knock you into pie!" McCorkle roared at Crawford. Buck James laughed and tossed the bottle over the fire to his protesting friend. Some comfort sloshed out of its open neck onto McCorkle's pants, but he was beyond caring. He tilted his head back for a hearty swallow and then went back to the hog he was roasting, poking it with a length of cut sapling. Juice flowed, sizzling over the coals below.

Another long mutter from McCorkle's gut pronounced the meat blackened enough. With his Bowie knife he cut off strips and started a new story about that day's attack on the Yankee supply wagons.

"I tell you, Pool was about as excited as if he'd done shot an elephant, or maybe I should say, giraffe. 'John,' he says, 'I just killed the damnedest, longest yellow nigger I ever saw.' So I go to where he was pointing and hell, yes, I'm telling you, that nigger looks like he's nine feet long, legs sticking out of them Yankee pants."

The melee that day occurred on Goslin's Lane. The guerrilla bands had swooped down on more than a dozen wagons escorted by some Third Missouri State Militia cavalry. They were taking military supplies, as well as officers' baggage, from Sturgeon to Rocheport.

Some of the 80-man militia escort had been stealing apples from a roadside orchard, like guilty little boys. And they had been punished. As with most such affairs, the fight was bloody, quick and one-sided.

"All of the soldiers were shot in the head, showing that they had been murdered after being captured," General J. B. Douglass would report. The surviving militia fled in every direction. The teamsters, trapped with their lumbering cargoes, suffered most. The bushwhackers took all that could be carried off, then heaved some of the dozen corpses into wagons and set the wagons on fire — except, oddly, the one carrying ammunition. The mules were shot in their traces.

Riley had taken a couple of the winesaps himself. So had his horse. As she snuffled through the high grass for the fallen fruit, Suzy, always dainty with her hooves, took care not to step on the dozen dead Yanks.

Now, as the guerrillas sat around the campfire, they heard sounds from the direction of the Rocheport Road. Riley put his hand on his gun and checked to see how far he was from Suzy. Union patrols seemed everywhere these days, and after the action in the lane, the Federals would want revenge. Some men stood from the various fires and bedding-down spots. McCorkle didn't even look up from his tin plate.

A friendly shout signaled that it was only more of the boys arriving. Since Todd had got word that General Price was coming, the bands had been gathering for something big.

This new bunch was Bill Anderson's. Lately they had been raising twelve kinds of hell in the counties north of the river. Men hailed comrades. The wind shifted, making Riley's eyes water. While he blinked out the wood smoke, he recognized a voice:

"'Lo, Buck. What you got cooked for me? Me and Archie here are riding on the light side of things."

"'Lo, Dingus. Come rest your frame and get yourself a piece of this sow."

Dingus was Buck James' little brother, 17, same as Riley. He sat down real careful-like, which was not surprising because less than two months ago he'd caught a slug outside his right nipple. A finger also was missing down to the first knuckle. Not a lucky feller, he had been raiding with Anderson only since spring.

Passing his sibling a piece of hog on a whittled stick, Buck spiced it up with teasing about how a damn Dutch farmer, unhappy at seeing a saddle stolen, put the fresh hole in Dingus. Little brother didn't seem in any mood to talk about it. A sore spot all the way around, Riley figured. He watched as Dingus started to bite into the pork, stopped and jammed greasy fingers into his collar. He pulled out a chill-hardy wood tick and threw it into the fire. Riley knew enough about the younger James that he would not be calling him "Dingus." It was a word that had various meanings, but one was for that special part that let a fellow write his name in the snow. Just using "Jesse," his real name, seemed far safer, although Riley felt he could take him in a tussle that did not involve weapons.

The story behind the "Dingus" nickname came from the cleaning of a captured pistol, a type he had never used before. The hammer had snapped, taking a piece of finger. Jesse James hopped about spattering blood, shouting "Dod-dingus pistol! Dod-dingus pistol!" as the rest of the band split their sides.

Five years younger than Buck, Jesse was a little better looking than his jug-eared brother, had a more girlish nose. But he wasn't as well-liked. People were tender toward Buck and for good reason. Take the time when John McCorkle's brother, Jabez, dropped his Springfield from his horse and shot his knee off. Friends dragged Jabez McCorkle off to a cave to die, away from snooping Yankees. Buck rode in to say he was there to protect the doomed man in his last days and also the womenfolk with him. Until that night, John said, he hadn't even met Buck.

Also, the older James boy carried around a book or two of Shakespeare and sometimes read aloud. Riley didn't always understand what the Romeos and all the other fellows were saying in the stories, but he always enjoyed being read to.

The Jameses had ridden briefly together with Fletch Taylor, but when Fletch lost an arm they split up. Buck joined up with George Todd, with whom Riley had ridden much of the year.

Little brother was telling Buck in a low voice what a raggedy mood Bill Anderson was in. Jim Bissett and five of his boys got gunned down out on a tax-raising run, and, as Jesse said, "Their loss has added gall and wormwood to Bill's disposition." Bissett was so handsome Quantrill had called him, "Apollo," who Riley believed was some fine Roman fellow that ran around with Caesar.

Riley scanned the growing camp. Might be more than 300 partisan rangers here. He hadn't seen such a gathering since the burning of Lawrence, the place folks called Yankee Town.

In the Confederate capital, Richmond, they looked down on guerrillas — other than John Mosby in the Shenandoah Valley — though they grudgingly acknowledged their usefulness in pinning down Union troops away from the front lines. Attempting to exert control, the Confederate authorities in 1862 proclaimed the Partisan Ranger Act and immediately regretted it. Not only did it lure away recruits that were needed in the regular army, it ran counter to the established ideas of discipline and ended up licensing indiscriminate marauding even in the East.

Commanders in the resource-poor Western wing of the Confederacy also embraced the partisans at first, calling on the populace "to organize themselves into independent companies … arming and equipping themselves, and to serve in that part of the district to which they belong."

Major General Kirby Smith met Quantrill and came away thinking that some measure of his men were "the very best class of Missourians." Still, Quantrill had been denied the legitimacy of a colonel's commission, had to be satisfied to be referred to in Confederate documents as "Captain."

Federal officers, however, consistently refused to recognize the partisans as anything more than murderous brigands and executed many they captured. Bill Anderson did nothing to rebut this approach when he wrote a newspaper in 1864: "I have killed many. I am a guerrilla. I have never belonged to the Confederate Army, nor do my men."

At the battles of Cane Hill and Prairie Grove in northeast Arkansas in late 1862, the guerrillas had served with General John S. Marmaduke and then-Colonel Jo Shelby as light cavalry or infantry. Always badly outgunned and outnumbered, they had fought well enough before being forced to retreat with the Confederate forces. All this happened long before Riley Crawford joined up in early 1863, but as far he was concerned, all those around the campfires were Southern partisan fighters.

McCorkle offered Riley another smoking slice of meat. Riley thanked him kindly and stuck his knife into it. The hot fat burned his mouth, creating a sincere longing for his canteen, but he wanted to avoid giving the fellows any new reason to tease him. Whiskey was immediately available, but Riley had learned the hard way when just one more pass meant he'd be shit-faced. That would give the boys got yet more ammo to make fun of him. And one more headache on horseback he didn't need.

"Got to go see a man about a horse," he announced around the scorching mouthful.

"A pony, from what I heard," said Archie Clement, to mirth all around. Archie had slipped up noiselessly to the circle. Another of Anderson's bunch — the brains, some said. Hard to believe.

Riley tried to think of something to fire back, but he was still sober enough to consider Archie's skills with a knife as well as his nervous vigilance. Turning and walking away, Riley noticed that Jesse was laughing the loudest and longest. His was the meanest laugh, too, come to think on it. No, Riley thought, Jesse didn't resemble Buck much at all.

At the next circle, Captain Thrailkill was talking about his close call last summer. Thrailkill was recruiting alone when he came upon some fellows who seemed to want to join up. He was suspicious.

"So I tell them: 'There are two arms of the service to which I am opposed. One is bushwhacking'" That got some laughs from his listeners. "…'And the other is jayhawking. If you is so disposed, I don't wish you to join me.' An' the next thing, I'm looking at five Colts. They was Union spies as I had figured. Thought they'd shoot me or hang me right there on the road, but they were right touched by my speech."

Thrailkill had been wearing his Confederate captain's uniform, so no doubt that helped him avoid execution on the spot. Instead, he was imprisoned at Alton across the river in Illinois. As a civilian facility, Alton was so bad that the state had shut it down before the war. The Federals gave it a monstrous new life, feeding into it thousands of prisoners, many not surviving its conditions, a few not tolerating them.

The prison record of June 11, 1864, records this: "Captain John Thrailkill escaped last eve. From Stone Quarry (took the Guards gun along)."

Thrailkill promptly wrote home: "Dear sister you cannot imagine how badley I was treated whilst in the federal bastiel ... you wanted me to take the oath and come home — as dearley as I love you all, I would rather never See you then to take this oath, one that would force me to support an abolition is government, one that I do so bitterly detest.... Sister I am glad I am a rebble."

Riley turned toward another fire under a bare walnut tree, and he noticed John Lobb, who was leading three horses to graze beyond the circles of fire. Lobb's was the only black face in the bunch, so it wasn't hard to pick him out. Lobb had the reins of a big roan known to the bushwhackers as "Charley," the horse of William Clarke Quantrill.

Riley picked his way through the clots of partisans and saw a somewhat gentle-looking man cheerfully chewing the fat with some Jackson County boys. Riley sidled close with a shy grin. Noticing, Quantrill smiled back.

"Well, hello there, young Master Crawford." Before Quantrill could say much more, Riley's old chief was called to share a log with Anderson and Todd. Riley was relieved at the friendliness. He'd ridden most of last year with Quantrill, but the captain had had a bad winter in Texas with the bands splitting up, and an even worse spring.

Everyone knew Todd liked to nurse old grudges, but what had happened in a seven-up game in Lafayette County caught everyone by surprise, especially the captain. The cards hadn't gone Todd's way, and when Quantrill accused him of reneging on the stakes a pistol suddenly appeared in his face, with Todd giving every indication he was looking for a chance to shoot his captain.

Losing face, but not his life, Quantrill backed down and admitted that, yes, he was afraid of his lieutenant. After that, Quantrill knew he was done. He had lit out for the hills of Howard County, taking along Kate King, his 15-year-old bride, and a few of his faithful "old men." Riley and the other younger ones had elected to stay with Todd.

He heard George Wigginton telling a new fellow to get rid of the dragoon pistols he had in his belt. The greenhorn demanded to know why he should do such a thing, that'd he paid $20 U. S. for them in Ray County.

"Muzzle-heavy," Wigginton patiently explained. "You'll undershoot with 'em. Think yo're aiming at a milish belt buckle and be lucky to hit the horse's cinch. You take a practice with 'em, you'll see."

Si Gordon was there. Riley admired Gordon, who'd done his share of real soldiering in Arkansas and Mississippi with the First Missouri Cavalry before taking what some called French leave. But it wasn't that he was shy of fighting. He'd come home to Missouri to pick up bushwhacking and fuel the hatred of the Yankees.

Rumor was that in September 1861 Gordon had set fire to the Hannibal & St. Joe bridge over the Platte River. Intentional or not, the flames did not destroy the small trestle, only weakened it. The unknowing engineer of the west-bound passenger express suddenly found all the cars on top of him in the riverbed. The wreck killed perhaps 20 and injured 100. Federal soldiers headed for Fort Leavenworth were among the fatalities. After the wreck, Federal authorities immediately ordered that anyone caught at sabotage to be shot.

On December 2, 1861, Major General David Hunter gave Platte City 10 days to turn Gordon over or drive him out, or, "I shall send a force to your city with orders to reduce it to ashes, and to burn the house of every secessionist in your county, and carry away every negro…Col. Jennison's regiment will be entrusted with the execution of this order."

It was normal practice for Union troops to burn the towns where their men fell into deadly traps. While the ambushers might be guerrilla bands just passing through, the residents generally got held accountable.

"No better region than this could be selected for guerrilla warfare," remarked General Clinton Fisk about Platte County and the other regions north of the Missouri River. "The topography of the country and the hearts and consciences of the people are adapted to the hellish work. There is scarcely a family but what has its representative in either Price's invading force or in the 'corps de bush.' Men and women of wealth and position give their entire influence and aid to the knights of the bush. The hand of the Government must be laid heavily upon them."

Si stopped talking and looked over his shoulder. The chiefs were arguing, a bad sign. Todd stood and pointed toward the surrounding trees.

"Perhaps you should go hide in the woods with the other cowards," he said loudly, trying to make sure most of the bands could hear. A last group of men, who had been happily and noisily divvying up some foodstuffs from the Union wagons, grew quiet. Todd had called Quantrill out once again.

Quantrill didn't rise, just poked at the ground with a stick.

"What I tell you, I tell you from hard experience," he said, still looking down. "A milish behind a solid wall is a sight more hard to handle than one out on a horse."

One of the men near Riley muttered something about Quantrill being a clipped Sampson. Riley figured he knew who done the shearing — Kate King. The captain had got her away from old man King over near home last summer. Some said she'd run away; others that the captain kidnapped her. Either way they had holed up somewhere near Boonesboro.

Everyone said she was beautiful, buxom, jolly, a brilliant rider. Probably she was 16; Quantrill was 27. Between the humiliations of the card game and titillations of a teen-aged wife, Quantrill was just a shadow of his old self this year. A Union scout would report that hundreds of men under Todd "are making preparations to act in concert with Price. We hear nothing of Quantrill."

But now Quantrill had showed up.

Anderson motioned for Todd to sit. He was the one pushing for this action in Fayette and didn't need bad blood complicating matters. Riley could feel the mood of the men around him. Apparently Quantrill could, too, tossing his stick into the embers of a dying fire.

"Well, let's go give it a shot," he said.

SEPTEMBER 24 — 9 A.M.

Williamsburg
Callaway County, central Missouri

OUT ON THE DOGTROT, LITTLE MARY Elizabeth Hays was churning butter and complaining of being set to the chore so early. Her sister Elfelda was there, too, with a dull knife and a bowl of apples to peel. Both were to be entertained by Jane, the littlest of the sisters, with her fresh-found litter of sightless kittens. John, their brother, had left before sunup to help a neighbor pen and cut shoats.

Their mother, Margaret Hays, now had a room to herself, a little space to think and compose. It had been a while since she had written to her mother out West. She wasn't sure how good her letter would be, so low-spirited was she. She had no one to talk to now. Sometimes it helped to let it all out on a clean sheet of paper.

"Dear Mother I wish you were hear with me, what pleasure it would be but alas my pleasure days is gone. I am Doomed to see no more pleasure in this world.... Their is a great deal of sickness in the country, there has been more Deaths than I ever knew in one season. Scarcely a day without I hear of some one being Burried..."

Should she mention that the country was buzzing that General Price was coming with his army? Folks had preached it all summer. An invasion would be a good thing, Margaret supposed, if evil men got their due, if Yankee interlopers were driven out. Yet no army had appeared. And even an army of the most gallant and best-hearted southern men could not set things right now.

Her beloved husband, Upton, was gone. Their farms south of Westport were long burned. She was a widow and refugee.

When the war began, the jayhawkers had wasted no time absconding with her husband's freight caravan. Upton Hays had taken to the brush, organizing a defense against the Kansans. For that he had become a much-wanted man.

Neighbors had been made to suffer, but it was not until November 1861 that the brigands came to the Hays farms for the livestock and equipment. And Negroes.

"They took two wagons loaded full from hear, my carriage and every negro on the place even. They was all willing to go. The idea of being free was a great inducement. Reason ran off some time ago. It was very agrivating to see (my carriage) drove up to the door and the negros jump into it and drive off."

Reason and the other slaves had belonged to her mother, except for one that Upton had owned. Margaret didn't miss them. They were the cause of all this suffering, weren't they? That's what the Yankees like to say. Good riddance and begone.

The first times the Federals had come by her place about a mile due east of the Wornalls, they had tried to draw her out with clever and provoking talk. She had replied mildly, and they had gone away leaving the roof over her head, at least. But in December, after Upton whipped them in a fight on the Little Blue, they had come to take out their revenge on her and the children. Margaret had been eight months pregnant when they pushed into her rooms. After taking all they could carry, they'd fired the place and made sure she had no chance to beat out the flames. That had been a cold December, too.

She had been treated better than some. At New Santa Fe, a little settlement just a pistol shot over the state line from Kansas, the jayhawkers burned a great many houses. Several men were shot, including one whose womenfolk tried to shield his body from another bullet as he lay on the ground. The Federals threatened to ride their horses over them. They might have done it. They had already done that very thing to a neighboring widow.

"She was standing in the yard. They came charging in and run over the old lady, came very near to killing her, cut her up so bad she had to send for Dr. He sewed her wounds up. It was 18 days before she could stand on her feet."

Then there was the sick woman ordered to leave her house so it could be burned. To get her moving, Margaret wrote, they gathered "two or three chunks of fire and throwed them in bed with her." That was unusual, ruining the bed-clothes.

George Caleb Bingham sarcastically noted in early 1862 how jayhawkers sent home to their bleak prairie homesteads, "a full supply of comforts, blan-kets, counterpanes, quilts... our Jackson county matrons may console them-selves in their losses with benevolent reflection, that many a Kansas spouse and lass, lies as cosily as the silk worm in its cacoon during these long winter nights, as the result of their involuntary contributions."

The action in New Santa Fe was the work of Captain John Brown Jr., son of the Harpers Ferry martyr, and the Seventh's Company K, which the younger Brown had raised and led. They struck at the homes "of every man in that neighborhood known to be in arms and found away from home," according to

Captain Levi Utt, whose own regiment "redestroyed" the town of Columbus, Missouri, and burned all but one of 46 homes in Dayton.

Margaret scattered her brood among households, then took another old house on their land, soon burned as well. Still she had coped. But almost two years ago — to this day it was — came the worst news. Upton had fallen at Newtonia, gallantly charging a third Wisconsin picket. They said he was undone by bad powder in his pistol. She had been 16 when they wed. She would be 28 in six days.

Finally, a year ago came that awful decree, the one the Union general called Order No. 11:

"All persons living in Jackson, Cass and Bates Counties, Missouri, and in that part of Vernon included in this District, except those living within one mile of the limits of Independence, Hickman's Mills, Pleasant Hill and Harrisonville, and except those in that part of Kaw Township, Jackson County, north of Brush Creek and west of the Big Blue, are hereby ordered to remove from their present places of residence with fifteen days...."

Margaret had lived south of Brush Creek.

"Mother they have done all they can do, burned me out three times and at last drove me from my country. They have nothing against me, they say. My Husband did his Duty, now he is gone. They will take their spite out on myself and little Children."

She had $600 worth of crops standing in the fields and had to leave it all behind to be destroyed or reaped by another.

"If the land would sink, I would be satisfied."

Many Missourians forced to join the exodus wrote accounts of it, much like Lone Jack's Martin Smith: "I thought I had witnessed and felt the hardships and privations of civil war and martial law before, but it was reserved for this ... to teach me ... On ever road that led eastward from the county of Jackson came the moving mass of humanity, seeking an asylum they knew not where; some driving their flock and herd along with them; others, again, as I was, with nothing but a makeshift of a wagon and team — some not even that. Women were seen walking the crowded and dusty road, carrying in a little bundle their all.... Others, again, driving or leading a cow or a skeleton horse ... on which the feebler members of the family road by turns."

Margaret Hays and her brood ended up in central Missouri, where they relied on the Christian generosity of family and friends.

"Mother, you heard that Dick was killed some time ago."

Dick Yager, her cousin, had been riding with Todd when he was shot in a July 20 raid, forcing the guerrillas to leave him in a cornfield. Southerner friends had tried to care for him, but the Federals found him and finished him.

"Oh Mother it is hard to think of, he was wounded at Arrow Rock in the head. He fell from his horse, did not come to hisSelf for some time, was run over by horses,

brake one leg but was getting well of his wounds when he was come upon by the D..... They murdered him in a most cruel manner.."

Margaret remembered how she giggled when Dick used to tease her when they were children. Upton had thought the world of Dick. The two men had freighted and spent long hours on the road to New Mexico or Utah. The Yankees had been holding Yager's wife and daughter up in Leavenworth but now had exiled them.

"It nearly kills his poor old father, his Mother I fear for her for she is sick and this news will go hard with her altho she has been expecting it. Dicks wife and Chile is in Texas.

Little Jane Upton Hays stormed in with arms full of mewing kittens, demanding to sleep with them in her cot that night.

"Betty and Fleda say I can't, momma, but I can! Please, Momma, please?"

"Let me have them, Jen Uppy." Hays said, using a pet name. She took a kitten, gray with white socks and nose, and set it in her aproned lap. She gently pried the rest of the creatures from the arms of the little girl, who was squeezing a mite too tight.

The tiny helpless things were worn out by all the attention. Frightened, not understanding, they wanted to go back to their nest. Cupping her hands, Margaret held "Socks" to her cheek and closed her eyes, mimicking the young animal.

"Yes," she breathed, "we all want to go back, don't we?"

10 A.M.

Fayette
Howard County

QUIETLY CROSSING BONNE FEMME CREEK, ONE fellow said the name meant "Pretty Lady." To Riley Crawford the stream looked like just one more Missouri mud hole.

The different bands had strung out on the road, so the lead riders paused at the edge of Fayette to let the others bunch up. None of the folks in the streets conducting their Saturday morning affairs seemed bothered by the guerrillas' presence, but then the wolves mostly wore blue sheep's clothing. Disguise let them get up right close. Hell, Riley once rode behind a milish flag they'd picked up.

"We captured from the Federals clothes, horses and ammunition," Frank James would write one day. "We generally carried our coats and overcoats fastened on our saddles. Most of our clothing was the blue uniform of the Yankees."

Fayette always had been a pro-Union stronghold. This time, Anderson and Todd reckoned most of its garrison was out trying to track down who hit the wagon train. Some had argued to sack the town, but Anderson wanted to burn out the milish more. He was hankering for revenge against the Ninth Missouri Cavalry, which had caught and scalped Jim Bissett, the handsome comrade-in-arms.

Riley looked around for trouble but saw none. The plan was to break into two columns, take different streets north toward the fancy-pants academy on the hill, then swing east toward the militia post below.

Now came the report of a pistol. Riley saw the cause immediately. Some fool among the rangers ruined the surprise by shooting at a nigger who was wearing blue.

Townspeople were running now, closing doors. Roundly cussing the shooter, the guerrillas split up. Well ahead, Riley saw two uniforms race across the street into what turned out to be a courthouse. He crouched low over the horse's neck in case they were of a mind to make trouble.

"We dashed into the town up the streets leading from the graveyard to the courthouse square," John McCorkle would remember, "all of us riding at the top of our speed and were passing down a side street when the Federals from the courthouse poured a perfect volley into us." Thundering up the hill, the band swung right and streamed down a street sloping toward the enemy position. Up the line, a sentry's ball knocked a guerrilla from his horse. Racing by, Riley glanced down. Hell, that was Thad Jackman. Unlucky.

Then right quick it got more unlucky. Anderson was leading the gallop straight at the log barracks that formed the militia post, but whoever told him the milish was undermanned had to be bad at ciphering. And if these were the sick fellers left behind, Riley would be glad to let the next man tangle with the healthy ones. From the smoke erupting from chink holes, none had left their guns at home, neither.

"Not one of the enemy could be seen," Hamp Watts would recall, "but the muzzles of muskets protruded from every porthole, belching fire and lead at the charging guerrillas. Horses went down as grain before the reaper."

Riley emptied one pistol close enough to see wood splintering. He turned away from the lead tempest, and then Suzy folded under him. Riley went head first into dust and horse apples. His ears rang, and he was having trouble with his breath, but he pulled another revolver from his belt and blasted wildly at the little log fort. He rolled back behind his mare, heard minié balls striking her flesh. Her thrashing stopped. He grabbed a third Navy from the saddle holster that was clear of the animal.

Another rush, this one led by Todd, thundered by, the men screaming and blasting away with both hands. A riderless horse loomed out of the drifting powder smoke, and Riley snagged a rein. He leapt for the saddle, but his left foot would not work. Falling flat on the ground once more, he didn't let go of the rein. He tried again, hobbling around with the frightened mare. A tug on his shirt — a bullet. Devilish close, that one. He made another lunge at the wild-eyed horse and clawed his way onto her back, turning her away from the fight. Staying so low over her neck that his chin became wet — the previous rider's blood in the mane, he realized — Riley took her up the hill, passing some of the boys on foot heading back down with a blanket to retrieve Oll Johnson in plain view of the blockhouses.

"When I saw the situation and knew just what was coming, my heart almost ceased to beat," one of the rescuers would recall. "Could the ground have opened up and engulfed me (I) believe it would have been a relief. When we succeeded in getting him on the blanket and started over the hill it appeared to me that every inch of space around us was filled with musket-balls. Strange to say, not one of us was touched."

Good luck to you, boys, Riley thought. He wasn't about to spend any more time in this turkey shoot. He dug his heels into the horse's flanks. Ah-h-h-h, pain in his boot.

Escape was north up the Glasgow Road, and soon he was part of a pack. Out of the town a ways, the guerrillas slowed their lathered mounts to take stock. Other riders, including Todd, joined up. Thrailkill was there. More came up the road — Bill Anderson with Buck James and maybe three dozen fellows, some slumping in their saddles. Apparently they'd tried a third run at the blockhouse with the same result.

Anderson was beside himself with rage. Riley felt like cursing, too. The ball that brought down his horse had knocked the heel off his boot and taken a little of his foot with it. He was just beginning to feel sorry for himself when he noticed Willie Hayes slip from his saddle before a comrade could grab him.

Men were recounting the ones they'd seen go down. Newt Wade, somebody shouted. Newt! Newt had given him some hard candy wrapped in paper last night. Riley patted the deep pocket of his guerrilla shirt, felt the hard lumps amid spare cartridges. He looked around. Both Tom Garrett and Tom Grosvenor were gone. Tom Maupin, too. Damn! The Yankees had been hell on Toms.

Lee McMurtry was trying to staunch the blood around one eye and look around with his good one for his brother. But George McMurtry hadn't made it out. Like maybe a dozen others. It was becoming clear that twice that was cut up. Oll Johnson was shot through the hips, could barely keep his saddle. Si Gordon had his horse close, trying to help him. One fellow was giving off a bad stink, a sign he had a hole in his bowels. Two others had arms hanging uselessly, blood streaming from coat sleeves.

"Where's Quantrill?" shouted Todd. "I didn't see him."

"He and his bunch didn't go in," McCorkle replied.

"I'll kill him," Todd roared. "Where did he go?"

"He headed toward New Franklin. We came up with Jim Little. He was shot up all to pieces. Quantrill said he'd go take him and get him to cover."

"That coward can't hide behind Little," Todd exclaimed. "I tell you, I'll shoot him the next time I see him."

"Never mind that, now," Anderson snapped. "We've got to move. The Ninth is going to hear about this and come at us."

Buggies and wagons had to be found for the worst-off. They would be left with friends on the way, who would slip them off to remote barns and caves to be nursed, away from snooping Yankees. Some of them Riley didn't expect to see again.

III

The gathering storm

"Hot times are upon us."

— Union Brigadier General Clinton Fisk, writing for
reinforcements as Price's army moved north

എഎഎഎഎ

SEPTEMBER 24 — 6 P.M.

Fredericktown
Madison County, southeast Missouri

SWALLOW THE YELLOW PUPPY OR CHOKE on Yankee oppression. That was the way in this garrison state. William McPheeters had refused to take the loyalty oath, the "yellow puppy," so the Federals had blocked him from practicing medicine. When the doctor also refused to pay his assessment, which was levied on Missourians considered disloyal, the soldiers twice dragged furniture out of his St. Louis home, even while his little boy lay dying. Figuring a Gratiot Street prison cell awaited him sooner or later, McPheeters left his family and medical practice and fled south two years ago.

But now he was going home at last. So it wasn't surprising that the army medical chief was in a better mood than Sterling Price had seen in quite a while. The doctor had wandered into the house chosen as Price's headquarters and plopped smiling into an empty chair.

"Care to change your breath, gentlemen?" He waved a bottle of brandy toward Lauchlan MacLean, who was Price's adjutant, and then toward Price, his close friend.

MacLean said he'd have a sip just a little later. Price decided to follow his aide's example. If Lauchlan believed they were too busy for a drink, then they probably were. The task at hand was coordinating the three columns under Price's command. They were riding north on parallel roads to maximize foraging. Jo Shelby's column was to the west and a bit ahead. To the east Marmaduke, naturally, was lagging behind. His path was closest to the Mississippi River, which meant navigating swampier terrain, but the man never failed to disappoint Price. The commander of the Army of Missouri was riding for now in the center division, Fagan's. Price had decided to stay in Fredricktown a second night until all the columns were near enough to support each other.

Price admired Jim Fagan, but he was an Arkansas man, not completely under the sway of Price, even though he now commanded the District of Arkansas. And Fagan's division, the largest, was made up almost entirely of Arkansas regiments, mostly mounted infantry. Price did not know much of their mettle other than that General William L. Cabell was very good.

Better than John Sappington Marmaduke, who for some reason known only to God was being promoted to major-general, even after killing a fellow general in a duel. Price despised Marmaduke. He knew the feeling was mutual, ever since Price had left Marmaduke holding the sack back at Boonville in '61. Price had tried to strip him of his division, yet here he was. Thomas Snead, who had been Price's adjutant and remained his biggest co-conspirator after becoming a Confederate congressman, warned him of "the hampering influence of Marmaduke's incompetency."

On the other hand there was Shelby, Price's very best cavalry officer. With Shelby, all things were possible. Price wondered what he was finding ahead. Shelby had caught up with and killed some of the Federals who'd burned Doniphan. The destruction was a cruel thing.

The Confederate army now was less than 100 miles from St. Louis, and McPheeters was talking about what he would do first, after kissing his wife and children, of course.

Price looked forward to St. Louis, too. He aimed to enter its streets the way Caesar had entered Rome, and also to prove Jefferson Davis a fool.

The general would never forget that first audience with the little Nero in the Confederate capital, Richmond. It was in '62, after Price and his 10,000 Missourians were deployed from Arkansas to Tennessee to tangle with Halleck and Grant. His men had fought well. Their charge into the Federal batteries at Corinth still made Price weep for its bravery and the bitter losses.

The meeting between the general and the Confederate president quickly broke down into a shouting match, with Price threatening to resign his commission. He said he would raise another army of his Missourians and win in the West — under the "Bear Flag" of Missouri — in spite of Richmond.

"Your resignation will be promptly accepted, General," Davis responded with contempt, "and if you do go back to Missouri and raise another army, and win victories for the South, or do any service at all, no one will be more pleased than myself, or more surprised."

Price had slammed the table so hard the ink splashed out of the silver wells and roared:

"Then I will surprise you, Sir!"

Davis later cooled off and promised to let him and his men repair back across the Mississippi to fight for their beloved Missouri. The promise was half empty. Price was allowed to return west, but there was never a good time for his remaining 4,000 men to make the trip. In summer 1864, Missouri State Guard General M. Jeff Thompson came across the remnants in the defenses of Atlanta and wrote, "I found the noble army corps that had followed Genl. Price across the Mississippi had become reduced to a single Brigade."

Price knew that Davis had described him as "the vainest man I ever met," but brushed it off like a horsefly on a mare's rump. For a Mississippian and a former military man, Davis had a weak grasp of the realities of the Western theater. Missouri was key, but they had let her be stolen away and ravished. Oh yes, they had sewn another star on the Confederate flag, but it was just lip service to enlist Missouri men and send them east to fight far away from their own tyrant-trampled soil. Price's Missourians, his poor Missourians, deserved more.

He wasn't the only one to realize Davis had no appreciation for the Trans-Mississippi. Take Kirby Smith's gambit. It was obvious to Price, who considered himself a master of political games. Davis wanted yet more infantry sent east to help Hood and Lee. Smith wanted to keep the infantry on his side of the Mississippi. The solution was to unleash Price on Missouri, which meant the southwest would be naked if the infantry were pulled out, too.

Besides, did the president of the Confederacy think it was easy to get divisions over the Mississippi these days? Did he miss the fall of Vicksburg the year before? Was he unaware that Federal gunboats were so thick that a man could walk on the waters like Jesus, really, stepping on Yankee iron all the way from St. Louis to New Orleans?

Price noted that McPheeters was talking now about a letter he had written to Sam, his brother in Kentucky, a man of the cloth and like the doctor, driven out of St. Louis. That was just the kind of tyrants the Yankees were, driving the ministers from their flocks.

Price had heard all the stories, too. That his Missourians were subject to such outrages just meant it was past time for them to break the shackles. Now. Price knew Davis was watching as the Missouri invasion unfolded. Oh, yes, Price would surprise him. Capture St. Louis, spur the uprising and watch the Yankees interlopers scramble. Price admitted it was optimistic, but it paid to be optimistic, to make your own luck.

A major came through the door and placed a newspaper in front of Price.

"Courier from General Shelby, sir," the major said. "He believed you would need to see it."

Price smiled at Shelby's name. Good, some intelligence. The courier placed a three-day-old copy of the *Missouri Republican* on the table. Price picked up the St. Louis sheet and quickly spotted the headline: Rosecrans had brought up Union infantry divisions from down the river — A. J. Smith's people.

The defense of St. Louis was no longer just home guard and 100-day enlistees. Price would be pitting his cavalry against "old regiments," battle-hardened infantry and artillery.

McPheeters was going on about a book he had read. Price vaguely was aware of the author's name, but never read him.

"Dickens is a bad man," the doctor was telling Thomas Jefferson Mackey, Price's chief of engineers, "and by making hideous his characters who profess piety, he clearly seeks to prejudice the public against religion. It's a damned mean mode of attack."

Behind a cloud of smoke from his golden meerschaum, Mackey suggested that perhaps the doctor was taking *Little Dorrit* a little too seriously. McPheeters repositioned, pointed with his cigar.

"His characters are over-drawn and not true to life and…," but then he noticed the general had lowered the newspaper and sagged in his chair.

Price realized that McPheeters was watching him closely.

"Perhaps, William, I will have a little of your brandy now."

SEPTEMBER 25 — 5:15 A.M.

Southbound from St. Louis

So Cump's in Atlanta, Grant's got Bobby Lee bottled up in Petersburg, Sheridan owns the Shenandoah and our ironclads cruise the Mississippi from Cairo to New Orleans. The Confederacy is retreating on every front.

General Thomas Ewing lowered his newspaper. It was still too dim in the car to make out anything more than a headline. He gazed outside the train window into the dark.

So who in hell forgot to tell Pap Price?

Ewing's thoughts about his successful foster brother — "Cump" was a shortening of Tecumseh, William Sherman's middle name — were interrupted as the locomotive gave a sharp tug on the cars. As the chain reaction bumped down the rails, a captain lurched into the seat across from him.

"We're all aboard, sir," said the young officer. "Name's W. J. Campbell, by the way." Ewing grunted. The 14th Iowa infantry, of which Campbell was a part, was supposed to have been on the train already when Ewing arrived a half hour ago. He also wasn't happy about his orders to take just a few companies of the Iowans down to Mineral Point and figure out what Price was up to. He wanted the whole brigade.

"Assigned the guard units we're dropping off?" Ewing asked the harried captain.

"Yes, sir."

Another grunt from the commander of the District of St. Louis. Part of the general's orders was to beef up the squads protecting the southern reaches of the Iron Mountain Railroad, but Ewing figured that amounted to a fool's errand. If Shelby was out there, the trestles would burn, no matter what the Federals did. It was just sucking away yet more fighting men who might come in handy farther south.

Ewing sighed, started to raise the newspaper, but then folded it and gazed at the captain's infantry uniform. Lucky for the Union side that Major General A. J. Smith still had his divisions in Cairo at the tip of Illinois when the call went out to help St. Louis. Still, Ewing would have preferred cavalry for this job. Can't scout with foot soldiers. Once off this train, it'll be slow marching to Cape Girardeau if that's where we're needed.

"Excuse me, sir, what are our orders?"

"Well, Captain Campbell, we're going to try to get a look at the famous Jo

Shelby. See if he's really got Pap Price with him and whoever else. You familiar with Shelby?"

"Just heard the name. Iron Brigade, tough nuts, I suspect, doesn't stay in one place long. They say the same about Bedford Forrest. We whipped *him*."

Another grunt from Ewing. From what he heard, Forrest was a fellow who didn't know the word "whipped." Some said the reb general had two dozen horses shot out from under him. "Well, this is Shelby and last reports are that he's north of Fredericktown or that some of his people are. Price supposedly was seen back in Poplar Bluff."

Their train was crossing the Meramec bridge now, and the rocking of the car was having its usual effect. Ewing had gotten up very early in St. Louis. A little nap might not be out of order. He tried to get his shoulder comfortable against the window, tilted his hat, and through nearly closed eyes he saw the captain shrug to a subordinate officer. From under his hat, Ewing called for his aide-de-camp.

"Captain Hills. Please be so kind as to scare up a map of these parts for our Iowa comrades." Wait until they realize that Fredericktown is almost exactly halfway from Arkansas to St. Louis, he thought. There's none too much time to do whatever is going to be done.

His mind briefly strayed from the military to the maternal, he thought of Ellen, nearing the end of confinement with their family in Ohio. Ewing had promised to get a furlough and be with her through the birth of the baby, but that was out of the question now.

A transplant to Kansas Territory from Ohio, Ewing had made a name for himself nationally by exposing voting fraud under the pro-slavery 1857 Lecompton Constitution. Poll-watching in Kickapoo had been dangerous with all the liquored-up, pistol-waving Missourians from Weston peering at him as they lined up to vote, many more than once. But finding that candle box of false ballots hidden under a woodpile in Lecompton had been the key to under-cutting President Buchanan's machinations to impose the pro-slavery constitution on Kansas. The Free-State men finally had triumphed, and Ewing, at 30, had been elected as the first chief justice of the Kansas Supreme Court.

The state salary, however, would never get him out from his land-speculation debts. Besides, the job had been boring, and he knew his chances for a high place in national politics after the war would be swamped by all the returning heroes. So it hadn't been hard to trade the bench for a colonel's shoulder straps in the 11th Kansas Volunteers.

Ewing had led them well enough at the battles of Cane Hill and Prairie Grove in Arkansas in 1862. His gallantry at the latter got him his star — to the surprise of everyone in his family — and, later, command of the Department of the Border. Headquartered in the little river town of Kansas City, he had been responsible for north Kansas and the corresponding part of Missouri.

Just in time for Quantrill to hit Lawrence. He grimaced, turned his mind to better things, to Cump's plan to head off to Savannah. Not so crazy now, is he? Ewing had gotten him to come west to Leavenworth to manage the Ewing, Sherman & McCook law practice. Although admitted to the bar, Cump had no taste for the courtroom and soon left Kansas. Their partner, Daniel McCook, had died on Kennesaw Mountain in Georgia only two months earlier, leading one of Sherman's brigades. Ewing could have gone east as well. He recalled the shock of his wife and aides when he told them that he had declined Cump's offer of a division in his army. Ewing still wasn't sure he'd made the right decision. Frank Blair had gone in with Cump, and no one was more politically ambitious than Frank. No one could put away the drink like him, either. When Ewing had gone down to Vicksburg to congratulate Cump and the others, Blair had gotten him wallpapered.

After more than an hour of fitful dozing, Ewing stretched his stiff neck and put his hat down on his newspapers.

"Mineral Point's just up ahead, sir."

Ewing nodded and began concentrating on the possibilities. Reports of enemy activity were coming from everywhere, not surprising for a large army looking for forage. At first, Ewing had thought Shelby was providing a screen while Price reduced Cape Girardeau. But the rebs would have been outside Cape by now. Their destination still could be Rolla, but the best rumors pointed to St. Louis, where the Home Guard was feverishly entrenching on the city's outskirts.

But now, Price would have to fight through A. J. Smith, ordered upriver by the frantic Rosecrans. General Thomas in east Tennessee and Sherman were said to be angry at the diversion of the tough, dependable Smith, but to Ewing, the move seemed only common sense. The Department of Missouri had been stripped of 42,000 "effectives," two-thirds of its regular volunteer regiments. With so many sent to other fronts, the Missouri militia could barely control the countryside in many parts of the state. And now an invading army?

The engineer hit the train whistle. Ewing was sure telegrams would be waiting for him at the station. Perhaps the Shelby puzzle had been solved.

Less than an hour later, it was clear that it had not. As Ewing reread the telegrams to make sure he hadn't missed anything, he was growing more certain that Cape Girardeau was safe. The main body of Price's force now seemed headed to Fredericktown.

A few minutes later, Captain Campbell was sitting across from him again, trying to steady a large map across his knees. Other officers gathered around.

"Know what's waiting for us there?" Ewing asked, stabbing a finger at the words, "Pilot Knob," "Ironton" and "Fort Davidson." On the map, Pilot Knob was the tail of the twisting Iron Mountain Railroad.

"Think of the fort as an ugly dwarf guarding the railhead to St. Louis. Hexagonal earthworks, with, I hope, some rifle pits outside that I ordered dug some months back. It may have more heavy guns per square foot than any place I can think of in Missouri, but don't be fooled.

"Fort Davidson is indefensible against a large force."

He paused for a bit of effect.

"So naturally, General Rosecrans wants us to defend it."

Campbell didn't blink. Ewing liked that.

The captain and his men of the 14th Iowa already had seen about the worst the war had to offer. In the Hornet's Nest on Shiloh's horrible first day, they and another Iowa regiment resisted 11 Confederate charges. They finally were shelled into submission by 62 massed cannon firing at almost point-blank range — but not before they had given Grant precious time to regroup and win the battle the next day. Sent to the Camp Oglethorpe prison in Macon, Georgia, Campbell and his Iowans were exchanged and returned to the Union Army to fight some more.

"At least for a bit," Ewing softened his tone, "our orders are to keep the rebels out of Fort Davidson, but to evacuate if Price's main army should show up.

"It's more likely he will pass us by to the east on these roads here and here, but I'm sure that someone will poke into this valley to cover their flank. They also probably know there are supplies here. I've already sent word to Major Wilson. He's got some Third Militia cavalry down there, to scout south and block the Shut-In Gap.

"There's also most of the 47th Missouri Infantry at the fort now and some enrolled militia. With the companies we have left in these cars, that adds 400 rifles, plenty to make it warm for anybody who comes our way."

He did not point out that the 47th had not even broken in its brogans, and the Enrolled Militia would be just as green, although in this part of the state they tended to be loyal. Nor did he sound his misgivings about an easy evacuation. Anyone glancing at his engineering map would immediately recognize it might not be simple at all. Fort Davidson sat on no high ground, but instead at the bottom of a bowl, a small valley hemmed in by big hills. The locals called them mountains.

No one was more aware of the fort's inadequacies than Ewing. The previous summer he had sent engineers to select a more defensible site, but the terrain left them baffled. So he'd ordered hillsides cleared, the parapet built up and the dry moat around the fort deepened.

Campbell put his finger, literally, on what was worrying Ewing.

"There's Fredericktown," he said, tapping the map. "Wasn't Shelby supposed to be there yesterday?"

He didn't have to complete his thought for the officers gathered around. Fredericktown lay less than 20 miles almost due east of Fort Davidson. Because Shelby apparently wasn't in front of them, by implication he already could be circling behind them.

6 P.M.

Warrensburg

Johnson County, western Missouri

"You don't have to tell me. I've already heard."

Lieutenant Colonel Thomas Crittenden wagged an accusing finger at his commander: "You're going off and leaving me here — after all I've done for you."

Colonel John Finis Philips shrugged as his friend plumped into a chair with a heavy and theatrical sigh.

"Orders are orders, Tom. I'm sure you'll follow along pretty quickly."

Headquarters had sent word for Philips to take the bulk and the battery of the Seventh Missouri State Militia Cavalry from Camp Grover here in Warrensburg back east to Sedalia. Everybody was on the move east. Philips could feel the machine of Mars grinding all over the state. Price had the place stirred up.

"Leaving me with just two companies, though. What am I supposed to do with 130 men, Finny?"

Crittenden had used Philips' disliked middle name to nettle him. Philips was the last of a large brood. His parents had named him Finis, the end, showing a humor their son rarely saw displayed when he got older. Ever since the two were classmates at Centre College back in Kentucky, Crittenden had delighted in pronouncing Philips' middle name as obnoxiously as he could. The colonel refused to take the bait.

"Just hold the fort," he replied. "That's all I expect, anyway. If Price shows up, you might let us know. But a word of advice. Pull a Keytesville and your chances of a glorious military career will be severely diminished."

Crittenden snorted at the suggestion. Both men had been shocked to hear of the surrender of Keytesville to bushwhackers a few days before. Even if the central Missouri hamlet was defended by nothing more than an Enrolled Missouri Militia garrison with a muster of shop clerks and farmers, the defeat left a bad taste. Not a single shot had been fired. The marauders simply threatened to burn the town, including the courthouse with the timid militiamen inside. Their commander, a milksop lieutenant named Pleyer, had watched the courthouse torched anyway, the town looted and two strong Union men, one of them the sheriff, marched off and executed. Worse, at least seven men in the garrison joined up with George Todd and John Thrailkill.

The Enrolled companies were a dodgy bunch at best. One regular officer dismissed the militia as "utterly worthless for sober fighting." Some units were in fact distinctly southern-leaning. The Unionists scornfully called many of the Enrolled Missouri Militia "Pawpaws," after the wild fruit that hid in the Missouri woods —just like the southern bushwhackers.

"The Keytesville affair smacks of something stronger than mild treason," fumed General Clinton Fisk, commander of the District of Northern Missouri. He deemed the county disloyal and levied a $50,000 fine on residents to pay the families of the slain men and to build a new courthouse.

The Enrolled Militia were created in 1862 by Governor Hamilton Gamble's Order 19, which disbanded the ineffective Home Guard. The order said, in effect, pick a side. That required every able-bodied man of fighting age, if not already in a volunteer unit, to join the local regiment — even southern sympathizers or Confederate soldiers returned home. In southern-leaning areas, this forced many residents to finally depart for the rebel army in Arkansas or disappear into the brush with the guerrillas.

More animosity was created when recruits assembled to organize a militia unit. Some would accuse their neighbors of disloyalty simply because of old feuds, subjecting them to heavy assessments — as much as $5,000 — needed by the Federals to pay for the units. The assessment process became so abused and onerous that Lincoln eventually outlawed it, but not before much damage was done.

Forcing everyone to sign on and take a rifle had stirred concern as well among those leaning Union, thinking it might be the first step of a draft. The Kansas City *Western Journal of Commerce* noted in July 1862, "It really is astonishing that we have so many men, crippled, blind, maimed, and otherwise unfit for manly duty…. There is an epidemic just now raging in our midst called Gen. Order No. 19…."

Philips and Crittenden belonged to another, earlier militia breed, as different from the Enrolled Missouri Milita units as a red-tailed hawk is from a robin red-breast. They led one of the Missouri State Militia Cavalry regiments, unique to Missouri and its place in the war. Unlike regular volunteer regiments raised in Missouri and marched off to reinforce Union armies under Sherman or Schofield, they were created by the state, but paid, uniformed and equipped by Washington to take the fight to the guerrilla on the home ground of both. The Seventh, stationed in west-central Missouri, Quantrill country, had a reputation for enjoying a good fight. The sides seemed about even.

Crittenden scratched a foul-smelling match and worked to light his pipe. "How's the 'shining dome' holding up?" he asked.

Both men liked their bald-headed commander, Brigadier General Egbert Brown. But they worried whether Brown was up to the task these days.

"He's feeling rode hard and put in the barn wet," Phillips replied. "Now Rosy wants to know what he's doing about reports of large outfits crossing through Carroll County. Brown telegraphed back that if it had happened he would have known about it."

Crittenden tried to snort in derision, but ended up choking on his pipe smoke. He made a show of pounding on his own chest.

Philips chuckled. Everyone in Warrensburg — hell, most of Missouri —

knew what was going on out there. The guerrillas were nowhere and everywhere. On July 22, Major L. C. Matlack reported that his Illinois troopers had arrived in Chillicothe from Glasgow, "hearing much, but seeing nothing on the way." The same day, less than 30 miles away, Colonel A. J. Barr reported: "I found the brush full of bushwhackers at Kingston. They charged into town while (I was) there. I made my escape...."Even with 37 military posts spread across 120 square miles, the Missouri militia could not crush the rebels. The Seventh Cavalry's patrols had been brushing up against bushwhackers for weeks, but rarely brought them to serious battle.

"Brown's fretting about all that hay stored over at Pleasant Hill," Philips said, "but you'll be stretched too thin to send anybody over there." The town was just a little ways into Cass County, one of the counties depopulated by Ewing last summer. While no row crops were grown over there, there had been plenty of hay for Union horses and mules.

"I'm sure the folks there are happy to have something fresh to burn," Crittenden said sourly.

Philips understood the grim joke. It was amazing that anything flammable was left in Pleasant Hill by this point. In August of the previous year, Cole Younger's gang had tried to burn out the town's northern sympathizers, as well as any structure they thought the militia could use. Some stables, the Campbellite church, the Oddfellows Hall, a couple of shops, and a dozen houses had gone up in smoke. Next night, the secesh came back to torch more. Then the following evening, some area militia took revenge against the southerners in the little town by making bonfires of the steam mill, blacksmith and carpenter shops and more businesses and homes. They didn't call it the "Burnt District" for nothing. It had made the Kansans happy to empty out the border counties, but to Philips it just meant the guerrillas were pushed deeper into Missouri.

"Come in," he bellowed to the knock on the door.

Private Barnes, temporarily his orderly, stepped in with papers in hand.

Philips took them, peered at one sheet briefly and put his signature on it, then took another and began to read.

Crittenden took advantage of the quiet to tease the private, a favorite of both officers: "Barnes, I see the scabs are finally off your face, but sadly you've grown no more beautiful. Have you retrieved Uncle Abe's property yet, or is Captain Henslee finally going to charge you with aiding the enemy?"

The tiny private flushed. Near Wellington a few months earlier, Philips had got word of the Sunday wedding of a local desperado and sent a squad to investigate. The result had been mayhem, with screaming women and children pouring from Warder's Church and trying to keep themselves between menfolk and Yankee pistols.

Barnes had been stationed behind the church and quickly found himself in a race with a fellow traveling toward the shelter of deep timber. Just as Barnes was aiming his revolver, his horse tripped and threw the trooper over its neck. Stunned, Barnes had watched his horse right itself and trot away, following the disappearing reb like a faithful dog.

Both officers thought the world of the little private, writing in his report: "Barnes is a mere boy and quite small, but is as bold and dashing a trooper as ever looked an enemy in the face."

Six other "bushers" hadn't escaped, though. Whether the bride, the daughter of the hard-shell preacher, ever got her band of gold wasn't known, but the notorious Jefferson Wilhite got his ration of lead, 28 balls. In his report about the church raid, Philips praised his men's success in getting the women clear of their men, and "the work of death went bravely on."

Philips signed two more documents and gave them back. "That's all, Barnes. Oh, if there's any coffee around, we'd appreciate a couple of cups."

As the teenaged boy retreated from the room, Philips picked up a slip of paper and waved it to his second-in-command.

"Box reports in." Reading the telegram, he intoned sonorously: "I am here. Had a skirmish with the enemy. Killed a lieutenant. Drove the gang across the river."

"'I am here,'" Crittenden nodded. "The fellow has a way with words, doesn't he? Killed a lieutenant, did he? Probably one of ours."

Crittenden had a low opinion of Captain Box, Philips knew, so he threw his friend a bone. "As a final favor to you, I'm ordering Box and H Company to come back here. As soon as he makes it, you start your people east. I'm leaving you Combs."

"Eases the sting of your betrayal only a little. So, Finny, you think this Fredericktown noise is for real? Price is coming up that way, not through Rolla? They've been saying Rolla for ages."

"If that's where Shelby is, then Pap's got to be around there somewhere. You were him, would you want to stick your neck into Missouri without Shelby close by?"

"Well, Jo does like to go on his sprees," Crittenden mused as he watched his pipe smoke. Crittenden, like Shelby, had immigrated to Missouri from Kentucky and had attended his old friend's rather fancy wedding in Waverly back in '58.

Everyone in Missouri had respect for Shelby. The previous fall, the fiery little hemp baron had led his 1,600 men, who'd honestly earned the sobriquet "Iron Brigade," up out of Arkansas, saying he intended to visit his home on the Missouri River. Philips and Brown had spent four days chasing and shooting after him and had nearly got the squeeze on the slippery reb at Marshall, but the trap had not quite closed. Shelby had gotten home to Waverly, all right, but with Philips on his heels had had no chance to exchange pleasantries with his traitorous friends.

It was the second time Brown had topped Shelby that year. When Marmaduke's raiders got into Springfield, the Federal general had been able to beat them off. Shelby got a licking, and Brown got a bullet high in his left arm, rendering it useless.

A whaler in his youth, Brown loved to tell stories of his days at sea. Philips had likened him once to old Ahab in that book by Melville. The captain had lost a leg, Brown the use of his arm. Brown didn't seem bitter, like Ahab, but you had to wonder. And now here comes Shelby again.

Pondering the similarities once more, Philips had a startling thought. That last meeting with the whale had not gone so well for Ahab's crew.

SEPTEMBER 26 — 10:35 A.M.

On the road to Ironton
Iron County, southeast Missouri

SUTTON TROTTED HIS NAG UP AND reached into a bulging pocket: "Here, have some pawpaws."

R. E. Holley took them and thanked his friend and fellow private. It was all they would have for breakfast. Somebody with a heart of grindstone had stolen their little poke of corn meal, probably one of the deserters Shelby rounded up in the north Arkansas hills and dumped on their division. Laboriously grated off a much-punctured sheet of tin last night, the corn meal would have made some morning coosh — mixed with grease and water and fried in a pan, a mainstay of the often famished Confederate Army.

The pawpaws probably meant a case of the shits down the road, but ah, that was down the road.

Messing with the soft fruit, Holley let his Enfield slip from its perch balanced across his pommel. Instinctively, he stuck out his stirruped foot to catch its fall. One point of the wooden butt caught him just above his bare toes. Damn! Damn, that hurts!

Like many in this column, Holley had no shoes. He'd started out with a shabby pair, but they had fallen apart halfway across Arkansas.

"Should have let it fall," Sutton remarked, a large bit of pawpaw fruit caught on his beard. "If it had gone off and shot you in the foot, probably wouldn't have hurt so much."

Between clenched teeth, Holley thanked him for the helpful advice.

"When we going to find some shoes?"

Sutton, who sported a pair in a condition so poor as to make a cobbler weep, shook his head.

"I had high hopes for goods in Fredericktown, but wasn't nothing left of them but their shadows."

Sutton was Holley's best friend in L Company. They shared blankets at night and jokes about the officers. Sutton had the water jug, Holley had the frying pan. Everything was share and share alike but the ammunition, and that was because Holley had a muzzle-loader, while Sutton carried a huge LeMat grape-shot revolver. Besides packing nine pistol rounds, it had an extra barrel that carried a 16-gauge scattergun load. It was a marvel in up-close fighting, but held no lure for Holley. He didn't particularly like to get that near a Yankee 'less he was well dead. Holley preferred his Enfield. It threw a ball a mile.

Both sides used the British Enfield — 900,000 of them were on American battlefields — but the Confederates more: They did not have the 1861 Springfield being mass-produced in northern armories. Both weapons fired the .58-caliber minié ball. The British rifle, which had done its bit to expand the Empire, was believed slightly more accurate than the Springfield.

Besides shoes and arms, Price's army — as well as just about every other fighting Confederate command — needed everything: cartridge boxes, canteens, tents and even blankets. Where the Federals used eight nails to shoe a horse, the rebels settled for six.

In the west, a complete Confederate uniform was the exception, unless it was a higher-ranking officer's. "In this army one hole in the seat of the breeches indicates a captain, two holes a lieutenant, and the seat of the pants all out indicates that the individual is a private," wrote a Texas soldier.

"You notice how the sun is behind us?" Sutton asked. "Ain't St. Louis north? Why ain't we going north? I just know there's gunboats in St. Louis." He was using the vernacular for the low-topped brogans issued to the Federal infantry. Word was that there were some Yankees over to the west. Apparently, Fagan or Cabell or Price thought they needed working over. Holley had no problem with the idea. He just wanted to find a dead Yankee with feet as big as his.

"Sutton, what was in that coffee we had last night?"

His friend just laughed and said it didn't bear discussion. Then he softly sang a few lines of an old marching song:

"Some hot smoking java, it makes my mouth lava,
I wish I had some in me now, don't you?"

Just then, Captain Wolfe came trotting down the line.

"Hey, Cap'n, where we going?"

"Ironton, they say."

He offered nothing more, kept his horse heading east. Turning his head to watch the company commander ride away, Holley mused, "Acts like he forgot something in Fredericktown."

"Maybe yore shoes."

"Yeah, that's pra'bly it, my shoes." He looked down at the raw place on his foot. "Hope he hurries back with 'em."

They were quiet for a couple miles as the column followed the post road west, ascending an ancient, nature-hewn valley of pink granite, boulders jutting between slope-clinging pines. Below, a stream ran over wide sheets of stone.

"Looks like a place that could have an Iron Town," Sutton observed.

"We ain't in Loggy Bayou no more," agreed Holley. His horse chose that moment to give its head a good shake. This time Holley grabbed the Enfield with his sticky hands as it started to slide. The Enfield was a fine piece, but it wasn't made for horse soldiers. Couldn't load it in the saddle. Had to get down.

He shivered. A Yankee overcoat would go well with them shoes. The problem was that he and Sutton were not well placed in the column. Too many soldiers ahead of him; they would forage out the easy pickin's.

Up ahead past Shut-In Gap, in fact, an advance guard of about 400 cavalrymen in Slemon's Brigade had come across the Arcadia Valley home of Cyrus Russell. Russell was ill in bed and could not flee. The rebels dragged him downstairs and outside, where one hit him in the head with a pistol butt. His wife, with a baby clinging to her, begged them not to kill him. While Russell was left alive, he lost everything from the clothes on his back to six boxes of honey in the cellar. "We had time now to look about us; and what did we see?" a relative later wrote. "There was not a room, nor a nook nor a corner which had not been visited; trunks were turned upside down; every bureau drawer was emptied of its contents; every article of food eaten or carried off; the orchard stripped of its fruits; the farm wagon and five horses taken; the carriage cut to pieces."

Holley looked up at dark clouds building over the mountain nubs ahead. "Think that'll turn to rain?"

"Well, we'll just get snug in our tent if it does." This was just more of his friend's wit. Sutton had a ragged scrap of canvas, barely a yard square, rolled up behind his saddle. He called it their tent.

"If it does," Holley said, "I get the side without the hole for a change."

"Ain't nothin' guaranteed in this world, R. E. Ain't nothin."

SEPTEMBER 27 — 8 A.M.

Pilot Knob
Iron County

THE SURGEON AWOKE FUZZY-HEADED FROM A troubled sleep. The night before, Colonel Seymour Carpenter had felt the occasion warranted a heavy dip into his medicine chest, and now his head told him the dose of whiskey had been a mite high.

Eyes still tightly closed, Carpenter listened to his tentmate muttering to another officer outside. Not surprisingly, the news was nearly as depressing as the previous evening. Myriads of rebels stirring already.

The train whistle blew. Still here, was it? No doubt it was filled with refugees.

As Carpenter got off the cars from St. Louis the night before, scores of locals scrambled to get aboard.

"I never saw such a panic as prevailed there," Carpenter would recall. "The streets were full of people, loaded with plunder, while more fortunate ones were moving off in great haste, in every kind of vehicles. They said the 'Rebs' were at Arcadia two miles below, just about 100,000 strong. I asked for the General; they said he was at the front fighting, but most probably killed or captured."

What nonsense. Ewing had come in about 7 o'clock, cheerful and ravenously hungry after the fighting down the valley. The general, an old friend of Carpenter's, had skillfully concealed a couple pounds of bacon and biscuits while discussing strategy with his officers. Carpenter, to make himself useful, had held a lantern as Ewing scribbled out orders on a barrelhead.

The day before, the Federal forces had pushed back the advance elements of Price's army, but the weight of numbers foretold what would happen. As Carpenter listened, he understood the Federals had been forced out of Ironton but were still resisting on the hills.

The doctor diagnosed the dull throb in his head: He would live, but just barely. Muskets began firing down the valley. When the first big gun of the fort opened up, Carpenter jumped a little. Maybe he needed another soothing sip from mother jug. He dug out his watch, pried open an eye and groaned. Only two hours sleep?

Carpenter decided it was past time to join his surgery staff at their makeshift hospital. The day before he and Ewing had decided the hospital would be set up in a church a couple hundred yards from the earthworks. As left his tent, Carpenter noticed two men with light wounds walking by and directed them to the church. Not enough to concern him yet.

"Check them all over," he yelled in to his staff. He drummed that into all the surgeons under him. It stemmed from the campaign in Arkansas, when a rebel soldier had complained bitterly about a finger that had been shot off. Carpenter hastily dressed the hand and was astounded when the man dropped dead on the floor. Looking more closely, the surgeon found an almost bloodless bullet wound in the rebel's abdomen.

Smoke appeared on the hill to the west. "Here the enemy opened on us with two guns from the summit of Shepherd's Mountain at about 800 yards, and two from the side as a less distance," Ewing would report. "The guns were well covered and we could not silence them, the two nearest getting and keeping our range exactly."

Carpenter watched the Union crews still outside the fort working their own field pieces. He had thought it noisy at Bull Run, where there were surely much more artillery, but that time he hadn't been so close.

Ewing had asked him to keep an eye on the town's telegraph office, the link to the Union forces supposedly building up at Mineral Point. Outside the little

Catholic church, Carpenter saw the telegrapher running his way, nothing in his hand. The wire was down. Carpenter directed the man to make sure Ewing got the word.

From one side of the church came a sharp *whap*. Then another. One of the surgeons, wiping his hands with a bloody rag, came to the door to join him.

"Doesn't seem our hospital flag's doing a lot of good, huh? Rebs must be coming to St. Louis to get fitted with spectacles." A round shot that had missed the fort went rolling down a street like a fat terrier on a mission. Carpenter had seen the damage cannon balls could do, had treated men who had playfully stuck out a foot or a hand to arrest a rolling ball, only to have it ripped off by the hidden energy.

"We're too close," his fellow surgeon said. It suddenly occurred to Carpenter that the enemy was overshooting the fort. Fool, he told himself, why didn't I see that before! We need to set up farther away. Where is Ewing?

Carpenter's dignity did not allow him to crouch or duck behind buildings as he approached the lines of Federal riflemen. Besides, as best he could tell, the sound of firing seemed to come from almost every direction. He caught Ewing's attention and began to explain the need to shift, but the distracted Ewing interrupted him, saying to do whatever pleased him. Before Ewing moved on, Carpenter remembered.

"Tom, you know the telegraph is cut?" Ewing nodded, looked to the north. Now the probability of being surrounded was dangerous reality.

Carpenter spent the next half hour making the move to what he hoped was a safer spot, a house in the middle of the settlement. The wounded were clearly relieved; the church siding had been holed in a couple places.

On their last trip, shifting bandages and surgical instruments, a ball tore into a horse a few yards away. My God! Carpenter thought. One could throw a hat through that hole! The surrounding mounts shied and danced, eyes wide with terror. One broke his reins and galloped away. Very smart horse. It occurred to Carpenter that perhaps he should be riding him just now.

IV

Hell fire

"The very air seems charged with blood and death. East of us, west of us, north of us, south of us, comes the same harrowing story. Pandemonium itself seems to have broken loose, and robbery, murder and rapine, and death run riot over the country."

— T. Dwight Thacher, editor of the Kansas City
Western Journal of Commerce, 1864

e⁄⁾e⁄⁾e⁄⁾e⁄⁾e⁄⁾e⁄⁾

SEPTEMBER 27 — 10 A.M.

Centralia

Boone County, central Missouri

THE GUERRILLAS' LOSSES AT FAYETTE STUNG mightily. Afterward, they had ridden up to Huntsville, where Bill Anderson sent in a message for the Union garrison to surrender.

Pretty clear what the answer was going to be. The commander there was a fellow named Denny. One of the bands had hung his pa in August. "Tell him if he wants us to come for us," was Denny's reply.

It just made Anderson look that much worse, 'cause Huntsville was his own hometown. So he was all for charging in, but George Todd wanted nothing to do with attacking any more garrison towns, and they had moved on. Nobody desired to treat the milish to another turkey shoot, but here was the biggest gathering of partisan rangers in forever, and for what?

So the band turned its horses southeast and camped on Young's Creek, where it cut through Singleton's farm a couple miles south of Centralia.

Anderson got up from his blankets deciding he required newspapers, information to let him know how Price was doing, so he declared he'd go into Centralia. Todd, John Thrailkill and Si Gordon's people just wanted to stay in camp, some to clean wounds, others to sober up. With his foot burning and seeping blood, Riley decided he'd go along with Bill and maybe find some ointment or something. Buck James and his snotty brother came along, too. They made maybe 60 in all.

Centralia had little reason to exist except as a spot on the railroad, where the stage south to Columbia crossed the tracks. The hundred or so folks who lived in the hamlet gave them no fuss. Anderson was sitting outside the saloon eating some cornbread out of a basket when Archie Clement came up with a couple newspapers.

"Well, Bill you're famous, but they spelled your name wrong."

Bill stopped chewing. "How can you misspell 'William Anderson?'"

Archie grinned. "It's right here in black and white. Says, 'The devil is loose in Chariton and Carroll counties with scarcely three feet of chain to his neck...'"

Laughing and spraying cornbread into his beard, Anderson snatched the paper. His study of the article hardly had commenced when a stage swung into view. It was quickly covered by two or three dozen pistols. Riley hobbled after Bill to see who they'd caught as some fellows were shouted out of the coach. One gentleman claimed they should not be robbed because they were Southerners.

"What do we care? Hell's full of all such Southern men. Why ain't you fightin'?" snarled Jasper Moody and snatched away the whiner's valise. Opening it up, he whooped and pulled out a gleaming white shirt with ruffles. He immediately began pulling off the red-checkered number he had on. It was nearly in rags, but Riley wondered how good a trade it was. That white linen would make a better target, at least till he'd got it his usual level of bad filthy. Buck agreed, remarking how Moody appeared to be dressing up for his own funeral.

Meanwhile, explorers in the freight house discovered four crates of boots and a huge barrel of whiskey. Another wild night in camp, Riley predicted. Men tied pairs together and then slung them over their horses' necks as extra saddlebags to fill with loot. Some of the footwear sloshed with the liberated liquor.

But the excitement did not end there. No, sir. Far, far from it. The partisans' heads suddenly whipped around as if all were on the same string. A train whistle to the east. Nobody had even thought to inquire about the North Missouri's schedule.

Running to the station, the boys still wearing their Union jackets got out front and waved from the platform. The rest hung back out of sight. The engineer was a wise old cove, though, and smelled a rat. Still down the line a ways, he began to try to get his steam back up, but then saw the stack of ties being piled onto the track. That forced his hand. The locomotive, with three passenger carriages and express and baggage cars, sighed to a stop right up next to the depot. When the boys pushed through the passenger coaches, it was a sight — among the riders were 23 Union soldiers on furlough from the war back east. Claimed they were from engineering brigades with Sherman, that they hadn't killed any of our men. Just a couple had pistols, but gave 'em up real meek.

Pushed off the train and lined up, they looked shocked at the shouts to strip down to their drawers. Two had been shot on the trains for not moving fast enough, so they knew it was bad, of course. When Anderson stepped up and told them who he was, they knew it was worse.

Riley thought they held up pretty well, even when some of the band spat on them or slapped them with their revolvers. One was on a crutch, and a few had other healing wounds. Another was ancient and wore tattered blue. No one could understand what he was babbling. Riley was sure he was no soldier, but Archie waved the old man into line, anyway, and then asked Bill what to do with them.

"Parole them," Anderson replied. If the Yankees took heart at that, then they didn't understand what was in Archie's cold laugh. For once though, he wasn't thinking of slaying everyone in his hands, but suggested hostages might help to get Cave Wyatt exchanged back from the Carroll County militia. Bill nodded, said just one would do fine. He called out, Was there any sergeants among them? They all just stared at him. When he asked a second time, a curly bearded feller stepped out, said he was Thomas Goodman, First Missouri Engineers.

Buck muttered to Riley that Goodman had real sand, figuring probably that he was about to take a bullet for his boys. Real Christian. Riley could tell the others — there was surely other sergeants who'd stayed mum — were relieved. But Bill had a never-ending number of tricks to surprise a Yankee.

Anderson led Goodman away and nodded at Archie, who suddenly fired both pistols, felling two men at once. That commenced the killing. Most of the Feds died where they stood. "Oh! Lord, I am gone up," one screamed. Some begged, some prayed, but as one bushwhacker said, "We slew in the face of prayer."

A big man knocked some rangers down, and although he'd stopped numerous bullets, got between the cars. The Yankee crawled under the station platform, so the boys set fire to it. Smoked out, his fate was no better than before.

"I expected every moment to be called forth, and to become, as it were, the last victim upon the hellish altar of Hate, erected by these demons, and reeking with the blood of innocent, defenseless men," Thomas Goodman wrote later. "Every one who passed me, in the preparations they were making, heaped abuse and curses upon my head, and not unfrequently a carbine or revolver was placed in close proximity thereto, with the threat: 'I would like to kill the d–n Yankee — Hell-fire is too good for you, you son of a bitch!'"

Screaming from women passengers just added to the mayhem, especially when a couple civilians ended up getting shot for holding back money and watches. One fancy-dressed fellow got bluffed into admitting he had $100 hidden in his boot. For holding back he was promptly plugged in the head, right in front of his mama. One lay unconscious with what looked like a ball in the lung, a heel of his shoe scraping back and forth, making a little rut in the dirt. Archie, the little piss ant — was he even five feet? — swaggered over to enjoy the fellow's last moments.

"He's marking time," Archie giggled as he broke open a Navy and began retrieving fresh charges from his pocket. Riley felt his gray eyes turn on him.

"Didn't see you doing none of the shooting."

"Wasn't of a mind," Riley answered and then crossed the tracks to find his horse tied back in the village. Turned out a patent medicine feller was on the train, and Buck James had secured various bottles and tins for Riley's foot. He'd also scared up another white shirt to rip up for a bandage. Riley thanked him very kindly. He appreciated how Buck seemed to pay attention to him.

One of the woman passengers timorously asked Anderson if they could continue on their way now.

"You can go to hell for all I care," he snorted. But that trip would not be on *this* train. It was set on fire and sent rolling on down the line to give the militia in Sturgeon something to talk about. The men sorted out their mounts and started back toward Singleton's farm.

But hard as the day was for them Yankee mamas, turned out the scythe had just been whetted a little.

1:15 P.M.

SUSAN SNEED HAD TO SIT DOWN.

The hotel's watering trough seemed the most likely place. She might need to splash a little of its murky water on her face. This was no time to faint. She had never swooned in her life. But then she'd never witnessed hell ride in on 50 horses, either.

Twisted grotesqueries wearing blood-soaked long johns covered much of the road between Ball's store and the tracks. Some had been scalped. The heads of some had been caved in. Parts of one were on the track where a locomotive had been driven over it.

"The maimed bodies of the Union boys lay where they had fallen," Thomas Goodman, the only Federal survivor, would recall. "Here and there wandering listlessly among the slain you could observe some few civilians, while others stood idly at their doors, or near the depot grounds, gazing half amazed and wonderingly, on the scene, as though they had not fully recovered from the shock of the revolting spectacle they had so recently witnessed."

No one made a move to gather the dead. The depot, the cars and the little storehouse across the tracks were almost consumed by flame now, hopeless. No one had lifted a hand to fight the fires. Anderson had warned them against it, hadn't he? And he couldn't be that far away, could he?

Congressman James S. Rollins, who'd hidden jammed in the garret of the Boone House, had taken off with a group walking smartly down the tracks toward Mexico. He and Boone County Sheriff James Waugh had been on their way to the Democratic Congressional Convention there. Rollins, a strong Unionist although opposing emancipation of the slaves, would have been in serious danger.

Only God knows how they escaped being recognized when their stage was robbed. Rollins had done a fine piece of acting, insisting he was a preacher of the Methodist Church, South. The "South" part had been clever, she thought. In the end, only the arrival of the train had distracted the bushwhackers long enough for Rollins and the sheriff to get out of sight. Eventually Anderson discovered the trick and thought of searching for the congressman, but one of his men talked him out of it, saying Rollins might already have sneaked out of town.

She looked around. What they hadn't robbed from the store, the guerrillas had thrown into the street. They had galloped down the streets streaming bolts of calico behind them. She thought someone could roll it up and still get something for it. But the dish sets just got in from St. Louis were a lost cause.

Riders! someone yelled, coming on the Paris road.

Oh, Lord, Susan Sneed thought to herself, have we not suffered enough?

The little railroad stop sat upon a flat and soggy prairie, so the new party, coming slowly, could be seen clearly. Blue uniforms. Not that that meant anything. Anderson and most of his men had been wearing blue. As she watched the riders approach, Achilles, her brother-in-law and the town's doctor, came up to her.

"Susan, are you all right?"

"No, but I ain't shot, if that's what you mean."

"I guess that's what I mean," said Achilles. "You haven't been misused...." She was surprised that he was blushing. He had delivered her babies, after all.

"No, they didn't try anything with me or any women that I know of."

Achilles surveyed the debris outside his brother's establishment. "Anderson come into the place?"

"No, he did his drinking with Joe Collier at the Eldorado, not that it helped us none. Had to fix breakfast for a passel of 'em. Cleaned me out, except for some potatoes and lard." She fluttered a hand toward the bodies. "Anyone out there *not* gone to Kingdom, Achilles?"

He shook his head.

Her husband, Thomas, came out the door, saying he had got settled those passengers who were not up to traveling on just yet. The wind shifted, and he tracked the sparks soaring from the fire.

"Has to be Union troops, looking for those devils," Achilles said, watching the oncoming riders.

Turned out that it was Major A. V. E. Johnston, leading his just-organized 39th Missouri Infantry (Mounted) out of Paris looking for marauders. He had been drawn by the smoke. Now he pulled up before the Boone House and gazed around with his mouth open. A wall of the depot collapsed in a swirl of embers, some floating far enough to land on the soldiers' horses, making them hard to control.

The woman stayed where she sat, but Thomas Sneed and his brother deferentially approached the major. Both knew how the Federals often took out their frustrations on the townspeople for these things. They seemed to assume that Missouri hamlets should rebuff Anderson — just throw him out like some old town drunk. It was not unheard of for government troops to burn a town where their comrades had only been shot at. Here they had been slaughtered like hogs.

"It was Anderson," Achilles said.

"How many with him?" the major asked.

"Not sure, maybe 40, 50?" Achilles asked Thomas.

"Maybe a few more," he replied.

"So they went south?"

"Down that way, yes," Achilles pointed, "they may be camped on Young's Creek, but...."

"They will not get away with this!" Johnston said angrily, waving at the bodies. "For God's sake, someone cover them up! Have some damned decency, damn you!"

The Sneed brothers offered to take the officers up to the attic windows of the hotel that looked to the south. Susan kept to the street, observing the farm boys in their new uniforms. They sat their mounts talking to themselves about the shapes in the dirt. She thought that whoever sold them those horses could either get a medal for sharp dealin' or be shot as a traitor.

Her gaze turned up to the men upstairs, but it stopped at a second-floor window, where a little blonde girl was peering out. Susan didn't know her name. She was one of those off the train. As the bushwhackers had begun firing the train, Thomas Sneed had raced through the carriages to make sure they were empty. As he had feared, the bushwhackers had been so drunk that they'd missed a mother and her brood cowering under a seat. He had led the woman off the platform. She'd walked like she was in a dream, her arms limp and the babies hanging onto her skirt. He had put them into that room, No. 3. They'd been in no shape to make the trek to Mexico, which was about 14 miles east.

The girl was young, but not so that she didn't understand the meaning of those twisted shapes in the street. Turn away, child, Susan willed her. Turn away before those poor men find a home in your dreams. The little face, blurred by the dirt on the pane of glass, disappeared. Before long, Johnston and his captain came stomping down again. They had spotted a small party of guerrillas just down the south road toward Singleton's farm.

M. G. Singleton was a wealthy farmer and a founder of Centralia, but having once served in the Federal-fighting State Guard, he'd been careful to give the Yankees no excuses until now to bother him. It was hard, though, to say no to 400 guerrillas. His wife even thought it was a fine idea. The previous year, about 20 Union militiamen had come to their house and demanded dinner. When she refused, they flew into a rage, insulting the woman, having two armed Negroes eat at the family table, throwing food and ruining the rug.

Susan was surprised to hear the major ordering his "H men" to stay and guard the town as he took the two other companies out after Anderson. Were it her, she thought, she'd take every man and gun that could be slung 'cross a horse. Course, were it her, she'd then whip that horse as fast as it would go in the other direction. 'Twas pure evil that came to this village this Monday.

Achilles was begging them to be wary, that there might be too many out there. But that Johnston was a determined cuss, didn't seem to want to hear any of it. As the major stuck his boot into his stirrup, Susan distinctly heard him mutter:

"I'll kill that son-of-a-bitch Anderson or eat my supper in hell."

1:40 P.M.

Young's Creek
South of Centralia

It might be all in his head, but hobbling away from the turbid little stream Riley thought his foot seemed a mite better. After the pus was squeezed out, he had soaked it and washed away the crusted blood. Then he applied the strongest-smelling ointment from the tins on the theory that it was the most powerful cure. Wrapping scraps of shirt around the heel, he'd eased on the stiff new boot, two sizes too large, he got from town.

The new footwear was nice, and he was kicking himself for not thinking to bring the mate of the smaller boot for the time when his heel returned to normal. But he did not believe he would be riding back to Centralia to claim it. No thank you.

As he grabbed saplings and pulled himself up the slippery creek bank, he heard a hubbub ahead. A fight between some of the boys? No, guerrillas were hieing through camp in every direction, collecting gear, untying reins. A rider was addressing the upraised heads of the leaders. Riley now could make it out what he was saying: Feds in Centralia, at least a hundred. Todd turned to Pool.

"Take a dozen men 'round about up there and demonstrate a little on the road."

Anderson offered to send Archie, but Todd ignored him. Earlier, Todd had made it clear how unhappy he was to hear of Anderson's doings in town. Pool waved over a few of his band, and they were gone. Nobody needed to be told what was happening. A little bushwhacker bait was about to be cast out for the Yankees to see.

The chiefs conferred quickly on tactics. Before too long, maybe 300 men were dividing in three directions. Both Jameses stayed with Anderson, so Riley did, too. They walked their horses out of the woods into a broad clearing and waited. Riley glanced over and saw their Federal hostage still in his drawers, on a horse behind a ranger.

And there came Pool and his people, galloping back toward them over the gentle rise ahead. Reaching the bottom of the slope, the bushwhackers slowed their blowing horses and got in the line. Yep, pretty quick, the militia came into view at the top of the rise. Seeing the rebels waiting so patiently for them, they stopped, wanting to recalculate the odds. It might have looked even. But what the milish up there didn't realize was that toward either side of their little ridge the woods reached out arms that held nothing good for them. Then their officer had 'em dismount, figuring their rifles could handle the rebs from there.

"Why, the fools are going to fight us on foot," Riley heard John Koger say with a laugh, and then more somberly, "God help 'em."

The officer up there sounded mad, not scared like if he had any sense. "Stand

and fight!" he howled, and Archie giggled loudly. Riley had to agree. Fight, surely; stand there, no, thank you, ma'am.

Someone reported a signal from Thrailkill, off unseen in the brush to the right. Over on the left somewhere were Gordon and Todd. Riley wished he were with them, not grasping early on the role that Anderson wanted in this fight. Riding straight into all them muskets could make a fellow a little wobbly.

They began with their horses at a walk, but then Bill waved his hat and screamed "charge," and Riley was shrieking with the rest as they thundered up that gentle little slope, suddenly crowned with gunsmoke. Riley noted that the Federals' volley was too hasty. Missed, too high, can't shoot worth a … And then his face and rein hand were splattered with something warm. Just ahead, Fred Shepherd toppled out of his saddle, nearly falling on Buck's horse, his head a wreck of black hair, brain and blood.

"Up the hill we went, yelling like wild Indians," Frank James recalled decades later. "Almost in a twinkling of an eye we were on the yankee line. They seemed terrorized. Hypnotized might be a better word.…" Some of the militiamen were fixing bayonets, other were biting off their cartridges. "Yelling, shooting our pistols, upon them we went."

The militia line never got off another round. The Navy bucked twice in Riley's hand, and a soldier crumbled in the act of trying to get the ramrod out of his rifle barrel. As Anderson's bunch blasted through the line, cutting off retreat, Todd and the others swept up from the sides. Johnston himself was killed. Some Yankees threw down their rifles and cried for mercy, but mercy was in ragged supply in these times.

"I always spare prisoners!" one officer entreated, clutching the reins of a guerrilla mount.

The bushwhacker's response was to level his pistol barrel. "I *never* do." And he pulled the trigger.

Riley didn't look back but kept the little mare pointed at the milish who had been assigned to stay back holding their mounts. Most had managed to get on the horses and kick them frantically toward Centralia, but a few just sat there with mouths open and hands up. One gray-bearded man fumbled with a pistol, having dropped his rifle. Riley gave him one in the stomach, heard a groan.

Then Riley was heading for the road, popping away at the backs of several escapees but doing no discernable damage with the last three rounds in his Colt. Buck passed him, going like blazes on Little George. Then McCorkle, Todd and some others roared by, whooping like at a fairgrounds race. Riley pulled up to watch as Federals, one after another, tumbled back-shot into the road. Most were doomed by their sickle-hammed plow horses. When the boys had gone out of sight, Riley turned Folly — and was startled that behind him the graybeard Federal was still in his saddle holding that pistol. But he was slumped, the only movement from his sway-backed nag as it contentedly chomped grass.

Riley swung wide around them. He heard another low groan. Let someone else finish him, he thought. I've done enough today.

The pursuers finally returned, their horses blowing, covered in foam. Mc-Corkle's, in fact, was broke down. Turned out that the Yankees had left a small detachment in Centralia, which neither fought nor rode any better than those on the ridge. Buck reported that a few made it across Scattering Creek — pretty good name, when you think about it — but he surely had pinked one of them good. Those that had escaped may have been ploughboys, but they'd found some decent horse flesh somewhere. Generally, for such steeplechases of life or death, the guerrilla always was careful to have a better mount than what was scraped up by the Federal quartermaster. "Anderson always made us keep our horses in good condition," Frank James would recall.

The poor bastards of H Company left behind in the hamlet were hunted down. Two Yankees hid in the Eldorado Hotel privy but were coaxed to come out and be taken prisoner. When they opened the door to smiling faces, as one busher would recount that night, "They were both shot to shit." A guerrilla asked a woman for drink of water, but before she handed up the dipper, a Federal broke cover and leaped over a fence. The bushwhacker spurred his horse in chase, put a fatal bullet in the running man and then trotted back, saying "I'll take that drink now."

Young John C. Rowland, the assistant railroad agent, was about to transport some women, perhaps passengers of the ill-fated cars, out of town after the massacre. Seeing the trouble, he drove his wagon behind a barn, but was found there by Tom Little. One of the women said something, and Little slashed her across the face with his pistol barrel. Rowland grabbed the gun barrel, his foot slipped off the brake and his team jerked the wagon, nearing dragging him out of the wagon box. Unimpressed by chivalry, the bushwhacker discharged a slug into the handsome face, riding away amid fresh female lamentations.

The boys remarked on the stoic toughness of one private, apparently one Frank Barns. Sergeant Goodman recorded this exchange: "We have got a prisoner, one of Johnston's men. We had to chase him a long way, and only settled him by putting six balls in his body."

"Ain't he dead yet?"

"Nary dead. The devil can't kill him, an' seein' as how he's good stuff, we shall care for him. We were ordered to carry him to a house below, so you see we will save him yet." Federal Lieutenant W. T. Clarke, who rode into Centralia later, also told of a wounded man "who has six holes in him," mockingly laid by the road by Todd to count the enemy as they rode by.

As usual, the bushwhackers stripped bodies of whatever was useful and smashed the rifles. Some of the drunks were having too much fun, however, using knives and bayonets in ways that did not bear comment.

Scalping had become common in Anderson's band. And some militia responded in like manner. The bushwhackers' methods varied. From some, according to the *Columbia Missouri Statesman,* "almost the entire scalp was skinned off; from others only a small piece was cut out about the size of a silver dollar. From the foreheads of others small strips of skin were cut off; all to be carried as trophies by these incarnate fiends."

Sergeant Goodman had been in the war out East and was not aware of how things were done in Missouri.

"Hell had suddenly been transferred to earth, and all the fiends of darkness summoned to join a carnival of blood," the captive would recall. "No treatment too cruel to satisfy the greed of that hellish crew."

Riley figured that maybe 100 bodies were in the grass on that slope. That should be enough killing for one day. Dave Pool hopped from corpse to corpse. He was either counting them, checking for possum-players or proving he could get the length of their line without touching the grass. Todd complained about disrespect, but Pool wasn't fazed.

"If they're dead," he laughed, "I can't hurt them."

V

Assault

*"Oh, what a sight! The enemy everywhere!
They came pouring in over the hills from all
points — a procession without end."*

— Mrs. C. J. Pitkin, recalling the arrival of
Price's army south of Pilot Knob

e/ɔe/ɔe/ɔe/ɔe/ɔ

Pilot Knob
Iron County

THE YOUNG SURGEON'S SAW WAS A Butcher's, Seymour Carpenter observed. He preferred his own Teufel, with its "trigger finger" hole, but you couldn't beat a Butcher for finesse.

The patient, an unlucky private, slumped in the operating chair almost beyond caring. Before succumbing to the dreams of chloroform, he had been resigned to waking without a right arm, already smashed into pulp and splinters by a ball in the elbow. When a sergeant had led the wounded man up to the door of the makeshift hospital, orderlies moved to help the patient off his mount. The private had cursed them, swung off the horse by himself and walked in almost defiantly.

Once the flesh was carved from the humerus, orderlies tightened their hold. Bone dust drifted above the swift, sure strokes. Carpenter figured on getting his own hands bloody today, but now he was acting in his role as medical director. The blade went quickly through the bone, and the strong, young fingers tied off the artery, knotting the thread and leaving a long tail dangling from the wound. In the post-operative days, the doctors would gently tug on the thread to see whether the knot had dissolved. If the thread slipped out, that meant the artery had clotted. It didn't always happen that way. For the unlucky ones, removal of the knot was followed by a fatal hemorrhage.

Carpenter watched approvingly as the cutter — stripped to the waist like most of the others to avoid ruined clothes from squirting blood — wiped his saw blade on his stained apron. A clean surgeon. Carpenter like that. As the skin flaps were sewn over the stump, he noted that the artillery exchanges were diminishing. What, was the battle over?

He went to the door, stepped out....

The stable across the street exploded, throwing hay, splintered wood and shingles in an impressive arch. Carpenter was staggered and sprinkled with dirty straw but did not fall. Despite the ringing in his ears, he heard the screams of rebels swarming out of the brush on the hill to the west. He moved to a corner to get a better view. The blue-jacketed line of pickets was scattering, pushed like chaff in that first gust of wind before a thunderstorm. Some dropped their rifles for more speed in the footrace for the fort or for the rifle pits outside. Behind them a wave of butternut. God, how many were there?

A shriek and a crack above. The yellow hospital flag with its large brown "H" fluttered down. A horse screamed and fell on its side, pawing the air. Suddenly, an ambulance began racing away. Carpenter roared for the driver to slow down and then realized there was no driver. The panicked beasts had not been hitched tightly enough. Oh, no!

He watched the vehicle tilt and tilt and then it was being dragged on its side. Wounded men spilled out. They rolled cursing in the dust behind.

It had been *his* suggestion to place the injured in the ambulances to keep the operating areas clear and have the hurt men ready to be quickly removed on their way to Jefferson Barracks when the time came. Well, they were removed, all right.

Running with his staff to catch the ambulance team, he sensed that the attack from Shepherd Mountain had quieted considerably, beaten down by the galling cannon and rifle fire from the fort. Then a new roar of yells and explosions, this time from the east. A mass of enemy rushed through the outskirts of the town. The fort — my God! — its little drawbridge was still flat! A rope dangled. Broken or shot through! A rallying cheer from inside the earthworks. Blue jackets were coming out and holding off the foe, knocking them into the ditch, shooting point blank into the rebs! There was Ewing!

"At the climax of the battle, I saw the stately form of Gen. Ewing, his arms folded, his mouth tightly closed, and his face, slightly pale, but firm as a stone wall," wrote Union Sergeant H. C. Wilkinson. "He was walking erect from side to side, looking here and there at the surging mass around us...."

Amid the dense and sable smoke, he caught a glimpse of another officer, insanely brave, striding atop the earthworks. It was Lieutenant David Murphy, the Irish artilleryman, fully exposed, exhorting his gun crews and even throwing rocks at the attacking forces before Ewing ordered him down.

Later, when hundreds of pinned-down rebels waited for darkness to slip away from the fort's guns, Murphy could not resist rising again on the rampart. Colonel Thomas Fletcher would recount how he "proceeded to address the audience in our front as it lay in concealment, daring and defying them to come on, and in a voice so loud that it woke the echoes of the mountains reflecting on their courage and parentage."

Carpenter saw the Federals pull their men back in and somehow get the drawbridge up, all the while under fire. Hearing the buzz of a couple shots, he threw himself against a sheltering wall. By God, that was something! He had never seen so many rebs!

When Tom Ewing had decided to fight last night, Carpenter had declared the idea "Bully!" He figured his friend could use a good battle to help his political ambitions after the war. It was false bravado on Carpenter's part, a pitiful effort to cleanse his own conduct at Bull Run. No one here was aware of how he had scampered white-tailed with the rest of the medical staff at that first battle in Virginia, panicked by the cries that the Rebs were about to cut them off from Washington. He could remember plunging into the run, losing his cap and later joining a mass of men knowing not what to do or more accurately where to find safety. Then the cry again that the Reb cavalry was coming, and a whole new rout. It had left Carpenter's spirit deeply wounded; his drinking and joking were a thin cover. Yes, his nerve seemed fine down in Arkansas, but that skirmish was hardly a test.

Carpenter worried that his empty bluster might have influenced Ewing the previous night, affected the balance somehow in bringing this fight and perhaps doomed these thousand men and his childhood friend. But Tom had already rejected the offer to surrender, hadn't he, even before Carpenter got off the train?

"They shall play no Fort Pillow game on me," the general had said, referring to a Tennessee fort in which perhaps 200 African-American defenders were massacred after surrendering to Confederate soldiers under Forrest. Inside Ewing's little fort were several black civilians, including some manning one of the guns.

The rebels that had swarmed off the Knob were running away now, leaving hundreds on the field behind them. Carpenter exhaled. It was a victory for Tom on a grand scale. One of the surgeons inside called out: Was the battle finally over?

Carpenter was about to assure him that it probably was when the screaming and shooting began again, this time from the west. Confederate riders were galloping in from the north, too.

"No," he called to his staff. "I'm not sure it will ever be over."

2:30 P.M.

PRIVATE R. E. HOLLEY WAS UNHAPPY about what was about to happen. They were going to charge that cursed little fort. As they were coming down off the knob, it kept disappearing in its own smoke.

General William Cabell was out front waving his sword. 'Course, being a general, Ol' Tige felt he had to stay up on his horse. His colonel, having more sense, was afoot, calling out: "Form up, Sixth! Form up, Sixth!"

"Forward!" the colonel yelled and started toward those cannon, so calm he could have been walking to church on a Sunday morning. The first rank stepped off. Holley's Company L was in the second of three.

"Step lively, men, just one good push, and we'll have them," Captain Wolfe shouted.

Holley was hardly sure of that. There were a lot of good old Arkansas boys from other brigades lying on the ground ahead. He didn't blame those that could for running away like startled shoats. As his friend Sutton had said, we might have done the same, but we had our good reputations to keep up.

One step, another, another. The fort was quiet for a moment, but a smattering of rifle fire was coming from the rifle pits outside. Another step, another,

another. He stepped over a man blowing blood bubbles.

"Somehow, I always pictured St. Louis as bigger, more friendly," said Sutton, staying in step beside him. A good joke, but Holley couldn't get a laugh out.

"Steady the lines," the colonel shouted.

Holley's rifle felt like it weighed 30 pounds. His right eye blinked uncontrollably.

"Got more damn cannon in there than I got lice," Sutton muttered.

One of the big guns boomed ahead, then another, making the ground and his legs tremble. Screaming on the right. He tore his eyes off the fort. Big hole in the front rank over there, officers hollering to close it up, close it up. That's fine, Holley thought, just keep them things aimed away from here.

"Quick time, boys, quick time!" called the captain. The ranks were trotting now.

One quick step, another, another.

Three men just ahead went down at once, like they'd tripped over the same log. Rifle fire was getting hotter now, a healthy sputtering between artillery blasts. A grunt behind him, he knew that sound, a man falling to the ground like a sack of bones. His bare feet moving faster now.

"Shit!" Sutton said. "Shit! My knee!" And he was behind.

With Confederates streaming off Shepherd's Mountain, Private James H. Campbell would recall: "All of a sudden the artillery from the fort, as well as the small arms, opened fire on our lines and as I remember distinctly, casting my eyes up our line to the left, I saw our boys pitching forward, as we advanced every step, like wheat before the reaper." Campbell believed some rebel shells fired from Shepherd Mountain — where cannon had been pulled up by "some twenty or more span of mules hitched to each piece" — fell as well on unlucky Confederates.

At the fort, smoke cleared some. Holley saw Yankee heads on the top like pickets in a new fence. He watched one man fire, then suddenly the Yankee had another rifle and was firing again. Hadn't been time to reload, must be Federals below that Holley couldn't see, handing up loaded rifles to the ones shooting. A big gun over on the right side of the fort was knocked over.

An odd whistle and the ground erupted about 20 feet ahead of the first rank. One man spun around, sank to his knees, holding his groin. Mortars, too? What don't they have crammed into that little dung hill? Suddenly, amid the smoke, a Yankee officer was standing on top of the earthwork, pointing — God, pointing straight here.

Didn't hear the order over the racket, but suddenly everyone was screaming and running. A shrill yell coming from his own mouth. Cabell ahead still on his horse. No! He's down!

Holley was running for the black smoke, trying not to trample the twisting bodies of the first shattered rank, jumping that fellow, God, it was a colonel, his face was half gone!

Almost there. Some were standing, firing, going down. Cabell, his horse killed under him 40 yards from the fort, was trying to get to his feet. In the smoke now, a blast of flame ahead in the haze that only the Devil could love, then two lesser ones. Holley sensed death whistling by. Can't breathe. Can't swallow. Suddenly, a ditch ahead — fort's moat. He was there! He was there! He gathered his strength to leap to the sloping wall of the fort. And suddenly, he was spun around, his momentum bringing him to topple backward into the ditch. The fall seemed to take forever, but was cushioned by a few inches of water and mud. Gasping, he twisted around and got on his elbows and knees. Overhead, a siege gun went off again. The ooze between his fingers quivered. And then … silence.

Holley crabbed his way forward again, threw his back against the towering wall. The giant belched again, the earth shook, but Holley heard nothing. More men tumbled into the moat. Their mouths, their eyes, open so wide. Screaming, Holly knew, but his ears, brain, weren't working. He was dizzy, his butt was soaked from the freezing water. His hat was gone, he realized. He liked that hat, brother gave it to him. As he felt his head, the water from the ditch dripped off his hand, felt good on his face. Right hand exploring his left side, now. Diluted blood on hand, sluicing it down into his sleeve. Hit, then, but no pain yet.

Some of the men huddled around him were pointing their rifles up the wall, hoping for a foe to poke out his head. A soundless flash to his left. He turned his gaze that way, but his slow curiosity was distracted. Something had fallen between his feet, almost hit his bare toes. Hard to make it out in the haze of burnt powder. Cardboard tail sticking out of a round ball of iron. What was this? He looked up. One of the men near him was shouting something. Holley wanted to say he couldn't hear him, then realized the man wanted him to throw the thing away out of the ditch, away from them. Ah, Yankee bomb? Fellow from Vicksburg talked about 'em once. You just toss 'em back. He leaned forward, his right hand reaching for it. There, had it, about to throw when the muzzle blast of the siege gun just overhead made him shudder again. The devil's device fell out of his hand, weak, slippery. As Holley grabbed for it, he watched it drop on its nose, pushing the little plunger in ….

10 P.M.

Night had come before the fighting finally winked out, seemingly extinguished by the steady, cold rain that was now drumming on Seymour Carpenter's hat. His staff's first duty had been to deal with their own Federal wounded. No shortage there, more than 80, at least six so grievously he expected them to join the 10 bodies already laid out behind the building.

A light toll, considering Tom Ewing had won himself a glorious and gory victory — so far, at least. Exploring outside the fort now, Carpenter was following an orderly's lamp, its weak circle of illumination showing rebs white-faced and still. Some of these poor beggars had been bleeding for eight hours. Ewing had not wanted him to go for fear of being shot by a skulking reb, but the pleading for water was too pitiful to be ignored any longer.

Carpenter also had brought out whiskey, but his nostrils detected that the wounded men had enjoyed a swig or two before the attack. Some in the fort insisted the Confederates had to have been liquored up to have made their assaults. They would complain that the stench of the bodies "was fearful, smelling like an overcrowded grog shop." Shivering in the rain, Carpenter took a nip for himself.

He heard one stretcher-bearer talking to the man on the other end: "Can't really say I believe you there."

"It's a Biblical truth," insisted his workmate, helping to flop a moaning man onto a door removed from a house. "Rebs rot faster than our boys."

A north wind added to the wretches' misery. So many were scattered between the fort and the Knob that it would take a while to get them to the houses Carpenter had assigned as new hospitals. He was bending over one when he felt a tap on his shoulder.

"The general begs to impose on the colonel," said the staffer. Leaving careful instructions to his attendants, Carpenter found his way into the fort; the rope system had been repaired and the drawbridge was down for the moment. He passed a campfire and the rectangular mound of earth that held the ammunition and saw Ewing leaving a tent. A meeting was breaking up, and the officers were making preparations for something.

He could not read the face of Colonel Fletcher, who commanded the 47th Missouri. His boys had been green, but Carpenter heard they had held up pretty well. The night before, Thomas Fletcher had voted for retreating, and Carpenter had teased him that it would hurt his chances in the governor's race next month. Fletcher had winced.

Ewing motioned that he wanted to talk privately and led Carpenter to the north wall and a large overturned gun. Carpenter started to congratulate his friend, but Ewing began talking quickly.

"It's down to this, Seymour. We hurt them today, much worse than I could ever have imagined, but our luck is going to run out. Their blood is up, and we can't hold them forever."

Carpenter was surprised. Ewing had been ready for a fight the previous night, but now that had changed. Could the situation be all that bleak considering the day's success?

"But we're surrounded, aren't we?" Carpenter asked.

A groan from a wounded southerner rose from the ground just beyond the ditch. Ewing pulled Carpenter a little away and lowered his voice.

"I've had two scouts come back to say there's camps north on both sides of the Potosi pike, but it doesn't seem actually blocked. No pickets. Went up a mile, they said, and came back without trouble."

"You really think you can slip out of here?" Carpenter almost added that his friend must be mad.

"I do not know if we can pull it off," Ewing replied, "but I'm pretty sure we have got to try. This valley holds nothing good for us. We used up much of our ammunition today and more rebel guns can be taken to the heights to rain shells upon us. Some of the officers are for giving up, but Campbell says he and his men will fight on alone, if necessary. Say they have seen enough of southern prisons."

Ewing talked of the letter, carried into the fort by an old woman, from a Confederate colonel, who had known Ewing before the war. "His note pleads that I give the place up before tomorrow's attack," Ewing said. "He says he will guarantee my safety, but how can he? He makes no mention of the Negroes, just predicts dire results for us if we do not submit."

In the more civilized corners of this war, the killing of a captured general would be unheard of, Carpenter thought. But this was Missouri, where hatreds ran deeper than the guts of volcanoes and maybe twice as hot. He had been with Ewing when they hunted the murderers after Lawrence last summer. Troopers found a wounded guerilla under the bed at a house and dragged him into the yard. He had begged to be treated as a prisoner of war and disclosed that two of his comrades were hiding in nearby trees. Carpenter had been checking the man's wound when a trooper walked up with a shotgun and splattered the rebel's brains. The two men in the woods were hunted down and similarly dispatched. Yes, that was war in Missouri. So Ewing had to get away, just as Quantrill had gotten away, again and again.

Although it was a night when the moon was swallowed whole by thunder clouds, they could see each other clearly enough. The huge charcoal pile near the iron works had been fired by artillery rounds, and now its white-hot core pulsed light across the valley. The surgeon's thoughts were interrupted by a boy's mumbling in the moat about someone named Sutton. Carpenter could detect the delirium in the lad's voice. He shuddered in the cold wet. We'll get to you sooner or later, son.

"How is our 'Captain Jim?'" Ewing asked, referring to one of the Negro contingent, who had been given responsibility for one of the fort's guns. His bravery had so impressed Lieutenant Murphy that the mad Irishman had personally searched out a stretcher to bring him to Carpenter. Shot in the groin, Captain Jim believed himself mortally wounded, but Murphy would not hear of it.

"Bleeding out, I fear."

Their tour of the haunted dark had brought Carpenter and Ewing back to the drawbridge. The general cleared his throat.

"Seymour, what I need to tell you is that you will not be coming with us.

You'll be safe, I'm sure, especially after what you're doing for these poor bastards. But I just can't risk a wounded man crying out on the road, and we will have to move with dispatch."

Carpenter couldn't say anything for a minute, then: "Whatever you think best, Tom. God grant you success. Ride like the devil." Better yet, ride like Quantrill, he thought, but this was not the company in which you might offer that salute.

Ewing asked him whether there was anything inside the fort that he needed. Carpenter made a feeble joke about always needing more whiskey, but suggested a few more boxes of foodstuffs, just in case.

"Get your rations quick, and then get back to the hospital and sit tight through the night," Ewing said. "We'll both have to see what morning brings."

It seemed time to shake hands. "Thank you for all that you've done." The grip tightened. "And whatever you do, Seymour, don't come near this fort again, you hear me? No matter how much whiskey I have to leave behind."

SEPTEMBER 28

GUIDED BY THE TWIN PILLARS OF smoke, Thompson spurred his horse through Ironton, passing a string of wagons moving north toward Pilot Knob. Wagons and buggies were coming the other way, too, hauling a moaning cargo back through the gap, heading for Arkansas.

Most of the smoke was coming from the iron works at the foot of Pilot Knob. What must have been a huge heap of charcoal still glowed like a suburb of hell.

Thompson's attention was on the earthen fort, which produced the thinner stream of smoke from behind its nine-foot-high walls. A siege gun, a 32-pounder, lay on its side up there. He trotted his horse toward the little settlement, noticing a patched tent where a Confederate major sat writing. The major looked up him. That face is familiar, Thompson thought.

"Jeff Thompson!" the major exclaimed. "What the hell are you doing here? How are you doin'?"

"Well, howdy there," Thompson answered safely. He pulled up his jenny and smiled at the man although he could not place the face. "I guess I could ask the same question."

A sobbing wail broke out from a nearby house.

"Better than that feller, I reckon," the major said, still smiling. "Git off that bony excuse for a mule and set a spell." A sergeant, missing an eye from some old engagement — or, considering that scar, maybe a tavern fight —came up with a sheet of paper. The major tapped the sleeve of the Cyclops.

"William, would you kindly get that bottle from my kit?"

Thompson took a moment to make up his mind. Now he was hearing moans from another of the houses. But he was short on intelligence, needed to know what happened here and how it might affect his chances up the road. He swung a leg over his mount's bony rump and tied her to a little dogwood tree. If the major thought the mule looked bad now, he should have been there when Bedford Forrest offered her over in Mississippi. Either the Confederacy was running dangerously low on mounts, or he had pissed Forrest off somehow. Despite their long odyssey, she'd actually fleshed out some. The major motioned to a wooden case branded "U. S." on the other side of his makeshift table. Whatever had been in it was long gone. Thompson sat, still trying to put a finger on the man's name.

"Well, I'd like to say yer a vision for tired eyes, but you look too rough," the major said. "I'd say the Yankees didn't feed you much, but you always was stovepipe thin. Get paroled?"

"Exchanged this summer back east," Thompson replied. "Heard Pap was rumbling about up here in my old haunts with Marmaduke and Shelby, so came hustling back. If I can catch up, I hope to find a place."

"Well, I believe there are a few vacancies," the major said, picking up the papers before him and waving them for effect. The sheets were lists of Confederate dead or wounded, Thompson realized.

A tall, bearded man with a bloody apron stepped out of one of the houses to stretch his back. He gave a glance Thompson's way and wandered away toward a wagon.

"Pap must be pulling some purdy big cannons to do that kind of damage," he joked, motioning to the smoking fort.

"Bless me, wish we did have such guns," the major drawled. "But we don't. The Yankees did that themselves. I was sleeping under my wagon when the powder house blew. You never seen such confusion. Shells flying everywhere. Horses breaking loose. One stepped on my leg, paining me something fierce."

Federal Colonel Thomas Fletcher, slipping away to the north, recalled: "Suddenly the heavens were lighted up by a grand column of fire ascending hundreds of feet … and making the whole region reverberate with a sound as though a mighty earthquake had riven Pilot Knob."

So the magazine went up. Hell of a fire probably, Thompson thought, hell for the men inside. "Did many of the Federals perish?" Thompson asked, glancing at the pile of arms and legs outside one of the houses.

"I'd like to say a fair number, but that'd only be true if some stubbed their toes and fell into a well in the dark," the major mused. "We were s'posed to attack this morning, been building siege ladders all night to get over that damn ditch. Old Ewing decided not to wait up for us, skedaddled with a lit fuse smoking behind him."

Thompson stared at the officer. "Ewing? Tom Ewing? He was down here? And he got away?"

"Yep, so far he has. He musta figured that some of the boys might have plans for him."

"So he got his men out, too?"

"All of 'em, is what I heard, sir. All that weren't dead or shot up, anyway," said the major. "I heard the old man marveling 'bout it this morning before he finally got hisself back on the march: 'Was Ewing a West Point man? Was Ewing a West Point man?' Like that would explain how we sat on our collective asses last night and assumed that bastard was still in there. Ewing had some grit. Refused surrender twice, said he'd shoot the next man that came at him with a white flag. Then, last night they used tents to muffle the horses' hooves and the caisson wheels. We found some laying on the road."

Thompson felt that old twinge of his own shame for not being admitted to the Point, the disappointment of his father, an Army paymaster, who wanted nothing more than for his son to wear the officer's uniform. "Which way did Ewing go? Not north to the Meramec?"

"We'd already cut the Iron Mountain line. Jo Shelby was waiting for him at Potosi. So they say he's turned toward Rolla," the major said.

"Down the road, word was you had them ringed in."

"So we reckoned. Colonel Dobbin's boys must be heavy sleepers 'cause Ewing tiptoed right by them. You shoulda heard Marmaduke. Said Dobbin had better check to see if Ewing hadn't stolen his watch while he was at it."

Fletcher would later tell of the Federals' escape: "On either side of the road the enemy lay about his campfires; pickets and sentries stood idly by the fires not twenty yards from our path. Mistaking us, no doubt, for a body of their own force moving into position."

Ewing had started north to join the rest of Major General A. J. Smith's infantry at Mineral Point. Learning, however, that Smith had fallen back toward St. Louis and that Shelby's Confederates were just ahead, Ewing promptly swung west.

"What a way to begin a campaign," the major sighed, but then the Cyclops sergeant shuffled up with a brown bottle and mismatched glasses. The major nodded thanks, uncorked it and waved it toward Thompson, who smiled and shook his head.

The major poured into his own glass.

"As the Irishman said, 'What is a quart of whiskey among one?' although I don't think he meant it just this way." He raised the amber liquid toward his lips, then paused and said, "To a new command, general."

Taking a moderate swallow, the major went on: "The leg aches so that this will hardly signify. I tell you, Jeff, it was a double-bill tragedy from the get-go. Pushing the Yankees off those mountains chewed up precious time. Then the assault on that fort yesterday? Nothing short of slaughter. Four brigades went at 'em but badly timed. Each got hashed in turn by the guns. Only Cabell's people reached that damned ditch there, and they got nothing for their trouble but red-hot rifle fire."

Thompson suddenly thought he had seen this major as a lawyer in Memphis. Sells? No. Shelton? Singleton?

"Certainly we could have used some more captured rifles and powder," the major said, "but all we've got to show for it is smoke and a thousand men down."

Thompson whistled. "A thousand!" He looked toward the papers before the major.

"At least that," the major said, jerking his head back at where the sawbones still labored. "It were a licking, that's for sure. Pap can recruit as many boys up here as he wants, but he's not going to be able to replace some of them Arkansas men we lost."

"All this makes me makes me wonder how we're going to break into St. Louis," Thompson said, then added. "You know, I've always said the best way to deal with the place is to send in spies and burn the breweries. Then the damn Dutch'll all shrivel up and die within a week."

The major laughed politely — it was not a fresh joke — then leaned over to confide.

"Let me tell you a secret, Jeff. We ain't going to St. Louis no more; they got seasoned infantry now. Price is still sending some of Shelby's boys up there to feint and scare the Dutch some, but it seems pretty clear we'll head to Jeff City now."

A scream broke out in the house behind him, followed by a furious: "Damn it, private, hold him down!" Then a moment later, the angry voice again: "Well, soak the rag again, fool!" A long, loud groan, then muffled. The major decided it was time for another swallow, a good-sized one for this time of day. At least he wasn't holding the scalpel.

Thompson realized his own head seemed a little thick just now. He rose and looked north. The jenny was finishing off the last of a dogwood's leaves.

"Think Pap is up in Potosi?"

"Probably not yet. Ain't no Bedford Forrest, you know. Just follow the wagons and keep an eye out for his outfitted ambulance. Be the one with sagging springs."

Pawnee Fork of the Arkansas River
Central Kansas

"RIDER COMING, GENERAL," THE MAJOR SAID quietly. Blunt jerked himself awake. He peered through gritty eyes to where the officer was pointing.

He was grateful for the distraction. Hard to keep from dozing.

James G. Blunt had been more or less banished to the wastelands. Instead of licking Confederates, an art in which he considered himself a rare talent, he was chasing Indians 250 miles west-southwest of Fort Leavenworth. It was the backwater to a backwater of the war. He was a major general, for God's sake. Others of his rank were directing army corps. Blunt had these 600 alkali-covered troopers.

The puny campaign had gone much as he had predicted. He'd kept his column in the ravines during the day and traveled only at night. The Delaware scouts found the big band of Cheyennes. The troopers killed a few, chased the rest and then lost them. But at least the damned savages were punished and scattered — for now. Stock exhausted by the running fight and supplies getting low, Blunt decided it best to break off the Indian hunt for now and return east to Larned.

This was the "Cheyenne War," which had ignited the prairie. Soldiers in Colorado were shooting at every band in sight, even if not hostile, ensuring that they became hostile. Up near Marysville, 16 souls lost their scalps just in August. In Nebraska, overland mail was suspended for hundreds of miles.

The dust came nearer. Obviously a cavalryman, he pushed his mount pretty hard. Blunt hoped it wasn't another Indian depredation to his rear. Blunt's own weary beast stepped on a shifting rock, stumbled.

"Major, we'll break here and wait for that fellow. Rest the horses."

"Sir!" the major replied and shouted the dismount order.

Blunt pulled up his canteen and let the water roll into his mouth. He rinsed the liquid inside his mouth and swallowed once. He would have spat out the thin mud, but water was precious out here.

"General! Sir!" the rider shouted, not waiting to make a more decorous report. "Message from Fort Leavenworth! General Curtis!"

Blunt scowled. The courier pulled up hard, holding out a grimy paper amid the swirl of dust that settled lightly over the older strata on Blunt's sunburn. Taking the dispatch from the eager young man, Blunt fixed him with a glare.

"Keep your mouth shut, you whore-poxed imbecile," he hissed into a shocked face. "Any information for me is for *me*, do you understand, not for the ranks! Now fall in at the rear. And I advise you not to say another God-damned word to anyone."

First peering east as if he could see over the earth's curvature, Blunt began opening the dispatches, beginning with the one dated the 23rd from Major General Samuel Curtis. Blunt's respect for his District of Kansas commander was shallow, and as he began reading it did not take deeper root. More of the old man's meddling. He looked up at the curious major who had trotted his horse back to his side.

"Curtis says we're after Kiowas."

"Those Cheyenne we just killed will be glad to hear it, I suppose," the major replied.

"Hello! Stand Watie's run off with the supply train at Cabin Creek. Going to be empty bellies at Fort Gibson."

General Stand Watie was one of the Confederate Indians still lurking down in the Territory. The chief, three-quarter Cherokee, was a threat to the pro-Union clans clustered near Fort Gibson, refugees who had to be supplied by wagons from Fort Scott, Kansas.

"We going to have to do something about Watie?" the major asked. Blunt had resumed reading.

"Curtis is bellyaching again about having to protect all of the Kansas Department. He's telling us?"

Kansas is said to have sent 20,000 men to the Union Army — seemingly not a large number until the tiny population of the state is considered — yet Curtis had fewer than 7,000 troops on hand to handle the vast Department of Kansas, Nebraska and Colorado. He had just gotten back from an Indian expedition himself when word reached him that Price finally was on the move.

"Wait, here's the news down at the bottom." Blunt lifted his head. "Curtis says Price is boiling up out of Arkansas with 26,000 men." That earned an appreciative whistle from the major.

Talk of an invasion had floated for months. Now it solidified into a hard fact. Major General George Sykes already had alerted the more eastern 11th and 15th Kansas cavalry that Price probably was "making his way to Missouri, and it is thought he may wheel to the left and cross into Kansas."

"He wants us to shift to Council Grove," Blunt continued, "be better positioned to act on whatever threat is the most serious."

"Any position is better than Larned," the major observed.

Blunt wanted to ask the major whether he believed in redemption. Instead:

"I've got to get back immediately. I'll pick up an escort and fresh mounts at the fort, but I can't wait for all this bunch. You'll take them back, rest them up and then get them to Council Grove."

"Sir!" The officer spun his horse, rode toward the men, calling for company lieutenants.

"So they need me again, do they?" Blunt muttered. He was hardly surprised. He was convinced Curtis was past his prime. Major General John Schofield, who hated Blunt as much as Blunt despised him, had been sent away to Ohio, thank God! While he'd had few dealings with Rosecrans, he ranked him along with the last tit on a boar hog.

Blunt, who had come to Kansas to practice medicine, had risen fast under the senator/general, James H. Lane, leading a regiment of Lane's brigade into Missouri in '61. Once Lane dropped his military ambitions, he became Blunt's patron, using him to keep control of military matters — and government contracts — in Kansas. Blunt went on to whip rebels in Arkansas at Cane Hill and Prairie Grove, pulled off a brutal winter march over the mountains and captured Van Buren. This time last year, many believed Blunt could do no wrong. Now, he mused, what was he?

Commander of something called the District of the Upper Arkansas, tasting the bitter dust of an American Siberia.

Just because of Baxter Springs.

All of his enemies had used Baxter Springs against him. In his mind, it had been bitterly unfair. He'd been sick, Blunt told himself. The troops were inadequate in every regard, a column of cowards, really.

It all happened just a little less than a year ago. Blunt was moving his headquarters from Fort Scott in Kansas south to Fort Smith in Arkansas. He had been riding in a carriage with an escort of two companies — one of green Kansans, the other of more seasoned Third Wisconsin troopers, both indifferently armed with Merrill carbines. Blunt's eight baggage wagons, another one carrying his musicians and two ambulances had fallen behind a half mile or so.

Blunt had been keeping his eye out for the turn off the Military Road to Fort Blair, often referred to as Fort Baxter after the nearby spring. The newly constructed, earthwork-and-log installation was hidden from the road by a little rise. The general had been seriously ill in earlier months and might not have been as alert as he should have been. On the other hand, no one else in the column heard the firing of pistols, rifles and even a mountain howitzer erupting beyond that knoll, either.

Who had expected Quantrill to head for winter quarters in Texas early? But a ferocious guerrilla hunt stirred up by the Lawrence raid gave him a good excuse. Unknown to each other, the columns of bushwhackers and Federal troopers were moving south in parallel. They might never have collided except the guerrillas learned of the little fort and decided to give it their attention.

Quantrill sent ahead a party with Dave Pool and Bill Gregg, who discovered the fort was missing one of its four walls. Cocky or careless, Lieutenant James Pond had ordered it leveled as part of an expansion. When the rebel horse swarmed out of the timber, they caught and gunned down some men foraging or target practicing, including Johnny Fry, the first Pony Express rider. Many of the fort's defenders, including Pond, were taking lunch with their families. Some of the little garrison had married war widows, who were living in tents just outside the stockade. In the crossfire, one woman was hit in the foot and a little girl was wounded in the shoulder. Another woman, just made a widow, picked up the pistol of her slain man and emptied it at the rebels.

Some attackers even rode into the fort, but did not stay long because the Federals had scrambled back inside to grab their rifles. Many of them were former slaves, these men of A Company, Second Kansas Colored Infantry, who "fought the best of any men I ever saw," Pond said. "I don't want to be without a company of Negroes if I can help it." The lieutenant went outside the earthworks alone to work the fort's little howitzer, an act that would win him the Medal of Honor.

None of this was apparent to Blunt's men. Nor was it to Quantrill, bringing up the main body of bushwhackers. Lost, Quantrill blundered out of the tree line along the Spring River north of the fort — directly east of Blunt and his escort.

As usual, many guerrillas wore captured Union coats, so Blunt's first assumption was that Fort Blair had sent out a welcoming party. He called his escort to halt to let the bandwagon catch up and make the affair a little grander. Bill Tough, one of Blunt's scouts, trotted his horse out to get a better look and quickly came back with a strange look.

That's Quantrill out there, Tough reported. Blunt, perhaps a little confused from his illness, perhaps a little drunk — guerrilla John McCorkle wrote later that a five-gallon demijohn of whiskey was in the general's buggy — couldn't believe it, even as the riders from the trees fanned out into a line facing his companies.

But the general ordered his troopers to form their own line of battle and heaved himself out of the buggy, only to realize his fine horse tied behind was not saddled. Cursing, he took a saddled mule. As he'd steered the steady beast forward to get his own look, more horsemen appeared to the south, these having left off the attack against the fort. The line of riders to the east, hundreds of them, began walking their horses toward Blunt.

Harboring no hopes of a band concert now, Blunt recalled, "I turned toward my escort to give the command to fire, when I discovered the line broken, and all of them in full gallop over the prairie, completely panic-stricken. Seeing the disorderly and disgraceful retreat of the escort, the enemy made a charge, using their revolvers...."

Many of the Kansans, led by an unsure 18-year-old second lieutenant, had tossed aside their weapons in their flight. The Wisconsin company briefly returned fire, but melted in the chaos. "Sell out the best you can," one called out.

The band wagon had come up, and its driver had tried to make a dash for it, drawing a pack of amused Missourians. Jovial old William Bledsoe — he was one of the few middle-aged bushwhackers —rode alongside trying to get the musicians to stop, when someone in the wagon shot him out of his saddle. A moment later the front left wheel fell off, and the band members were frantically waving kerchiefs, trying to surrender.

George Todd, infuriated by the mortal wounding of his rotund friend, retorted that they should have waved to Bledsoe, who, as the story goes, said, "That outfit have shot and killed me; take my two pistols and kill all of them." And so it was done. The bodies were tossed into the wagon, and all was set ablaze, with the music sheets as kindling. One of the dead was James O'Neal, a part-time artist-correspondent for *Frank Leslie's Illustrated.*

On another part of the prairie, Blunt adjutant Major Henry Curtis, with his fine staff uniform and beautiful gray horse, had drawn bushwhackers like a murder of crows on an owl. Curtis had raced toward a gully, intent on clearing it and shaking off his pursuers, but his mount took a bullet in the rump and crashed into the ravine. Getting to his feet, surrounded by his attackers, the son of Major General Curtis offered his pistol in surrender. A horseman accepted the weapon, then shot Curtis through the head with it. "I've killed Blunt; I've killed the old son of a bitch," was the cry.

Although portraits of Blunt show him in full dress, almost ridiculously so in one case, he often wore civilian clothes. At Baxter Springs, his garb reportedly was more that of a wagon master. This goes far to explain how he, riding his underappreciated mule surrounded by the rebel steeds, slipped away into the timber when so many didn't.

As Blunt wrote the next day, "I was fortunate in escaping, as my effort to halt and rally the men I frequently got in the rear and got considerably mixed up (with) rebels who did not fail to pay me their compliments… Revolver bullets flew around my head thick as hail but not a scratch."

The Federals counted almost 90 bodies the next day. No one the guerrillas could catch was spared, except, the story goes, one freedman, Rube. In his Kansas City barber shop, Rube once overheard a plan to capture George Todd and had gone out to warn him. Now, about to be shot by the guerrillas, Rube asked for Todd, who rushed over and announced: "The first man that hurts this nigger, I will kill!" Switching sides again, Rube went along to Texas to cut Confederate hair.

The Federals later found Sergeant Jack Splane still breathing despite being shot in the head, chest, guts, arm and leg. He was able to gasp out what his inefficient assailant had instructed: "Tell old God that the last man you saw on earth was Quantrill." Another survived with five gunshot wounds to the face, which, according to the post surgeon, "could not be recognized as belonging to a human being." Federals reported following a scorched path through the high bluejoint grass to the body of the 12-year-old drummer. He had crawled away from the band wagon while on fire.

Quantrill declined to attack the fort again as Todd and some of his men wanted. He had his victory, and it had come very cheap, indeed. That night he had swaggered amid the bodies in a rare drunk, declaring: "By God, Shelby could not whip Blunt, neither could Marmaduke. But *I* whipped him!"

The disgrace hung on Blunt like the smell of shit. Even Lane couldn't cast off the odium. Now, he gazed east again, watching a dust devil. A trooper, having transferred the general's gear, was holding the new mount, which looked little fresher than his old one. Blunt ordered the soldier to recheck the cinch. He was no great horseman, and his men knew it. It was one of the reasons the ranks seemed not to like him. They called him "fat boy." But Lincoln had liked him once. He could again. Price was coming, offering a way for Blunt to come out of this wilderness, to save Kansas again. He would not let this chance slip away.

By damn, he was back!

VI

Flesh and blood

*Dont be uneasy my children.... Your Miss Kaitty
said that I tried to steal you But I'll let her know
that god never intended for man to steal his own
flesh and blood.... I once ... had some respect
for them but now my respects is worn out and
have no sympathy for Slaveholders. And as for her
cristianantty I expect the Devil has Such in hell...."*

—Private Spotswood Rice, former slave and tobacco roller, writing
in 1864 from St. Louis to his children in Glasgow, Missouri

✐✐✐✐✐✐

Paris

Monroe County, northeast Missouri

THE SHUTTLE SLIPPED THROUGH THE YARN like a cottontail through milk-weeds. Ann's calloused fingertips performed the quick strumming of the loom, back and forth. White fuzz from the crude homespun snowflaked to the dirt floor. Back and forth.

The cloth, growing so slowly, was in a race against winter. Ann needed the rough cotton fabric to clothe her and her toddler. Old Marse Hogsett certainly would buy no replacements for the rags they were wearing now. He was, in fact, likely to sell too much of what cloth she was making.

But Ann's mind was not so much on the cold that was coming as on the husband who was gone.

Andy had slipped off the Hogsett place months ago to enlist in the Lincoln army. One of his letters had told her that the army gave him new shoes, which was a fine thing, but also a musket, which worried Ann. Hogsett had taunted her that the old general was coming home and would put paid to the nigger army and her Andy. At the thought of someone shooting her husband, tears began to streak her cheeks, and she made a mistake with the warp.

Trying to bear down on her task, Ann did not notice the approach of the old woman until the open door cast an unsteady shadow.

"Child, does you have a spot for me to set?"

Ann jumped, then grabbed an old chair, its cane bottom so worn that a kitten could fall through it. "Mama Jo, I didn't take your presence!"

Mama Jo pointed to a spot just inside the door, where she could enjoy the day's dying light. The one-room cabin had a fireplace, and now Ann set about laying sticks on the coals.

"Thank you, child. I am the nearest worn and my feet is weary."

Ann was happy to see the old woman, who, with an inventive mix of sighs and groans, placed her ample bottom on the chair. On the farms in these parts, Mama Jo was the next best thing to a slave telegraph. She gathered news and spread it, taking a cup of raspberry leaf tea and whatever was in the pot, sleeping on the straw ticks with the occupants of one cabin before moving on to the next with just a little more to tell.

Mama Jo had once belonged to the Shortridge place, but now in her last years, no one there seemed to mind her wanderings. Certainly, they had more to distract them now, Mama Jo had mournfully reported. Not so long ago, the Shortridges had learned that Flavius, the son who'd rode off with Porter, had died in a Yankee prison.

The old woman knew the deer trails and cow paths better than the beasts themselves, and she stuck to them. Although the slave patrols seemed to be gone, some ugly-minded white folk sometimes took it upon themselves to whip blacks who were caught out at night. And the bushwhackers were known to treat their own race cruelly, so what chance did an ancient negress have in their hands, especially if they were liquored up?

"I have things to tell, missy, things to tell. But first, how you be? Have you heard from your husband? I see the child sleepin' there, I see she be well."

Ann's little girl was curled up with an old dog on hemp bags filled with corn shucks. The quilt covering them was so patched that the original pattern was lost in time. Little bits from the cotton work were stuck in her hair.

"We are just barely getting by," Ann told Mama Jo. "My man is well, as far as I know. Ain't got no letter for some time now. 'Course, Hogsett may have got his hands on it again. He took one my others, supposed to have five dollars in it, 'cordin' to the next Andy sent."

Still furious that Andy had left the farm to fight for his freedom, the master was taking it out on Ann, forcing on her many of the outside chores that her man had once done. It was Hogsett's way. She had asked Andy to let her bring the baby and go with him, but he told her of the miserable "contraband" camps outside army installations where the runaway families of black soldiers were still at the mercy of slave-catchers. At first she had worried that Hogsett might sell her in Kentucky, but had soon figured out that she weren't going nowhere. She simply did too much work around the place.

The old woman's tiny, hooded eyes settled on the chickens, which patrolled the bare earth in front of the two slave cabins, one cabin empty for years now. Mama Jo knew Hogsett might drive her off, but this time of day, the farmer would be yonder in the fields with his boys trying to save their harvest.

The women could not see it from their vantage, but Missouri slavery was in its last throes. It would finally be abolished on January 11, 1865.

"Thirty-five contrabands crossed the river at Kickapoo, night before last, from Platte county," the Leavenworth *Daily Times* had noted a year earlier. "The stampede has become so general that Platte is almost denuded of negroes. They leave at the rate of thirty or forty a day....Few owners pretend to stay the exodus."

Eleven months ago Major General John Schofield had issued General Order 135, which allowed the enlistment in Missouri "of any able-bodied man of African descent, slave or free, regardless of the owner's loyalty or consent, with freedom for slave enlistees and compensation ($300) for loyal owners."

After the years of bloodshed and destruction, many southerners had become fatalistic about slavery, among them Margaret Hays, who wrote her mother January 25, 1864, from central Missouri: "We still have peace hear but the country is full of negro recruiting officers. Some negros go and enlist and get their arms and them get a furlough and go back home and stay until their time expires. If their Masters say anything to them they are cursed and told that they are as free as they are. If any white person insults they have them arrested and sent to St Louis. Negro familyes are leaving by wagon loads ever day. All the harm that I wish them is that they were all in Liberia or somewhere where I could never see one for they are all the cause of this war."

Manpower shortages led former slaveholders to pay wages or grant sharecrop rights to the African-Americans who were left, just to keep them on the farms.

Mama Jo passed judgment on Hogsett: "He a evil man, ain't no doubt, rotten inside like a bad tater. They like to say they follow the Jesus road, but I've done read the Book, and I don't see no slave owned by Jesus in there. But Hogsett don't bid you come to his featherbed in the night, and his son's too young, dat's something. Count your blessin's on that. There much more evil about. Has you heard about the children they caught trying to join the blue men in Hannibal?"

Ann had. It was a terrible, terrible story. Three young men had run away to join the Lincoln army but had got caught and been returned to their farms. One slave owner, an old widder woman, had got beside herself with anger. She declared to the white men standing about that she would pay anyone five dollars to kill her slave Alfred right there. And one had pulled a pistol, put it to Alfred's heart and shot that boy dead. Ann wondered about the Lincoln soldiers. They came around saying they wanted the colored men to put on the blue coats, but then they let such things happen.

"Well, I fine with that," Mama Jo said to Ann's having already heard the tale. "Didn't have the heart to tell it again, so evil is it. Lord of Glory, where are you lookin' when such things happen? Wish I had some good news, other than fresh babies and such. You heard about the Lincoln soldiers taken off the train nigh south of here and sent to Kingdom?"

Again, Ann had overheard Hogsett tell the Centralia story to a son.

"Child, why I comin' round here tell you things? You already know all this."

"Oh, Mama Jo, you know I can't bear not seein' you. What would I do without? See, I need you to take down my words and help get 'em to my Andy, again."

Unlike Ann and most slaves, Mama Jo had her words, learned years ago from a little white girl who'd thought teaching her old mammy how to read and write was a delicious secret.

Under the Black Codes, teaching a slave to read meant at least a $500 fine and up to six months in jail. A ferryman who took a slave across the Mississippi without the owner's permission had to pay the cost of the slave, about $1,000 in Ann's case, or $1,300 for her husband. The punishment for slaves themselves generally was whipping, 39 stripes for many offenses, 25 for giving another slave liquor.

The old woman nodded.

"I got the pencil, but I got nothin' to do the letters on."

Ann went to a corner of the cabin and found the piece of paper she had saved.

"Tore out a sheet from an ol' ledger Hogsett left around."

"Light's fadin'. You got a candle? No? Well, shift that table."

Mama Jo got up and peered outside again. Settled again with chair and table near the doorway, she swept grit and bits of food from the already rough-hewed surface. A stub of a pencil was pulled from a deep pocket of a patched wool coat, its point licked. Then she lowered her face to within inches of the ledger sheet.

"So, what you want to say?"

Ann stepped over by the door to keep a lookout. The dog was chasing something in its sleep, but its twitching paws were directed away from the little girl. She'll be hungry when she wakes. Ann closed her eyes and ran her tongue over her lips in thought.

"My Dear Husband…. I r'eed your letter … but have got no one till now to write for me. You do not know how bad I am treated. They are treating me worse and worse every day. Our child cries for you…."

Already Mama Jo was having trouble keeping up. Ann paused and collected herself a bit. Feeling sorry for herself, she knew, but it was so powerful hard right now. Never been easy, but some nights she would weep and wonder what would come next. She had heard the Lincoln soldiers were winning and had hoped freedom might find them before winter. But now the old general was coming back from the south. Would Andy have to go fight him and his cruel men?

Mama Jo grunted that time was wasting.

"Send me some money as soon as you can for me and my child are almost naked. My cloth is yet in the loom and there is no telling when it will be out. Do not send any of your letters to Hogsett especially those having money in them as Hogsett will keep the money. George Combs went to Hannibal soon after you did so I did not get that money from him."

She stopped again to give the old woman time. She heard her mumbling to herself. "Combs went to Hannibal…" The letter, Ann realized, was so unhappy. She was miserable, but Andy thought he had done right and deserved better for it. Didn't want him doing something foolish, not now. Mama Jo lifted her head.

"Getting too dark. Be quick with it, child."

Ann nodded. There wasn't much more to say, anyway.

"Do the best you can and do not fret too much for me for it wont be long before I will be free and then all we make will be ours. Your affectionate wife Ann."

They can't keep us here forever, she told herself again. Her child stirred again on the coarse hemp bagging. And the child inside her stirred, too. They will not be slaves, like me.

"Wait, Mama Jo, I got another thing to say:

'*Sind our little girl a string of beads in your next letter to remember you by. Ann.*'"

"That nice," Mama Jo said. She folded the sheet and carefully tucked it and the pencil into the safest pocket. "Is your man still in Hannibal?"

"Don't know. Last letter came from there, but he spoke of going down to the big place, St. Louis? If you take that to the Carney place and ask Mr. Jim to post it, I'd be so much obliged, Mama Jo."

"Well, I'm goin' thataway, so won't be no trouble. So did you hear about the Wilkins' child getting run over by that hay wagon? Oh, it was terrible, I've known that child since he come outta his momma, oh, I was dere. I said then, he got the biggest head on him, like to never come out, he's gonna fret his moma all her life, and now he's got two busted legs…"

Ann poked the fire, put on the pot for the tea and settled back at the loom, listening to the news.

VII

Up the Missouri

"Ho Boys! Make a Noise! The Yankees are afraid!
The rivers up, hell's to pay —Shelby's on a Raid!"

"Shelby's Mule," a Confederate song

თავდასხმა

OCTOBER 2
Bolton's Ford, Osage River
Cole County, central Missouri

"**All right, lieutenant, are you ready?**" Colonel John Finis Philips asked the man sitting cross-legged next to the morning's reluctant campfire. The sun was still beneath the horizon and far to the east, waking men in Virginia to a new day for killing. Here in Missouri it was not yet time for such work.

The young officer shifted, trying to find the fire's best light. Getting an affirmative, Philips began:

"I reached this point at 9 o'clock last night. Had to lie here on account of artillery, miserable road. Sent three companies across river last night to scout and look out. Nothing heard yet. I find this to be the main crossing...."

The younger officer cursed, so softly Philips hardly heard him. His pencil had ripped through the paper. Everything in the camp was soggy after a gully-washer last night. Looking around, in the dark of the morning, Philips could hear his wet troopers stirring, coughing, trying to blow out mucus. Some would be on sick call if they were in camp. More fires sizzled and popped, accompanied by a crunching sound — a cloth-bagged ration of beans being crushed between convenient rocks. This trooper was lagging; the colonel's nostrils reported that some companies already had their coffee boiling. A prescient captain brought him a finger-burning cup of it.

Philips needed to get this message back to General Brown and get the men moving. He turned his gaze toward the sound of the current, felt the river's rising mist. Even in the dark he could tell the river was up a little, but nothing to worry about.

"...The ferry amounts to nothing. I leave a picket of ten men at ferry and thirty men here to watch this and a ford three miles ..."

The paper ripped again. "Sorry, colonel, keep going."

"Just so the general can read it, son. Uh, where are you?"

" 'Three' is the last I got..."

"Yes,.... *three miles above. I move to Gasconade at once.* Sign it, you know, *Very respectively, your obedient servant.*"

"Yes, sir."

"You better shift yourself before that coat catches fire, son."

Steam was rising out of the sodden wool. Philips stopped pacing — his boots were so soaked they leaked water — and began gnawing on a bit of coffee-dunked sheet iron as he considered the coming day. He felt something wiggle in his mouth and spat it out.

"Sheet iron" was just one of the nicknames for the standard 3-inch by 3-inch hardtack cracker, the Federal soldier's staple. Usually it was riddled with weevils and worms; one soldier wrote home that vermin was "all the fresh meat we had." Another joke was a soldier saying that while chewing on his tack he'd bitten on something soft, a 10-penny nail.

Philips whacked the rest of his "Weevil Castle" against a tree to dislodge any other inhabitants. Hell, forgot something.

"Lieutenant, I've got to add a P. S."

The report was unfolded, and the pencil dug back out from within the heavy caped overcoat. "Yes, sir."

"Say, *Found Lt. Stephens' Fourth Cavalry Missouri State Militia at Castle Rock, and leave it here on picket duty.* Just initial that part."

About time we heard from those companies, Philips thought. Old Brown can't get enough news, but I don't have much. He smiled to himself. The general had had the shovels and mud flying up at Jefferson City. Egbert Brown, like Philips, was pretty sure the enemy would turn west eventually.

Philips considered whether his second-in-command, Thomas Crittenden, and his two companies of militia were having any better luck. He'd heard that Brown had sent them to patrol the Missouri River looking for Bill Anderson to cross. Rocheport is where I'd go, Philips thought. That's where the bastard is always hanging out.

Poor little Rocheport, a once-prosperous river town just down from Boonville, was terrorized so often by Anderson that he called it his "capital." About this time, the *Daily Missouri State Times* in Jefferson City noted that the "thieving, murdering, misbegotten, God-forsaken, hell-deserving" guerrillas had established themselves around the town "and they are having things entirely their own way."

On the evening of this very day Rocheport would be "badly scorched," one general would report. "All the business portion destroyed by an accidental fire."

"Accidental" was not what Thomas Goodman had seen. Still a captive of Quantrill, the captive Federal sergeant later wrote of watching from the bluffs above as Union troops went from building to building torching the town.

In the summer, Anderson captured the steamer *Buffington* at Rocheport, killing its captain and using the boat to transport his band on a raid. The Federals fined Rocheport's "disloyal citizens" $10,000 for the incident.

Bushwhackers also enjoyed peppering the steamers. Some of the boats had iron plates around the pilot houses and boilers now. Philips heard pilots were demanding a thousand dollars to take a boat up from St. Louis. For one run! It made a man question all those hours spent reading law.

The men were frying fatty chunks of pork and skillygully, the paste made of soaked and mashed hardtack. Sometimes they just wrapped a string of the dough around rifle ramrods for cooking. The morning's entertainment was a sergeant loudly berating a trooper for pissing upstream.

Philips bit off another piece of coffee-soaked hardtack.

Who will get to the Gasconade first? The Seventh or Shelby? And where was the First Missouri, anyway? Philips wasn't much impressed by its commander, but the second-in-command, Bazel Lazear, was one of the toughest sons-of-a-bitches in the militia cavalry.

Lazear ran down and executed guerrillas like a man possessed. "There is no punishment on earth great enough for the villains who have brot this Rebellion about," Lazear wrote to his wife. "We have put a good many of them out of the way lately. I yesterday had one publically shot. He was the prisoner we took the evening after we had the fight with Quantrill and was in the Lawrence raid. He is the second prisoner I have had shot and will have everyone of them shot I can get hold of. As such inhuman wretches deserve no mercy and should be shot down like dogs where ever found."

In Saline County, where rebels burned the courthouse in Marshall and gunned down nine local Negroes, Lazear summed up his feelings: "This county needs rough handling."

And it got it. A half-century later, a book titled *Past and Present of Saline County Missouri* remembered events this way: "The Federal militia were equally merciless towards citizens, guerrillas and bushwhackers." Anyone giving them a bit of information or a bite of food "or had seen them and failed to report their presence to the Federal garrison, if captured, was shot down with but little ceremony or none at all." The author described the arrest of an Arrow Rock man named Marshall Piper, "always peaceable and inoffensive." One friend "remonstrated, expostulated, and entreated Colonel Lazear to spare the poor man, and so did others; but he was inexorable, would listen to no explanations, would give no time for the procurement of testimony establishing the innocence and harmless character of the condemned — would have nothing but his blood."

Lazear's version of the same event was blunt: "Piper was shot for harboring and feeding bushwhackers, and refusing to give information concerning the same: and you will please allow me here to say that it had more good effect in giving the Union people of Saline peace and protection than any one act I had done during the war."

The tales reaching St. Louis were less positive. In early September, General Egbert Brown's adjutant wrote Lazear: "Colonel: The commanding general is informed by Major-General Rosecrans that your troops are causing a reign of terror in LaFayette and Saline Counties and that it should come to your attention. He is also informed that their officers are permitting them to rob the people of their property for their own benefit, to murder peaceable citizens, and commit other outrages upon the people while the pursuit of bushwhackers is abandoned by loading the troops with plunder from the country."

By the second dose of caffeine, Philips' morning gloom began to lift. He washed down some of the sodden mass of hardtack and his tongue probed gaps in his teeth to dislodge the clinging dough.

Where are those scout companies? He needed information. If he had to grope out into the dark countryside and touch Price's army, he'd prefer not to draw back a bloody stub. But scouts in or not, in about an hour he'd have to take the regiment across the Osage.

A bit of his law reading came to him: *nolens volens* — "willing or unwilling." That was why they paid him a colonel's salary, wasn't it? Why they gave him all the hard biscuit and weevils he could eat. He took the last sip from the cup, but the liquid offered no warmth now. He flung the rest at the river, a meager sacrifice.

OCTOBER 3

The road to Mount Sterling
Franklin County, eastern Missouri

THE ADJUTANT SHIFTED THROUGH THE NOTES and dispatches, trying to distill the previous day's disordered tramp of twelve thousand men into a clear track for their Confederate command. He dipped his pen and began:

"*Oct. 2 (Camp No. 33). — Joined Marmaduke and Shelby early in the morning, found Cabell; returned, burned a bridge east of Franklin, and in the dawn burned the depot and destroyed the railroad. Lieutenant-Colonel Wood also returned from burning the bridge on the southwest branch of the....*"

Lauchlan MacLean frowned. What stream was that? So many ran between the granite ribs protruding from this poor country. The lieutenant colonel pulled his map closer and peered at the squiggles. He did not admire the craft of the chart; the school teacher in him gave the unknown topographer poor marks. Hmm, the Moselle. Named by a homesick Frenchman, he did not doubt. Probably on a day just like this under cold, frowning clouds that intermittently wept.

"*...Moselle. General Clark went to Washington, on Missouri River; Federals retreated across the river. Marmaduke...*"

Here a drop of the cold drizzle found its way from a leak in the roof of the porch under which the general's secretary, given the unwieldy title of assistant adjutant general, had gathered his freshest paperwork. It had traveled down a roughly cut beam of black oak to a junction with a piece of white pine. From there, it dropped onto MacLean's official journal below, badly smearing the name of the disfavored general. Uttering an oath, MacLean blotted the paper. The name and a few surrounding words were still discernable in the light blue mist, but his work was now marred. He dragged his table away before the drop received reinforcements.

"… ordered to Hermann with his division. Fagan and Shelby encamped on road to Mount Sterling, eight miles from Union, making in all…"

MacLean, who had dragged a surveyor's chain across a good part of west Missouri and then Kansas, now pulled a little string from his pocket, positioned the required length between his thumbs and marked off the distance.

"… fifteen miles."

Fifteen miles. The old man was certainly taking his time. As he blew on the ink so as to put the journal away, MacLean heard a sound that everyone around found disagreeable. It was the voice of Missouri's governor-in-exile, Thomas Reynolds. On Price's staff, one was encouraged to see the worst in the pudgy politician, who, upon assuming the place of the dead Governor Claiborne Jackson, had had the temerity to ask to look at the general's state accounts.

"Sir Knights, morning dawneth," Reynolds had cried, fiercely rapping the box of an ambulance, where, inside, his aides stirred under the wet canvas cover, foiled in their attempt to steal more sleep.

"I'm buckling, I'm buckling," moaned one, jumping to the mud. He threw his blanket back into the vehicle and ran fingers through wild blond hair.

MacLean had to smile at the exchange. Clever. Unless he was mistaken, the lines came from a printed proclamation to rise up against the Yankee tyrants and join the Price occupation.

It had been signed by one mysterious John H. Taylor, the Missouri commander of the Order of American Knights, the secret Copperhead organization. Although some assumed that Price was the actual author, this was doubted by MacLean, who was in charge of his chief's official communications.

Said to be waiting in St. Louis for the right moment to "buckle on my armor," Taylor declared readiness to — how did it go? — "greet many thousands of you in the camp of our friends."

So far, however, the uprising had not materialized. After three years of violence all around them, many Missourians simply feared to declare and leave their homes and families to the mercies of the Federal militias or bandits. It was obvious, also, that the Confederate armies were hard-pressed and exhausted, and that Europe was not coming to help.

Price, as MacLean knew very well, was disappointed by the reaction and low turnout of recruits so far, yet still held great hopes for their friends in the counties farther west, counties where Price and MacLean had made homes.

Perhaps the only persons who believed as fervently as Price in his Order of American Knights insurgents were Major General Rosecrans, the state's Federal commander, and his intelligence officers. They estimated as many as a quarter million Knights skulked in Missouri, Illinois and Indiana.

"Rebel agents, amnesty oath-takers, recruits, sympathizers, O. A. K.'s and traitors of every hue and stripe, had warmed into life at the approach of the great invasion," Rosecrans would write. "Women's fingers were busy making clothes for rebel soldiers… women's tongues were busy telling Union neighbors 'their time was coming.'"

Accordingly, he sent detectives to ferret out the "dark lantern" societies with their romantic names, such as Knights of the Columbian Star, Sons of Liberty, Circle of the Mighty Host, Democratic Invincible Club. Arrests were made.

In July, the Leavenworth *Times* published the confession of a 22-year-old captive from Platte County, Andrew E. Smith. Besides admitting briefly riding with bushwhacker John Thrailkill, he went on to say: "I am a member of the Knights of the Golden Circle. I joined them at Platte City, and was sworn in by David Jenkins of that place. All of the Pawpaw militia, so far as I know, belong to them…. The sign of recognition is the open right hand across the breast." The OAK password was nu-oh-lac, the letters of "Calhoun" spoken backward.

Reading the smoke from the Pawpaw uprising or whatever had occurred in Platte City and Parkville that summer, the Missouri Confederate commanders hundreds of miles away concluded the state was ripe for revolt.

"The Confederate flag floats over nearly all of the principal towns of North Missouri," Price's letter had exclaimed to Major General Kirby Smith. Shelby, too, bought into the dream, telling Smith of uprisings in more than 20 counties.

Both generals should have known that pawpaws spoil rather quickly, just as did the takeover in the two Platte County towns. Almost as soon as Federal troopers in surrounding counties could get into the saddle, the Pawpaw revolt was crushed, three months before Price even got to the state.

It was violent while it lasted. From Parkville, Captain Thomas J. Wilson of the Enrolled Missouri Militia sent this account to the *Times*:

"Between the hours of 5 and 6 o'clock A.M., on the 7th inst., just before sitting down to breakfast, myself and wife saw quite a body of men, dressed principally in Federal uniform, coming down Main street, in the direction of my house. When nearly opposite the house, my wife cried out, 'My God! they are bushwhackers!' I stood still until they had passed, and then got my revolver and ammunition and started for the quarters where our men were. My wife, who was in the door watching them, told me not to try to get to quarters, that they had them surrounded, and were firing on the company. They took possession of Widow Williams' house, which is directly opposite the door of the quarters, on the side of the hill above, raised two windows, took two Union ladies, Mrs. Jackson and Mrs. Pollard, and placed them in the windows, firing from behind them."

The Union garrison officers surrendered under promise of parole. Wilson offered a snide and probably untrue note that the militiamen had to compose their own paroles as none of the guerrillas could write. More: "Among the other outrages committed out in town, was the murder of Isaac Brink, of company F, 16th K. V. C., who was at home on furlough. His wife was lying at the point of death, and he had come into town to get ice for her, when he was stopped by young Sewel and another man. Sewel asked Brink for his belt. Brink replied that he had a revolver, and wished to know what would be his fate if he gave it up. Sewel replied, "You shall be respected." He then took Brink's revolver with his left hand, pulled it out of the scabbard with his right, and shot him in the left cheek. Seeing that he was not dead, the other demon shot him through the heart, took his horse, and left him lying there until the hogs had eaten off one of his ears."

The guerrillas commenced plundering, stealing thousands of dollars in cash and value of goods from stores and homes.

"They asked old man Clark for his key. He told them that Major Clark, in command of the Paw-Paws of Platte, at Platte City, was his son. They told him Major Clark was all right, but that that would not save his goods. They then went to Mrs. Dainbon's whose husband is in the 6th Kansas, and took $400 in money. Next they went to my house in squads of from three to eight, five times, and took all my clothes except my old ones. They also insulted my wife by calling foul names, and cursed and yelled around the house like savages…

It is useless to give further details; therefore, suffice it to say, that they did as much or more than the demons of hell would require of them to make them fit subjects of association."

Eighty-two of the paroled men of the 82nd Enrolled Missouri Militia then switched sides. A frustrated General Clinton Fisk had complained about the 82nd earlier, noting it would fight only Kansans.

Three days later, Platte City was similarly taken over by Lieutenant Colonel John C. Calhoun "Coon" Thornton, a veteran officer sent north to recruit, and Fletch Taylor with a large number of guerrillas. Captain John Thrailkill also showed up with more than 50 men. Again, many militiamen shed the Union blue and donned as best they could the Confederate uniform. Some looting occurred, but apparently it was not as widespread as Parkville. Most of the guerrillas then scattered before the avenging Yankees appeared.

MacLean put a weight on his papers and stood. The general was calling him, perhaps to dictate some thoughts for a speech to be given in Jefferson City. MacLean figured they should just use parts he already had written up for St. Louis. Going back inside to attend the commander, MacLean still wondered about the decision to turn away from St. Louis, even with its fresh infusion of infantry and cavalry. You had to make your own luck, Price knew that better than anyone.

Now Price was asking about Shelby's whereabouts. MacLean was very fond of Jo, but had to admit that his hero had let him down. When they had chased Tom Ewing after Fort Davidson, MacLean had wanted to ride with them, to deliver a pistol ball into the arrogant son of a bitch himself. The old man had not let MacLean go, said Shelby would handle the pursuit well enough.

But they had let Ewing slink away like a miserable cur. When he rejoined the column, Shelby had not been able to look MacLean in the eye. The adjutant had gotten seriously drunk that night.

OCTOBER 4

Hermann

Gasconade County, eastern Missouri

"TELL YOUR GENERAL THAT I'M HERE to build him a bridge!"

Major General John Sappington Marmaduke raised his head from the order he was writing. Outside the room, the confusion of the young lieutenant was evident.

"What bridge? I do not understand you, sir."

"Well, I'm afraid I do not know, either, son. But I always serve at the general's pleasure, especially when it is a bridge that is required."

Marmaduke chuckled and called out into the hallway: "It's all right, lieutenant. Please ask the general to join us."

The door swung open to reveal Jeff Thompson, looking even skinnier than usual in a threadbare black suit. Marmaduke rose from behind his table to shake hands with the scarecrow. He decided his usual formality would not do here.

"Jeff, old friend, it has been too long. How are you?"

"And it is a pleasure to gaze upon you, too, John. It has been a coon's age, certainly. Captain Moore, you have grown stout," Thompson added to the grinning adjutant in the room.

"Something I fear we shall never say about you," the captain shot back.

Marmaduke motioned Thompson to a chair and said he needed to finish just two things, and then they would talk. He completed the report, blew on the paper and handed it to the aide with instructions that Price's adjutant, MacLean, receive it immediately. Then he scratched out a quick note to the commander of his largest brigade and handed it over, too.

"Please give this to General Clark and ask him to give me a few minutes at his pleasure, say around 10," Marmaduke ordered, then turned to the nervous man tapping his fingers on the chair arm.

"Well, rumor was you'd caught up to the column. I didn't believe it at first, thought Grant had eliminated the exchanges, but here you are."

"Caught up? John, this army is moving so slow, I almost passed it twice."

Marmaduke let out a sigh. It was true.

"Giving the recruits time to show up, is what I'm told." He looked toward the door to make sure it was shut. "Giving Rosecrans time, too, I fear."

"So we're heading for Jefferson City," Thompson mused. "Given up on St. Louis. A pity, I've always said the key to Missouri is St. Louis and Missouri is the key to everything in the west. One of the few things on which I've agreed with Price. Is there anything I can do for you, John? I'm at loose ends right now."

"Well, I don't need any bridges at the moment, Jeff," Marmaduke smiled. "In fact, my boys have been pretty busy burning those we have come across."

But he had needed one last year, both men were thinking. Marmaduke's raid into southeast Missouri failed to take the well-fortified town of Cape Girardeau. In retreating, the Confederates had nearly been pinned against a flooding St. Francis River. As Marmaduke held the Federals off at Chalk Bluff, Arkansas, Thompson had gone to the rear to assemble a rickety wisp of a floating bridge.

With every wagon they dragged across, the sweating men had feared the thing would disintegrate, but they made it over to safety. The heavy guns were broken down and rafted in pieces, the still-saddled horses driven in to swim the full river. Sadly, many of the saddles slipped back over rumps and tangled hocks. The drowning of so many horses had not been pretty to watch. But Thompson had saved Marmaduke's division and his reputation.

"Of course, it would be a pleasure if you would ride with us, Jeff, but there is no place yet for someone of your rank."

Thompson was so flamboyant, so quick with a verbose speech that some didn't take him seriously enough. But Marmaduke had learned to trust him.

"Nothing opened up at Fort Davidson?" asked Thompson. "I hear it was pretty bad there."

It *was* bad there, Marmaduke thought. He was not particularly proud of it, but several of his regiments had not gotten any farther than a creek bed and had stayed there until it got dark enough for a safe withdrawal. Then Ewing added insult by escaping. He and Shelby had taken to the chase, but the stubborn Federal had stuck to a ridgeback road through thick timber and bad ground that allowed no flanking or getting ahead of him. Ewing had played it all very shrewdly, using his field pieces in the rear to keep the pursuing Confederates back, whipping his men along until they'd reached Leasburg, a stop on the St. Louis-Rolla line. There he'd dug in, building a little fort out of rail ties and fought them off. It was all very distasteful and time-consuming.

He shook his head, watching how Thompson's jaw sank into his neck in disappointment. Thompson, he knew, had almost no teeth and could make the strangest faces. He wondered why he did not grow a beard to help disguise his empty jaw. He did have a decent mustache, which he was smoothing with thumb and forefinger.

Thompson then shrugged and leaned forward in his chair and asked quietly, "Is it true what I hear, that we marched those prisoners up here, and then took them out and shot them?"

Marmaduke nodded. "So I understand. I had nothing to do with it."

"The Federals will have a fit. They may decide to shoot a few of our boys to even things."

"Just so. Try not to get captured."

"Been captured just enough, thank you," Thompson smiled. "So what's happening here?"

"We strolled into the town — well, that's not quite true. Some old Dutch gentlemen dragged an ancient cannon from hill to hill, firing it enough to make my first ranks believe a Federal force lurked here. When the men figured out the bluff, they grabbed the old piece and threw it into the river."

"Lucky for the old Dutch fellows that your men didn't throw *them* into the river."

"It was the most fighting spirit we've seen up here in the river towns. Most of the militias paddled across the river, both here and in Washington. Seemed like every house had fresh bread and pies left out, their women hoping we wouldn't burn their homes."

"Think they have got fresh pies baking in Jefferson City?"

Marmaduke shook his head.

"What they are cooking up, I suspect, will be nothing good." He was told General Egbert Brown was in Jefferson City, and Brown had fought like a tiger last year in Springfield.

"Riding up here, I was puzzling on Hannibal a bit. You know, he failed to take Rome, which I believe was his undoing. I was wonder if St. Louis was our Rome?"

Marmaduke knew Thompson had no great regard for Price.

"Just so," he agreed. He had read his classics at Yale and Harvard before studying at West Point the tactics of the doomed Carthaginian.

"And I am reliably informed that we have been issued no elephants," Thompson joked.

"Actually, we began with two," Marmaduke smiled. "The men ate the last one before we reached Fredericktown."

Thompson laughed heartily at this. Marmaduke joined in a little, pleased with his own joke. He had not laughed much on this expedition. He had expected nothing good and so far nothing had lifted his gloom. The brigade of Louisiana cavalry had not arrived before they left Arkansas. The soldiers he did have in his division had seen the damned elephant at damned Fort Davidson, and it had eaten *them*. He felt worn down. Just 31 years old, he knew he looked 50, gaunt and hollow-eyed. After Vicksburg and Gettysburg and now Atlanta, Marmaduke believed the South was teetering toward defeat. This thrust into Missouri was of little strategic significance no matter how much Price tried to gild it.

Thompson was telling a story from his days in the prison camps, something about a big snowball fight, but Marmaduke was only half listening. Should Colonel Kitchen take the lead tomorrow? He was worried about him. Normally sound on the goose, now Solomon Kitchen had to be distracted about his son,

Cortez. He had brought the 12-year-old along as his orderly, and now the child had gone missing.

Marmaduke had told MacLean that his division would move out tomorrow, destroy the Gasconade railroad bridge and then swing south to a ford. He reflected on the great heavy pontoon boats Price had dragged up through Arkansas. Believing Thompson would appreciate a story with a bit more history, he recounted the scene when Price decided they should be burned at Dardanelle on the Arkansas River. Marmaduke cleared his throat.

"Well, it has put me in mind of another of history's great invaders. Cortez. He burned his boats, didn't he? To let his Spaniards know there was no turning back?"

"It has never once occurred to me to compare our commander to a conquistador," Thompson reflected.

"Just so," agreed Marmaduke.

OCTOBER 5

In the brush
Boone County

"PLUNK, THIS BREW'S AS BAD AS your ma's."

The joke was worn through nearly to daylight. Plunk Murray gave a little moan, but not because of any last squeeze of humor. He'd taken a bullet that broke his arm and bounced off a rib on the first charge at Fayette, but wouldn't let the band leave him behind. Then damned if he didn't fall off his horse on the same arm.

Plunk Murray's ma was famous for trying to poison some Union men who'd slaughtered her milk cow. Her coffee trick did not go undetected, and the Yankees were about to string her up when an officer asked whether she was Plunk's ma. When it was ascertained that the woman in the noose was indeed the lad's kin, he made the soldiers let her down. Seemed as if Plunk, who was always sweet-natured if a tad shy of hay in the loft, had once gotten the officer a dipper of well water on a hot day.

Now, it was Plunk, fevered, who asked for water. He was lying on a blanket, and the men tried to joke with him a little, take his mind off his hurt.

Riley had heard a lot of stories come out of this fighting, but few as heartening as Plunk and his ma. Goddamned Union men were always quick with a rope. When you studied on it, almost made sense to chop down every tree around a southern homestead, not make it so easy for the bastards.

Jesse James put down his bedroll a couple yards away and snugged a couple Colt sixes where he could grab them quickly. Jesse's daddy was one, Riley thought, strung up by folks wanting to know where brother Frank was. Jesse had cut him down, but not soon enough. The old man was never right in the head after. He mused on how many of the partisan rangers were sons seeking revenge: Bill Reynolds, Dave Pool, Sam Kimerlin, George Barnett, John House, well, hell, even Bloody Bill. And Quantrill was avenging his brother. Even Uncle Henry Younger, a staunch Union man, had been shot and robbed after a cattle sale by one of those sons of bitches who made up old Penick's hounds.

The commander of the hated Fifth Missouri State Militia Cavalry, headquartered in Independence, was Colonel W. R. Penick. His policy was to shoot any bushwhacker as an outlaw. A radical Unionist, Penick liked to say that Jackson and Clay counties could be tamed "if hemp, fire and gunpowder were freely used."

By the spring of 1863, Penick was advising Major General Samuel Curtis, then in charge of the Department of Missouri, that his area was not tamed: "It will be impossible for the U. S. soldiers to drive them out of the country until the government can afford to send 10 soldiers for 1 guerrilla. The only way to get them out is to destroy all subsistence in rocky and bushy parts of the country, and send off their wives and children…"

The foul reputation of the Fifth eventually got it consolidated with the First Missouri, but not without more trouble. The commanders in the area worried about a mutiny, and once the reorganization was completed, a newspaper reported that "a great number of Penick's men have deserted since his removal, and altogether the county is in a greater degree exposed..."

Guerrillas took revenge on every former member to fall into their hands. In early January 1863, guerrillas got hold of five of Penick's troopers and artillerymen, leaving their faces showing the impressions of boot heels and even exploding loose gunpowder in their ears, which then were sliced off. Within days, the slain soldiers' comrades would retaliate, and Riley's life would never be the same.

Although the Crawfords had tried to stay neutral, Penick's bunch had ridden up to their place and demanded to be fed. After that, they rode away with Riley's 50-year-old father, Jeptha, and a neighbor, Colonel Sanders, for "questioning" in town. The bodies of both were found in a foot of snow along the Independence road. The family barely got Jeptha buried before the milish came back to burn the homestead. Riley had watched one devil snatch off his mother's little lace hat and fling it into the blaze.

The family had kept a couple mares and a foal hidden in a shelter in the timber south of their Round Prairie acres. Momma had put what little was left in the wagon and took her brood to stay with kin. On the way, Riley had counted seven columns of smoke in the Blue Springs area.

Then one early spring evening, Momma, her lips so tight they might have been stitched by her own embroidery needles, told him to hitch up their wagon again. She threw a gunny sack in the wagon bed, and took his hand up onto the little seat. He took his place beside her, but she didn't give him the reins. It had turned cold again, and they lurched over frozen ruts as she encouraged the mares in the direction of Pink Hill.

He'd later wonder how she knew exactly where to turn off the road. The wagon had trundled past an abandoned house, through a pasture gone to weeds, across a creek and then there they were, about 50 or 60 men standing around a fire.

"Captain Quantrill, I'm Betsy Crawford," she had announced.

One of the watching men had stepped away from the warmth of the blaze. Unlike many of the others who wore long unkempt beards, Quantrill's chin had been clean-shaven. Mild looking, he wore an Imperial style mustache that Riley thought fine.

"Yes, Miz Crawford. We've heard of your loss. You have our sympathies and can be assured we will…."

Elizabeth Crawford had cut him off, no time nor inclination to play the grieving widow right then.

"I know you will and I've brought you some help."

She'd turned to Riley and told him to get down. That was all the words she spoke to him. Inside the bag she handed down, he'd felt some clothes inside, a jar of something. She'd turned back to Quantrill.

"You take him, Captain. You give him a gun and you tell him what to do. The Crawfords have a score to settle."

"It's a hard life for a lad, ma'am," Quantrill had said, studying the shivering, bewildered boy. The woman had clucked at the horse, pulled the reins toward back the way they'd come.

"You *take* him, Captain," Momma had said sharply. She never looked back at Riley, as far as he could tell. He'd watched until the buggy was swallowed by the dark. Quantrill had gazed after it, too, and then addressed the fair-haired, smooth-faced lad.

"You look cold, boy. Dick, get him a blanket," and then he'd returned to the talking around the fire. A minute later, a bad-smelling man had handed Riley a thick covering, smelling different, but just as bad.

"How old are you, son?"

"Little over 15, sir," Riley had answered between chattering teeth.

Many teens were in the bushwhacker ranks; the youngest was probably Allen Parmer, who began riding with Quantrill at age 13 and was with him at Lawrence and at the end in Kentucky. Archie Clement was 18 or 19, and Jesse James had turned 17 the month before.

Decades later, Frank James would recall, "At night and when we were in camp, we played like schoolboys … as rough as football. The truth was we were nothing but great big boys, anyhow." Only a couple were over 25, James later said. "If ever you want to pick a company to do desperate work or to lead a forlorn hope, select young men from 17 to 21 years old. They will go anywhere in the world you lead them. As men grow older they grow more cautious, but at that age they are regular daredevils."

Now, Riley's teeth were chattering again. It had been cloudy and frosty all day, and he'd gotten soaked to the waist when Folly, the little mare that had pulled him out of Fayette, stepped into a hole crossing Bartlett Creek. "Folly" wasn't such a bad name for her. He decided to take off his trousers and stand in his drawers next to the fire, see if he could get something to dry.

Riley unbuckled his belt and had his pants down when the blanket was thrown over his face and chest. He was pushed flat, McCorkle straddling his chest, and Riley figured what was coming next. He squirmed and kicked with his good foot, but he felt Frank James pulling off his sock with gentleness and heard him whistle.

"Damn, Riley, this don't look good." Riley knew what he was seeing. The whole foot was black.

He felt a cold wetness and then a cloth gently but painfully rubbing the caked blood away from his heel. Then alcohol reached raw flesh. Riley started hollering. Frank said, "Hush, you're as girlish as Dingus."

From the nearby bedroll came, "Go to the devil, Frank." McCorkle, who was having a peck of trouble holding Riley down, asked over his shoulder, "How's it smell? I've got this damn runny nose and can't smell nothin'."

The older James brother sniffed, "No, don't think it's any worse than Dingus's feet on the regular day." No rise out of Jesse this time.

Frank poured a little more on the foot. Riley almost heaved McCorkle off with that wave of pain.

"Damn it, Riley," Frank said. "I'm wasting enough busthead on this damn foot as it is, and now you've made me go and spill more."

And he swigged what was left of his antiseptic.

OCTOBER 7

Along the Moreau River
Cole County

STERLING PRICE WAS DRAGGING UP THE old story about how Thompson had climbed to the top of the St. Joe post office and ripped off the Union flag back at the beginning. God, Thompson thought, he had been so drunk that day.

"Well, sir, being as I had once been mayor of the city, I just felt it was my duty," Thompson joined in. Price roared. His staff officers chuckled. In the weedy yard of an abandoned house, a roaring fire sent up sparks to compete with the stars.

General M. Jeff Thompson could entertain the officers all night, he was full of stories: He had inaugurated the Pony Express and helped build the Hannibal & St. Joseph Railroad. Early in the war, he had had a giant Indian bodyguard called Ajax, who liked to pretend to be a wild savage. In Memphis, Thompson had organized the futile defense of the "cotton-clads," white-bale-covered river rams against the Union's iron-plated gunboats. After that, it was the swamps again, this time in Louisiana, where he bedeviled Union General Ben "Beast" Butler for a time.

And he had just completed a fairly thorough tour of Yankee prisons, having been captured the year before in Arkansas. Thompson had been exchanged in Charleston Harbor, of all places, after Federal admirals briefly had placed prisoners on boats in the line of fire from Confederate shore batteries. Once on land, he went to Richmond, where he learned of Price's invasion, and beat it home.

On this night, Price was playing genial host more than commander. Thompson privately believed the older man was better suited for the former, but he was happy with "Old Pap's" judgment this night, putting him in command. Oh, yes!

He might see action very soon. Word was that the Yankees were pouring into the state capital. Might be a pretty fight there. It had been hot enough getting across the Osage River, apparently.

On the fifth of October, Federal commanders had received stern instructions from Jefferson City: "Failing in driving the enemy across the Osage, they will contest every foot of ground, fighting them fiercely on their approach to Jefferson City, holding the banks of the Moreau until the last moment."

General Shelby had sent the Confederates' Fifth Missouri Cavalry to make a demonstration at Castle Rock while the main force attacked at Prince's Ford. One unit ran into a Union scout patrol and, according to Shelby's report, hit them "so hard that they (were) like the swine possessed of the devil and ran over a steep place and thirteen of them drowned." The next day, the rebels easily crossed the last shallow moat, the little Moreau River.

A sharp ripping cracked the chill air. Some of Price's officers were tearing more planks off an outbuilding and stomping the planks into pieces to feed the blaze and beat off the chill. Others turned the beef that was roasting on the tips of their sabers arranged over the embers.

Thompson watched the shadows flicker over the circle. These men admired and respected his predecessor, Colonel David Shanks, who forced the crossing. They said he likely would die from his wound, the fourth in about a year. Shanks' bad luck was his good, but Thompson couldn't let on how happy he was. The Iron Brigade! To be handed Shelby's band, famous across the south, some of the best riders and fighters in the whole Confederacy. Hell, they had ridden rings around the Yankees last fall on that recruiting run up here. His men liked to boast: "Stuart rode around McClelland. Hell, Shelby rode around Missouri!"

Thompson would have to prove he deserved to command them. He had waited so long for this. He'd tried again and again to secure a regular army commission. Despite fighting for the Confederacy in four states, he was still just a Missouri State Guard brigadier.

He again shook his head at the offer of the jug. No more of the drink until after the war, he'd sworn to himself. The conversation was turning toward food back in civilian life. Thompson thought he might offer one more story and then get out of this quilting circle.

"Say, did I ever tell you about the big dinner I charged to the Yankee command when I was being held in St. Louis? Well, I knew my days under genteel house arrest were about over, and I knew that the victuals were going to be a little less than sumptuous at Alton, so I went down to the best hotel...."

Price was already roaring and the other officers were beginning to really laugh this time. God, it was good to be back in Missouri.

OCTOBER 8

Jefferson City
Cole County

As GEORGE CALEB BINGHAM, TREASURER OF the State of Missouri, strode past the Virginia Hotel, a passing fellow doffed his plug hat.

"Afternoon, Mr. Treasurer."

"Yes, a very good afternoon," Bingham replied, touching his own headwear.

Good because it had just been learned that Sterling Price's Confederate army had declined to attack the capital and was headed on west. For Jefferson City, the danger was over.

The city's salvation had come cheap. General Egbert Brown had managed to pull in about 7,000 defenders behind Jefferson City's defenses. General Clinton Fisk arrived from across the river with his seniority and a few more troops.

On the Confederate side, Fagan had the head of the column and drove in the Federals' pickets, and Shelby cut off the western approaches to the town. Price, however, believed his men faced 12,000 Federals in those rifle pits and blockhouses, with 3,000 more just across the river. After his debacle at Fort Davidson, Price had little stomach for more assaults on earthworks.

Well, General Pleasonton took command today and should soon be riding west. God grant him success, thought Bingham. There was no need to return to the statehouse. The clerks would have the papers and such back in the office. Means, his secretary, would have everything under control.

Bingham wanted to share his good mood, so he turned off Washington onto

High Street to duck into a tavern where he took lunch some days. The talk at the bar, naturally enough, was of the passing crisis.

"Reckon Ol' Pap could turn back?" wondered a High Street merchant whose wares had just escaped liberation by Price's men. The merchant's companion, a young man Bingham did not know, shook his head. "If he didn't think he could crack us before, I doubt he'll think it likely tomorrow."

Bingham settled at a table where he could hear the talk at the bar and keep an eye on the street.

"Cider, Tip, if you please."

As the bartender drew a glass, the merchant turned to him.

"Good day, Mr. Bingham. Since you've probably been scurrying in and out of the vaults of our besieged capitol, perhaps you've got a little silver or at least some greenbacks to help us with our thirst. Defending the Union is mighty dry work."

Bingham decided not to tell the tavern crowd that the state's greenbacks were in a giant bank safe in St. Louis, certainly not that he personally delivered them there by ox cart one night soon after hearing of Price's crossing from Arkansas. Bingham insisted he would make the trip with the state's assets through guerrilla- and bandit-infested country alone, saying, "I have the Lord on my side, and if he and I need any help, I have a pistol with me."

He waved to Tip to fill the others' mugs. "Thanks to glory that brave men like yourself were here. Were you armed with a broom from your store, sir, or did you go for the new repeater mop that I've heard so much of?"

All the men laughed. The relief in the room was still palpable. The Confederates' Army of the Missouri had just knocked on their door, probing Jefferson City's hastily built defenses. Then it moved on up the Missouri River to spread its misery somewhere else, or with a little luck and Union pluck, be destroyed.

"You're high in the government," stated the merchant, "how many men are with Price this time?"

Bingham, who had been present at some meetings between the governor and the military men, had no intention of sharing everything he heard. But this was innocent enough.

"Maybe fifteen thousand in his column. God knows how many bushwhackers pitching in."

The fellow he did not know spat on the floor and began to declaim: "Traitors enlisting murderers. Scum who corduroyed the streets of Centralia with the corpses of unarmed men. Price should be hanged along with such recruits, I say."

Bingham thought of his best friend, James Rollins, saved at Centralia only by merciful providence.

"Sir, I don't believe you've introduced me to your friend," Bingham said to the merchant.

"Oh, sorry," said Mr. Dry Goods, motioning with his mug for a refill, offering a name that Bingham did not recognize. His loquacious friend was a member of the Bohemian Brigade, correspondent for the *Missouri Democrat.*

"And this old cove is the honorable George Bingham, treasurer of the state," Dry Goods continued. "He's an artist, too, when he's not counting my money in his vault."

"Yes, I thought it was you," said the St. Louis scribe. "I'm familiar with your work. You rendered a very fine likeness of my uncle. And I must say I've seen copies of your electioneering paintings gracing many St. Louis drawing rooms."

The compliment pleased Bingham. His lack of production these days could be blamed on the distraction of his state appointment and the terrible events around him.

"You're too kind," he replied, thinking a little mention in the *Democrat* would not be a bad thing; he was not on the best of terms right now with the radical St. Louis sheet.

"Are you working on anything now? Portraits, perhaps? Plenty of officers around, willing to stick their Napoleonic hands into their coats, I'd wager."

"Oh, Governor Price didn't seem to want to stick around long enough for a sitting." A chuckle from his listeners on that. And then for reasons he couldn't understand, Bingham added, "Actually, I've got something I'm working on now, in my spare time, of which I seem to have so little."

Why did he bring that up? God, the ego of the artist, always hungry.

"And the nature of this work?" asked the scribe, eyebrow arched. "Not something as bland as portraiture, I wager. Could be worth a few lines in the rag."

Bingham didn't answer, trying to think of a way to pitch the talk in another path.

The merchant, now on at least his third mug of a dark German brew, answered for him. "A battle, of course. A glorious battle with our Union boys charging over the battlements and blowing the goddamned rebs to bits. Wait, how about the glorious battle of Pilot Knob and its hero, General Thomas Ewing? That'd be the thing."

Hardly a hero, Bingham thought to himself, but the merchant had a theme now.

"Yes," said the newspaper wretch, catching something in Bingham's face. "That's not a bad idea. Ewing really did pull it off, you know. Held Fort Davidson against 20,000. A leaden tempest, surely. They couldn't crack him, and he only had a thousand men or so. Genius." The reporter smiled. "But then you know Ewing, I recall."

"We are acquainted," Bingham replied noncommittally, thinking how it would look criticizing the general whose holding action probably had saved St. Louis as well Jeff City. All those rifle pits and stacked logs on the town perimeter had not been there a week ago. No, feuding with Ewing right now would not go over well.

The merchant egged on the reporter, saying, "Read him your letter about our events here."

The scribe also had an ego, needed no more urging. He reached into a coat pocket, pulled out some wrinkled papers and began to read.

"Here's a good part about Price, I think. 'He mounted his white horse, Bucephalus, and made a display that was terrific to behold. Not knowing the man, General Grant would have been staggered by it, or Napoleon would have been driven back over the Alps. All day on October the seventh, he raved and frothed, formed and reformed, and marched and countermarched, but never once did he or any of his cavaliers venture within range of the frowning Federal guns, backed as they were by a line of true blue, eager for the fray.'"

"But that didn't happen, did it?" Bingham frowned. "Someone spotted Price with some of his guns over to the east, but 'raved and frothed, formed and re-formed'? I recall nothing of that."

"The license of the poet," the reporter said, grinning and showing very bad teeth for such a young fellow. The truth was, however, he wasn't sure his letter would be published. The *Democrat* was fairly strait-laced about its news columns, and many of his writings of late had been spiked.

"It's getting late," Bingham said, draining his mug. "I must be going."

The hack gave up, placed some scrip on his table. He was weary, a little tight, and there was still work to do. "Well, yes, so must I. Got to dispatch my letter. See if there's any steamers to take it. The wire's cut all to hell by the rebs."

Outside, Bingham hesitated, letting the other make the first move in whatever direction he was heading. He had no intention of walking with the reporter, who was now complaining about his poor lodgings at an old inn: a varying fraction of a bed, served with a bottomless buffet of vermin. Bingham grew itchy just listening to him.

Damn, the hack was stepping off to the left. That was the direction of Bingham's home, so the treasurer said good evening and turned the other way. He would walk a couple blocks out of his route toward the river before turning supperward.

The talk of Ewing was unsettling. He was no hero to Bingham, but now the general's adventure would make his reputation whole again.

He silently thanked God that the reporter had not known or at least said anything about the Kansas City jail episode. Some people here were aware of it, of course, but the whole thing was so distasteful that few ever broached the subject. Five southern women crushed dead in Bingham's own building on Grand Avenue, others grievously hurt. And Ewing had let it happen. Hell, the Kansan had crammed those women onto the second floor, and then did not act on reports that the structure was growing unsafe. And now these hosannas!

The dead were all bushwhacker womenfolk, of course. The Democrats had accused the Federals of conspiring to cause the collapse. The Republicans insisted the women, all spies, had brought the thing down on their own heads trying to tunnel out. Tunnel out? From the second floor?

So, what do the guerrillas do a week later? Launch the biggest raid Kansas has ever seen 40 miles into Union territory and burn Lawrence, kill every man and boy they could find. Oh, the papers had screamed for revenge, then. The jail scandal was forgotten. Lane had climbed Ewing's back. The Constitution be damned. It was war.

So Ewing made it all worse, him and then that damned Order No. 11. Bingham was as pro-Union as any in Missouri, but to turn Jackson County into abandoned wasteland! Ewing had driven everyone out, loyal or not. Homes, crops, livestock left behind.

"It is well known that men were shot down in the very act of obeying the order, and their wagons and effects seized by their murderers," Bingham would write. "Large trains of wagons, extending over the prairies for miles in length, and moving Kansasward, were freighted with every description of household furniture and wearing apparel belonging to the exiled inhabitants. Dense clouds of smoke arising in every direction marked the conflagrations of dwellings."

Given just 15 days to get out, the refugees trudged away mostly on foot to find shelter wherever they could. Bingham had seen them "crowded by the hundreds upon the banks of the Missouri River" begging steamboat captains for charity and transport to wherever. Ewing had seen them, too, writing on September 17, 1863, "The boat was crowded full of them and god knows where they are all going for I don't nor do I care so (long as) we get rid of them in Missouri…"

Bingham turned another corner. His front door was coming into view. The idea was that the marauders would no longer have a base, that those feeding them, sheltering them would disappear. And did the raiders disappear, was evil just wished away? Hardly. They simply moved east and brought new circles of hell to central Missouri, which had its share of bushwhacking already.

Bingham scraped his boots outside before entering. Hanging his hat, he greeted Eliza with reassurances that Price was indeed gone and that General Pleasonton had things well in hand. He'd be in the dining room in a minute, and they could talk more about it, he said, but first he wanted to freshen up. He mounted the stairs but did not go to his bedroom, turning instead to the makeshift studio. He picked up some pencil sketches, flipped through them.

Ewing the hero? Bingham personally had asked Ewing to set aside his Order No. 11. "Rescind it?! Rescind it?! That is impossible," Ewing replied. "I wouldn't if I could. It is a preposterous request and reveals a lack of knowledge of the military requirements of this department."

To which Bingham responded: "I do not take issue on whether I lack or possess any military knowledge, but I do not lack a sense of what is just and right, and that order is neither… If you persist in executing this order, I shall make you infamous with my pen and brush so far as I am able."

Months later, Ewing had softened the order, letting some return under conditions, but return to what?

Looking at the penciling, Bingham mused. Pilot Knob might not save Ewing. He got to a favorite sketch, a white-haired grandfather in a pose of defiance, a daughter holding to him in despair. It would be a big canvas, he figured, his biggest. In his mind, he was thinking of the balance. The house being looted would loom in the left background, smoke of burning farmsteads on the horizon on the other side. A story that anyone could understand: the tragedy of the Greek, the cruelty of the Roman.

He dropped the sheets in their pile and turned toward the smells of dinner. He might come back later and work up a drawing of Ewing's arrogant face.

OCTOBER 9

The Boonville Road

Moniteau County, central Missouri

"By God, if Boonville holds no horseshoes for me, I am going to shoot that idiot quartermaster."

Thomas Reynolds was talking aloud to himself, and his remark got an appreciative laugh from a man greasing an axle of an overburdened wagon. Here he was, trapped another day on that damned instrument of torture of an ambulance pulled by footsore mules, when he had wanted to be back up at the front of the Confederate column when Boonville was taken.

Back in Arkansas, the imbecile quartermaster had given his guarantee that Reynolds and his aides did not need to bring their own supply of horseshoes.

"Now, when my horse can hardly walk, I get nothing but studied neglect from the whey-faced fool," the Confederate governor in exile muttered to himself. "Were his brains lard, he couldn't grease a skillet!"

Stalking back from the barren forge wagons along the endless line of vehicles, Reynolds stopped and stared. He was badly nearsighted, but this wagon bed clearly had a cargo including not one, but two towering hall clocks. More procured "military supplies," he supposed. Like the iron beds, women's clothing, spinning wheels and such loot that could be found in many of the other wagons. Well, time is a weapon. Why not assemble a battery of clocks?

He froze. A hen, clearly an escapee from some container, clucked by. Amazing that it survived last night's dinner hour. The hen bobbed away into some sneezeweed. Make a dash after it? The plump executive realized he could look ridiculous, and that would never do.

The thought of the chicken made him snort. The night before, Price had made a production of paying for his room and stewed bird at the Wallendorf farm, counting out 27 Confederate dollars. What a joke! Outside the house, meanwhile, Price's men had slaughtered every piece of livestock on the place and taken the horses, leaving their jaded beasts behind. Every farm is stripped for miles around by this rabble of deadheads. Even their stolen negroes are riding stolen horses. But can the governor of the state even buy a fresh mount? No.

Reynolds mostly blamed Price, but in truth he had to blame himself as well. After Senator Peyton died of the ague, the generals in Arkansas had practically begged Reynolds to appoint Price to the vacant seat and pack him off to Richmond. It was common knowledge that the man had never met a commanding officer who couldn't be driven to distracted fury by his ravenous self-importance.

"I apprehend that no officer can serve where he is without lending himself to fractious schemes and losing sight of discipline or else becoming involved in endless disputes," wrote General Thomas C. Hindman. Similarly, General Ben McCulloch and Price, like children, had gotten to the point of not speaking to each other. Reynolds had first clashed with Price over disbursements from the shrunken Missouri Treasury.

Davis and the others believed Price always put Missouri before the Confederacy. To South Carolina-born and Virginia-educated Reynolds, a personal friend of Jefferson Davis, it was more that the general always put himself, his fame, his ambitions before *everything*.

Oh, Price was brave enough, but brash — a poor administrator, yet a master manipulator. No one dares slap him down for all the howls that pour from Missourians every time Price believes himself slighted. As Price's insufferable former aide, Thomas Snead, had said, "Price is Missouri!" And, Reynolds conceded bitterly, he had foolishly bought into that. He had believed no one could bring Missourians to the flag like the general.

Of course, a Senator Price would have been an absolute disaster in Richmond, an immense aggravation for the president. Davis never would have forgiven Reynolds for such an appointment.

Always secretive, Price moved through a swirl of rumored plots. One was that he would bolt from the Confederacy, just like his traitorous son sitting not so many miles from here, getting rich off the family tobacco operations.

State Guard General Edwin Price had been captured in 1862 trying to bring recruits south to his father. Davis helped get him exchanged for a Union general, and he rejoined his father, in Mississippi at the time. Then came the startling conversion. The younger Price resigned his commission, took the oath of allegiance to the United States and received Lincoln's pardon.

When Edwin tried unsuccessfully to visit his mother in Texas, some smelled an effort to persuade his father to defect. The odor reached the other side. Missouri Congressman James Rollins wrote to Lincoln that Price's "vanity and ignorance induced him into the whirlpool of treason" and that he could be returned to the fold. Price insisted that such stories were fabrications.

Another theory had once worried Reynolds more, that Price might try to become generalissimo of a Northwest Confederacy, a murky conspiracy in which states from Indiana to Minnesota might break away from the Union themselves. Considering Price's success so far on this march, this seemed absurd now.

"Ye Knights" of this humiliating crusade had reached Jerusalem and then marched by its walls. Indeed, the capitol dome was already 20 miles behind. Reynolds had dragged along from Texas the state seal and several pre-written proclamations for a triumphant return. To retake Missouri's capitol after three years' absence would have rattled Washington. But no, the old tortoise let the Federals reinforce the city.

What might have happened if Jefferson City actually had fallen? Many saw Price as always alert for the bigger stage, one reason Reynolds had accompanied the expedition. If the old general, the white-haired hero, *did* capture the state, he might have tried to make himself a military governor, pulling off a quick election to evict Reynolds.

What is clear is that Reynolds was always uneasy about his status after Governor Claiborne Jackson died in exile in December 1862, a victim of stomach cancer. The Missouri Constitution required an election soon after a governor's death, something impossible for Reynolds to organize as long as the Federals held the state. This was used against him the next year, in fact, when Price sneeringly referred to "Reynolds, who pretends to be, and styles him self in it, the Governor...."

Reynolds' young aides were bringing up four sad-faced mules. Only two of them were in any shape to pull. Wonderful.

"Let Albert handle the hitching, William. Get out the writing box. I've got a letter in mind. Here, Albert, that chain is tangled, do you see? Watch her, she kicked yesterday."

Her mood is exactly mine, Reynolds thought. He puffed his rosy cheeks, then let out a long sigh. He needed to kick a little bit.

"Are you ready, William? Let's get this done before the column starts to move. The letter is to Major General Price. Date it tomorrow." As he began to dictate, he realized that he could not let it all out, but he would certainly register his frustration. And he'd have William make a copy for his file, too.

"*...In fact, in an expedition designed to re-establish the rightful government of Missouri, the Governor of the State cannot even purchase a horse or a blanket while stragglers and camp followers are enriching themselves by plundering the defenseless families of our own soldiers in Confederate service....*"

Kirby Smith had foreseen the possibility. His orders to Price had said, "You will scrupulously avoid all wanton acts of destruction and devastation, restrain your men, and impress upon them that their aim should be to secure success in a just and holy cause and not to gratify personal feeling and revenge."

Well, it was a lovely thought, but Price had never been considered a disciplinarian. To protect his personal supplies and own foodstuffs from the many thieves in his army, Price had assigned a company of Shelby's brigade to ride with that part of the train.

Some of our finest men guarding the old man's luxuries, Reynolds fumed. This was not the way it was supposed to be. We said we would secure our people from Union predation. But this rabble, this locust army? We *are* the predation!

The host of "recruits" Price was picking up was unlike anything seen elsewhere in the war. Besides the deserters rounded up by Shelby in Arkansas — who performed poorly in the attacks on Fort Davidson — some saw themselves as amateur cavalry gentlemen. Others made no bones about being slackers, the trash of many a small town, out on a lark, carrying off anything they could steal from southern families as well as Unionist. "A large number of unarmed men who seemed to think themselves not amenable to orders," was how Major James Shaler would describe them.

The small, springless vehicle lurched over ruts. Swaying, bumping shoulders with the younger men, Reynolds frowned. Use of the ambulance, smaller and more nimble than a wagon, was fine for his attendants, but a governor had no place there.

Until Reynolds' horse had lost that shoe he had acted as volunteer aide to Shelby, enjoyed the general's excellent company and the action usually surrounding him. Price had fretted about it, suggesting Reynolds ride back with the wagon train. But that was where you could find Price, wasn't it? Reynolds earlier had written to Price that in an army endeavoring to restore him to the executive chair, the proper place of a Governor of Missouri is in the front.

No, when the story of this shameful exercise was penned in history, Reynolds wanted no scribe to find him in the rear. He chewed on that for a moment, reviewing his reading of history, wondering what past invasions had been as weak as this one. Price's folly would be lost in time, he concluded.

OCTOBER 10

Gasconade River
Gasconade County

SAMUEL BEREMAN GRITTED HIS TEETH. THE water was now up to his personal parts but he was nowhere near his destination. He stepped on a sharp rock, then floundered into an unseen hole. Suddenly the freezing stream was nipple high. Back on the bank, the sergeant's men hooted afresh at his discomfort.

His horse had got him into this misery. As the Fourth Iowa Cavalry forded the Gasconade, it became clear that the bottom on the west side of the river had been churned into a morass by the soldiers who had already crossed. Bereman's company determined to go upstream a bit to find a cleaner place to cross and water the mounts. As the horsemen waded in, Bereman let his gelding get into a boggy part along the bank. Too late, he tried to turn away.

His panicked horse, hooves sucked into the mire, thrashed and struggled. It broke free in a wild, snorting heave that nearly unseated Bereman, but could not get fresh footing and finally capsized — into a deep pool. The saddle girth broke, leaving rider and gear slipping off its back. His men caught the beast as it plunged to the other side. Fortunately, one end of its halter was tied to the saddle, so that it was dragged out.

"But very unluckily my carbine was not tied to my saddle & so it dropped in the creek," Bereman would recall. "Aside from being without a gun in close proximity to the game — I did not like to pay $25.00 for losing it ... my Spencer Carbine ... my seven shooting carbine which was lost in the creek."

The baby-faced sergeant stripped off his wet wool uniform, thought about it, and then took off the rest, asking a private to wring it out a little. The private asked whether he should apply a little soap, but he said it with a smile. The sergeant replied that he did not need starch, thank you, and then turned to the river as another company forded, pointing and laughing at him.

"Then accoutened as I was (not) I plunged in '&c.' Oh! how cold it was. It makes me shiver to think of it. But I 'stemmed it with heart of controversy.' But ere I reached the point proposed it came to my neck. Oh how cold! Ugh!"

He calculated roughly where he had been dunked, judged the current and adjusted his search. A sharp rock stuck his heel, and then his toes telegraphed the good news. With his foot, Bereman foot dug into the gravel under the barrel and lifted his beloved carbine. The current strove to upend him as he carefully balanced on the other foot.

Wading back to shore, he redressed in everything but his heavy caped overcoat while a private repaired the saddle girth. Another soldier attended to his carbine, giving it a quick cleaning and reloading from his own cartridge box. Bereman thanked them all and gave a private the reins to the gelding.

Their impatient captain yelled for the company to get moving, and Bereman began trotting on foot to get warm. His teeth chattered. He was looking forward the fire that night.

It was well past dark when the column stopped in their never-ending slog after Price's army. Having started from Little Rock, Arkansas, with General Joseph Mower and his infantry, the Iowans had been ordered to move ahead and try to catch up with the Seventh Kansas and some other cavalry regiments nearer Jefferson City. Bereman wasn't sure the whole thing was not a wild goose chase. The rebs seemed to have a pretty good head start, and Bereman couldn't imagine how the infantry could be brought up in time, considering how the railroad was so cut up.

After hammering his picket pin into the rocky soil, Bereman pulled the saddle off his horse and ran his fingers gently over the animal's back. At the ford, he had seen a deep scratch at the loin where his gear had dragged off. The cavalryman wrested open a greasy can of ointment by which the company farrier solemnly swore and smeared its contents liberally. Then he bent to feel around the cannon bones for swelling. The gelding, perhaps abashed by its earlier silly behavior, allowed all this without a twitch.

The sergeant had been lucky on the draw at the corral in St. Louis and knew it would not do to have to find a remount in this country, already stripped by the enemy. Coming out of Arkansas, he had been forced to hobble on foot the last miles to Cape Girardeau, leading a miserable mare with a volcanic running sore under the saddle and grossly swollen withers. It would take a month to heal and hide her ribs under fat again. Even though much of the chase of Price had been done at a walk, even a pace of four miles in an hour for such long days had been brutal on the horses.

Bereman patted the gelding with his messy hand, and the name "Grease" came to him. "For the slickness of your little trick of saddle shedding," he explained to the horse. A private had suggested "Poseidon" as a joke, but that was too much for this horse to carry. Despite the day's adventures, he was a pretty good animal. A little cow-hocked maybe, but fairly bridle-wise and better than many of the nags scraped up for the outfit.

He thought of the story going around about how Lincoln, upon learning that one of his brigadier generals was captured as well as many horses, remarked that he could always make more generals but horses cost money.

Bereman could only agree that the average horse was worth more than the average general any day.

VIII

Regulars and irregulars

"It is cheering to see the bright faces of the ladies at the prospect of being rid of the Dutch and Yankee domination."

— Major William McPheeters' diary, October 2, 1864

c/ɔc/ɔc/ɔc/ɔc/ɔ

Boonville

Cooper County, central Missouri

THE WHITE-HAIRED GENERAL, OUT ON THE City Hotel porch to welcome the riders, stiffened at the sight of Bill Anderson and Archie Clement. Other officers and a chubby civilian were looking hard-faced, too, although some army fellows were grinning.

Riley Crawford walked Folly forward a couple steps to get an idea what was up. He followed their gaze to the bridle on Bill's mount.

Oh, those: The scalps.

General Price turned and went in. A staff officer stepped down to the street and talked softly to Bill, who frowned, then decided to laugh it off.

"Reckon regular soldiers don't take to hair," he said to Archie, who smirked as usual. Archie had some ribbons taken from a Centralia store streaming from his hat. "Let's go get a drink and come back all 'presentable' for the general."

Riley had little truck with scalping, himself. But he was surprised that a general who'd let the Union invaders run roughshod over his people for so long would make a fuss over it.

Guess Ol' Pap hadn't caught word of how Al Collins was treated by some milish patrol a couple weeks back. A grapevine caught Al in the throat and pulled him out of the saddle as he was fleeing. His long curly hair made the militiamen think they'd caught Bloody Bill at last. So what'd they do? Shot out both his eyes as he was lying there. And *his* hair was tied to *their* bridles. By God, scalping was too damn good for some of them milish. He'd be happy for a chance to take a gutting knife to the ones that murdered Pa and the girls.

Riley had crossed the river the day before with Anderson's bunch a little east of Rocheport, taking skiffs and swimming the horses over in long lines, reins tied to tails. Now in this southern town so strongly garrisoned by Yanks for years, the men scattered like a busted covey to see kin. The army reached here two nights ago. Apparently the local guard thought it was Bill come visiting and was ready to put up a scrap. Once they realized it was Shelby, though, they'd surrendered peaceful enough.

Riley had carefully drifted away from Buck James, who had this notion that some army surgeons should take a look at his foot. He was studying on a string of bony horses some farmer was trying to sell and didn't have to time to scoot before Buck appeared with a giant, red-haired man named Pringle.

"Com'on with us," he said. "Get a move on."

"Where we goin?" Riley protested, thinking the long-faced James brother had found a saw-bones.

"Gotta find Bill to tell him something. He was headed down that away a while ago."

"Why the hurry?" Riley asked. He couldn't keep up with the red-headed Pringle even without a hole in his foot.

"I think I saw a spy."

"A spy? Where?"

"Down closer to the river. Ducked into an alley. I never got a fair look, but he powerfully resembled a fellow called Hickok."

"Who's Hickok?"

"A Union man, supposedly a rare hand with a pistol. I saw him stand down a mob in Independence that wanted to take a wagon train he was guarding. He's a cool number, all right."

They were heading south on Fifth Street toward a saloon where someone thought Anderson might be. Riley's limp got worse.

"You and your damned foot," Buck complained. "Gonna' git you a doc, I swear, but this Hickok business comes first."

They had reached the defensive works erected around an imposing building fronted by the most massive pillars Riley had ever seen. "You go rest on them steps, and I'll come back for you."

Riley felt reprieved. Looking a little torn by his priorities, Buck looked up at one of the soldiers holding up one of the brick columns. "Wherebouts is the surgeon tent?"

"Right where it's always been. When Shelby come through in '63, it was 'ere, too" the private said, jerking a thumb behind him. "And wouldn't I know it, cause I was in it, caught one in the butt, but I wasn't running, no sir, don't you go getting no ideas! Gol-danged feller 'hind me was shifting his gun to get a better grip on ah ol' rooster he'd liberated, and it went off and took a piece outta my ass, the gun, I mean, not the chicken, and I said to him, I said, 'I'm gonna put that rooster up ....'"

"So I can leave 'im here," Buck interrupted, pointing to Riley, "and you'll watch 'im?"

Riley had been enjoying the story. So had Pringle, who applauded the teller with an appreciative smirk and said, "So you're the fellow with two assholes that I've always heard about."

"Sonny," the soldier grinned back, "you ain't the first body to suggest I can be twice the ass-hole as any...."

"Well, yer heading for triple in my book," said an exasperated Buck. "Will you make sure a damn doctor sees him or not?"

"I believe the bone-cutters are doing business right now on some fellows brought in from the skirmishing out south. But I'll keep an eye on your boy."

Buck made Riley swear he wouldn't run off, that he would go inside and see a doctor about his foot. Riley watched him and Pringle stride down the street.

He got up and wrapped his arms around himself. "This is the biggest church I ever seen."

"Church?" Two Holes exclaimed. "Ain't no church, you bumpkin. It's a playhouse. That's what they call it, 'Thespian Hall,' tho I don't reckon there's been much play acting lately."

Riley tried to imagine the grandness of seeing actors at a place such as this. He'd never been to a real theater, but his sisters had put on little performances he'd gotten a great kick out of. Then he began blinking.

Mina and Suzy. Crushed in that hellhole jail in Kansas City. It was a terrible thought that dogged him mercilessly, made him merciless at times. Everybody knew the Kansans had weakened the walls, had plotted to murder the girls as spies. John and Bill's sisters had been in there, too. The Federals caterwauled over Lawrence — Yankeetown — but that was just payback. And we didn't kill no women, neither.

Crawford's older, married sisters, Armenia Crawford Selvey and Susan Crawford Whitsett Vandever, were arrested on a trip to Kansas City to buy flour and cloth, alleged by the Federals to be destined for guerrillas. They and perhaps a dozen other southern women were confined to the second floor of the three-story Thomas building on Grand Avenue. The building collapsed on August 13, 1863, killing immediately Crawford's sisters; Bill Anderson's sister Josephine; and Charity McCorkle Kerr, sister of John McCorkle, who would say: "We could stand no more."

Conspiracy theories were floating before the dust settled. Southern sympathizers accused Union soldiers of purposely murdering the women by removing key building supports. Northerners protested that the building was dilapidated and felled by a high wind or rooting hogs or the victims themselves.

Most believed that the Cockrell building next door, used as a guardhouse, collapsed, sagging into its common wall with the jail and bringing it down, too. The first floor of the Thomas Building was occupied by a business, so it was logical that it was the Cockrell building that was structurally compromised by soldiers removing beams. Some argued those modifications were made innocently; others saw a murder plot.

Eleven years after the disaster, Dr. Joshua Thorne, the Union surgeon responsible for the medical care of the women prisoners, would come forward. He would testify that, while the second floor was occupied by the southern girls, and the first floor housed a grocery, the cellar held women "of bad character and diseased." To reach this harem, the guards barracked next door tore out large holes in the common cellar wall, weakening both structures.

But the deaths of the womenfolk, while a strong motivator, were not the main reason for the Lawrence raid. Days before, Quantrill had discussed with his lieutenants the possibility of such an attack and already had spies there to determine the strength of local Federal forces.

So the guerrillas had ridden all night, dozing in their saddles, nearly slipping from them at times, 40 miles into the enemy's lair, to slay Red Legs and deliver revenge. Riley hadn't heard that they'd caught any of them, not George Hoyt, the Red Leg chief, nor James Lane, the jayhawker senator, he knew that. A lot of other folks had been home, though, and wished they hadn't.

"Kill! Kill and you will make no mistake!" Quantrill had shouted. "Lawrence should be thoroughly cleansed, and the only way to do it is to kill. Kill!" It had seemed right at the time, avenging the death of pa and the sisters.

Riley had missed out on some of it, being light on substantials, and had stopped with some of the boys at a house where cooking was to be had. A northern women had obliged his request for a meal, but took into the raiders about killing unarmed men. Riley had gotten pretty warm of manner. What did she know about it?

"I had two sisters arrested in Kansas City by Union men for entertaining Southern sentiment," he told her. "One night that building fell, and my two sisters, with three other ladies, were crushed to death. Jennison had laid waste our homes, and your 'Redlegs' have perpetuated unheard of crimes, I am here for revenge, and I have got it."

Then Riley finished her buttermilk and cornbread and had gone out to get some more — revenge, that is.

Riley was thinking of those bodies in the Lawrence streets when the guard motioned.

"All that talk of my assholes done put me in the frame of mind to find a place to empty my bowel," the guard said. "Supposedly, I'm guarding the hall 'ere, but from what I ain't zakly sure. Ain't the season for mad dogs, and no Union man's gonna poke his head up in this town. Come on up here and stand in my place. I'll be back in a minute."

Once the private was around the corner, Riley turned to the doors. He would just do his guarding from the inside. Propping the private's Enfield behind a column, he opened a door a bit and peered in. The place had some benches shifted around up front, where men were standing by some tables. Several townswomen were helping out. He heard the medical men murmur, saw a flash of some silver instrument. Some soldiers were lying in the bench-pews, a couple sitting up, patiently waiting their turn, watching intently. One fellow's bubbly wheeze gave every indication he would not make it through the night.

Riley was weary, decided he'd just do his guarding laying down, and so he slipped in and stretched out. He hadn't run off, he told himself, he'd gone inside, and now he'd seen the doctors, yes, from about 50 feet maybe, but then Buck didn't need the details. That should take care of his oath.

A couple of the women sat down a few rows ahead. They didn't notice Riley, but he heard much of their gossip. One was from New Franklin, the other from Boonville and the two had not visited in a while.

Riley strained to listen, could tell that the Boonville woman was complaining about the behavior of some of the Confederate soldiers in town. Apparently, quite a bit of thievery was going on. The country woman insisted that it couldn't be as bad as some of the milish.

"Why, they would steal the coppers off a dead nigger's eyes," she exclaimed and began to relate some depredations she had witnessed or personally suffered. While completely agreeing with that assessment of Yankees, Riley had to concede that from his brief experience Price's army did seem as intent on liberating the Missouri chickens and horses as liberating their owners.

He was getting sleepy. If the women spotted him, he'd say he'd been asleep all this time. Didn't hear nothing. He closed his eyes, preparing his act. His act. He smiled. Today's performance in — what was this place called? yeah, Terrapin Hall — will be by the amazing Riley Crawford.

11 A.M.

QUANTRILL WAS NOT HERE. REYNOLDS PONDERED THAT.

Had he and Anderson — over there in the street, laughing at some private joke with his lieutenants — had another falling out? He understood that rough-looking fellow in the ragged Confederate coat was John Thrailkill. And George Todd, where was that sullen guerrilla?

Men looked toward the hotel entrance. "Himself" had finally gotten down the stairs and was coming out, obese but still regal in his gray uniform with the three stars wreathed on the collar. No salutes from the guerrillas. Would Quantrill have given one? Probably. Even if Richmond had denied him his coveted colonelcy, Quantrill was still considered a captain. Besides, he was a gentleman.

Anderson turned to a mischievous-looking little tad called Archie, who handed over an ornate wooden box. Anderson — he was a handsome pirate, even if barbarous, all curls of dark brown locks and beard — in turn presented the box to Price.

"We're mighty glad to see you, General," Anderson said jauntily. "To show how glad, me and the boys wanted you to have these." He opened the case to display two revolvers, mounted in silver. The older man beamed at the pieces.

"Why thank you, Captain Anderson, thank you, gentlemen." He took one pistol out, sighted along it down the street. Very handsome pieces, Reynolds thought, but if a name is etched on them, it's not Price's. Out in those Missouri hills is another gentleman missing them right now. Or, Reynolds frowned, was he really missing them now? Probably not. Probably murdered, perhaps by one of the men here on this porch. His scowl deepened as Price turned back to the guerrilla chiefs.

"If I had had 50,000 men like you. I could hold Missouri for as long as it takes," the general happily declared.

Reynolds actually shuddered at that, thinking of the scalps Anderson's gang had brought into town. Having these men as allies was much like winning the elephant in the raffle. Once you have him, what can you do with him?

Reynolds, the unhappy governor in exile, later wrote that, "at Boonville, the hotel occupied by General Price's own headquarters was the scene of drunken revelry by night...." He also took note of the guerrillas, "with human scalps hanging to their bridles, and tauntingly shaking bundles of plundered greenbacks at our needy soldiers...." The Union commanders would hear of this meeting and protest. Rosecrans wrote to Price on October 22, "to express my surprise and regret that you have allowed to associate with your troops bands of Missouri guerrillas ... whose record is stained with crimes at which humanity shudders." Afterward, Price tried to put a little air between himself and the bushwhackers, noting dismissively how they'd done little damage during his campaign.

The leaders soon went inside to get down to business. Anderson was supposed to take his crew back down the river to destroy the North Missouri Railroad bridge not far out of St. Charles. When Price talked about Quantrill taking the Hannibal & St. Joe across north Missouri, Reynolds noticed that some of the partisans gave each other glances.

What is afoot? Have they killed Quantrill? Anderson remarked how he'd just smote a heavy blow against the North Missouri line at Centralia and would be happy to do so again. Reynolds had an idea of what had happened at Centralia, it was hard to avoid it. Spies were bringing in newspapers. People in Boonville were shaking their heads over it, some quite frightened at the idea of Anderson's men being in their midst. Those outrageous scalps certainly allayed no fears.

Down in Texas, an appalled General Henry McCulloch wrote that "They regard the life of a man less than you would that of a sheep-killing dog ... Quantrill's mode of warfare, from what I can learn, is but little ... removed from that of the wildest savage." And McCulloch hadn't even seen these scalps.

The bushwhackers caused almost as much trouble wintering in Texas as they had in Missouri, and the regular army commanders quickly got fed up by the partisans' refusal to enlist and their overall bad behavior. McCulloch tried to get them out of his district, "which they have nearly ruined, and I have never got them to do any service."

When Quantrill tried to impose some order on the bands, Anderson had split off in a huff, saying, "I won't belong to any such damn outfit." The unraveling of the band did not stop there. George Todd tried to get some of his men to shoot another Quantrill lieutenant, William Gregg, but Gregg got away. Then two Confederate officers were murdered, and while it was pretty clear that Quantrill had not pulled the trigger, McCulloch still considered him responsible one way or other.

Quantrill resisted arrest and escaped into the night, taking Todd and his men with him. Anderson and his gang even took up the pursuit. The climax came with them blasting away at each other across a road while Todd and Anderson roared that the other led a "damned set of cowards."

Bad blood there, Reynolds thought. And now Quantrill is missing.

OCTOBER 12 — 9 A.M.

AT BOONVILLE LANDING, THE STEAM FERRY to take them back to the north bank of the Missouri was filling up. Men walked on board holding tight to the reins of their nervous mounts, some fresh from trades made with family members or supporters, some contracted for at the point of a pistol.

Riley muttered reassurance to Folly, who wasn't at all at ease with the give of the leaky planks beneath her new iron shoes. Nor did the hiss of the boiler please her. She wasn't as spooky as some, though.

"You're a mighty good lady, ain't you?" he murmured, stroking her quivering neck. "Got me out of Fayette."

The bottom shuddered as one more horse clattered aboard, and the ferryman told those on the bank that was it; he'd have to come back for them.

Pipe smoke and talk wafted over the wind-whipped channel as the craft set out. Men were shaking their heads at their orders; they were to stir things up in the north to draw off Federals. Just how many more stirred-up Federals they could deal with was a serious riddle. After Centralia, it had gotten very feverish north of the river. At one point, he and some others were feeding their mounts ears of corn in one end of a field and heard noise among the stalks on the far end — the pursuing milish cavalry doing the same. Riley and the others meekly walked their horses out of the rows and down the road a bit before laying tracks.

A fellow he had not seen since Texas was talking to Joe Hall, who also was from Cass County, it seemed. The captain, now with Shelby's bunch, was talking about some girl who might marry him. He recalled that his name was Gregg and that Todd had had a powerful dislike of him.

Riley gazed downstream at all the sandbars in the low water, at some ducks paddling hard against the wind, and then at a cluster of bleached snags — sycamore limbs. That was a body! Somebody in a white shirt caught in the tangle.

"Hey!" Riley called. "Dead man over in that snag down there." The others stopped talking and craned their necks. Some younger ones moved to get a better look, leading their horses with them. The ferryman shouted at the damn fools who were going to capsize them all. "Dead men feeding the catfish ain't nothin' special, not in these times," he snorted.

"Hope it's Goodman," said Plunk. Riley didn't even bother to explain to his dim friend that the Union sergeant had disappeared miles *downstream* of Boonville in the confusion of crossing to the south side. Plunk peered at the corpse diminishing in the distance. "Nah, I'm pretty sure Goodman had on that red-checkered shirt that Grubbs give him."

Goodman slipped away from his two guards the night of October 7, after 10 miserable, nerve-wracking days as captive. Many guerrillas had expressed the wish to kill the Yank sergeant in the first days, but they'd got used to him. The burley former blacksmith did nothing to irritate them. Assigned to curry Anderson's mount, Goodman wrote of tucking into the job so earnestly the horse would remember the grooming "as long as he is a horse."

Weasel, as Anderson liked to call Ike Berry, cleared it up. "Ah, that's just Shoemaker. Captained the Boonville Provisionals. Captain of the catfish now."

"Thought they was all paroled by Shelby," Riley said.

"Yeah, that's the truth. But some of our boys had a grudge against ol' Horace, I think from afore the troubles. Got him out of his bed and took him down to the river and tucked some gunpowder in his ear." Weasel was nearly as bad as Archie about scattering folks' bones about the country.

Riley stared down at the water until the ferry grounded in the mud of Howard County. He wondered again whether he done right deciding to ride with Bill Anderson. Riley admitted to himself that he was tired of this war, although he'd like to be in a real battle for once, with flags and cannon.

It hadn't been hard to break off with George Todd, who was becoming ever more gloomy and sullen. But the main reason Riley was on this ferry was the strong likin' he'd taken toward Buck James, and Buck had decided to keep an eye on Jesse, and Jesse said he liked Bill's style and wanted to stick with him. Still, Riley was real sad that McCorkle had gone off with Todd and Pool. Before the split up, McCorkle had divided what was left of his percussion caps. Over the summer McCorkle's cousin, Mollie Wigginton, had gone to Illinois with a double-bottomed trunk and brought back 35,000 of them.

Many farm boys, having vengeance on their minds, agreed with Jesse. One Clay County man, Jim Cummins, would later write, "Having looked the situation over I determined to join the worst devil in the bunch. While (Quantrill) was fierce, he was nothing to compare with that terrible Bill Anderson, so I decided it was Anderson for me as I wanted to see blood flow in revenge for the outrages the Jayhawkers had committed."

Bill supposedly spoke himself of growing weary of killing Yankees, but it hadn't shown. Anyhow, Buck said battles were not all they were cracked up to be. He'd been at Oak Hills and Prairie Grove and said nobody ever knew what was going on, that a feller could get hurt that way, and Riley was already hurt.

As the rangers settled in to wait for the ferry's next load, Riley found himself eavesdropping on the banter between two new recruits picked up in town. They were not much younger than him, or so it seemed, and apparently great scholars back in the Sunday school. And rivals, for each tossed questions of scripture at the other.

"Who threw 10,000 off a mountain?"

"Easy. Amaziah. So who did the Lord kill with hailstones?"

"Uh, the Hiv…ites, no wait! The Amorites!"

Once the unit was whole again and began moving, Riley kept the two within earshot. It seemed the boys had memorized all the bloodiest parts of the Old Testament. The thousands and thousands slain for God eventually grew tiresome, though, so Riley nudged the horse with his good heel and moved up the line.

The scouts out front were wearing Union blue and before long they came across a fellow in a wagon and pulled their usual trick, asking whether he had seen any bushwhackers. This fellow advised that Anderson's bunch had been reported back in New Franklin. This was true, but the wrong answer, as the informer realized when the rest of the band rode up and joined them.

The farmer was swinging from a convenient oak as they rode off. He'd sworn he had a boy in Georgia with Hood. The rangers had heard it so many times before, and sometimes even allowed themselves to be convinced. Riley had been convinced this time, in fact, but Bill's heart was that of a walnut, black and hard.

"Joshua 9:83," smirked one of the new recruits, riding away. "Who was hanged?"

"Old Al, the King of Al," the other shot back.

Well, Riley thought, Sunday school was good for something.

IX

Marching orders

"Move forward with your troops to Hickman Mills or to Shawneetown as fast as you can. This is no time for paper warfare."

— Major General Samuel Curtis, telegraphing October 14 to Colonel Charles Jennison in Paola, Kansas

ᘒᘒᘒᘒᘒᘒ

OCTOBER 13

Grand Avenue, Kansas City
Jackson County, western Missouri

The glorious weather and a chance to stroll on actual sidewalks had put Ellen Williams in a better mood than she had felt in days.

A little browsing in Bullenes hadn't hurt. She could afford almost nothing, but then fingering the silks and daydreaming of new gowns had cost nothing, either. She had not been in such a large store since her husband's regiment, the Second Colorado, was reconstituted in St. Louis. Certainly the poor shops in Independence could not compare. As she wandered, however, clerks were grabbing armfuls of dry goods and disappearing into the back. Upon inquiring, she learned that the owners were moving much of the stock onto a steamer to take upstream, out of reach of thieving rebel hands.

The whole area is in an uproar, she thought, turning off Missouri Avenue onto Grand. With the day to herself, she decided to wander south toward some of buildings that could been seen up there. Trenches were being dug not far away.

She passed a woman and three children, all looking distinctly pinched and shallow. *My word*, she thought, *if I were back at the wagon, I'd find something to eat for those babies.* She looked back again and saw no one; the sad little family had turned down an alley.

The day before in Camp Smith, about three miles southwest of Independence, she had packed up her and Charlie's few things into a wagon, and she and the other camp followers were driven into Kansas City for safety. With Price approaching, all of the Second Colorado's companies, her Charles among them, would be out to the east looking for him. She was not sure how much she wanted Charles to find the old traitor and his evil men.

"... the brave bugler trilled,
the notes that so thrilled,
the hearts of the horsemen..."

What rhymed with horsemen? Norsemen. Hmmm. She wanted to greet Charles with a new poem. Gallant riders? This was going nowhere. Oh, she prayed her bugle boy was all right. No one knew better than the Colorado regiment that the western Missouri countryside was as safe as a snake missing its rattle.

After fighting in the New Mexico Territory, the Second Colorado Volunteer Infantry had been merged with the Third Colorado, reorganized as cavalry and sent to occupy southeast Missouri in late 1863. Then, the unit was transferred to this side of state, a bitter Christmas present, indeed.

Was Sergeant P. F. Russell of I Company the first to discover this? This spring, he had ridden to meet up with what he thought were comrades ahead, but who were not comrades. They were the foe, disguised in Federal garb. "He evidently did not discover his fatal mistake until arriving in their midst, and was surrounded and hurried away utterly unable to offer any resistance," Williams would write. It was just one of many evil bushwhacker tricks to be learned at the cost of blood.

Because of their more spirited horses, George Wells and John Freestone got too far ahead of the column on a chase and paid with their lives the price of the lesson. Tom Herrington and Pat Ford, both A Company boys and friends of Charles, were carrying dispatches between Hickman's Mill and Pleasant Hill when stopped by a uniformed but, again, false and fatal messenger, who told them to turn back toward the mill and ambush.

This summer Captain Wagoner went on a scout with two dozen men of C Company and got lured into chasing four riders spotted on the Independence-Pleasant Hill Road. Perhaps 100 bushwhackers came storming out of the trees, killing the captain and seven others. Partisans said Dick Yager slew Wagoner in a horseback, hand-to-hand melee, the captain's pistol blast so close it sheared off half of Yager's mustache.

When the full extent of the Grinter Farm disaster was understood, Ellen, whose poetry was admired in the regiment, was asked to compose some lines for the handsome obelisk that marked their resting place in Independence. The words were etched as deeply in her heart as in the white sandstone. As she walked, she quietly recited the lines:

"Brave heroes rest beneath this sculptured stone.
In unfair contest slain by murderous hands.
They knew no yielding to a cruel foe —
And thus, this tribute to their memory stands
Our country's honor, and a nation's pride
'Twas thus they nobly lived and bravely died.'"

Ellen's steps had taken her to McGee's addition and a much better view of the sweating men who were deepening some rifle pits. A major and his men watched over the work of dozens of civilians pressed into service. She had no sympathy for the men with their picks and shovels; she had seen many of their kind in Independence, lily-livered sympathizers.

"Too cowardly to openly espouse the cause of the rebels, (they) chose to remain at home out of the way of bullets and gun powder and discourage Union sentiment and feelings by their contaminating influence and intolerable hypocrisy," she wrote years later. "Some of their leading characters possessed this contemptible quality to the most astonishing and alarming extent."

She knew that General Fisk liked to call the Second Colorado, half of whom had left their mines back home, "his mountain hogs." Ellen hated the expression.

If there were any swine around here, it was these men in the mud. It was gratifying to hear their grunts.

OCTOBER 15

Sedalia

Pettis County, western Missouri

THE GENERAL UNHOLSTERED HIS ADAMS, RODE up to the drunken looter who gleefully waved a pretty basket of silver to his friends. Taking careful aim, Thompson fired.

The private's mule collapsed without a sound, rolling and crushing both the silver piece and the man's leg.

"The next round is for you, thief." General Jeff Thompson was furious.

He had been using the flat of his saber to whip rumps and was finally restoring some discipline, when the loot-laden fool wandered up. He should have shot the man instead of a good mule, but Thompson was having enough trouble with his Iron Brigade, many of whom had managed to quickly sniff out Sedalia's significant liquor stocks.

The operation had been successful. Having spooked the pickets, the Confederates had raced the enemy back to town. Thompson had decided to bring up the two guns to fire on the redoubts on the outskirts. They proved to be abandoned.

Quickly convinced of the futility of resistance, hardly any blood was shed among the 300 men guarding Sedalia. "On the first explosion of shell, my citizen support deserted me. And one general stampede of citizens and home guard took place," wrote Captain Oscar B. Queen of the Seventh Missouri State Militia. His unlucky M Company had been sent by Colonel John Philips to fetch ammo for the regiment.

October 15 was an alarming day for the Federals in Missouri: Not only were Sedalia and Glasgow sacked, but a bushwhacker siege of the Glenn Hotel in Paris ended in the surrender of the milish holed up inside.

Thompson tried to hurry their task, gathering arms, supplies and livestock to be given over to the quartermaster. He shouted at a sergeant to break up a fight. The sooner he got back to Shelby and the main command at Waverly, the better.

It made little sense for the division to be so scattered, especially in light of the considerable Yankee force shadowing Price that he had seen from the timber. The intelligence gleaned from two captured Yankee stragglers was it was some of a division of Pleasonton's cavalry, and Union infantry wasn't far behind.

Thompson had sent a courier to Price with another ominous bit of news: A massive Union force was said to be assembling at Kansas City.

He thought about his anger. Some of it came from the trail of thievery witnessed in just about every town this army had "liberated." Thompson was in love with the idea of commanding this brigade and did not want to see it diminished by dishonor. He could sympathize that the men had not been paid in more than a year, understood that civilians would inevitably suffer in the seizing of legitimate war material, but this looting for individual gain infuriated him. No army could operate on such a pinchbeck ideal of every man for himself.

"I had only to try to control my own Brigade, to save their reputation from the demoralization which was seizing the army," Thompson would write later. "The plunder of Boonville nearly completed this demoralization for many officers and men loaded themselves, their horses and wagons with 'their rights' and now wanted to turn southward and save what they had." It was not just the looting, but the melting away of the Missouri men to visit families on the march. He had granted some brief furloughs, but the roll calls indicated that maybe 600 of his brigade could be off somewhere at any point.

He looked around the streets. Sedalia, no doubt, was benefiting from the railroad, but it still wasn't much of a town. Pretty soon all those Dutch in St. Louis would be riding the cars out here, settling. The thought of St. Louis led to his suffering wife. He had been moving around so much, no letters from her had caught up with him, assuming she was in any condition to write them. Was it her last letter that spoke of how a "congestive spell went to my brain a little?"

A good-sized herd of horses and mules, maybe 300 much-needed remounts, was being driven north out of town, cattle, too. One of his staff came up grinning and leading a beautiful stallion, calling out, "This one ought to be yours, general."

Thompson was tempted. He'd had terrible luck with horseflesh on this expedition. Shelby had given him a grand-looking charger to replace Forrest's trusty mule, but turned out it was too heavy for speed and wore out quickly. Later in Boonville, Thompson had watched over the gathering of 32 splendid horses, and had ordered a guard on them. The next morning's trip to the corral to pick one out had revealed just broken-down stock left by the thieving troopers. He was still riding one of the bony leavings.

So he nodded to the officer, and minutes later, they had the stallion saddled. Thompson got his foot in the stirrup and heaved himself up.

"First thing I knew I rode over two soldiers and at the house to which I was going, the horse went straight in the door." Thompson later reminisced. Practically housebroken, he assumed, and continued up and down the street giving orders and paying too little attention to his new mount. The horse proceeded directly to a ditch easily too wide to jump, and Thompson drew up the reins.

"You damned fool, I believe you'd try to jump it," he said. Hardly had the words left his mouth, when the stallion squatted like a lion for the spring — and away they soared.

A second later, Thompson found himself in the ditch, face down and gumming the grass growing in the ditch. Several of his men came running to see if the general was injured in the "heels over head" fall.

"Well, be damned if that horse ain't stone blind!" one sergeant drawled.

"Either that," added a smirking private, "or he was tender toward that mule the general shot."

OCTOBER 16 — 7:45 P.M.

Westport
Jackson County

THE NEWSPAPER RATTLED WITH FEMININE INDIGNATION.

"Did you read this, Em?" Bettie Palmer asked from behind it. "The *Journal* advises us to keep cool. Keep cool? With Price and his cutthroats in Missouri once more?"

She began reading:

" '*The danger is never half so great as people's exaggerated fears make them think it is. No military force is going to ride into our town rough shod....*'

"That's certainly easy for a fool of an editor to say, snug up in Kansas City with its fortifications and cannon to protect him. But what about us here in Westport?"

Captain Henry Emerson Palmer smiled. It was Sunday afternoon, their reading time. Bettie enjoyed nothing more, well, almost nothing more, than to devour newspapers, novels, plays and whatever could be found printed on a page. And then to pepper him with what she found remarkable. And as poor a rag as the *Journal of Commerce* was, she could always find something remarkable.

He was going to have to get back to camp, but he was dawdling at her father's home in Westport, in part to give Bettie more of her beloved routine. He was so smitten with his bride, still wasn't sure how he had won her. He had been brought up rough, frontier farming in Wisconsin, prospecting in Colorado. Now he was a 23-year-old cavalry captain wed to the daughter of Solomon Houck, a man who'd made a fortune in the Santa Fe trade and was in California during the Gold Rush. He glanced at the clock face sitting above the fire, a Brewster "chapel" clock, prized by the family. Another hour more perhaps.

"Price is far away, darling, probably already running back south to Arkansas."

"That is what the paper suggests, that it would be madness for Price to come this far west. Do we really have 30,000 men waiting for him, Em?"

Palmer thought only a few thousand were on the scene so far. Wide-scattered cavalry companies and some of the closer militias had been dribbling into the camps along the border. His company was stationed here so it had been fairly easy to win permission to spend his Sunday in Westport.

"Oh, I'm sure we've got at least that many," Palmer lied.

"Well, where are they? I certainly have seen very few soldiers. And do you have adequate numbers of cannon?"

"Quite a few." But most of their pieces were mountain howitzers with half the range of a Parrott gun.

"Oh, and here it says, and I quote: 'But suppose Price does take the town, does anybody suppose he will be able to hold it?'" She raised her head, brow furrowed. "But up above they said they wouldn't allow him even to come in." She continued reading. "'He cannot hold the state, nor any portion of it. Momentarily depressed the Union people may be, but they are bound to hold the state. Let those, then, who would wreak vengeance upon Union men, beware!'"

Laying the sheet in her lap, she exclaimed, "I wasn't depressed until I read this!"

"Darling, you know how newspapers are full of steam. Price, Shelby, Marmaduke have made raid after raid into Missouri over the years and they've never come close to Westport."

Bettie wasn't convinced about Westport's lack of attraction to rebels. Just last summer, George Todd brutally slew several Federal cavalry — not Em's boys, thank Heavens — coming in on the Fort Scott Road. Soon after, her husband had assured her that he would take care of Mr. Todd, much as he had assured her that he would take care of a wasps' nest on the back porch. The wasps were gone, but the bushwhackers still buzzed around. She had said nothing to Em, of course.

"Price was in Lexington," she countered, mostly for fun, "and that's only forty miles away."

"That battle was three years ago, love. And Price promptly skedaddled."

"It's a charming city, maybe he wants to come back," she smiled. "And who are these 'forces' chasing behind the rebels?"

"Well, as I understand it, Rosecrans has General Pleasonton, some fierce fellow who used to be chief of the cavalry out east, about to catch up with Price. He's got many regiments, and then there's divisions of Union infantry on their way, too… "

"Pleasonton? But he was replaced with General Sheridan. Is he any good?"

He had learned to never be surprised at the breadth of her knowledge.

"I'm sure Pleasonton's just the ticket, darling. Last year in Virginia, I recall, he gave Jeb Stuart a hard knock at Culpepper."

Bettie's father could be heard in the hall, talking to another daughter, it sounded like. Bettie rustled the paper, clearly not convinced by anything he had said.

"Hmmm, here is an article about a Mister Perry of Independence."

Solomon Houck walked in at that moment. "Could that be the Perrys we know?"

"I can't tell, father, no first name. Here's what it says: "Mr. Perry of Independence was attacked by a couple of bushwhackers beyond the Blue between here and Independence. They robbed him of his money and his arms and then thinking that a squad of Federal soldiers were after them withdrew into the brush. Mr. Perry improved the time by putting the whip to his horses." She laughed, so prettily, Palmer thought.

"Probably weren't bushwhackers, just thieves," he said.

"I concur entirely," said Houck, sticking a splinter into the glowing fireplace and then lighting his cigar. "Do you know what I heard in town today? The eastbound coaches of the Hannibal and St. Joe were captured this morning by eight boys. Boys! Robbed the passengers and then let the train go on its way. Wasn't anybody on that train armed? It's ludicrous!"

His mother-in-law poked her head into the room. "I'm so sorry, Captain, the girls have repaired your coat, but your other pair of trousers …."

"Please, do not concern yourself. I'll retrieve them later."

Although he and Bettie were married a year ago, this had been their home because he was so often away on duty, and Bettie could not be expected to live alone on his officer's pay. She was used to the benefits of the old Spanish silver her father surely had socked away, and it was best that her confinement be among her family.

A bit later, Palmer kissed his wife goodbye and told her that he would return the moment he could. Her father had retreated discreetly to the porch with his tobacco. When Palmer followed him into the cool October air, Houck offered his hand.

"Good luck, Captain. And take care. Don't go sticking your neck out. You've got a family in there." He nodded to the parlor. It had been a poorly protected secret that Bettie was with child. One could barely tell, but his mother-in-law was not to be deceived.

"No fear, sir. And thank you again for taking care of Bettie."

Palmer found his horse ready for him, rose to the saddle and waved to the silhouette in the parlor window.

What had Bettie said the *Journal* had written? "Let them who'd have vengeance on Union men, take care!"

No, that's not it. No, it was "beware!"

OCTOBER 16 — 3:30 P.M.

Hickman's Mill
Jackson County

BLUNT'S MOUTH DROPPED OPEN.

"Snoddy is doing what?"

"Taking the Sixth out of camp, general. Says he's marching them back to Linn County."

"The hell you say! Why isn't Fishback stopping him?"

"From what I gather, sir, General Fishback approves of the whole affair," explained the aide to the beet-faced Major General James Blunt.

He would have the colonel shot, Blunt thought. It would be an excellent example to the men.

Lieutenant Colonel James Snoddy had asked that his regiment be allowed to go home, a request Blunt denied. The man was an anti-Lane newspaper editor, so there had been no friendliness between the two, but this! Kansans marching away just as Price's horde was swarming over the horizon. Of course, that was the problem. Price still hadn't shown up, leading many to believe this was all a hoax. Once his cavalry was gathered and provisioned, Blunt was thinking of probing ahead, perhaps to Lexington.

Well, Snoddy would be put down. If one regiment walked away, they all would. And as pusillanimous as these militia poltroons were, he needed them. Blunt chewed it over just a minute; this would require the volunteers.

He had Tom Moonlight's people, but Doc Jennison had come in two nights ago with several companies of the 15th. Moonlight's 11th was easily the more disciplined. On the other hand, Doc was now in Governor Thomas Carney's pocket. Having him arresting H. M. Fishback, a state senator, and Snoddy, both Carney allies, might be uncomfortable for him. All the more reason to do it.

"Get me Jennison. Now!"

"Sir, I don't believe the colonel is around just at the moment."

"Goddammit! Where is he?"

"Don't know, sir," the captain shrugged. "Perhaps playing poker. He left Hoyt in charge."

Lieutenant Colonel George Hoyt, his second-in-command, his toady-in-chief.

"Then, get *his* ass in here, *instanter!*"

Blunt began to cool a bit. Fishback was just a pawn. His official position would be that neither Blunt nor Major General Samuel Curtis had the authority to take Kansas militia outside the state. But Blunt knew the real problem. The pompous whoreson was seething that he, a general, even if of shabby militia, had been subordinated to a mere colonel, regardless that he was a proven fighting volunteers officer.

No, the real traitor was the Kansas governor, who had opposed Curtis's bringing Blunt out of his banishment among the hostiles. The governor was running for re-election in November, fighting the powerful Lane, who believed Carney might use a victory to challenge him for the Senate seat in January. The governor and his bootlickers, Fishback and Snoddy, wanted the 30-day men closer to the state line to get back home in time to vote.

Hoyt stepped into the tent to offer a shadow of a salute.

The bird-like Massachusetts lawyer was something of a frontier celebrity, having been part of John Brown's trial defense team. Once the war began, Hoyt had come west with John Brown Jr., captain of a bunch of Ohio fanatics, to join Jennison, then commander of the Seventh. When Brown went home, Company K fell to Hoyt.

Dismayed by the regiment's deployment to Tennessee, however, Hoyt convinced his superiors that the climate "would prove fatal" to his health. When he resigned his commission to return to Kansas and his mentor Jennison, "the company and regiment were well rid of him," said then Private Simeon Fox. To him, Hoyt represented "a combination of ambition and cruelty."

The prospect of a free rein and free Missouri horses must have been rejuvenating, because the delicate Hoyt soon was at the center of some Kansas toughs terrorizing both sides of the border. These were the infamous Red Legs, who held all the records for horse stealing and didn't place far behind in most other crimes.

Blunt and General Thomas Ewing both used Hoyt's paramilitary outfit until learning better. Soon Blunt was discharging twenty of the so-called "detectives, Provost Marshals and Special Agents" and ordered "The band of irresponsible men, popularly known as 'Red Legs,' or 'The Forty Thieves,'" to be dispersed and arrested.

The Red Legs were not particular. They robbed in Kansas as well as in Missouri and even from the U.S. Army. In April 1863, a letter ran in the Kansas City *Journal* signed by the "Fifth Cavalry," which was still headquartered in Independence. The writer sneered at the Leavenworth *Conservative's* recounting how 30 of Hoyt's men killed 32 bushwhackers, losing none in the fighting. After suggesting that the dead men likely were unarmed Southern farmers, the letter went on to say that the Red Legs had stolen two of the Fifth's horses. When the cavalrymen tracked down their horses, the Red Legs tried to threaten the soldiers but were faced down. The writer went on:

"I believe the Red Legs will kill any man in this country for a good horse; and they have glorified themselves considerably over finishing some unarmed sympathizers. The fact is, they have carried on an immense stealing operation, and have endeavored to conceal it by a huge story that would hush the indignation of Union men."

To Blunt, it seemed that, "Officers, soldiers and citizens had become infected until the leaders became so bold as to defy interference with their operations. A reign of terror was inaugurated…" Some of Hoyt's Red Leg associates now ran companies in the 15th. He rose from his camp table and reached for his hat.

"Colonel Hoyt, are you aware of the excitement in the militia regiments?"

"It has come to my attention. I assure you that the 15th is solid."

"As I expect it to be, Colonel, but that is not why I ask. Colonel Snoddy, with the support of General Fishback, is removing the Sixth from our ranks."

Hoyt offered a twisted little pout. "And miss their chance at glory, sir?"

"Exactly," said Blunt. "Come with me. I need your regiment for a little exercise." Heaving himself on his mount, Blunt watched impatiently as Hoyt organized some companies to go turn the Sixth around. When out west, Blunt had heard how Jennison, as the new colonel and cock-of-the-walk up at Fort Leavenworth, had set up in style, even building a fine new guardhouse. That lock-up better not be comfortable. He did not want Snoddy or Fishback to be comfortable.

Blunt really wished he could shoot them.

OCTOBER 17

Union Hotel, Kansas City

CHARLIE GRAY DID NOT ENJOY BEING in the Yankee jail. It was boring, except when his mother wept and argued with Aunt Susan and Aunt Martha. Then it was unsettling and sad.

They were all prisoners on the top floor of some old hotel building on Main Street. Only six blocks away was the landing where Charlie once loved to watch the steamboats come in. Kansas City had been his favorite place back when his folks would hitch up the buggy and come in for special things. Usually some hard candy had been in the deal, too.

But Charlie was now 10, and although the Union guards made him a bit of a pet, it still was a very hard thing to be cooped up with all these women for months. Having his two brothers, Richard and Josiah, there helped only a little. They were just babies.

The door unlocked from the outside, and he looked up to see grandma Mary come in. His mother and aunts rushed to her.

"Oh, have they arrested you, too, Momma?" exclaimed Susan. She was Charlie's aunt, but was only 15, so he just called her Susan. She sometimes called him "Cornsilk." Because his hair was yellow, he reckoned, but she insisted it was because his skull was stuffed with it. His other aunt in the room was Martha. She was about 20. She was a Lindsey now, having married Brinard Lindsey.

Uncle Bree was in Gen'rl Price's army and was coming to get them all out of this room. Aunt Martha promised.

Charlie's grandma had not been arrested. "No, not yet," she said. "I don't know why they'd want to."

"Oh, Mary!" said Charlie's mother, stamping her slipper at her mother-in-law. "They want to arrest us all! Why can't you get that through your head? Did they question you again? What did you say?"

"Hush, Nancy!" said Susan. "Let her be! Let's get away from the door. Come, Momma." The two sisters took their mother to one of the beds and sat her between them, providing a buffer from their sister-in-law.

Charlie discreetly scooted over the floor to sit nearby. He thrust his hands into his pockets to empty them of his coins. Busily sorting them, he tried for the appearance of absorption, lack of interest in listening in. First, he arranged the "fish scales" given to him by one of the friendlier guards. The silver 3-cent pieces were so small they were easily lost.

"Well, what did you tell them?" Nancy hissed again.

His grandmother looked nigh worn out. She shook her head and recited what she had confessed: "All my troubles have arisen because I have friends and relations in the Brush, also from having many acquaintances who are friends to the Bushwhackers, but who pretend to be friends to the government." She hesitated, trying to remember whether she'd left anything out, then concluded. "I am a Union woman."

Arraying his half dimes along a seam in the planking, Charlie frowned at that last part. His family was not Union people. His stepfather was riding with Colonel Quantrill when killed two years ago. And brave Uncle Jim had been hanged by the Yankees last year at Fort Union. And Uncle Dan was still with Quantrill. Then it flashed on him that his grandma had lied to the Yankees. The same grandma who'd switched him mercilessly for denying shooting the hole through the barn roof. This was a revelation. She was still talking.

"They say Daniel has two of their men and that if he doesn't give them up, they will keep you until Daniel is killed."

"Well, the food is so poor here, it's an excellent place to starve," Susan remarked. "But it sounds like we'd better get used to it."

As if signaled by the word "food," the littlest girl began to whine. Martha glanced at Charlie, shifted away and began fighting her dress buttons to let the child suck.

Charlie's mother and aunts were arrested at the end of August, supposedly for aiding bushwhackers. Special Order 76 was clear: "Having been informed that Daniel Vaughan (Bushwhacker) has in his possession Sergeant John Bay and private B. M. Fox, of Co. "A," Second Colorado Cavalry, it is hereby ordered that his sisters, Nancy J. and Susan Vaughan, now in custody at this place, will be held as hostages subject to the release of the two prisoners now in his custody."

The authorities seemed little concerned about keeping children in their prisons with their mothers. Simply tiny traitors, many of them.

"It is much easier to catch a rat with your hands in a warehouse filled with a thousand flour barrels than it is to catch a band of guerrillas where every, or almost every, man, woman or child are their spies, pickets or couriers," complained Missouri General Ben Loan. Later, the Kansas City *Journal* noted how "the bushwhackers lie concealed in the brush, and at the approach of the troops, a boy, or girl, or woman slips out into the thicket and gives the alarm. So perfect is the spy system, that a squad of troops may march and counter-march all over the country, and not find a single bushwhacker…."

Charlie studied the "In God We Trust" pressed over the shield on a bright bronze two-cent piece. He had traded a fish scale for it the other day. No other coins had those words. Usually they declared, "God Our Trust."

The sisters tried to comfort and coach their mother. They repeated what they had told the Federals so far, to make sure she did not undercut their stories. It was clear that the Yankees intended to harass the frightened old woman until something damning was wrung out. But Grandma Mary kept wringing her hands and saying she wished she had stayed in Illinois, where she had gone for months to escape the troubles.

"Yes, you should have," Nancy said through clenched teeth. "But you didn't, did you? This is no place for the weak-hearted. You have to toughen your hide against these people, give them nothing that could hurt us or Dan. They will kill him and all of us if they get a chance."

At that, Charlie, who was striving to keep three the large copper pennies spinning on their edges at once, looked toward the ceiling. The little boy had heard the women discuss what happened last year in Kansas City at a place like this.

Charlie wished Gen'rl Price and Uncle Bree would hurry up and get here.

X

Skirmishes

"Give them no rest until they are squelched out, it is Fight or die. There will be no trifling."

— Union Major Frank bond, aide-de-camp to Major General Rosecrans

◡◠◡◠◡◠◡◠◡◠

OCTOBER 18

Lexington

Lafayette County, western Missouri

Doc Jennison tossed his thumbed and greasy cards on the table, stood and stretched. He yawned mightily for one so tiny. Hoyt was still in, so were Laing and Swain.

Captain Curtis Johnson rubbed his nose at the three treys in his hand.

George Hoyt, their wisp of a lieutenant colonel, made a show of shoving four half eagles into the small pile of paper scrip in the pot. Major John Laing put his hand down. Twenty dollars in gold. Most likely a bluff, Johnson figured, but he couldn't afford to find out.

"I'm out," he said. "It's up to you, Swain."

Joe Swain dug into his pocket. One hand produced a fat gold band that he dropped into the pot; the other produced aces and tens. Hoyt giggled a bit shrilly and tossed in his cards, face down.

Johnson got a glance at the ring before it disappeared back into the captain's pocket. Could it be the old lady's? The one that his boys supposedly cut off her dead hand?

Would Swain still have it after so many months?

The whole regiment had heard the story. Swain had taken some of his K Company out to visit old man Lawrence at his place not far from the Blue River. Just happened that they arrived the day the old man's wife had croaked. She was already reposing in a nailed coffin perched on parlor chairs.

The troopers decided to distract the widower from his grief by hanging him three times in the front orchard. Lawrence had been a slaveholder and was considered well-to-do. He claimed his money was banked in Canada, however, and it well might be because the boys tore the place apart and didn't find much. Just some silver serving pieces.

On the way out, one of the fellows wondered whether the money could be hidden in the coffin. So they ripped the lid off, felt around. Came up empty again, but there was that big ring. An arthritic knuckle was a problem so out came the Bowie knife. As captain, some said, Swain had claimed it. They told the distraught daughters: "If you want to plant the old lady, drag her out, for we are going to fire the ranch."

Now their colonel retook his seat, picking up the cards for a fresh deal.

"Boys, I'm hoping we resolve this Price business pretty quick," Jennison said. "All this martial law and being called out here is not helping the business much."

"Amen to that, Doc," said Laing. "I'm not making any money on these cards."

All the officers of the 15th Kansas Cavalry around the table were in "the business," one way or another. After leaving the jayhawking Seventh Cavalry, "Doc" Jennison had started up a livestock business and then later had a freighting company, Losee and Jennison, to ship stuff from Leavenworth or Lawrence on to Colorado. The stock and goods, naturally, came mostly from Missouri, although Hoyt's old bunch, the Red Legs, weren't known to be choosy.

Johnson himself had been making pretty good money that summer running cattle out of the Indian Nations. He'd been caught once with a herd rustled from some Creeks, but everything was so confused down there, he thought he'd succeeded more or less in talking his way out of it. Besides, pretty much everyone was doing it.

Johnson drew a second nine. The captain's hand resembled a three-legged dog, pretty much worthless but still hard to put down.

Swain just snorted and threw his cards in. Jennison didn't care for his, either. Now it was Laing, George Hoyt and Johnson, who was rubbing his nose, again.

"Wish we had more wine," Jennison said.

Reaching Lexington the day before the Confederates, Blunt's brigades had sent scampering a detachment of rebel recruiters and then gone into camp. Moonlight's 11th Cavalry took the old battleground around the college, and the 15th settled in at the fairgrounds south of the city.

For regimental headquarters, Jennison had gleefully chosen a large brick house on the west side of the road, the property of Thomas Shields, an officer in Price's old State Guard. "That evening a requisition for supper was served on the remaining 'chattels' of the gallant rebel, and the feathered effects of the homestead suffered to some extent," according to the colonel's report.

"I have grown fond of wine," Jennison continued. "When this war is over, I intend to open a saloon and drink it by the crate load. It is a genteel beverage, suitable for an officer of the United States."

Two queens took the hand. Johnson lost another $28 that he couldn't afford right now. Hoyt saw the moment had come. "I could not help but take note how that fine chestnut of yours carries a Cherokee brand on him," he asked helpfully, his girlish fingers tickling some more half eagles. "Might I take him off your hands for you?"

Johnson said he'd reckon not. He was mighty fond of that pony.

"Well, I know a lady in Leavenworth who's looking for one of that color for a carriage team. You have a bill of sale for that beast?"

"Got it somewhere," Johnson laughed. The idea that Hoyt, of all people, would worry about an honest bill of sale was rich.

"Yes, I'm sure you do," sniffed Hoyt.

Johnson had joined the 15th, like many others, expecting plunder. Jennison and Hoyt, after all, had called for the general destruction of the Missourians after Lawrence. Hundreds more than could be enlisted had clamored to join. An undated clipping, probably from the Kansas City *Journal*, mockingly, or perhaps resignedly, remarked: "All kinds of stories are afloat in regard to Jennison coming down here with various numbers composed of whites, niggers, Red Legs, Blue Legs, and Blue Bellies, with orders to sack, burn, destroy, tear to pieces, &c., &c."

Although large incursions, such as the one to Platte City after the Paw Paw rebellion, were authorized, the agreement behind the 15th's creation specified defense of Kansas, not invasion across the border. While some over-the-line freelancing by troopers of the 15th still occurred, the policy redirected much of their illegal efforts toward fellow Kansans.

A new deal — Hello! — two kings. Johnson asked for three new cards.

"Where's Orren gone to?" asked Laing.

"Sent him out to watch the Sedalia road," Hoyt said.

Johnson slowly picked up the fresh cardboards, a five, a seven, and — hello, again — another of those crowned gentlemen.

"Is he sober?" asked Laing, frowning at his hand.

"Is Orren Curtis ever sober?" Hoyt shrugged. Shouting outside now.

"What the hell?" Jennison said, going to the door. He listened for a minute and then yelled back to Hoyt and Laing.

"Scouts have found Shelby camped just to the east. George, John, you come with me. Blunt wants to talk on it."

The two men threw down their cards. Swain shrugged, threw in — three jacks — and picked his bills out of the pot.

Curtis Johnson just sat there, looking at his cards.

<hr>

OCTOBER 19

On the Dover Road
Lafayette County

NOTHING SPOKE AS ELOQUENTLY TO CONFIRM Henry Palmer's fear as those muddy three miles behind him. The road back to Lexington was empty. No one was coming. Price's army had cut them off.

The captain paced behind his thin line of men, ignoring the occasional z-z-zip of a minié ball, the thipp! of a miss into the moist soil.

It was time to get out. Hell, it was way past time to get out.

He'd heard the battle flare up off to his right, a rattling that sounded just like beans pouring on a tin pan, then it faded back to the west an hour or two ago. Palmer, commander of Company A, 11th Kansas Cavalry, was sure that the graybacks were in Lexington by now. So that put them in front of him, to the right of him and behind him. And to the left? The Missouri River.

Captain Palmer had three times sent a rider back to find Blunt, each one with the message: "Can I be of better service elsewhere?" A polite way of saying one's goose is cooked if one stays here. No reply.

"I shall depend on you, Palmer," the general had declared. Hold the Dover Road and don't pull back until called back. Had a ring to it: Sparta? Don't come back with your shield unless carried on it. No shields — the quartermaster was out. He'd distributed plenty of ammunition, though. The two companies of the 11th had packed more than enough out here last night. And Captain George Grover showed up with his few but well-armed provisionals from Warrensburg.

Between the cold rain that had moved in and the increasingly hot rebel fire, this qualified as a miserable day. Palmer's men had been nudged out of the timber and now had a fencerow as decent cover. He glanced at the prisoners he'd taken in the first clash that morning. They were gnawing at some donated hardtack, staying low so as not to catch any lead from a friend away in the woods.

His watch showed almost 5 o'clock. They'd been in this noisy but largely harmless duel for hours.

"I shall depend on you, Palmer." Damn. This was ridiculous. He closed the watch. Dark soon. Was that a good thing or a bad thing?

He saw Grover looking toward Lexington. A rider, thank God!

Sent by Jennison, he brought warning that Shelby had got behind them. Time to break for it. That was all that Palmer needed to hear.

He went to turn loose his 17 favorite rebels, the only ones he knew who couldn't — at the moment, at least — shoot him. He paroled them, told them not to take up arms again until some exchange was worked out. Smirks in the eyes of a couple; they knew well enough what was going on: Their side had the better hand. Their captor had nowhere to go, would soon be in their holey shoes, a prisoner. Was that one looking at his boots, measuring them for size?

As soon as the skinny rebs were jogging down the road to rejoin their friends, he ordered his men formed up in columns four across. No bugle calls; the less attention the better. He waved his arm forward, glanced behind. The mounted men, around 250 of them, were in good order, moving westward. But most were looking over their shoulders, just as he was. No rebel horsemen emerging from the trees yet. Pass the word. If all revolvers and Starrs weren't reloaded, do it now.

Grover left his men, galloped to catch up with him. "I figure half of Price's people are 'tween us and Blunt."

Palmer nodded.

"I figure, too, that walking to Texas is a terrible thing for a cavalryman to contemplate. And the grub will undoubtedly be bad." Grover smiled. Through the drizzle, they could see rebs moving on the road behind them now. "I've got to send down to Sergeant Cameron on the Berlin Road, tell him that we're withdrawing."

"Do it, and let's scyugle," Palmer said. "They're coming."

Now appeared eager John Lindsay, wondering what he was telling Grover.

"Lindsay, I cannot tell you just now what we will do until the hand plays out a little more. Just keep cool, old boy."

So naturally, the young lieutenant wheeled his mount to race down the line to his F Company bellowing, "Keep cool, boys, for God's sake, keep cool!"

Palmer slumped a bit. But Lindsay's men were grinning. Seeing another man's fear can either cause panic or resolve. That was resolve back there. Good. Damn good. Then the rebel rifle fire intensified as the Johnnies began to fill the road, and Palmer called for the gallop.

Before long, they had left the pursuit a hill or two behind and found themselves on Lexington's eastern edge. Grover called that he would wait for Sergeant Cameron there. Palmer grudgingly decided to stay with him. Anxious minutes passed.

Women came out in the drizzle to their yard fences to see who they were. One all in black cried out: "That's right, you old Lincolnites, come in and surrender."Palmer looked ahead, as if he had not heard."We welcome you," trilled another, across the street. Little love for the Union here.

The enemy could be seen going to and fro deep in the town, but none heeded the column on its outskirts. Private Edwards made an appreciative sound in his throat, and Palmer caught the scent of chicken frying. Maybe a home-cooked meal meant more to the rebs than Palmer's boots. The gloom was deepening, but it wasn't just dusk that was nullifying curiosity about them. The front ranks of Palmer's column were his scouts. Their garb looked more bushwhacker than Union uniform. This illusion would only get better as night fell. Good. Damn good.

"I reckon we'd better go," called Grover, "I don't think my people are coming. Wait, who's that?"

A body of riders had appeared on a ridge a few hundred yards away. Palmer could not make them out. One of their number rode ahead and called out to them. Grover replied, and the Federals heard:

"Yankees! Charge them, boys!"

A few shots were fired in the confusion, and the Federals had no place to flee, but into the town. Just when everything seemed up the spout, Palmer's men found a quiet alley to gallop into. Grover signaled that he knew the town, and Palmer let him take the lead, and they turned into a street lined with fine houses. At one intersection, rebs made an attempt to halt them, but Private Edwards shot an officer off his horse. That was a signal for the nervous troopers to begin blasting away, sending surprised rebs diving for cover. Grover shouted that the Wellington Road was just ahead, and in a moment the column swung toward the low sun and out of Lexington.

Palmer dared to think he might not be walking to Texas after all. As the town fell away, they passed evidence of fighting, rails knocked down, cannon ruts, hoof-churned fields.

Blunt had put up a scrap southeast of Lexington. Outnumbered and outgunned by the rebels' longer-range artillery, he pulled out by the Independence road with Moonlight forming the rear guard. Confederate General Jeff Thompson's brigade followed hard on Blunt's heels.

"This was the first real indication of the immediate presence of a concentrated force in our front," Confederate General Jo Shelby would report, "and I knew now there would be heavy work for us all in the future."

Finding the fork he wanted, Grover stopped and peered at the hills ahead. Darkness was settling. Time to send a pair of scouts out front. And a few men should ride well in the rear, too.

Palmer checked his companies and was assured no one was hit or left behind. Grover learned one of his, somebody named Talbot, had been killed stone dead, a head shot, in the dash through town.

It must have been obvious how much they wanted to get west, because by a house — a smiling woman was in the lit, welcoming door — two dismounting rebels yelled at them: "Give 'em hell, boys!" One waved his hat at them and then grabbed the laughing woman in a fierce hug. We'll do just that, Palmer smiled. Just not on the Dover Road.

OCTOBER 20 — 7 A.M.

Rocky Fork River
Ray County, western Missouri

THE LIGHT WAS GETTING BETTER, SO Riley broke open the first, the offending Colt Navy. Two misfires with it the day before when the band had brushed up against a milish patrol made him uneasy about his arsenal. He had six of the trusted revolvers, favored by horsemen over the heavier .44 "Army" model. But the Navys were hardly perfect.

Cross-legged back under a sheltering limestone outcrop, he picked through his loading stuff on the dry blanket folded beside him. A pattering rain swirled with the wind, trying to decide whether to become ice or snow, so it was not the perfect time to do a reload. Riley thought it best, anyway, if some of his rounds had gotten damp.

Some of the other men had the same opinion, fiddling with their pistols under soggy horse blankets draped from limbs or bushes. The bushwhacker camp was on the side of a wooded and time-worn bluff fairly high above little Rocky Fork. The wide, accessible ledge they had chosen the night before did not offer a 360-degree view, but no one had voted to sleep at the top, where the wind had real bite. The horses were tied on another ledge about 40 feet below, there not being room for all on the flat spot.

With a whittled stick, Riley carefully probed the six chambers, working out the balls and the unburnt powder that had hung fire. A rub between finger and thumb detected no deficiency. The one round that had fired had left its usual gummy residue. He cleaned all of the now-empty chambers, blowing sharply into them. No paper cartridges left, so he began pouring in the prescribed level of powder from the brass pistol horn, set a .36-caliber lead slug on top, then worked the rammer under the barrel. He rotated the cylinder, with its pretty etching of some sea battle — Buck James said it was the Texas navy fighting the Mexicans — and repeated the process again and again, with each load tightly pressed. He clamped the pistol between his knees and wiped his hands on his filthy trousers. One could not be too careful. More than one man had had a misfire during loading. He'd heard that explained the missing tip of Jesse's finger, another bit of "dingus" luck.

He smiled at the thought, and at that moment heard Jesse's voice. He looked up guiltily and saw the younger James coming up the slope through vines after his morning movement, laughing at something a fellow guerrilla said. Jesse pointed to a miserable-looking man sitting nearby. Riley had gotten his name the night before. James Crowley, a milish the boys had caught and kept alive as guide.

Wouldn't wish to be him, Riley thought, and reached for the grease to seal the loads from the wet. That messy chore done, he turned the piece around, dug into his deep shirt pockets for the crucial percussion caps. Made of copper, they contained fulminate of mercury that would explode when struck by the pistol's hammer. He looked at the first one closely, blew on it, then carefully fit it over the nipple projecting from the rear of the chamber. He pressed gently. A loose cap could jam the whole weapon. He reached into his pocket for the next and....

The whistle was long and carried an order with it.

A militia sergeant, leading one of the companies searching for Crowley, had been the first to spot the bushwhackers on the hill. He would recall dismounting and leading up his horse, "when reaching the bluff, he discovered the picket, who instead of firing on him, blew a shrill blast from a metallic whistle which aroused the enemy..."

Every man in the camp froze, looked into the brush around. Then it was a mad scramble for cover, just as the first ragged volley cut through the camp. Riley leapt up, forgetting he was under the rock overhang, smashed his head and collapsed.

Several sock-footed guerrillas bolted toward a heavy stand of hardwoods, shots kicking up leaves after them. Others were jumping out of sight toward the horses below. Grasping his throbbing skull, thanking the Almighty that he'd kept his hat on, Riley looked around. Most defenders were staying close to the little stone cliffs, pulling on boots or jumping up to throw a shot and then crouching again. The Federals' slugs seemed to be about hailstone level now. Riley tried to clear his wits. Besides the milish above and below, smoke showed they were coming from along the hillside, too. Riley looked at the pistol in his hand. Without the caps it was nearly innocent of value. He jammed it in his belt and grabbed another from his holster. He saw nothing to shoot as yet and wasn't about to stick his head up.

Bill Anderson was hollering orders. Mostly to get the hell out. But then he and Buck were beside Riley. Buck uncoiled his frame and squeezed off one shot, coolly paused to let the breeze take the smoke and got off another, then hunkered back down.

"We are up against it! Time to light out!"

"Where's Jesse? *Jesse?*" Buck roared. "*Jesse!*"

"Comin', Buck, hang on!"

Jesse and another fellow burst from the hardwoods firing with both hands. The other one promptly went down holding his groin. Down the bluff, men were hollering that they had the horses, to come on! Here came a guerrilla with the captive, who didn't look any less miserable now that his friends had arrived for breakfast. Anderson grabbed the coat lapels of the milish.

"Guide us out of this, and I'll let you live. If you balk, I'll kill you myself," he snarled.

White-faced, the man looked out at two bootless dead. He nodded, motioned and then they were slipping down a ravine past where the horses had been. Riley looked to where he had left Folly under an oak. Two horses were on their sides, and the tree was shedding its leaves, clipped by minié rounds. Folly was not there. A root caught Riley's boot, but a desperate grab saved him from plunging head-first down the rocky path. Off to the left, unseen milish crashed through brush as they navigated to lower ground to cut the rangers off. The shooting slackened above, although a few pistol shots indicated one or two boys were still back on the ledge, fighting it out. Good luck to them.

Riley and the others caught up with a like number of panting fugitives, who had hesitated to see whether their chief would escape. Crowley raced by them with Anderson just behind, gasping out a question about where the goddamned horses had gone. Down below, said one guerrilla. And suddenly all were plunging down an even steeper part of the hill face, grabbing at vines to keep their feet, bouncing off tree trunks, falling, sliding on the ice-slicked leaves. By the time their plunge found bottom, Riley's hands were raw and bleeding, and he'd felt his heel rip open again. The noise of horses, not far, came coming from down the Slipup Road. With his thumb on the hammer of his Navy, Riley turned to limp away. And there was Archie Clement and Clell Miller and Bill Anderson's brother, Jim, holding the reins of about two-dozen mounts, some saddled, some not. Relieved, Riley saw one guerrilla had Folly. Going to her, he listened as Anderson took charge again.

"Head for that timber that way. Buck, you and Jesse are going to be our rear guard. Keep 'em in check for a few minutes and then get out quick. Clell, you stay with them, too."

Riley frowned at that. To him, Clell seemed a small-caliber type of fellow, just a kid brand new to the gang and a bit of a clown to boot. How much use would he be? Riley bellied up aboard Folly, lamenting his lost saddle and extra guns back on the hill. Anderson found his own still saddled mount, swung up.

"Grand Pass morrow night!" He motioned to Crowley, who had taken an unclaimed horse, to lead. "Let's go!"

And the band plowed into the deep brush and kept going. Riley started to follow and looked back. Buck and Jesse had pulled their horses into a willow thicket, waiting for a chance to ambush the first Yankees to show their faces. Folly snorted, enjoying the missing weight of the gear, impatient to canter away.

Suddenly three militia men were coming through the trees, and the thicket erupted with white smoke from the James boys' pistols. One Yankee spilled from his saddle, and the others turned away, but here came a half dozen more galloping into the ruckus.

Riley gave Folly his good heel. He steadied his arm, the Navy spat flame once, twice. Screaming at the top of his lungs, he raced back to Buck.

XI

Opening fire

"Arms and ammunition have arrived and are being distributed. I will soon have everything in fighting trim. The men are eager for a fight."

— Major General James Blunt, to Major General Samuel Curtis

ↄↄↄↄↄↄ

Little Blue River
Jackson County

THROUGH BRISKLY FALLING SNOW, MAJOR GENERAL James Blunt peered east along the road that led back to Lexington. Shapes and sounds took definition across the little river where he stood. In minutes the last companies of the 11th Kansas cantered through the covered bridge, hoof beats magnified by the planks of its floor.

No indecent haste there. Perhaps 20,000 Confederates had snapped at his troopers' heels much of the day, but apparently had tired of the chase. Blunt was nervous. Reinforcements, mostly the Second Colorado, hadn't moved up from Independence yet.

And he wanted to meet Price here. While the Little Blue, which ran north to the Missouri a mile or so away, certainly wasn't deep or wide, it had cut deep in the silt discarded by countless floods. The stream's banks must be eight to 10 feet above the water level, much of it straight up — certainly enough to slow down cavalry.

On its west side, where Blunt paced, were medium-sized bluffs, some close to the stream in key spots, especially near the bridge. He had the 15th Kansas, Jennison's men, preparing firing positions from up there. Across the Little Blue to the east, the flat bottomland stretched away for miles, no cover to speak of. At first Blunt had recommended withdrawing to the south to block the rebels' escape until Rosecrans could get here to pin them against the Missouri. But then he had seen these fortress-like walls complete with moat carved by nature. Farther west, along the Big Blue River, Curtis was frantically cutting trees to make abatis at the fords, but *this* would be the place to squeeze the Johnnies between us like grapes.

Colonel Thomas Moonlight's officers were trotting over. They had covered the Federal retreat from Lexington, and it had been sharp at times. At one curve, Captain B. F. Simpson and another man had been pinned by a caisson in a deep road cut and were under pistol fire from advancing Confederates. Moonlight had learned of their plight and personally led a charge to rescue men and caisson.

"They followed us right close for awhile, general," Moonlight bellowed to Blunt. He waved to the south. "Bushwhackers on our flank, too, but don't see them now."

Hearing that hint of Celtic burr, Blunt thought again about his and Moonlight's similar beginnings. Weary of the hard ways of Scotland, Moonlight had caught a westward-bound ship and sailed to a home in the tiny U. S. Army. Moonlight — what a ridiculous name, practically Indian — eventually left the army for some dirt farm around Kickapoo, Kansas, but was one of the first to enlist when the war broke out. He had handled the Lane Brigade's meager artillery before moving to the regular infantry. Blunt, too, had left a rockbound family farm, this one in Maine. Maybe he'd been a year or so older than Moonlight. And he, too, had found adventure on sailing ships. But his past was superior to that of the Scot. He'd soon risen to captain of a schooner and then decided to go to medical school.

"You're here," Blunt replied. There had been no salutes. Blunt had the distinct feeling that Moonlight had not missed him during his banishment among the hostiles near Fort Larned. Moonlight agreed that the placement of his mountain howitzers should cover the bridge and went off to direct his sleepy troopers. He came back briefly to say that another road was not too far downstream. It did not have a bridge, but the river apparently was passable there. He suggested sending a company to guard it. Blunt nodded again.

"Captain Greer," Moonlight shouted to an officer who'd apparently lost his hat and was wearing a light laurel of snow. "Take the company and watch the ford downstream." The officer threw up his hand and wheeled his mount.

One of the officers around him mentioned Shelby. Reportedly it was his division that had been chasing Moonlight's rear guard. Hell, Blunt thought, he had whipped Shelby in Arkansas in '62. Now he'd beat him all over again here, him and Marmaduke. And Quantrill? Would Quantrill bring his men to the fight? By God, he'd like another go with that bastard.

A captain rode up, horse lathered.

"From General Curtis." He saluted and handed over an envelope hidden in his blouse.

The staff officers quieted as Blunt looked at the directive.

"General: I have no time to explain. Your troops must take position here where dry corn and provisions are arranged. The militia will not go forward and the Big Blue must be our main line for battle. We must not break down our best regiments, the Eleventh, Fifteenth and Sixteenth, and Ford's must have some rest. Leave two howitzers and, say, 400 men...."

Blunt raised his head and looked east across the little river. God, what a plague of fools. He thought of ripping it up, but decided he might want it for evidence in case of a court martial. He finished reading.

"... The blow you gave the enemy is doing good in the rear. It is crushing some of the silly rumors that had well nigh ruined my prospects of a successful defense...."

Your prospects, old man, he thought. Blunt's prospects were right here.

He called for the brigades' officers to join him.

"He wants us to fall back," he said quietly.

"Sir?" asked Lieutenant Colonel Preston Plumb, Moonlight's second-in-command.

"Curtis says we're to fall back to Independence. He is enamored with his wood cutting on the Blue." The other officers looked at each other. They had been commenting appreciatively on their position on this stream.

"This is the place to fight!" Jennison declared.

"You're right! It should be here!" Hoyt chimed in.

"The old fool is losing his grip!" Now it was Lane joining in. Being a senator and not a subordinate officer, Lane could put voice to such verdicts. Well, being Lane, he'd bellow them no matter what. He'd risen from his sick bed, Blunt had been told, and come to the fight, supposedly acting as an aide-de-camp to Curtis. But Curtis had shucked him off on Blunt, or Lane had preferred being here.

Lane's recovered good health was probably one part chance to shoot Missourians and three parts need to shore up his political standing. Both Blunt and his former patron had much to gain or lose in this contest. Lane's reputation had suffered badly at Lawrence, despite his howls for hellfire to be rained down on Missourians.

Blunt knew what was going on. Curtis was having trouble getting the Kansas militia to venture more than a few miles into Missouri. Reading the anti-Lane Oskaloosa *Independent, Lawrence Journal* and Leavenworth *Daily Times*, more and more had become convinced that Price's army had turned south — their militia general even agreed.

Only the day before, John Spear, who had just arrived in camp, wrote a warning to Curtis that he found "considerable restlessness among the troops."

"An impression is being created that all the danger is over," Spear continued, "and with some persons there are, in my opinion, efforts being made to dissuade the militia from crossing the line, and if there is a necessity to keep the Kansas men in the field such impressions are calculated to demoralize them." What he may have seen was Lane was burned in effigy and a donkey with a "Blunt" sign on its rump paraded through the Shawneetown camp.

Blunt fumed as he considered the order. It gave leeway to leave pickets. Pickets! A good seven miles out of Independence. Pickets! I'll give him pickets, he decided and spat.

"Colonel Jennison, get your men mounted up. Where is Colonel Moonlight?"

He found the Scot fussing with his tiny howitzers. Moonlight loved his field pieces and was a bit deaf as a result. One of the men noticed Blunt and informed the colonel, who looked up and approached.

"Colonel, a word. I have here orders from Curtis, who wants us to retreat west. Obviously, he fails to grasp our superior position here. I will go back and try to impress on him that this is the place to hold them, not on the other side of Independence. I believe he can be convinced."

The old man can be swayed, too easily swayed. The problem was Blunt was not there to keep him swayed in his direction.

"I want you to keep your whole regiment here tonight. With your four guns. Don't give up this line unless you're pushed out. You know what to do?"

"Aye," the hairy-cheeked Scot nodded, "burn the bridge."

3:30 P.M.

Road to Independence
Jackson County

HUNCHED IN HIS SHABBY BEARSKIN COAT, the senator cursed the early snow, especially the flakes that insisted on finding their way down his neck. He was as chilled, bone-weary and hungry as the Kansas troopers, who kept trying to pull the capes of their overcoats over their hats, only to be frustrated by the gusting wind.

As Blunt's column fast-trotted west toward Independence, Lane studied the thick back of the major general, his creation as surely as if Lane had fashioned him from clay and breathed life into him. The man had the vanity of Pompey, a taste for whores, a tongue filthier than a teamster's and, the senator knew better than anyone, was not above a little innocent corruption. Like Lane, Blunt had made so many enemies that he could hardly be choosy about his friends. But if Blunt did not make his poor mother proud, he was still the fightingest general to come out of Kansas.

Except for me, maybe, Lane told himself. With the old "Lane's Brigade," Texas would have been conquered by now. Good God! That would have been great fun. Much like Osceola, but on a much grander scale.

That was back in '61 when the senator had briefly been a general, given his commission at Lincoln's order. The president had not forgotten the April after Fort Sumter, before Union troops were organized and when the capital seemed so defenseless. Lane, a fledgling senator, had pulled together his "Frontier Guard" down at Willard's hotel to protect the White House. Kentucky's Cassius M. Clay showed up with men, too. "Kansas had Supreme possession of the White House," wrote the proud Lawrence *Journal*, "and fifty of her 'Old Guard' slept sweetly on the President's rich Brussels (carpet), with their arms stacked in martial line down the center of the hall...."

Impressed, Lincoln had written to Secretary of War Simon Cameron, "We need the services of such a man out there at once; that we better appoint him a brigadier-general of volunteers to-day, and send him off with such authority to raise a force...."

Those who knew Lane better than Lincoln were appalled. "It is rumored that Lane has been made a brigadier-general," wrote Major General Henry Halleck. "I cannot conceive of a more injudicious appointment...." On this letter, Lincoln simply noted: "I am sorry General Halleck is so unfavorably impressed with General Lane."

Lincoln had urged Cameron to impress Lane that energy was needed to put down the rebellion. "Tell him when he starts to put it through," the president insisted. "Not to be writing or telegraphing, but put it through."

And Lane had put it through at Osceola. He had marched his little army of 1,500 or so down to Fort Scott. After Nathaniel Lyon perished at Wilson's Creek and Sterling Price began moving north, the Kansans marched into Missouri and the Osage River valley to punish secessionists who weren't so well armed. One September day, a dozen rebels outside Osceola fired on them.

The brigade required no more encouragement to wipe the place off the map. The rich river town was exhaustively plundered. Bank, stores, stables, homes and churches were robbed, then put to the torch. The courthouse was shelled by Captain Thomas Moonlight, and at least nine residents were given drum-head trials and shot.

Captain Henry Palmer had been sent to smash large casks of liquor and spill their contents, but the men were not deterred. As Palmer wrote, "The 'mixed drinks' filled the side-hill cellar and ran out of a rear door down a ravine, where the boys filled their canteens and 'tanks' with the stuff, more deadly for a while than rebel bullets." Some became so incapacitated that they were loaded into the stolen wagons and carriages with their loot.

Wiley Britton, a onetime Federal soldier and later a historian, would write how Lane destroyed the property of the loyal "with the same recklessness that he did the property of the secessionists. He was incapable of seeing that the loyal people of Missouri were entitled to the protection of the Federal Government...." A correspondent for *The New York Times* was shocked by the scene: "I found all through Western Missouri a deadly terror entertained towards Lane.... Everywhere he has been, he carried the torch and knife with him, and has left a track marked by charred ruins and blood. An old man told me his story, told it with composure, while he said that they had taken his horses, mules, grain, his wife's dresses, and then fired the log shanty that afforded his gray hairs shelter from the pelting rain and nipping frosts. He told all this in detail with a firm voice, but when he added 'They even stole the clothes of my little dead grandson,' his lip trembled convulsively a moment, and then the hot rears gushed from his eyes and found ready channels down his time furrowed cheeks."

In Lane's eyes, these ravages were necessary. What better way to make the Missourians regret their damn treason? As the "Grim Chieftain," Lane bent the whole energy of his soul to this aim. Run the slavers out, free their human chattel. Take their beasts of the field, too, watch their farms dry up. Jayhawking was just punishment.

Good God, but they would have done it to us, if we had not got the jump on them.

Now, three years later, Lane did not doubt that Price intended to invade

Leavenworth. The fort and its prosperous port city were great prizes, much more than Lawrence had been. Lawrence. Well after a year, the outrage still burned hot.

Not just the disaster itself, but that his enemies had shackled him with it. Former Governor Charles Robinson at first claimed, absurdly, that Lane had aided Quantrill, then tempered his remarks to argue that Lane's earlier actions against the Missourians had brought it on.

After visiting Osceola, a State Guard officer named John W. Fisher was of the same mind. "It is enough to make a man's blood boil… steam boats even came here, a great deal of business was done here… in one place there are several hundred fine stores that are ruines (sic)… plates and dishes, cups and saucers, large quantities of nails melted together, salt ruined, and everything in like condition, and men are anxious to go to Kansas and retaliate…."

The line of cavalry slogged past a large stand of unpicked corn. Some troopers turned their horses to a place where the fence was down. Ears were pulled and stuffed into saddle bags, for their animals, Lane supposed. The senator kept his eyes ahead. He'd be damned if he would be seen in a cornfield. He would ride his horse past the brink of starvation before letting some fool joke that he was scouting out another hiding place.

It was widely known that Lane had taken to the corn when the marauders came looking for him in Lawrence last year.

Lane had understood what was happening only just in time, that Beelzebub had come knocking for breakfast. In his nightshirt, he'd chopped his brass name plate from the door, but it was in vain. Quantrill's killers had a guide to show them the way. The senator fled to a field and crouched in the green stalks of corn, watching the smoke from his new home rising to join the giant plume over Lawrence. The shooting had seemed endless, and he could not believe they would not come looking for him again.

Well before noon the Missouri cowards retreated back to their viper nests, leaving a scene from Revelation. Every building but one was burning on Massachusetts Street, the hotel, newspaper offices, stores, homes. Women and children wailed over slain husbands, fathers and sons.

A surprising number, like himself, had escaped into the fields, the river timber, the weeds of the ravines. He'd not stayed hidden long, but gathered some farmers and horses and rode through the town shouting for the remaining men to join him in the pursuit. Following the trail of discarded ladies hats, bolts of cloth and whiskey bottles, his little band had met up with Major Preston Plumb's company on winded mounts. Plumb, who had been in Kansas City as Ewing's chief of staff, had shown real grit. Gathered up 30 men and went looking for the demons, gathering up other groups of Kansans as he came across them.

Then had come the second cornfield. A rear-guard of the bushwhackers had lined up facing them about a quarter mile on the other side of a rail fence. The first of the Kansas posse had stopped cold upon seeing them. In his frenzy, Lane dismounted to tear down the rails to get his men through at the killers, but some imbeciles decided to fire a volley at the bastards, which panicked their green horses. The bushwhackers had seized that perfect opportunity to charge. Lane was still throwing rails down when he realized his Kansans were running for it. Just in time, he managed to get back to the embrace of tasseled corn, himself.

The Kansans' pursuit and subsequent scouring of the land across the border over the next few weeks had rubbed out some of the bandits, but hardly enough. George Hoyt, Doc Jennison's right-hand man, would say that a new coat on the back of a Jackson County man — it had to be stolen in Lawrence, didn't it? — was enough to have him killed.

"God damn Missouri," Lane had proclaimed then, calling for a counter raid that would leave Westport and Independence in ashes. "I want to see her destroyed, her men slain and women outcasts."

He called for "extermination of the first tier of counties in Missouri, and if that won't secure us, then the second and the third tier, and tier on tier until we are secure… There is no such things as Union men in the border of Missouri where these bushwhackers stay…. I want to see every foot of ground in Jackson, Cass and Bates counties burned over — everything laid waste. Then we shall have no further trouble."

The day after Lawrence, Leavenworth Mayor Daniel Anthony, the former jayhawker officer, had placed a notice in the papers: "All men in favor of the Lex Talionis will report at the market House this evening, mounted. Sharp's Carbines and Revolvers will be furnished."

Then that imbecile Ewing, who had so conveniently pulled his soldiers out of Lawrence, stopped the punitive actions. They had to settle for the general's Order No. 11 simply banishing those along the border.

Lex talionis. An eye for eye, Lane thought. It was all the rebels understood.

Or perhaps they understood it all too well, he considered. Hadn't some of them cried "Remember Osceola" as they burned Lawrence?

OCTOBER 21 — 9:30 A.M.

West of the Little Blue River
Jackson County

IN THE RACE BACK TO THE Little Blue, Blunt ran a familiar prayer through his head, the one that asked a benevolent God to save him from dithering fools.

He felt in his ample gut that he was too late. A half hour earlier in Independence, a private had run up with a message that Colonel Moonlight was under severe attack.

If Curtis had allowed him to stay out there with the First Brigade in the first place, he would have had another thousand men and four more guns on the high ground over the river. The closer Blunt got to the river, the more his fears seemed justified. The smoke that rose over the trees to join the low, gloomy clouds clearly was the bridge. Moonlight's howitzers had been at work, but suddenly had quieted. That worried him most. Also the steady rattle of musketry seemed to be spreading across a front wider than Moonlight could possibly stretch the 11th. Wounded were passing back, most on horses being led away, but they gave off no sense of panic.

He soon spotted Moonlight, who had been forced back west from the river bluffs — Blunt's fortress wall — but had found a decent position behind a stone fence that ran north and south. As Blunt rode up to him, the Scot saw him and bellowed cheerfully:

"Good to see you this morning, general! You better have brought ammunition. Some of the men are plumb out. We've been singing at the rebs in the last half hour as much as shooting at them. The Johnnies, they're a wee slow, but I think they have begun to figure it out."

Moonlight filled Blunt in. It was Marmaduke's division's turn at the fore of Price's column that morning, and it had gone straight for the covered bridge. Anticipating that, Moonlight's troopers prepared for its destruction, pulling a wagon of hay onto the structure, ready for firing. It had been lit, and the troopers fell back to defend the howitzers and the high ground with a withering fire. Pushed back, the Confederates began probing the flanks, with Shelby crossing south of the bridge. That and the rapidly diminishing supply of cartridges had forced the Kansans' first grudging step back toward Independence.

Major J. Nelson Smith led up the first of some Second Colorado companies. Their uniforms, with their long gauntlets and their companies mounted on white horses, added to their appearance. The regiment, with detachments of 16th Kansas Cavalry and the six 3-inch rifled guns under Captain W. D. McLain, made up the Fourth Brigade.

"Where are they?" bantered some of the Colorado men. "Shall we take care of this for you?"

"Just keep going straight ahead, children. You'll find them," jeered one of Moonlight's sergeants.

Blunt shouted for the Colorado officers to form on the right side of the road, then sent a man back to hurry up the ammunition for Moonlight's people.

As Moonlight's regiment shifted to the left side of the road, it became more obvious that the Confederates were crossing both upstream and downstream of the bridge. When Jennison and Hoyt rode up, Blunt assigned them the south flank to the right of the Coloradans. The few companies of the 16th Kansas he sent to help Moonlight.

"The Second has the center," he told the jayhawker. "Take your brigade down there and cover his right. And watch to your own flank. Graybacks in those woods. Lots of them."

Those rebs quickly showed themselves, but hesitated at the arrival of more than a thousand fresh Federal troopers. Recognizing a chance to retake his coveted high ground over the river, Blunt ordered an attack. His line gave a cheer and surged eastward.

Private James Campbell of the 14th Missouri Confederate Cavalry recalled this moment: "As we dismounted and ran to our position on the right of the road, and the right of Clark's Brigade, (we) hadn't any more than got in line when our skirmishers were thrown out and they hadn't gone more than thirty yards when they came running back and said: 'Boys, they are coming.'"

The rebs got off a few scattered shots and fell back toward the trees cloaking the river, probably to regroup with invisible comrades. Certainly, they gave no intention of going far back.

Advancing to where the road began its curving descent to the river, Blunt came to a cut in the thick timber that revealed that hundreds of Price's men, soaked to their chests, had waded the stream. And the fields on the other side seemed filled with dun-colored troops, red flags moving at double time on the road from Lexington. Blunt watched as his regiments took advantage of the rail fencing along a little lane that skirted the west edge of the river-bottom woods. Many of Moonlight's men settled around a church left of the crossroads.

How far away were Rosecrans and his divisions that supposedly were tracking Price? Blunt asked for field glasses and peered toward Lexington. Nothing encouraging, just a longer-than-hell line of Confederate wagons. As he lowered the glasses, a six-horse team towing a rebel cannon burst through the smoke of the bridge. Blunt nodded admiringly at the display of guts. Shouldn't the shit-heeled little bridge have collapsed by now?

Gunpowder smoke began to roll over them. The line was heavily engaged now.

Blunt decided he had not given enough attention to Jennison's position to the south. He found the situation there very hot, but under control. Attached to Jennison's brigade was a small battalion of Warrensburg volunteers. They were more than holding their own with their fast-firing Henry rifles. Damn fine guns. Blunt had one himself.

His commander, Major General Curtis, had now come up, Blunt saw, thinking, Just leave it to me, old man.

Retracing his route back to the other flank, however, he found Moonlight's mounts being led farther back. Already the line is giving away? Could not that damned Scot stay where he was put? But the answer was found in the trees to the north, where dismounted rebs were trying to work their way around to the west. Moonlight had pulled around some companies to create an angle. Cries for fresh allotments of cartridges were being heard. In a moment, the big colonel was towering over Blunt, gesturing toward the stone fence behind them, the one they had charged from so recently. He hated retreating, but the need was becoming only too obvious. Blunt growled approval to Moonlight and went galloping south to Jennison. Some guns already were withdrawing back west, their spinning spokes flinging mud skyward.

Just as he reached his right flank again, rebs came screaming out of the shadows of the timber, and the Kansans rose to meet the attack. It briefly became hand-to-hand, and again the Johnnies fell back. The success could only be temporary. Even more butternuts were forming up. He motioned to his staff to get out of easy range.

There was Jennison, filling the breech of a Sharps. Blunt had never admired the colonel, but right now had to admit that under fire the man was cool as an icehouse rat.

As he yelled to the Kansans that they would be reforming again on that fence back there, a horse hobbled by them on three legs, then fell with a shuddering sigh that could be heard above the musketry. Jennison pointed at some men in blue overcoats a hundred yards to the south. Blunt was confused. Reinforcements? Curtis has finally got up the militia? No, the militia had no uniforms. Then he realized it was the enemy, garbed in Union coats, working to get behind the right flank. Jennison sent a man to turn a couple of howitzers that direction.

Blunt recognized that, no sooner would his men retire to the stone fence than the gray tide would again lap around his line. It meant a leapfrogging withdrawal all the way to Independence, but would give the rebels fits. He sent orders to organize the retreat to a third line well behind Moonlight's wall.

General Jeff Thompson and other Confederates would recall, "we scarcely halted except (at) a stout fence until we drove them to and through Independence" just as night fell. On the Union side, Blunt would remember that the fight continued "until 4 o'clock p.m., when the enemy refused to advance upon our last line, formed on the east side of Independence… In this day's fighting our loss was slight while the enemy was punished severely." Dr. Williams McPheeters would write in his diary, "Dead Yankees were strewn all along the road." The fight that took place over seven miles of territory left perhaps 300 casualties on the two sides.

Moving back to the center of his line, Blunt watched as a couple hundred Colorado men trotted back to a new position, many reloading on the move, several helping injured comrades. One man was missing an arm and spraying blood over his Samaritans, who were trying to hold a wadded shirt to the wound. Giving an account of the fighting in the next day's edition, the Kansas City *Journal of Commerce* would report that: "Frank Gould, Orderly Sergeant… shoulder torn off by a shell, will probably die. The conduct of Sergeant Gould was heroic in the extreme. Though so terribly wounded, he hurrahed for the gallant Colorado as he was born from the field, waving the arm that was left."

Blunt felt something was wrong. What? The booming of his artillery seemed to diminish as the rifle fire grew hot again. His answer came in the form of Major T. I. McKenny, one of Curtis's staff officers, who was saluting.

"Sir, General Curtis's respects. He wishes you to know he has repositioned some guns for covering support."

"Goddamn it to hell! Why is he doing that!"

The shocked McKenny had no answer; concentrated on holding in check his horse. Blunt peered through the smoke. Yes. There were some rifled guns, exposed and without support, in a plowed field. As he looked, two artillery men fell to skirmisher fire.

Just more evidence for Blunt to view most of his superiors as fools not to be suffered gladly. The old man shows up on the field, and everything goes up the spout!

"Where is Curtis?" he roared. But before McKenny could bring his nervous horse around to lead the way, Blunt could see Major Robert Hunt, Curtis's artillery chief, was shifting two more howitzers, trying to remedy the situation along the Blue Mills Road that ran to the north of the Lexington pike. He was shouting at another major, it was Edmund Ross of the 11th.

But did they see the threat developing, the mounted rebs in the trees to the north! Why weren't they pulling the guns back? Then it occurred to Blunt. They were stuck in the mud! Those guns were about to be overrun!

11 A.M.

PALMER KNEW THE STANZAS OF THE "Charge of the Light Brigade" by heart.

As his company galloped toward a broken hive of rebels, he recalled the line about how some English officer "had blunder'd, charging an army, while all the world wonder'd." He prayed this action was not to be a faint copy, prayed that Bettie would not read about his death in the *Journal*.

Prayed the *Journal* would not write how Palmer died not wearing any pants. The morning had unfolded poorly.

Had it only been an hour since he had out his needle and thread, trying to patch the rip in the seat of his trousers? The sergeant sitting next to him had bellowed, "Rebs!" — making Palmer jerk and send the needle deep into his thumb.

He had stood on the rock ledge, his good hand holding the badly torn trousers. The sun was still low, so he'd used the injured hand to shield his eyes. Yes, there they had come, riding hard as if they meant to eat Union bacon. The Kansans' pickets placed far on the other side of the stream took their few quick shots, then bolted for the bridge. Moonlight had ordered his beloved little howitzers to open up, men had scrambled into their chosen firing positions along the low bluffs, and he had run to his company in his flannel drawers and boots, throwing his last pair of pants over the saddle of his horse. Private Edwards, who never seemed to be farther than two yards away, had been pretty tickled about it.

They had lost the high ground, then Blunt had arrived with more men to push the rebs back on their heels. But the numbers again had become too lopsided, and their colonel had told them to drop back to avoid being flanked.

Palmer had been withdrawing his weary company to a new position closer to Independence when Moonlight had galloped up, shouting, "The guns! Got to save those guns!"

Palmer twisted in his saddle and saw the peril. Some of McLain's crews had taken their pieces into wet plowed earth. Now the Colorado men were struggling to extract them. The rebs were coming up the Blue Mills Road and firing at them from ever-closer range. Somebody had to give the rebs something else to fret about.

"Eight front," he called to his troops. "On my left!"

The men resignedly wheeled and made their lines quickly enough. His bugler called the charge, and they were off. Why A Company? Palmer knew Moonlight bitterly disliked him, would not weep if he didn't come back from this little adventure. It stemmed from a year ago, when Palmer circulated a petition that got Thomas Ewing made colonel of the old 11th Kansas Infantry instead. Now Moonlight ruled the regiment, and Palmer's treason was never forgotten or forgiven.

His column scattered some rebs, but peripherally Palmer saw a cluster of rifles tracking them from a rock fence and little orchard on the right, his side of the rank.

"Get down," he screamed, trying to flatten himself over his horse's neck. Rifles erupted, and he felt his steed falter and then collapse. Palmer got his feet out of his stirrups and fell on the horse's neck. A weight slammed into his back, flattening him. He lay stunned a moment, trying to draw in breath, and realized that blood was running over his neck. Panicked, he twisted his arm to feel for the wound and found the blood came from a body lying on top of him. He rolled from beneath the weight. It was Private Edwards, the boy's jaw blown away and eyes empty. Palmer tried to gather his wits, looked for his pistol, couldn't see it. He pulled Edwards' Gallagher from his warm hand and fumbled for a few carbine rounds from the lad's cartridge box.

Momentum had carried his column past him, their hooves nearly treading on him. Now, his men turned back, trying to aim carbines from skittering horses and give him some cover. He screamed to his troopers to dismount and follow him. He ran toward the fence, firing the carbine, levering the trigger guard to open the smoking breech, thumbing in a load, and firing again as the enemy worked their ramrods. They were no longer looking so much at him, though, as the next threat.

Another Federal column, some Colorado companies, was roaring into the melee, as were some rebel horsemen, too.

Palmer was over the fence heading for the apple trees and the house behind them. A few more shots came from its windows, but when his Kansans poured in fire, rebs with empty rifles scrambled out the other side. He considered further pursuit, but it registered that the fields behind the homestead were crawling with graybacks, a battalion being formed for a charge. No place to stay, this! Turning to tell his men to remount, he watched shocked as the Colorado officer whose appearance probably saved Palmer's life slid lifeless from his saddle. It was Major Nelson Smith.

"If the guns weren't out of the mud by now, so be it!" Palmer shouted to no one in particular. As he cleared the fence once more to get back to the road, a projectile of limestone, chipped by a minié ball, stung him in the thigh. A clearly anxious trooper was bringing him a mount. He looked down at his filthy, torn drawers, then to where his horse and Edwards lay in the road. Palmer was judging his chances when the rebel yell came out of the trees.

This is no way to die, he thought. And he raced for his pants.

3 P.M.

IT HAD BEEN A BRUISING TUSSLE, but never in doubt in George Todd's eyes once Shelby got his people across the river. Shelby was a fighter as good as they come. The guerrilla chief was glad he had thrown in with him.

He turned in his saddle, looking back toward the army fellers forming up on the Lexington Road. Far beyond them to the east rose an exhausted rivulet of smoke.

"That stream needs a new bridge."

"I'll get the boys to build you one tonight," Dave Pool laughed. "You want it covered? Maybe whitewashed?"

Todd gave his horse a nudge, his boot slipping along its mud-slick side. Up ahead, he could see the jayhawkers falling back to another position much closer to Independence. Oughta figure out they can't stop us and just get the hell back into Kansas where all devils belong.

"Doubt any of you will be sober enough tonight to put a hammer on a nail, Dave. No, I just reckon a double stone arch would look fine back there." Pool showed his puzzlement, so Todd elaborated a little. "You know I cut stone afore the fighting? Dad and my brother, too, were masons over there in Kansas City. Learned a lot from him. Figure plenty of bridges need building after the war, lots of good limestone here."

Legend had it that Todd's father was forced into service to build Fort Union at Kansas City, the Federals imprisoning the younger Todd at starvation rations till his father started the stone work. Just one more fiction created to justify simple bloody-mindedness. Fort Union was not built of stone, despite its later depiction in crude prints, but was an earthwork fortification with wooden-frame buildings inside.

Truth was that Todd had grown bored with stonecutting, had liked the idea of a war stirring things up. His family had emigrated from Scotland, through Canada, where his father had some trouble with the damn English. While his family had had no use for slavery, Todd's social circle of toughs had definite secesh views. Soon enough, some Union men had come to search the house for him. His ma had berated them, screeching, "You wretches want to spill the best blood of Scotland, the noblest blood of Scotland!"

Forced to jump into the brush, he had joined up with John Little and Ed Kroger. It had been just upstream on the Little Blue where the three had been letting their horses water when the bank timber erupted with musket fire. Little and Kroger toppled from their saddles dead. Somebody forgot to aim at Todd, or aim well, anyway, and he got away, not a scratch on him. And before long, he was avenging his friends.

Possessing almost all the skills required, Todd quickly rose to become a bush-whacker lieutenant of Quantrill. The talent he lacked was taking orders. Didn't much care for it. Over time, however, he'd ciphered out how even Quantrill could be intimidated. 'Twas easier than bluffing his pa. Been some rough times with his old man.

Now, a thin voice piped up. "You know who puts up mighty fine rock bridges? Them Dutch fellas."

Todd and Pool turned. The speaker was a tad they didn't know, apparently one who had joined them at some point since Lexington. Most of the recruits had been placed with the train, but here was this sprout, riding a buggy mare his ma probably had been hiding for years and singing hosannas to the Dutch. A bit of blond hair had escaped the black felt hat jammed down to the ears. In his belt was tucked a flintlock pistol, a relic, for God's sake, his grandfather's? He considered asking about it, but Pool was already chewing out of the boy.

"Anybody ask you about the goddamned Dutch, you little turd?" Pool snarled. The lad's eyes went to silver-dollar size, but his trap was clamped tight shut now. Some of the others in the band were shaking their heads, muttering about the puppy up there taking airs with the captains.

"Reckon you ought go back that way to Cook's Store," Pool continued thrusting a thumb back east. "Have you a chat with them Dutch fellers we run across a couple weeks ago, just talk your little straw head right off with 'em. They won't butt in, not at all. Some of the best-mannered, sauerkraut-fartin' Dutchmen I ever met!"

That got a big laugh from several of the men.

"Dave Pool was a born comedian," Frank James would recall. "He could have gotten $500 a week on stage." And in the next breath, James would add: "Up in the old German settlements of Lafayette County the mothers still quiet their children by telling them to be quiet or Dave Pool will get them."

Todd knew the boy would be clueless about that miserable little Home Guard bunch. About two dozen of them and every one a Dutchman farmer. They sure shot like it, just winged a few rangers in their volley from a roadside thicket. "What occurred afterward reminded me of a rabbit hunt in the country," said John McCorkle of the Germans' fate. "The boys started in the brush and every few minutes out would run a Dutchman and the boys on the outside would start after him. Not one of them escaped."

Before too long, more of the German militiamen, mounted this time, appeared down the road, only to be scattered by Todd's charge. Hopping off their plow horses, they had disappeared into a corn field, hoping to find refuge. Hoped in vain, McCorkle noted. Hunted down one by one, "there were very few of this company that ever reached home alive."

Up ahead near town, the Yanks now clung like ticks to a fence row; gunfire was brisking up some. No Dutchmen there, for sure. It had been no easy thing crossing the Little Blue, and then all a sudden a whole new set of Kansans had come roaring in. If Shelby hadn't just got across upstream and flanked them, it would have been uglier than it was.

Shelby's people had brought their horses up and were beginning to mass in the field to the left. They'd all be galloping through the corn stalks in a minute, yelling like Injuns. Todd turned to Pool. "Get ready, Dave. Don't want to let Shelby's boys get to the whiskey in Independence first."

Todd loved a charge.

"Quantrill had always tried to hold him back, and yet he was Quantrill's thunderbolt," said one guerrilla. "Todd only charged. Were he attacked in front, a charge; in the rear, a charge; on either flank, a charge." Todd knew that Quantrill had said he wasn't long-minded enough, but Quantrill was a coward, wasn't he?

"Yeah, a saloon could come in handy right now," Pool agreed. "I could use a little smoothing influence from Mother Jug, if them Red Legs ain't stole it all."

Pool decided to dig a fresh pistol from a saddle bag. "Too bad that Bud and Fletch aren't around these days, eh?"

"Wonder how old Fletch is doing?" Pool mused. "Think he's going to try his *hand* at raiding again?" and then burst into guffaws at his own joke. Todd's lips, so often set in a sullen line, twitched. The boys let it be known that they, too, thought it was another belly buster, although a couple of Fletch's old band didn't find it so hilarious. They'd joined Todd and Pool after the chief's arm had to be hacked off. Fletch was a runt, but tough enough. He'd survived the shooting, the sawing and the Yankees' weed-beating hunt for him. One day he was back, said he had the itch to try life in the bush some more. When a comrade accidentally shot him in the other arm, though, that was enough for old Fletch. He retired from the field as the soldiers like to say. That itch was done scratched.

"Who's that bunch ahead?" Todd rose in his stirrups and pointed to a stone wall where some men were adjusting rocks to suit their firing positions. Then he saw a Federal holding a half-dozen white horses well back of the firing line, not far from the court house. Likely, it was them Colorado miners. The "White Horse Regiment," some called 'em, although as far as he could discern only two or three of their companies had such horses. Tough enough, but he'd whipped them before.

Frank James said they were the bravest Federals the bushwhackers faced — doubtful that he would have anything good to say about Kansans — recounting a tale about a day when a large contingent was chasing him, Pool and some others.

"You cowards, you, if there wasn't so many of you," Pool had shouted back, "I'd stop and fight you." To the guerrillas' surprise, the Federals pulled up and one rode forward to take the challenge. "And then those two men, Pool and the Yankee, sat on horseback and pecked away at each other until all their ammunition was exhausted. Pool had a slight flesh wound and the other man wasn't hurt. "Pool always said he would have whipped him if he hadn't been afraid of the other Federals," James said, "but we made fun of him for inviting a fight and then getting licked."

Todd nodded ahead and said to Pool, "I think that your Colorado friend may be up there." One, two puffs of smoke ahead. "Maybe you two …"

Thugt! Todd's head was jerked violently. He collapsed back on his saddle roll, conscious of a burning in his neck, felt himself sliding off his horse. Suddenly, on his side in the field, he could not get his hand to his neck, his arm was pinned under his body. I caught one, he thought. How bad? The ground conducted the pounding of hooves, Shelby's charge taking off. His cheek felt the roughness of a corn cob, something flowed wet and warm around his ear.

'Twas the noblest blood of Scotland.

XII

Respite

"We would shoot Jesus Christ or God Almighty if he ran from us."

— Bushwhacker of Anderson's band in 1864

☙☙☙☙☙☙

OCTOBER 21 — 5:30 P.M.

Glasgow
Howard County

RILEY SURVEYED THE SCENE: CHARRED BRICK husks of several buildings, including one that had been right handsome, up the hill a little ways. A mighty big fire had occurred here, but it seemed as if it had consumed all the warmth. He was cold, even wrapped in a light quilt found snagged on a fence picket.

Shifting his rump on the stone wall, he sat under a disagreeable sky in a disagreeable mood. Members of Anderson's band wandered here and there, happily finding whiskey, victuals and carry-away missed by the hurrying Confederate Army a few days earlier. Glasgow was a rich town that had gone unplundered for just too long. After the fracas on the Crooked River, several of the guerrillas needed to replenish their saddle bags, or in his case, to get a brand new McClellan saddle and U. S. Army horse blanket. That task had not been too hard, but Riley's mood was not improved by the acquisitions.

There'd been a battle, and he had missed it. Glasgow had fallen almost a week earlier. Shelby and John Clark had taken the town, and now the Confederate Army was back south over the river with Price again.

Riley had wanted to be able to go home, wherever that was now, and tell his mother and sisters that he fought with real troops with flags and cannons and all. Truth be told, he was getting so that he would just like to go home, period. Two knots in that plank, though. First, he wasn't sure mama would figure he'd killed enough Yankees. It was hard, certainly, to detect any lack of them about. The other was he was reasonably well known as a partisan ranger now. He couldn't be at all sure some milish wouldn't come for him just about any place in Missouri.

"Hello, do you care *awfully* if I share some of the sun with you? There seems to be so *little* of it today."

Riley was startled. He turned and saw a girl, perhaps his age, shivering in two, no, three shawls over a faded green dress. Her darker green bonnet had white lace streamers, probably sewn on by the girl herself.

"Uh, hep yerself." It occurred to him that there was no sun to be seen at all. She perched on the wall about three feet away.

"Thank you. I confess I'm a bit weary trying to find some items for my aunt. Some of our usual shops have been burned and the other practically emptied."

"Yep, Shelby did a job on your town, all right."

"Oh, it wasn't Shelby. It was that fool Harding who set fire to the City Hall, and then it spread from there. It was awful! One of my best friends lost her home to the conflagration."

"Harding?"

"The Yankee who surrendered. He was trying to keep the militia stores in the city hall from being captured. My aunt said the imbecile destroyed $100,000 worth of private property to keep from losing government supplies worth a pittance of that."

"Oh, well, I'm sorry your friend lost her home."

"It happens, doesn't it? My own home was given to the torch in Dayton, that's where we lived. That awful Jennison burned every house but one. This reminds me of it, but it was worse there. I am practically a salamander now, totally immune to fire. We moved in with my sister and her husband, but then we were told to leave last summer. We got out with very little, of course, mama and I having already lost most everything. We found refuge here with my aunt. She's daddy's sister; daddy's somewhere in Tennessee, we think, he hasn't written in forever. We worry so. We're living up there a couple streets. You can see part of it there on the other side of that church. Do you know what I thought when I walked to church past those buildings with the coals still burning in the basements? I thought I was peeking through the doors of hell, I really did."

She talked a lot, but Riley relished hearing a girl's voice again. He had been brought up in a big family with sisters chattering and fixing up things and rushing around minding everyone's business. Looking up the hill at her aunt's stately home of brick, Riley thought, we've both been burned out by Yankees. He stole a look at her. Reddish hair, not too red, he could tell it was curly under the bonnet. Looked pretty with the green dress.

Some of the rougher-looking guerrillas wandered by. Riley realized that he looked pretty rough himself, and only the good Lord could know when he'd had his last real bath. Some of boys looked keenly at her, and he could sense her discomfort. He wondered if she chose to sit here for safety. He knew his youthful appearance might seem disarming to her, it had seemed such to fellows with pistols a couple of times, and they had found they had been mistaken.

"Could I escort you home, miss?"

"In a minute, I'm enjoying the sun … and your company." She shifted her skirt a bit. Riley was pretty sure she was a good six inches closer. And he knew for a fact no sun was going to break through those clouds.

"My goodness, you've hurt your foot!"

Riley looked down as if a wounded extremity inside a knife-split boot had not occurred to him until now. Actually, he realized, his foot had been feeling better. He'd been so blue in general he hadn't noticed.

"Oh, it went and got shot down at Fayette a few weeks ago. It's healin', tho."

"You were in that battle? It must have been frightful. We've heard that many southern men fell there."

"Too many," Riley allowed. Too many who were friends. He did not feel the subject was suitable for delicate company. "But it was hardly a battle, just me and other fools trying to shoot pistol balls through logs."

"Oh, tell me about it."

"I just did. It wasn't much."

She looked at him with a little pout, very fetching. She seemed truly disappointed. She had the bluest eyes. He relented, but offered terms.

"You fill me in a little on what happened here, and I'll try to remember something interesting to say about Fayette."

"Oh, I can do that. I saw it all."

Riley was surprised. "You did?"

"Oh, my mama and my aunt tried to get me into the fruit cellar, but I said I had to find Claiborne first. Really, you know, I had no intention of missing a battle. Things are so dull here. I went up to the second floor and watched everything."

"Claiborne?"

"Yes, my cat. Claiborne Jackson." She gave a wicked little smile. "I gave him the name cause he stays away from home more than the governor."

Riley gave a sharp laugh. He liked this young lady more and more. She had sand, and she was funny. He looked down and noticed her feet, tiny and elegant in shoes — slippers, really — of blue velvet and leather, with their neat little laces facing each other. Suddenly he had a vision of her sitting, one leg bent out akimbo, its ankle resting on the other knee, skirt and shift pulled back as she primly laced the shoes. And he felt a tightening in his trousers. It might be a good thing he was inside the quilt, he thought. Buck rode by, gave them a glance and grinned at Riley. He lifted his hat to the young lady. Riley smiled shyly and offered a wave back.

"Who was that big-eared fellow?" she asked. "How did he get hurt?"

"A friend, Buck, or I should say, Frank James. He got grazed a couple days ago. Buck and me are best of friends. We're with Anderson now. I was in Pool's company for a while and then he joined up with Todd. I used to ride with Quantrill, but the captain hasn't been campaigning much this season."

"Quantrill not campaigning? Why he was here just days ago!"

Riley cocked an eyebrow at her. After Fayette, word was Quantrill was hunkered down in the Perche Hills.

"Indeed he was. Whole town's been talking about it. Came in a little after the army left. The Federals, since they had their guns taken away, they asked to cross the river with Shelby under his protection. Five hundred of them, local militia and all, just left. My aunt had a fit, said the town was left completely unprotected.

"Anyway," the girl continued, "Quantrill was the perfect gentleman, sent two men to fetch Mr. Dunnica from his home, had him open the vault and took $21,000, my aunt says." W. F. Dunnica of the Thompson & Dunnica bank had anticipated trouble and had buried $32,000 of his bank's money in his yard, leaving enough not to arouse suspicion.

Riley was shocked. $21,000! He's never heard of such an amount being won by any guerrilla. He wasn't sure if even the Yankeetown raid had produced that kind of money, but he'd never know. Old Charley Higbee had been given much of it to hold, and he'd promptly absconded, some said to Canada. That was a reason some of the men had turned against Quantrill. If Bill heard about this trick, he'd light up like a coal-oiled cat.

"Didn't shoot him?" Riley asked.

"Why no, of course not." She waved the idea away with one of her crocheted mitts. "He escorted him back home for his safety."

That was why Riley had a soft spot for Quantrill. Unlike Bill or Archie, he didn't put a bullet in you just for the pleasure of looking into the hole. Oh, the captain had killed more than his share of jayhawkers and Federals, but there was always some order to it. Even in Lawrence, when he couldn't find Lane to take back for hanging in Jackson County. Burning the senator's new brick house, he had allowed, even helped, the bastard's wife to take out possessions. Not only that, she'd fretted so about losing her piano that damned if they hadn't gone back into the burning house and tried to wrestle the thing out. If so many hadn't been drunk, Riley figured the men would have saved it, but he'd never figured out just why they had even tried.

"Well, I think you still owe me your history of the battle of Glasgow, miss. You didn't wave flags from the roof, did you?" He got a giggle. Lord, he was getting pretty good at this girl-talking thing.

"No, silly, but I rushed from window to window. It started with cannons, so early in the morning, it was still dark, I swear, there were four artilleries, I counted, and much musketry from just across the river. I believe that was General Shelby. My name's Ella, by the way, but everyone calls me Allie, I don't know why. You don't think it makes me sound common, do you? Oh, please don't tell me if you do! Anyway, the Union men all ran down there and got in ditches and were shooting back.

"There's the *West Wind* down there in the river. I just love the name. So sad that they burned it, don't you think? Poor thing, it couldn't get any farther down river on count of it being so low and all. Oh goodness, I'm supposed to be telling you of the battle, aren't I?"

The sidewheeler had been loaded in St. Joseph with six companies of the 43rd Missouri Volunteer Infantry to help General Egbert Brown and his Federals defend Jefferson City. Realizing the Confederates already had marched past the capital, the mission was abandoned, and Colonel Chester Harding decided he could help the small local garrison at Glasgow.

"So, then, all of a sudden, came this *enormous* noise from up on the bluff, and I went to peek out the east windows, and they had more cannons all the way up there. I couldn't see them, but there was so much smoke. This was about seven in the morning." She pointed at what was very high ground looming over the town.

Riley could imagine the shock that had run though those Union rifle pits. The Yankees would have known they were the fish in the proverbial barrel.

"Yeah, that was pretty slick, all right," he said. "See, they sent Shelby to pin 'em down on the waterfront, and Clark slipped over the river downstream and surrounded them before they knew what was happening. We'd 'a been here but Price needed us to cut the railroads and cover his back," he added, realizing he was trying to impress her a little with his superior military knowledge and at least some role in the campaign to free Missouri.

"Well, I'm quite sure they were surprised into idiocy," Allie agreed. "Before you knew it, our southern soldiers were in town fighting with the Federals. It was frighteningly fierce. I saw Yankees shooting from behind the front street fence through the yard at soldiers just behind the rear fence. They were that close! They retired into that fortification over there on that high point in town, isn't it just so ugly? But Harding saw that it was senseless and he surrendered. Not before trying to burn down the town, of course."

"And that was it?" Riley asked.

"Well, yes, I suppose so. It went on all day, though. I was quite famished, and when the shooting stopped I went down to the cellar. Mum and auntie were very cross, and I simply had to *beg* them for apples. After that, the southern men got very busy gathering the rifles and such. There was quite a lot. And oh, the steamboat had unloaded a great number of Union overcoats before the battle, and the southern soldiers seemed delighted with them. Why was that?"

"Uh, because they're cold?"

"Well, yes, many of them were wearing them when they left, but won't that confuse things? Won't they get shot by their own men by accident or something? I thought that sort of thing was against the rules or whatever."

Riley decided not to tell her about the Union jacket he had worn many times — after all, it was back on Crooked River with half his guns. He wondered if she would like to hear that story. That had been a pretty damned near thing, especially racing through the brush without a saddle on Folly. Folly! He had intended to find her some feed. He'd been sitting here for more than an hour, not noticing as the already gloomy sky had darkened. Allie noticed.

"Oh, must you be going? Well, would you oblige me with your very generous offer earlier of an escort?"

"I have to tend to Folly, that's my mare. She's the one that got me out of Fayette."

"Of course, let's get her. Folly, what a wonderful name! We've got corn and such at the house. Oh, you're limping."

Riley tried to walk as normally as he could, but to appear brave doing it, too.

He noticed that Allie was very close to him now. Through the acrid smell of the burnt buildings, his nose detected a reminder of home — some toilet water or perfume or something his sisters had favored. Smelled like a flower, hanged if he could say which one. He wondered if he could ask.

He realized she was talking again. About tobacco?

"Well, Mr. Lewis had a great many darkies working at his factory down there, and do you know, he set them all free last year. Then hired some back. He's positively the *richest* man in these parts, my aunt says. He's also the *blackest* Republican, too, in these parts, very much a Lincoln man, I believe, but despite that, he's very kind. I've met him, and he doesn't put on airs. You can't see it from here, but he's got the most *glorious* house, they call it Glenn Eden, which I think is a little *much*, don't you?"

"I reckon he took off with the Union parolees."

"I don't know, but auntie, she knows who is related to everyone in the state, I believe, she said this morning that Mr. Lewis is kin somehow to both General Price and General Clark, who was here, you know, with General Shelby. Surely, no one would bother Benjamin Lewis."

Much later, after Riley had walked Allie back to the home of the aunt — she had been much relieved to have her niece back and appreciative of the young guerrilla's courtesy — and gotten a reward of a fine meal, he was wondering where to bed down. It had been an astonishing day. Allie had told him that she and her mother were planning to move down to Tipton once the armies got out of the way. A sister's husband bought a farm there. Riley knew the little railroad town in Moniteau County. What he didn't know was: What would it be like to kiss a girl, right on the lips?

He turned Folly around a corner and saw several Anderson men clustered around a store front. There was some excitement about what was inside. He dismounted carefully, making sure to land on his good foot. The other one was throbbing after the homeward stroll with Allie.

"What's goin' on?" He couldn't get a good look through the door for the men in front. His arm was touched. It was Buck.

"Nothing pretty. Bill's got himself a rich man in there, and the fellow's pretty pulped up. The boys worked him over worse than I ever seen. Bill's in one of his tempers, but I don't know how's I blame him much. The sumbitch hired spies to sneak around southerners in this area and posted a $6,000 bounty on Bill's head, dead or alive. Now Bill says he's brung himself here, so the $6,000 is his. Lewis didn't have it up at his place, so they dragged him down here. His wife has to find it or watch Bill kill him. From what I can tell he's likely to die anyway of the beatin', but she's out trying to scrape up the ransom from town folks now."

At that moment a couple men turned from the door, giving Riley a better view of the shop's interior. A man lay on the shop's counter in a long sleeping shirt that had been white once but colored now in a way only the devil could appreciate. His face was unrecognizable, his body shuddering in convulsions. Anderson was sitting in a chair, not far from the man's head. He was studying the oozing, pistol-whipped mask.

"Good thing you didn't put $10,000 on me," the chief told him. "Yer woman might never be able to collect that much cash." Then he gently blew smoke into the battered face.

Riley had seen enough. Going back to Folly, he'd have bet a half-eagle that the smokes came from Lewis's own tobacco factory.

XIII

Clashing arms

"Death was everywhere but no one saw him. Only the gapping guns vomiting grape — only the infantry and cavalry beating the air with bullets ....
One swift, short, hungry yell now and no more."

—Confederate Major John Edwards,
describing the Mockbee farm fight

ↄↄↄↄↄↄↄↄↄↄ

OCTOBER 22 — 3:30 P.M.

Hickman's Mill crossing, Big Blue River
Jackson County

A BLACK CLOUD OF CROWS EXPLODED from the highest tree limbs, protesting the disturbance. Everyone in the regiment turned his head.

That had to be the howitzer.

Something was happening not far to the north.

Sergeant P. I. Bonebrake saw the officers of the Second Kansas gather with Brigadier General M. S. Grant for a quick conference. Bonebrake wished it were the other General Grant on the field. He had no confidence in this version.

They and other militia regiments had been sent to watch the upstream crossings of the Big Blue. Some, including Bonebrake's unit, got sent over the Hickman's Mill ford to scout on the south side for the rebels' supply train. From the high ground over there, their glasses had spotted an ominous dust cloud with flashes of guidons, and they'd come back to the other side of the river in time to meet a messenger bearing disturbing news: Jennison's people had given up Byram's Ford. The rebs were loose inside Curtis' line on the Big Blue River. Everyone was to get back north to Westport *instanter*. Bonebrake's colonel shouted orders, and the column moved off at a gallop.

Another *whump*. No other field piece was big enough to make that sound. The firing was not coming from Russell's Ford, the next crossing downstream, where the 24-pounder had been left on guard. Bonebrake glanced back at his company, didn't see anything to worry him, turned back just in time to be stung on the cheek by a frozen clump of mud. Well, at least it wasn't a horseshoe. The column carried over a rise, and then down to splash across a creek and then up a gentle slope toward the higher prairie. There the column found the howitzer, unlimbered in the road. Captain Ross Burns' gun crew cheered the arrival of reinforcements. Surprisingly, no other Union troops were around.

The artillery captain pointed to the north, where apparently some rebels lurked. Not many, Bonebrake hoped. A moment later, most of the Second Kansas was forming a mounted line in the field to the gun's right. Captain Horace Bush, who ran Bonebrake's company, however, yelled for his people to go to the left of the lane on the other side. The little stone farmhouse and barn nearby was the Mockbee place, somebody mentioned, adding that old Samuel Mockbee, who had put in some time with the Sixth Kansas, had been dispatched by bushwhackers some months ago. Just beyond the buildings to the north and west was a grove of locust trees.

"Company G, make a line here, make a line here," Bush shouted, motioning along a fence.

"Falling back to Westport might be easier said than done," Bonebrake volunteered.

"Might have to fight our way there," the captain agreed. He looked back toward the river timber to the south. "Where is everybody? Where's the 21st?"

One man dropped his Springfield, jumped down off his horse to retrieve it. Bonebrake heard the mumbled excuse of frozen fingers. It was chilly but not that bad. Just nerves. Like a lot of the company, the man had a sumac leaf in the band of his hat. Without uniforms, the Kansans looked little different from the average farmer or townsman or reb, so they had been ordered to wear something red. Bonebrake had a red bandana on his arm. But many had just plucked the scarlet leaves and called themselves the "Sumac Militia."

Burns yelled, "Fire!" and Bonebrake and his horse both jumped at the huge noise that engulfed the line. Others were fighting their spooked mounts, two men were being ridden away with, but they weren't any of Bush's men. Bonebrake looked back at the gun, the elevation of its barrel. Why, that shot looks to land in Independence. He caught the eye of young Guilford Gage, an engaging young Topeka fellow, and gave a quizzical look.

"Trying to lob some solid on the Johnnies," Gage yelled. "They're behind that rise. We got some canister on them when they fired at us from the grove. Sent 'em scampering."

After a few more of those, Burns spoke:

"That's enough. Let's wait for them to come and see us again. Double-C."

A loader jumped forward, cradling a heavy, cloth-wrapped cylinder in each arm. Into the muzzle went a powder bag, followed by the two large cans. Each round held nearly 50 one-inch balls. Bonebrake could not imagine charging into that.

"Here they come," yelled Hughes, a black teamster. He had come up with the crew. Staying back with the wagons apparently wasn't exciting enough.

The gun sergeant was spinning the elevation knob, dropping the muzzle of the beast inch by inch. Hurry up, Bonebrake wanted to say. Most of the horsemen in butternut had topped the rise ahead. He did a spotty census, at least 300, no, more. He tore his eyes off the men that were gathering to kill him and looked back to the gun. Gage was stepping back with his ramrod.

Voices screaming down the hill. The charge was on its way, six abreast down the Westport Road, with other foes dismounting and spreading out in the fields ahead.

Fire it! Bonebrake wanted to yell. Fire it!

Burns was coolly sighting down the thick brass tube, ordering it swung left about two inches, then a bit the other way. And he stepped back, knowing the recoil could crush a foot, cripple a man.

A few men fired off nervous rounds that had little chance of finding flesh. On the other side of the road, a sergeant creatively discussed the maternity of the offenders.

The approaching hoof beats drummed the ground.

"Eeeeasy, eeeeasy," Bonebrake told the preacher next to him, who was muttering, "He layeth me down in green pastures…"

Some muskets were beginning to rattle on the left. Still too soon.

"… deliver me from evil…"

At that, his colonel, George W. Veale, screamed, "Fire!" and the lanyard was pulled. The sound erupted around Bonebrake, smoke hiding the enemy for a minute, then dissipating in the raw wind. The crackle rippled up and down the line.

The howitzer bit hard into the rush of horsemen, who turned away and rode back over the knoll. He saw Gage's face, burnt powder on his cheeks, ramming a swab, Lear Selkin shoving down the next charge.

The other rebs decided to fall back as well. Well, hey, thought Bonebrake, that didn't take much. Veale was excited, riding out in front of the line.

"Hurray, boys, we have got them whipped." He called for an escort to ride out a ways to get a better look at where the rebs might have disappeared to. The order came for the companies to dismount and reload.

Bonebrake tore the end off a fresh cartridge, spat the paper, poured the powder, proudly noting that his hand did not shake. But the ball was a bad fit, just more of the questionable ammunition they'd gotten. He pulled out another cartridge, thumbed the bullet out of its paper wrapping, felt it drop it down the Springfield's muzzle.

Bush was naming horse handlers, every fifth man. Bonebrake turned his sorrel mare over to the boy collecting reins.

As he replaced the ramrod, Veale's party galloped back. They'd seen enough. Another attack was coming.

Within two minutes, officers were hollering to watch the left, rebel horse in the cornstalks, watch the grove.

"Cavalry moving around to the west of the farmhouse," called Sergeant John Kemp of D Company. The howitzer was swung around, a shell was sent at the procession racing by. To no effect, other than sparks from its blast setting afire the lane's rail fence.

Bush barked orders to face G Company in the new direction, just as riders were scattering leaves in the grove. "Go it!" Bush shouted. Picking out a bald rider on a shiny black horse, Bonebrake squeezed the trigger and watched the horse fall. He felt a moment's remorse, terrible to do that to a such a good-looking horse. Dispassionately, he watched the preacher's shot knock back down the bald man, who was trying to find his feet after a heels-over-head tumble.

The big gun's muzzle erupted, and Bonebrake saw the wadding fly. This time the head of a secesh turned to red mist, hat sent spinning. The rebs were on top of them now, some jumping their horses through the line over on the right. Preacher down. Kansans running.

"The enemy appeared to be closing in on us," Kemp would remember. "My horse and Wm. Elliott's were standing near each other. As I was loading my gun Elliott passed me and went to his horse, mounted and rode off in a gallop. My horse followed after and I didn't see it again."

Bonebrake stepped back as a spotted horse with blood on its withers thundered though the line. He willed his fingers to steady enough to place a fresh cap on the firing pin. The officers were screaming to re-form, stay put, re-form. The powder burned Bonebrake's lips. As he licked them, he put a color bearer over his iron sights and ... nothing. Hang fire! And then the rebs galloped away once more, and it quieted — except for the moans.

A glance showed Gage still standing, but Selkin slumped against a gun wheel — gone, it appeared. A few yards in front, a gut-shot reb was reaching toward a carbine on the ground. Bonebrake watched as an E Company fellow, a mercantile clerk, stepped out of the line to kick the carbine away. Then he thought about it and kicked the wounded man in the head.

Bonebrake looked down his own company's line. It was thinner, mostly because of runaways. The old soul mender's forehead needed a sew-up. A couple G Company fellows decided to drag him back a bit. "Just take him a ways and get yourselves back here," Bush ordered. Bonebrake picked up the preacher's Springfield. Seemed more reliable than his own. Maybe the power of the Lord was on it.

A young fellow wearing what seemed to be parts of a gray uniform galloped in from the east, went straight to Veale. "Hold this point at all hazards, and reinforcements will be here in a few minutes," he assured him. Bonebrake liked the sound of that. Hoped they got here quick. Then Veale did an odd thing. He seized the pistol of the young man — a boy, really — and called up an escort to take him away. Bush went to find out what had happened and came back with a big grin.

"You know who that was? That was Tecumseh Shelby, some kin to the general. He thought Veale was a Missouri officer in their brigade. It's Shelby's ass we've been kicking!"

Bonebrake felt a surge of pride. They were just militia, sumac leaves and old Springfields. He slapped a man on the shoulder. "Dang, if this ain't a fighting ..." And then it struck him. The lad had spoken of reinforcements.

Long shrill notes of bugles sounded behind the knoll. In a blink, the fields ahead filled with horsemen. More than twice as many as before, coming back down the lane, but thickly spreading out past both flanks, too.

The gun jumped back. Riders went down, but the rebel charge never lost a step. Raising his rifle, Bonebrake sensed more of the militia line melting. From the corner of his eye, he saw Gage pull out the swab. It was the lad's only weapon, Bonebrake suddenly realized. Lieutenant Colonel Henry Greene was screaming for men to get back in line. Bonebrake tried to settle on a target, squeezed off his shot, and the rebs were among them, screaming, firing pistols in their faces, swinging rifle butts at heads.

"I am killed," cried a captain of D Company and collapsed.

Clubbed from behind, Burns collapsed in a heap, holding his bloody head. The crew was surrendering. Where was Gage? Bonebrake started a sprint back for the mounts and — Damn their souls! — realized the horseholders had released them in their panic.

He swerved to the right to escape a horseman behind him. Over there in the farm yard: his sorrel! He hurdled the fence, reached to grab her reins. Couldn't get his boot in the stirrup, she kept spinning away. He followed her nervous dance until getting the chance to throw his weight against the sorrel's shoulder, penning her against the wall of the house. Swinging into the saddle, he felt a knuckle light on fire, looked down to see a bloody graze. Bonebrake janked the reins toward a south fence and dug in his spurs. Blind with panic, the mare didn't bother to leap. She just scattered the rails, stumbling, but collecting herself. As Bonebrake got her head pointed toward the mill crossing, he turned his own for a last look.

Not far from the howitzer, a kneeling Johnny unsheathed a huge knife. Had Hughes down. My God! Sawing at the black man's throat!

3:45 P.M.

Main Crossing, Big Blue River
Jackson County

THE REBS DID NOT SEEM INTERESTED anymore.

Observing a slouch hat drift by a blackened piling on the slow current, Lieutenant Patrick Henry Minor was considering the possibility that they had never been interested, really. Just too quiet here at the ford.

Then a bang made Minor and hundreds of others jerk. Startled oaths were uttered, musket hammers clicked back. Price was here!

But no. It was just some militia fool practicing on the hat. The brim was splashed. Not a bad shot, actually....

Minor's colonel was not so appreciative. He trotted up his horse and screeched in red-faced fury. Borrowing liberally from his hours-long sermons from before the war, Colonel James Montgomery promised hellish torment — but on earth, here, now — for the next man to fire without orders.

Minor didn't know what to think of this consumptive-looking fellow. Montgomery had showed up to assume command of the Sixth Kansas Militia after James Snoddy, its original colonel, got thrown in the guard house for trying to march the regiment back into Kansas.

But then, no one ever knew what box James Montgomery would fit in, really.

"He is not what one would call a 'Kansas Ruffian,'" offered Colonel Robert Gould Shaw, a Boston swell who also commanded a black regiment in South Carolina, the 54th Massachusetts, before getting slaughtered with it in front of Battery Wagner outside Charleston. "You would think at first sight that he was a schoolmaster or parson. The only thing that shows the man, is that queer roll or glare in his eye…."

Minor turned his attention to his two Parrotts, brought down from Fort Leavenworth by steamer. The lieutenant was part of Douglas' Battery, more formally the Independent Battery, U. S. Colored Light Artillery. The unit, still beating the bushes for recruits, was not officially mustered in yet. Minor's section was attached to the Ninth Wisconsin Battery under Captain James H. Dodge. All the guns were trained on the road between Independence and Kansas City where it crossed Big Blue.

Kansas militias, including five colored companies from Leavenworth, had spread out and dug in on either side of the guns, some using charred pieces of lumber that had once been the bridge here. One of the black captains was Minor's barber and brother-in-law, William Burnham, who had Company C. Over in Company A was Lieutenant Henry Copeland, whose brother had gone with John Brown to Harper's Ferry and had gotten hanged for his trouble.

The Kansas militia line stretched more than a dozen miles, north to the Missouri River and south to where Blunt's regular cavalry and then more Kansas militia guarded the upper fords. They totaled maybe 15,000 men, some said, but were badly outnumbered.

Hours ago, one of the militiamen had shouted that a reb was on the road on the other side of the ford. Minor got a glimpse of him, a horseman well out of rifle range, who had observed them for a few moments before turning back toward Independence.

An anxious murmur went down the militia line, and in no time at all enemy skirmishers were slithering through the heavy brush on the other bank. Suddenly, that side of the river spouted smoke from the sputter of dozens of muskets. Montgomery had bellowed, and the militiamen emptied their barrels nearly at once.

Minor had been shot at before, but his gun crews hadn't. He stayed close to them, made an example, did not duck. Dodge ordered them to shell the woods a couple hundred yards to the south of the road, where he'd seen smoke erupting. As the cumulus from burnt gunpowder had spread over the river, Minor wondered how Dodge had spotted this special puff. As best as vision allowed, Minor had pointed his Parrotts one by one at an almost theoretical foe. He'd stepped back and yelled "fire," with nary a clue if they were hitting anything. Didn't seem that the rebs had hit much, either. The militia companies nearest the battery had three wounded men, but none mortally. He saw Will Burnham moving around, clearly unhurt. That was good. He would not want to be the one to tell Josie she was widowed.

By 9 a.m. Curtis was suspicious. "Price is making very feeble demonstration in front. Look out for your position," he warned the units upstream. He told them to send out scouts "to see if he is moving on my flank."

After well more than an hour of this, it had settled down to a few scattered shots, then quiet. Three wood ducks, assuming the war was over, swooped in and settled with a ripple in the river. It all suggested the rebs were not that hungry for a scrap. Which raised the question: Were they fleeing to the south or fording somewhere else? Firing had been heard upriver, but it had died, too.

Minor watched the ducks bob, looked down river for the hat, but it was out of sight, heading for New Orleans. He wished he could go, too, to see how his mother was faring. Her last letter to Josie hadn't told them much.

"What we need here on dis ribber is one of them iron-coats from over on the big river," remarked one of his loaders, Daniel Cooper. "Dat would keep dem on the other side."

Minor wasn't inclined to join in the discussion, but puzzlement won out.

"Iron coats? Who's wearing iron coats?"

"Nobody wearin' dem, Lootenant, unless that ol' river."

"Private, what are you talking about? Make sense, please."

"Iron coats, suh, boats with guns sticking out."

"Ah, iron-clads," Minor smiled. "Gunboats. But there are none here. We've got a little steamer anchored down at the mouth with riflemen aboard, but…"

"Not what my woman say, and she reads good; she say the noospaper say …. got it right here." He reached into his jacket.

Minor had only a moment to wonder why an obviously illiterate former slave was keeping a newspaper until he saw it contained food within its folds. The man carefully pulled an oily sheet free of the package, some of the more deeply greased parts of the pages separating and staying with the raw hog belly.

Minor took the proffered sheet, which he could see was the *Daily Times*. He suspected its Leavenworth subscriber had cast it away, and it had been retrieved by a word-hungry young Negro. He knew about those.

Minor generally considered the *Times* a lying rag, especially after its August article about the battery's difficulties in enlisting. "We learn that three colored men were tied up by the thumbs, on Sunday, in order to compel them to enlist in the colored battery. This occurred at the camp…," the *Times* claimed. "We fail to perceive the lawfulness of such conduct in Kansas. It may work well in slave States, when practiced by rebel slave-drivers, but in free Kansas no human being — be he white or black — should be persecuted in such a brutal manner."

What the fool correspondent had seen was just men punished for some infraction. They were not exactly suspended by their tied thumbs, but made to stand on tiptoes for an hour or so, a normal practice. He descended the ladder of exclamatory headlines down into the narrow well of copy to where the first of the article dissolved into the grease. Yes, there were the words. "In a couple of days a Brigade of Iron-clads will meet their 'Pa' and give him welcome on the Kaw."

"Well, your wife read it right," he assured Cooper. "But it is surely all bosh. All the ironclads are way down the Mississippi now. I've never seen a gunboat on the Kaw, at most a couple steamers with some iron plates up around the wheelhouse." He looked again. The line said "*brigade*" of ironclads, not squadron or fleet. Ah, perhaps the editor was being complimentary, likening the Negro soldiers to iron.

The *Times* had it right, for once.

4:15 P.M.

Mockbee farm
Jackson County

Captain Bush raised his hands in surrender.

The horsemen approached between the trees of the grove, carbines and pistols level.

The leader of the butternut-and-blue-clad squad leaned over in his saddle, took the revolver and saber from the Kansan. It was a cold day, but sweat trickled way from Bush's scalp to his collar and then down his shoulder. Gunfire was still being exchanged on the road back to Hickman's Mill, but he dared not look away from the hard-faced men studying him.

"We taking officer prizners, Cap'n?"

Horace Bush realized the speaker had on a Union overcoat, better than anything Bush's own Second Kansas could have hoped for.

The leader said nothing, but just broke open Bush's surrendered revolver and confirmed that there were two unburned loads in the cylinder. He snapped the pistol shut, swung it around and aimed at Bush, standing just a yard away.

Bush's ears filled with the explosion, and he found himself flung to the earth, his chest seemingly bursting. He groaned and squeezed his eyes shut, his fingers fumbling with his coat buttons, as if he could open the garment and let out the pain.

"I don't think that shot did it, Cap'n," Bush heard the young rebel say. Then came another explosion, violently jerking the arm that now lay across Bush's breast. Then one or two more, but these were only echoes.

Bush assumed he was dead. But somehow he was aware of hands inside his coat, his tunic. "See, Cap'n, you hit his watch! Damn!" The searching went through his pockets. His midriff was jerked from the ground. Stealing his belt? Then he felt nothing, heard nothing.

He opened his right eye, its lid fluttering but functional. For some reason, his left eye wasn't working. Around him came shouts of men in the fields, an occasional shot, the call of a crow. A leaf settled on his chin. He closed his good eye.

He awoke again to the stamp of a horse. A voice.

"It's no good shooting him, he's dead as a stone already."

"Well, then I reckon he won't be needing that duster. Hell's plenty warm, they tell me."

"Suit yerself. Looks purdy bloody to me."

And Bush found himself turned over in the blood-stained leaves. He opened his eye, but could not focus on the fading vegetation under his cheek. They left. He closed his eye again and passed out.

"He ain't dead."

Bush opened his eye. He wasn't?

He tried moving his undamaged arm. No, I'm not dead, he thought. Maybe he could get through this.

"Help me," he whispered into the leaves.

Bush could not see him, but sensed a man kneeling beside him.

"Help me," he whispered again.

He heard a pistol's hammer pulled back, but lost consciousness before the shot.

And woke yet again.

To more voices.

"Well, you can shoot him, but it's just a waste of a cartridge. You can see he's dying."

No, Bush decided. He was not.

And once more, he passed out.

5:30 P.M.

Kansas City

THE GENERAL STARED OUT THE WINDOW of the Gilliss House, allowed himself to be hypnotized by the Missouri's milk-and-coffee current. The river was still low, forcing the Harlem ferry to negotiate a course between a long sandbar and a knot of snags guarding the north shore across from Kansas City.

"Sir, this message is from Senator Pomeroy, and this one is from General Deitzler."

"Ah, what does Pom the Pious want now?" Major General Samuel Curtis wondered aloud.

He refused to turn away from the dirty pane of glass. The Honorable Samuel Pomeroy was one of his volunteer aides-de-camp. Curtis had no use for him;

just one more thorn to bear in the painful crown of politicians.

Major C. S. Charlot stifled a grin and examined the paper. Pomeroy sends regrets; he would miss the evening council. At last, Curtis thought, some good news.

"The senator has volunteered to take some companies of militia down to the Kaw, to apprise you of any enemy movement around the right flank," his chief of staff recited.

Also, Curtis suspected, it kept Pom within hailing distance of the new pontoon bridge to Wyandotte, just in case a fast escape were needed. He swiveled in his chair, tiredly cocked his eyebrow.

"Well, at least we know our right flank is safe, eh?"

Charlot's grin escaped as he answered:

"I'm sure that's what Secretary Chase said, sir."

Curtis let out a sharp laugh. The first in days. Curtis was a fervent backer of the president. The rotund Pomeroy was anti-Lincoln, had fanned Treasury Secretary Salmon Chase's ambitions to push the president aside in this year's elections. He was behind the "Pomeroy Circular," that "strictly private" document, distributed by the thousands, that catalogued Lincoln's incompetence. The mailing of the circular, however, from Chase's own Treasury, illuminated the secretary's disloyalty and his standing had shriveled.

"What does Deitzler need?"

Charlot knew the answer without checking.

"He has expressed some concerns over the handling of his militia regiments by General Blunt."

Another heavy sigh escaped the commander of the District of Kansas, who was 59 now and feeling it. Just about everyone had concerns about Blunt, himself included. Governor Carney had been furious when Curtis gave Blunt command of the regular cavalry, angrier still when Blunt arrested two of Carney's favorites in the militia.

Blunt's pugnaciousness made him a fighter, which was why he was needed here. He had all the characteristics of a bull-fighting dog, save loyalty. Curtis had no doubt that Blunt was stepping on toes — no, jumping on them — while organizing the Kansas City defense. Curtis also knew he should be out there, too, but he was depressed. His make-do fortress along the Big Blue had collapsed just as Blunt had predicted. Some of the militia regiments had broken and fled back to Olathe, many miles to the southwest. Much of the Army of the Border, as Curtis had proclaimed it, was here in the town and could soon have its back to that river out there. It and the Kaw made a pocket of sorts, and Curtis was uncomfortably deep inside it.

After a knock at the door, Colonel Samuel Crawford came in.

"What is the situation in Westport?"

"Fighting to the south and west," Crawford replied. "Moonlight and Jennison."

"Have the rebels reached the Shawnee Mission?"

"Not that we've heard," Crawford said.

"Well, we're clearly in the hands of the volunteer regiments. Where is Ford?"

"In or near Westport."

"Nothing from the east, then, Sam?"

"Nothing about General Pleasonton."

Curtis frowned. He had so little information. The rebels had cut the telegram lines all across central Missouri. A messenger had been sent down the river last night to make contact with Pleasonton, but nothing was heard back.

Dan Boutwell, a veteran scout from Major General George Deitzler's Second Kansas militia, had volunteered to try to reach Pleasonton. After his skiff lodged on a sandbar, however, he waded to shore and crept through Independence, rebel territory where he was shot at by sentries. Boutwell found Federal pickets near the Little Blue early the next morning and was escorted, covered with mud, to Pleasonton's tent. Told of Curtis's plan to hold the Big Blue line, the cavalry commander began his aggressive attacks on the Confederate's rear.

Curtis continued his questioning of Crawford. "Have you seen General Blunt?"

"Yes, sir. He is striving to situate the militia," Crawford replied. "There is no end to the confusion." Colonel Charles Blair, a veteran volunteer officer placed in charge of several militia regiments, would write humorously in his report how that evening "whilst I was placing Colton's regiment and Eve's battalion in position behind the earth-works some officer, without my knowledge, carried off the residue of my brigades, and placed them so securely that I never found them until the next morning." Curtis could imagine. Let Blunt work it out.

"The general's profane proficiency never fails to educate me," Crawford smiled.

"I have found it indispensable in managing mules," Charlot said. "Blunt seems to find it so with men."

His son, Henry, used to say much the same, the general remembered. Henry admired Blunt's fighting spirit more than he deplored his many sins. Ah, Henry had been a good boy that way.

Curtis looked down at the piece of stationery before him, a letter he had started to his wife back in Iowa.

"It is certain that among the rebels killed yesterday the notorious Todd, one of the murderers of our son, was one…" he had written. Good news of a sort, but then his pen had taken him further:

"They are retreating southwest, but fighting us hard."

It was a lie. It was not the Confederate army that had retreated today, but his own. The words did not signify, though. They were just to comfort the poor woman. Henry had died at Baxter Springs last October. They also had lost Sadie, only 20 and Curtis' favorite, to the typhoid. In the family home in Keokuk, the mood was blacker than the crepe in the windows.

The old West Pointer rubbed the bristle on his chin for a few moments. He needed a shave. His cavalry regiments needed rest and food. He told Crawford to write up the orders necessary to withdraw them to Kansas City once their engagements were broken off by darkness. Crawford left to find couriers and an orderly to shave the general.

Charlot offered the reminder that the council of war was to start in less than an hour. Curtis was dreading it. Fractious, swollen-headed generals he could handle. But the politicians: confound them!

Lane, his other volunteer aide-de-camp/U. S. senator, would be there, so his presence would draw the anti-Lane faction like angry hornets. Led by the Kansas governor, they would strive to neutralize any advantage, real or imagined, Lane might gain. Curtis' aide, Crawford, was one of the dogs in the political fight, too, running for governor with Lane's backing. His election or defeat in two weeks would indicate whether "King" Lane's grip on Kansas was weakening. Meanwhile, Lieutenant Colonel John Ingalls, on the staff of Deitzler, was running for lieutenant governor on the anti-Lane ticket. He dismissed Charlot and decided he would finish the letter to Iowa.

Did any other general in the Union Army have to put up with such a creature as Lane?

Many considered the man mad. Curtis knew the stories. Back in '58, Lane had shotgunned a Lawrence neighbor. "No event has produced such excitement," wrote *The New York Times* correspondent. "Some were for hanging Lane at once, and the mobocratic spirit was intense for a time."

The killing was confused as everything around Lane was. A property dispute, a child's grave, use of a well, a locked gate and, of course, who had fired or tried to fire the first shot. Tom Ewing, the Leavenworth lawyer who often had opposed Lane politically, got him off on self-defense.

Naturally that had hung over Lane when it came time for Kansas to pick its two senators in January '61. Lane had been anxious, sitting outside the chamber. He had a revolver in his pocket, muttering that he would shoot himself if not chosen.

Cutis had heard another story, too. Last summer, the old reprobate had created a scandal by getting horsewhipped on the street by a Washington woman. Curtis did not know the whole story. Did Lane insult her by assuming she was a prostitute? Or was she a prostitute, and he still managed to insult her? Or did Lane's madman gleam, his hair blasting off in every direction, frighten her?

But he had done well for the president at the convention. In his short speech, Lane had warned: "If we nominate any other than Abraham Lincoln, we nominate ruin." Exactly, thought Curtis. Exactly.

Curtis knew that some considered him a "Lane man," but he did not like the senator, knew few of intelligence who did, but still had to be careful with someone so close to the president. Explaining why the senator always seemed first in line for political patronage for Kansas, Lincoln shrugged, "He knocks on my door every morning." This naturally increased Pomeroy's bitterness.

A little later, as Curtis approached the downstairs parlor, he could hear Blunt complaining loudly as usual at everyone else's incompetence, this time the militias' reluctance to stay put in the entrenchments around Kansas City.

"The north side of the Kansas River possesses peculiar attractions for them," the major-general was saying. "It was with great difficulty that I succeeded in halting and forming in line even a small portion of them."

Curtis quickened his step, hoping to head off an argument between Blunt and Deitzler, whose 30-day soldiers Blunt was insulting. The room was crowded with officers and their attendants. Curtis believed he had nine on his staff now, counting the politicians. Unhappy Deitzler, standing with Carney, had at least that many. Then there were Blunt's people. Lane was out of the room but not far. A hall tree was disgraced by the senator's bearskin coat, filthy and moth-eaten, worn in every season. Curtis found the center table and knuckle-rapped it.

"Well, gentlemen, we have much to discuss."

Blunt, naturally, demanded his attention first.

"General Curtis, I understand many of our supply wagons have been taken across the Kaw into Wyandotte. Who gave those orders?"

The bantam major-general had probably grabbed four hours of sleep in the last 48, but still Blunt brimmed with aggressive energy. His tone carried a challenge.

Ingalls started to say something about impertinence, but Curtis waved him off and answered smoothly.

"A miscommunication occurred, General. We are transporting the most important cargoes back over the river as I speak. Apparently some of the horses of Colonel Blair's regiments were taken over as well. We are putting priority on getting them returned."

Curtis was not sure he was believed. Some of his officers had lost faith in him, were convinced he had only one thought, retreat into Kansas.

Blunt had never had much respect for Curtis, but then there was a pantheon of superior officers for whom the man had no respect, starting with Halleck, whom he accused of shallow loyalty.

In Blunt's camp was Colonel Thomas Moonlight, who 17 years later would write of the events of October 22: "There was no commander, and each regiment had to act for itself and right here I may as well state that this was the source of all our trouble from the time General Curtis assumed command in person." Moonlight's experience that night did not change his view, probably. He sent an overwrought message to Curtis reporting that he had intelligence — from a captured prisoner who must have been a bluffing wonder at the poker table — that Price had 28,000 men and 20 artillery pieces. "We must be reinforced," he pleaded. "For God's sake send me rations, general. My men must eat, and they will fight."

That day also had been the funeral of Major Nelson Smith of the Second Colorado, killed at the Little Blue and buried at the cemetery between Westport and Kansas City. Curtis left before ceremonies ended, as recalled many decades later by musician Charles Waring, and ordered the band to follow across the Kansas River.

"At Wyandotte he could not be found," Waring said, "and the band followed him out to the 'Six-mile House,' on the Leavenworth Road, where he was found in camp." From that point on, Waring said, the soldiers had little confidence in Curtis.

Nevertheless, that evening Curtis was back at the Gillis house on the Kansas City levee.

"As you certainly discern," Curtis continued to this officers, "today's action has placed the command in some peril. Many militia regiments have been cut off to the south and cannot coordinate with us. While I am confident we can hold this city, we cannot protect Kansas from this position if, as has been reported, Price has his eyes on Fort Leavenworth. General Blunt recommends that we continue the fight in Missouri. What is worrisome is how the enemy has broken through two strong positions in two days."

He saw Blunt's flush, thick mustache quiver. The man could spot a slight in a fly's eye, Curtis reminded himself.

"No one could have engaged his cavalry more adroitly than General Blunt," Curtis continued diplomatically. "But the bare fact is that we face superior numbers."

Blunt was not assuaged. "We did not hold the Little Blue because the governor would not release his units. Too many have been sitting on their asses! Political perfidy!"

Ah, Curtis thought, what did it take for the politics to erupt afresh: two minutes, three?

"Too many newspaper editors trying to stir up mutiny," exclaimed Crawford, earning a glare from Ingalls, an editor from Atchison. Curtis agreed that Carney and his pets at the Leavenworth *Times* had gone way over the line with their bombast, confusing many militiamen and damaging their resolve.

Curtis wanted nothing to do with this brawl, having run into political problems when commanding Missouri. That was how he had ended up being sent to chase Indians out on the prairies. He was not sure now much farther away Lincoln could send him.

"General Blunt," Curtis replied wearily. "You know most are raw militia. Pitted against Shelby or the bushwhackers, will they fight? We all know the fate of the gallant Colonel Veale, cut to pieces as other regiments watched or fled."

No one was surprised when Deitzler jumped in to defend the honor of his militia. Deitzler was a good man. He had fought like a wounded bear at Wilson's Creek — took a bullet there — but serving Carney wasn't making his life any easier.

"Might not they fight with more resolve with their feet planted on Kansas soil?" asked Ingalls.

Today's action demonstrated that some of our regiments are not ready to take on Price's ruffians on any soil, Curtis thought.

Deitzler growled that the militia would fight where he told it to.

Now Blunt again: "General, falling back beyond the Kaw would pull away the anvil, just as the hammer is about to strike. Pleasonton will face Price's hordes alone. We would be shirking our duty."

Curtis was beyond tired of hearing Blunt's anvil and hammer speech. How long did it take for Pleasonton to get here, for God's sake? He left Jefferson City weeks ago, did he not, with stripped-down cavalry brigades. In that time, Curtis told himself, he could have walked to Kansas City.

"I would like the opinion of the officers who have shouldered the burdens of the last three days. Colonel Moonlight and Colonel Jennison should be here soon," Curtis said, noticing how the eyes of Blunt's staff shifted to their commander.

"I ordered them to stay at Westport and the mission," Blunt said.

Curtis stared at him. Good Lord. The man countermanded my orders, he thought. Didn't even have the decency to inform me.

Now the Carney people were criticizing Blunt for arrogance. They might as well complain that a crow was black. But Curtis did not stop them. When Lane got into the argument, Ingalls could not contain himself.

"Certainly, Senator, you've never thought of politics, yourself. Why you insist upon advising on this astounds me. You're not a military man. This is no place for your speechmaking."

Lane bristled, but then he always bristled. With his hair, he presented the appearance of an enraged porcupine.

Someone was at the door. Charlot went to see who it was.

"Young man," Lane said to Ingalls, "I was meting punishment on the secesh at Osceola when you were chasing your mother's laying hens."

Charlot was reading a message a courier had brought. The major straightened and walked quickly through the assembly and handed it to Curtis. The major general unfolded the paper and put on his spectacles. In a moment, he rapped his knuckles on the table.

"Gentlemen, the course is clear enough. This is from Pleasonton. He is in Independence and punishing the enemy."

As the room erupted in exclamations, Curtis motioned over Captain Meeker, his signal corps officer. "Get this to Rosecrans: 'I am preparing to renew the attack and pursue it at daylight with all my available cavalry.'

"Gentlemen," Curtis announced to the room, "we have work to do."

Blunt already was pushing through the others to the door.

10:30 P.M.

Southwest of Independence

Jackson County

IT WAS LIKE NOTHING SO MUCH as a knife fight in a damned root cellar.

Marmaduke did not care for it a bit. The Federals did not seem to realize that it was nearly midnight. No one fought this late! Were they drunk over there? Even with the little bit of moonlight, you could end up shooting your own men!

Several flashes erupted ahead and to the left. He was fairly sure it was Clark's people, still....

Shouts: "They're falling back... Watch out over there!" He peered toward the source of the voices. Falling back? Who's falling back?

"I think that's General Clark over there, sir!" said a nervous-sounding major on his staff. Their horses were steered to the right a bit and wove through the trees. Marmaduke, his nearsightedness even more troubling in the dark, ran into a branch that smacked him in the nose and scratched a cheek. He managed to catch his hat before it was swept away.

"Watch out, damn ya!" His horse shied at something, no, someone, on the ground. Lord! Almost trod one of my hurt boys, he thought. This is unnatural!

"Thus passed this long and never to be forgotten night of the 22nd," General John B. Clark Jr. would write. "The dark obscurity that enveloped friend and foe alike was relieved by the bright flash of our guns, and the deathlike stillness that reigned in the forest around us was only broken as volley answered volley." He said the fighting did not cease until 2 a.m. It probably felt that way, but others reported receiving orders to stand down at 10:30 p.m.

"General, over here, sir!" It was Clark's voice that Marmaduke heard. "Best dismount, sir. It's pretty wild up here."

Marmaduke did not need to be asked twice. Handing the reins to the major, he considered with whom he might trade to get rid of this hard-mouthed beast. His favorite horse had been killed at the Little Blue. It had been very hot at that crossing.

"How does it go, John?"

"Wearying, sir," Clark replied. "But they're being checked now. These Yankees are full of vinegar and gunpowder. Rushed us with a reckless fierceness that I have never seen equaled, but they are finally satisfied by the reception, I believe."

After eight hours of fierce fighting, Lieutenant William C. Ballard, Company D, Seventh Missouri (CSA), scrawled this in his diary:

"…the confusion in the night was terrible, the enemy sometimes in 20 paces of us and we could see nothing but the blaze of their guns. We fell back to Big Blue, here the enemy (Curtis) had fell a lot of timber in the road."

General Pleasonton, who had organized his 4,100 Federal cavalrymen into four brigades, had thrown them at the Confederates' rear like vicious kicks. He opened with General John McNeil's Second Brigade, which included the Seventh Kansas jayhawkers, forcing passage of the Little Blue and then driving straight into Independence. The Third Brigade under Colonel John Sanborn hooked in from the northeast.

It was Confederate Colonel W. F. Slemon's brigade that was knocked off the river and sent running westward. General William L. Cabell, one of General James Fagan's brigade commanders, had been escorting the rebels' baggage train and beef herd through the town. He turned back to help Slemon and immediately was overwhelmed by the rush of blue uniforms, some mounted, some on foot, through the streets.

It was a repeat of the day before, but with different flags. Yesterday, our army pushed Federals through Independence, Marmaduke mused, then today the Federals sweep us out. Both times going west.

Not sensing the coming disaster, Marmaduke had ordered Clark to take his brigade into camp about two miles west of Independence. Suddenly Fagan's officers came racing down the road looking for help, quickly followed by their broken regiments. Marmaduke had ordered Clark to form his regiments, then decided to withdraw a mile or so to another line.

Colonel William Jeffers and his Eighth Missouri barely got to their new positions before taking the assault head-on. The Eighth had been with Marmaduke forever, it seemed. He always relied on them, too much probably.

A minié sang its song, then another, not far overhead.

"And Jeffers? Is his bunch holding up?"

"His boys were roughly handled, but we got some ammunition up to them, and as I say, we're gaining some breathing room."

A burst of some language — what was it, Italian? — was heard from somewhere to their right. It was one of Clark's colonels, a multilingual fellow "down to cussing the Yanks in Italian, (having) ran through the English and French some time ago."

"Are all of Fagan's people through?" Marmaduke asked Clark.

"Any still out there are probably in the bag by now. Maybe 400 of Cabell's people surrendered; he lost a couple of guns, too. The general had a very hard time of it, had to jump his horse over some fences."

Mrs. Robert Smith watched the running fight from the balcony of her house and wrote her sister: "…. We had a clear view of the battle for more than a mile.

We saw the Federals capture a battery in Noah Miller's field. It was magnificently defended and no less bravely attacked. We could see the far-off flash of red fire coming out of the guns and pistols and men fell by the dozens. It was one of the most sublimely thrilling sights that no one could imagine."

The Yankees really had their teeth into it, Marmaduke thought. Price, alarmed at Pleasonton's rabid-dog nature, covered his bets by sending the wagon train south toward home. None too soon, especially with the scouts saying that the Union infantry that had followed them all the way from St. Louis was just a few miles south at Pleasant Hill. The news had finally given the old man a jolt. Marmaduke was glad that something had. Price's serene optimism as Union forces yapped at their heels across western Missouri had cost Marmaduke as much sleep as this night fight.

Now, as one colonel had worried, Price had brought them between "two impassable fires," to which Cabell had responded: "Yes, damn him, unless he jumps pretty soon, it will be too late to jump."

Clark was asking about where the supply wagons might have gone. "We'll be needing some substantials when those fellows figure out the sun has gone down."

"John, I regret there will be little time for victualing on this side of the Blue," Marmaduke replied. "You're familiar with the road back there that runs to the ford? That's the way to Westport. As soon as this situation allows it, you must shift your men over to the other side to a good hill that covers the road. I've just come from that way. The ground over the ford is very suitable from what I can see. You will have Parrotts there."

"What will keep the Yankees from flanking the position?"

Marmaduke pulled at his beard, fingers combing out a twig from his horseback encounter with the limb. "Can't promise anything, but I think this bunch will come straight at us. That's all Pleasonton has done all day."

A heavy burst of firing interrupted them. The clot of officers looked into the dark. A few minutes later, some men came back with a prisoner. Turned out to be an Iowan, who'd said he was with a cavalry brigade under a Colonel Winslow, who had been chasing them since deep in Arkansas.

"I think it's finally dying down out there," Clark said. "Shall I keep men on this side tonight?"

"No more than a regiment guarding the road," Marmaduke replied. "They will let us know when these fellows start coming at us again."

"What is the word at headquarters?" asked Clark.

"Shelby's people pushed almost into Westport without much trouble tonight, but have withdrawn to reorganize. Tomorrow morning they will strike north again. Shelby is very confident. The general in the meantime has the wagons moving south toward New Santa Fe to get them out of the way. A wise move, I think. Some of Fagan's people, once they pull themselves together, and the recruits will go with it. Another of Fagan's brigades will be on your left flank, but to your rear somewhat. I cannot emphasize enough that we must hold the river."

Both men knew that this additional brigade would be little help. It was made up of conscripted men and recruits who still were poorly armed. And Marmaduke knew that some of the untested men in his own division weren't much better.

Marmaduke asked for his horse. Just as he took the reins, the beast viciously kicked into the dark, striking the horse of Captain Moore, his adjutant. The victim squealed and stumbled. The major, barely aboard, offered some observations that could never be published in his Denver newspaper.

"Yes, I'm getting rid of you, don't worry," Marmaduke muttered. Securely in the saddle, he saluted in the dark. Assumed the men on the ground could see it.

"Good work, John. See you on the other side of the river."

And he realized how that must have sounded.

OCTOBER 23 — 4:30 A.M.

Kansas City

THE FOUL WEATHER SEEMED TO HAVE passed through. A cold waning moon offered a miserly light by which the gun section left its emplacement on Kansas City's western edge. Roused a little after 3 a.m., Lieutenant Patrick Henry Minor and his men had limbered their two Parrott guns and harnessed the teams. They rolled a few blocks down dark streets, found a place behind the Ninth Wisconsin's guns, then sat and shivered on the caissons. All waited for the order to fall in on the road to Westport.

Minor's gun crews were more bothered by the lack of food than the cold, and the lieutenant could not blame them. As the militia units pulled back from the Blue, all had been chaos as far as supply was concerned.

"Not appreciating the importance of position, a large number of the companies sought to pass into town and obtain food," Captain Richard J. Hinton, attached to the colored militias brought down from Leavenworth, would recall. "The scene grew animated. Staff officers galloped here and there, shouting hoarsely; portions of the militia obstinately insisting upon their right to do as they pleased; amusing colloquies and expostulations occurred, but at last the long line of works was occupied…."

The supply train had made it all the way to Wyandotte in Kansas before being found and turned. Some units got biscuit, Minor knew, and some residents in town had cooked for the soldiers, but his men expected little generosity and got less. Largely escaped slaves, they were regarded that way in Missouri.

At least the men had gotten the satisfaction of firing their pieces at a real enemy the day before. They'd talked of little else since, some choosing to believe their shells had chased Price off the Independence Road like rabbits. Never mind that Shelby had broken through some miles to the south.

The battery was ordered to tighten up. As some mountain howitzers rolled by, Minor heard the man sitting the swing horse make a joke back to the wheel rider. They both sniggered at the "baby" guns. The Independent Colored Battery, Light Artillery, was proud of their 10-pounder Parrotts, which had 74-inch tubes, compared to the 33 inches of the mountain howitzer.

A gap appeared in the column behind the Sixth Militia, and the order came to get on the road. Minor was hardly sorry to leave Kansas City. Arriving by steamer a couple days earlier, he'd decided the place was even uglier since last seen. The buildings, like the Gillis House down by the wharf, had grown even shabbier. The streets, cut through daunting bluffs to reach homes and stores perched above, were so steep and muddy that doubling up the teams was needed to pull the guns to the high ground. The town would never amount to much.

The column now was heading south, with the buildings thinning out. Some pasture to the west, hardly any trees around. In a few minutes, the road was taking them past farms. A few lights could be seen in the windows of some of the houses and cabins. Dogs barked warnings from under porches. Oxen, curled on their hooves, just chewed and contemplated the passing column, content perhaps that it was not them yoked to the heavy guns. Here and there, fires made of fence rails flared as men poured off excess bacon grease from skillets. We eat so much bacon in the army, Minor thought, it's amazing we don't oink.

A caisson wheel hit something hard, knocking a dozing gunner to the ground behind. He quickly rolled out of the way of the next team of snorting horses. The rest of his crew jeered as he ran cursing to catch up and climb back on.

"Harris House, it a mighty fine place," he heard Albert Jackson tell a comrade about the establishment up ahead in Westport. "My old mastah, he go there for the drink with the gentlemans." The 18-year-old had escaped a year or two ago. When he had made his mark on the enlistment papers, Jackson had said his occupation was "gentleman." Nothing wrong with that. Gentlemen, even those paid only $16 a month, were always in short supply. Minor's father had been one. Brave enough to marry his mother, not just keep her as a back-cabin concubine.

Minor watched the captain from Wisconsin ride back down the line. James Dodge seemed a pretty good sort. The fact that Minor was a Negro hadn't seemed to interest him a whit, which was better than could be said about a lot of folks in Mr. Lincoln's army, especially in what had been the First Kansas Colored Volunteers. The former slaves and freedmen filled the quota by August 1862 and were fighting and dying within two months, long before black units were organized in the East. At the Island Mound fight in Bates County, Lieutenant Minor had charged out of "Fort Africa" with his company, forcing a larger number of rebels to withdraw. "The black devils fought like tigers," one of the southern leaders said, "… not one would surrender."

Officially, the infantry regiment did not join the Union ranks until January 13, 1863, after the effective date of Lincoln's Emancipation Proclamation. That was when white officers were brought in. Minor and William Matthews, who had done much of the recruiting for the regiment, had resigned their commissions, incensed that they would no longer command their men. Captain Hinton, a friend of Matthews, had written to Senator Lane about the injustice: "The whole thing amounts simply to the idea, that 'niggers' (should) not be mustered as officers and not as to any question of competency." But now Minor and Matthews wore shoulder straps again as artillery officers. Matthews was still down at Fort Scott. He'd be sorry he was missing this fight. Minor smiled in the dark. For now, these were *his* guns and *his* men. What had Douglass said? Once the black man gets an eagle on his button and a rifle on his shoulder, nothing can stop him? Well, we have cannon, so that goes double for us. Captain Dodge had trotted up beside him.

"The rebs are still south of Westport and our people are around the town," he said. "Blunt's down there with Jennison's and Moonlight's brigades, waiting for us. Ford, too."

The night sky paled off to the left. Ahead, Minor began to pick up the patter of gunfire, which sputtered out after a few minutes, then picked up again. Somebody's getting busy up there.

The crews were listening, as well. They were only too aware that more was at stake for them in this fight than for the white men riding along with them. Poison Springs had proven that, yessir. It had happened about eight months ago, in mid-April, down in Arkansas. Minor's former regiment, now called the 79th U. S. Colored, had been sent to seize some wagonloads of corn. On the way back to Camden, they'd been hit hard by a force led by General Marmaduke. His old comrades had fought gallantly enough until the cartridges ran low and then they took off.

"Away trotted the poor black men into the forest clinging to their rifles, but not using them, while the pursuing Confederates cut them down right and left," recalled a Confederate colonel. The captured wounded were asked, "Where is the First Nigger now?" After the bullet was delivered to the brain, the rebels then jeered: "All cut to pieces and gone to hell by bad management." The bodies were found stripped and mutilated.

Disdain for black soldiers also was found in the Union army. A Rhode Island private thought that when it came to putting "whites and blacks on the same footing, I come to the conclusion it is about time to quit soldiering. I want to see the war come to a close, this rebellion crushed, and the Stars and Stripes waving over a united country once more, and I am willing to fight for it, but I am not willing to fight shoulder to shoulder with a black." After a sharp fight near Carthage, Missouri, among the 30 Union dead were First Kansas Colored. The Federals who came in later did not bother to bury some of the African-Americans, but simply tossed their bodies into a blazing house.

But none were as cruel as the bushwhackers. Take the *Sam Gaty*, forced by Gregg's band to land at Sibley last March. Contraband blacks were said to be aboard the Kansas-bound steamer, which was true, but only about 60. Boat Captain John McCloy inquired of the plans for them, and upon learning that it was "to blow their brains out," he held out stubbornly in favor of mercy. The bushwhackers compromised, agreeing to kill only the "bucks."

About 20 terrified Negroes were marched down the gangplank, the Leaven-worth *Times* chronicled, and "when the guerrillas drew their revolvers on the Negroes as they stood in line, the women on the boat screamed and cried, and begged them not to kill them; but the work of death went on."

How many had their brains splattered when the lantern's light swung their way, 10, a dozen? Thank God, the rest managed to break away and escape into the timber.

Minor had heard that bushwhackers had joined this fight. They might be down south there, near Westport, where the gunfire was picking up again.

In his days working on the riverboats, Minor had seen men place all they had on the green felt of the gaming tables. The stakes his cannoneers would be playing for today made those games look cheap, very cheap.

XIV

The battle joined

"Never was a more criminally foolish order given,
nor was one more gallantly and recklessly obeyed."

— Colonel John C. Wright, Arkansas Cavalry

ℯↄℯↄℯↄℯↄℯↄℯↄ

South of Westport
Jackson County

"ARE THE MEN READY, GENERAL?"

"Yes, sir, your Iron Brigade is chomping at the bit. The horses, too."

The smile inside the beard was thinner than Jeff Thompson's little joke. General Jo Shelby's arm, wounded in an earlier campaign, was hurting him in the chill.

"The 23rd of October dawned upon us clear, cold and full of promise," Major Edwards would write in his commander's report. Actually, it dawned with a fulsome chorus of coughing and expelling phlegm. The troopers had spooned under their thin blankets, like old married couples squeezed together for warmth on a night when puddles froze around them. When they made their pre-dawn fires in their camps not far from the Big Blue River, it was to try to heat hands, feet and rumps only, because no food was to be had.

In Sedalia, someone had given Thompson a neck shawl, and now he tucked the corners of it into his collar, rubbed his hands and dredged up memories of the Louisiana swamps. Anything for warmth, real or imagined.

Shelby had assigned General Thompson and his old brigade the center of the line, along the road that led south from Westport to Fort Scott, placing parts of Sidney Jackman's bunch mostly on the left of him. He could see Jackman peering west over the ground-hugging fog that submerged a rolling, but otherwise largely featureless prairie.

Fagan was to be the hinge. Some of his people were to guard Thompson's right flank, some to keep contact with Marmaduke's left. And two of his brigades, Slemon's and Dobbin's, would be in reserve behind Shelby's line.

"Sir, I hope you will do me the honor of buying you a toddy in Westport, say, in about an hour."

This time, Shelby responded to Thompson with a real grin. "Well, it's a mite early…" He made a show of checking his watch, "… but say, in one hour." He waved a lazy salute and then rode his sorrel back to confer with Price, who emerged looking a bit shabby from the farmhouse that was his headquarters.

Thompson and his officers kept an eye on the commanders. A black man rode up to Shelby, wearily shaking his head. It was Shelby's servant, Billy Hunter. Thompson knew that he'd been out all night looking for some trace of the general's nephew Tecumseh. After exchanging a few words with Price, Shelby looked Thompson's way and waved his gloved hand, and the long ranks of horses stepped out toward the Fort Scott Road.

When the bugle calls ended, Thompson picked up the thrill of meadowlarks snug in the frosty grass beside the road. A red-winged blackbird flitted along the strings of horsemen, for all the world looking as if it was trying to find its place in the line. Better fall in, Sergeant Bird, Thompson thought, smiling. We're going to need everybody for this one.

Everyone on this line knew what he had to do. Just north of them was Westport and beyond that Kansas City, both towns filthy with Federals. Price had made it clear: The Iron Brigade, with Jackman's, had to smash them, drive them from the field. Then they could dispose of the Yankees over in Independence. And all this to keep the wagon train safe. Price is determined to get all those wagons home.

Thompson was aware that many of his officers had the uneasy sense of betting high with low cards, but he figured it could be done. Shelby did.

Hell, it had to be done.

It was pretty clear that the southerners could not let the Federals link up. On the Sedalia raid, Thompson had gotten a good sense of the size of Pleasonton's force and was glad enough that it was Marmaduke who had drawn the job of holding the Big Blue this morning. The ease with which Jackman's people punched through the Yankees at Byram's Ford on Saturday showed it was no easy task to defend. And reorganized, those Federals had proved they could hold the Kansas line better than any Missouri river. The brigades of Moonlight and Jennison had fallen back, then pitched into the advancing rebel horsemen. Thompson had been called away before reaching Westport that day, but hadn't found the tussle until it was over. Night had fallen and neither side particularly wanted to fight anymore. Both sides had retired, looking over their shoulders.

Now, Thompson wondered, have those stubborn Kansas troopers been reinforced? There was talk of many militia regiments holed up in Kansas City. Would they stay there this morning? The Yankee cavalry was in a vigorous mood. Sun was hardly up before they'd crossed the creek and begun driving in the pickets.

He rode along his advancing column, nodding to Gordon, Smith and the rest of the Confederate officers. He was trying not to shiver. He was still in his threadbare black suit and broad-brimmed planter's hat from Charleston. No chance to get a decent uniform since his release. When he reached Slayback, who'd done some lawyering in St. Joe when Thompson was mayor, he called:

"Brisk this morning, Alonzo,"

"It's about to get warm, I reckon."

"Hmm," Thompson acknowledged. "Ah, there they are."

A sharp stab of flame, then another punctured the mists ahead. Yankee battery on the road.

Fagan's people were supposed to be farther to the east, but Thompson couldn't spot anything of them. That way the ground sloped away into mist and a heavy stand of timber. Wasn't sure what he could expect from them, anyway; they hadn't done well yesterday. He was peering east when ….

My God, like a guillotine! A cannon ball had taken off the head of one of Slayback's men. The body hung for a long second then collapsed to the frozen mud like an overcoat dropped to a floor. The troopers around him murmured, but did not falter. Where was Shelby's artillery? He scanned behind him. Ah, there was Dick Collins, his crews shouting for the cavalrymen to get off the road, to let them through. Another shell went sizzling overhead.

Thompson gave orders for the regiments to begin spreading out from the road. Fences, some split-rail, many of stones, chopped the prairie into domestic patches. Hard to work cavalry out there. Now came a blast from close by, Captain Collins' Parrotts announcing their day had begun. For a while, Shelby let the guns talk, and then called for the advance to resume.

"Let us commence," Thompson called down his line.

Through the thinning mist, a fairly heavy rank of Yankees appeared beyond a little swale ahead. Now both sides could see the other. A moment's hesitation, and enemy officers screamed orders to dismount. Their men knelt, melting into the low haze. Thompson and Jackman quickly called for their brigades to get down as well.

"Horses to the rear. Wait for the volley and then charge," Thompson called over his shoulder. "Drive them and drive them hard. Send them back to Kansas or hell, it's all the same to me!"

The gloom erupted with spurts of flame, marrying the gray mist with a wave of blue smoke. How fitting, thought the poet's part of his brain, and then his men were returning the volley and screaming the old yell as they began to run ahead.

The Confederate charge was having the right effect, Thompson believed. Some Yankees were taking second and third shots, but others were rapidly legging it back though a harvested corn field. Then, through the smoke, he could see that it wasn't any rout, but a disciplined move back to some rock fences. Another volley. The Federal battery on the lane looked to be six guns. Collins had four, so it was a fair fight. More smoke rolled from the gray stones. We'll have to pry them out, Thompson thought.

Then he felt his men wavering. Most were looking for cover instead of pushing ahead. Actually, some were already falling back. Thompson shouted encouragement, went out front to where he wanted his men to form a line. He wasn't getting many takers.

Slayback yelled to his captains. Thompson realized a young lieutenant was at his side. "Sir, the general wishes me to inform you that Colonel McGehee will make a charge on the guns in the road. He asks that your brigade provide support. Oh, and that he wishes you to know that he has taken on a terrible thirst."

Thompson barked a laugh. "My mouth's a bit dry, too, son. Please relay that, along with my apologies. We shall be there soon."

"Yes, sunnhh!" As he spoke, a scarlet patch appeared on the lieutenant's right thigh. He had caught a ball in the fleshy part. Probably the bone was spared. Thompson fished out his handkerchief to apply to the wound, soaking it crimson in a second.

"You'll be all right! Hold this tight." He looked up to see a couple of men moving low in their direction. Everyone wanted to help a downed officer back out of the fire and get to a safer place themselves for a while, Thompson knew. Just as well, he guessed, could be him next.

At that moment, he saw McGehee's Arkansas men galloping north up the road in columns of four. Thompson yelled for his dismounted men to push forward as they thundered by

Glorious, he thought, just glorious. He might have to write a poem about that charge.

8 A.M.

Byram's Ford, Big Blue River
Jackson County

BETWEEN WRACKING COUGHS THAT LEFT HIS lungs aching, Colonel John Finis Philips tugged off a boot and grabbed its mate. About to stand in the cold mud, it occurred to him that his only pair of dry socks was on his feet. Lady friend in Lexington, bless her, had made a gift of them — first item of clean clothes he'd had on his skin in weeks — as his regiment had gone through. He slipped off the socks, too, then hopped barefooted to his horse, and dug an old pair of damp shoes out of his kit.

Grimacing at the chill seeping into his toes, he returned to his log to be shod once more. If — no — when he got to the other side of the river he didn't want to be running around in sopping cavalry boots.

Lieutenant Colonel Thomas Crittenden stared ruefully ahead, blowing pipe smoke through his nose. Nobody was looking forward to what was coming. The Seventh was supposed to wade Byram's Ford afoot. Philips and Crittenden had taken a careful look across the sluggish little river just minutes ago. Much of the west bank was a tangle of felled trees, their branches tugged by a mostly indifferent current, although the ford itself had been cleared by reb axmen the day before to let their wagons and artillery across.

On the flats behind the downed timber was a fair helping of rebs poking rifles through the leaves, and behind them some rock faces and then high ground with enemy positions that promised trouble to anyone showing their noses at the crossing. Crittenden bet $5 that a battery was among the trees up there covering the road. Philips hadn't seen anything, but he didn't take the bet.

Philips assumed that it was Marmaduke's division over there. Those were the same people with whom his Missouri State Militia regiment had dueled the night before. His diary noted "terribly fierce" fighting on foot on the western edges of Independence. Colonel James McFerran found his First Missouri too far in front without adequate support. They were handled quite roughly before General Egbert Brown figured it out and sent up Philips along with the rest of First Brigade to even things a bit.

Before the long day ended, Colonel Edward Winslow's Fourth Brigade had moved up to take over the battering of the rebs. From the sounds of brief fighting before light this morning, some graybacks had lingered briefly on this side of the river to take some pot shots at Winslow's column.

Philips ran fingers through the greasy black curls of his long beard. He was sure he was running a high fever. Still 29 years old, he felt all of 59. Everything ached. It had been a rough night, men sleeping in the frozen ruts of the Independence-Westport Road, wrapping the reins of the horses around their wrists, no rations, nothing for the mounts. He blew into his hands before trying to tie the shoe laces. Crittenden came over, now fiddling with a pair of extra, loaded chambers for his revolver, obviously thinking about how to keep them dry.

"Oh Lord, lay me down, but it's cold. And that river's going to be colder," he predicted. "Don't get me wrong, I'm in no particular hurry to swim through that ice, and apparently old Brown isn't, neither, but weren't we supposed to be over there by now? The firing to the west of us has been going on a good hour. By the way, have I mentioned that you look like death?"

"Only enough times that I believe you, for once."

The attack at the ford was supposed to start at misty daybreak. Egbert Brown's brigade, made up of the Seventh, First and Fourth Missouri State Militia regiments, was supposed to lead it. Philips kept his voice low because their commander was riding back their way, probably to get the action finally underway.

"You were on that lane same as I was. If the ammo train had come up when it should have and had Winslow got his broad ass moved off, we'd been here before."

Philips noticed a commotion farther back on the road, troopers trying to make room for galloping horses. Several officers… Ah, that was Pleasonton's pennant. The big man himself here to see us off. Brown's few staff turned their mounts and saluted. Brown didn't, of course; his free arm hung uselessly. Nodding his respect, he began to address a clearly furious commander. Philips was standing at attention, one unlaced shoe on, the other foot still bare. And then Pleasonton began a rant at Brown unlike anything Philips had ever heard from an officer.

"Why isn't this brigade on the other side by now? My orders could not have been more clear! Attack at daybreak! Is daybreak somehow different for Missourians?"

"Yes, sir, no, sir," Brown tried to explain. "Sir, it's a damned tight road, and Colonel Winslow there hadn't pulled back far enough in the brush to let us through easily, badly broken ground and I'm …"

Pleasonton was having none of it. "If you can't push First Brigade through another Union column, you obviously can't handle the rebs on the other side!" he snapped. "I don't need any more ambulance soldiers in this command!"

The helpless Brown looked as if he'd been slapped, but Pleasonton wasn't through.

"I've already placed Colonel McFerran under arrest," he said. "You're relieved, as well. Go to the rear and consider yourself under arrest."

In his report, Pleasonton declared that Brown's First brigade was "so disordered as to be in no condition for fighting, and General Brown himself had made no preparations to carry out my order." He added that McFerran's "regiment was straggling all over the country."

"Winslow," he barked at his Fourth Brigade commander, "if you don't get this mess straightened out, you'll be joining him!"

Grim as the Sphinx, the Iowa colonel saluted again.

Pleasonton recently had been in charge of the Army of the Potomac's cavalry, just as it finally matured into a force that could rock J. E. B. Stuart's southern cavaliers at Brandy Station in June 1863. He deserved some credit for that, but always wanted more. Newspapers back east called him the "Knight of Romance" for his breathless reports and exaggerated claims. During and after the war, the major general was accused of hogging or falsely claiming credit for many Union successes.

Considered a martinet by many of his fellow West Pointers, Major General Alfred Pleasonton often carried a rawhide whip instead of a saber to shake in a subordinate's face. Hardly surprising, then, that he was disliked by most everyone who came in contact with him, the exceptions including his favorites, one of whom was Brigadier General George A. Custer.

Pleasonton's piecemealing of his forces during Gettysburg and Lee's retreat immediately after exposed his flaws, and Ulysses S. Grant, when he came east to take command of all the armies, replaced him with Philip Sheridan.

Philips glanced at Crittenden, saw shock. Brown was no Mercury on the march, perhaps, but the general was a good man, wasn't afraid of a fight. He had saved Springfield in '62, got wounded there, too. And he had just kept Price out of Jefferson City, for God's sake. Now you arrest him, simply on the grounds he hadn't got off the jump quick enough?

But the surprises on the road were not over.

"You, Colonel! Philips, isn't it?"

"Yes, s…"

"You have command of First Brigade. Take it and go down there, and put those people out! I've had enough of this timidity from the damned militia!"

"Yes, sir!" Philips hesitated, but decided to risk it and sit again, quickly putting his shoe on the painfully frozen foot. He was not leading any damned charge with one bare foot, even if he was nothing but damned militia.

Pleasonton decided to accept this and used the lost moments to fill in his new brigade commander. A Fourth Iowa captain, Dee, was just a ways downstream in a gully preparing to rush a battalion across the river. This was to be simultaneous with the Seventh Regiment's attack at the ford. The First and Fourth Missouri Regiments would follow Crittenden over.

The assault would be supported by Captain Charles Thurber's four, 3-inch ordnance guns of the Second Missouri Light Artillery. Philips had a lot of regard for Captain Charlie Thurber, with whom he'd spent time at Brown's Sedalia headquarters. A lieutenant in Grant's army, Charlie first took command of the First Missouri battery in Tennessee after his commander took a ball in the chest. He had been at Shiloh on the second day when General Lew Wallace remarked that to Thurber, "the sound of rebel cannon seemed a challenge no sooner heard than accepted."

Laces tied, Philips began to stand, then burst into a spasm of coughing. Getting his breath, he wiped his mouth and assumed an expression that said he saw generals arrested every day. After saluting Pleasonton, he faced Crittenden. "You understand the orders, Colonel. Get the regiment formed for the attack."

Crittenden snapped perhaps the sharpest salute of his life, turned and started rattling orders to the various company officers. Philips strode to the First Missouri, where some officers still looked in shock. But not Lieutenant Colonel Bazel Lazear, the tough-minded and by some accounts ruthless officer who would take over the regiment. It was hard to faze him. No, Lazear was enjoying Brown's unhappiness.

Brown had twice called Lazear to Jefferson City — everyone assumed he would be court-martialed — for overzealous behavior by some companies of the First. A month earlier Lazear had written his wife saying he had not been placed under arrest yet, despite an angry argument with Brown, who he believed had bungled a trap set for Shelby the previous fall. After the Westport battle, he again wrote his wife how both of his commanders had been arrested for "cowardice," and then added smugly: "The devils got their due at last."

A good trade for McFerran, Philips was thinking. He and Lazear had taken turns at the front in chasing the elusive Shelby last year. Yes, Lazear had all the grit that could be asked for in a fight. And Philips believed they were about to have a dandy.

8:25 A.M.

South of Westport

WHAT WAS DOC JENNISON SHOUTING?

The reb guns ahead, three Parrotts, were making a racket. Some Federal rifled guns, unlimbered in the lane, were barking back. Neither battery had a shortage of targets up on this prairie. Johnson's horse shied as a ball rolled by. No shortage at all.

Captain Curtis Johnson looked to where the jayhawker chief was pointing and saw the threat through a gap in the smoke. Massed rebel cavalry coming straight up the road at the Union gunners. Twisting in the saddle, he screamed. "Company E! Hit them!"

He buried his spurs and his prized chestnut leapt at the still unfamiliar and ungentle touch. The sound of hooves signaled that more of the 15th Kansas were just behind. Johnson glanced to his left, saw Captain Green's Colorado bunch coming, too. The Federals cut across fields to catch the enemy's column in the flank; the distance between the two masses evaporated in seconds.

The threatened battery roared, collapsing enemy horses 200 yards ahead, flinging off their riders. The rebs faltered, then saw the threat on their flank. The battery crews took advantage of the rebels' hesitation, whipping the limber teams to drag their guns out of harm's way.

Their mounts trampling comrades on the road, the rebs now tracked the oncoming Kansans with their rifle barrels. Johnson saw the mouth of an enemy officer form the word, and the lane filled with smoke. Beside Johnson, a horse collapsed, blowing blood. Just behind, another tried, off-footed, to jump the stricken horse, but went down with a whump and pinned a gasping private beneath. Now the Kansans were at the wall, firing at almost point blank. A gray forage cap went flying in a shower of blood. From 20 feet away, Johnson fired at a grizzled face with a chaw-stained beard, but it was a miss. From 10 feet, he fired again. Damn, another miss! Jesus, Johnson thought, couldn't hit the side of a smokehouse if I were shooting from the inside!

Pistol smoke swept back in his face. Don't empty it, he thought. You can't reach anyone over that wall with a saber. Then he saw that some rebs were on his side of the stone fence, had found a gate or cleared it with their horses. A sergeant aiming his Sharps into the road was rifle-clubbed from his roan by a coatless fellow in red-checkered shirt. Johnson leveled his weapon, but was too slow; crimson already darkened the enemy's faded shirt, and then it was under the hooves.

The fighting was boot to boot up and down "Bloody Lane," the Fort Scott road south of Brush Creek. Among the Colorado men, one Private Iker emptied his carbine and then used it to club a southerner to death. Then he fell from a fatal wound. Another private, James Ross, was taking three prisoners back to the lines when one wheeled his horse to escape. Before he could shoot, Ross was jolted by a musket ball from somewhere. He escorted the other two rebels back, however, dying the next day.

Now, the enemy column wavered, its men trying to shoot over their shoulders as horses skittered and reared. An officer appeared to be rallying them. Johnson applied the spurs again, headed for the reb, who sensed the threat immediately. A savage jerk of the bit, and the officer faced Johnson with his mount and pointed a large pistol. Amid the mayhem around them, the duel over the fence became very personal.

Charging along his side of the stacked limestone, the foe fired from 40 yards. Johnson was nearly hurled from his horse by the blow to his left arm. That hand dropped, the other convulsively fired off a worthless shot. At 30 yards, the baby-faced southerner looked hard at him, determined there was more to this fight, and steadied his piece for the killing shot. No, surprise showing in widened eyes; he'd either hung fire or was empty.

Johnson was now close enough to notice a missing button on the stained grey coat. The chestnut had never faltered. Raising his Colt, thumbing the hammer back, Johnson suddenly thought: How many rounds do *I* have left? The trigger seemed unnaturally stiff, then he felt the recoil. A puff of dust jumped not far from the unemployed buttonhole, and the young man stiffened, then sagged. Two heartbeats later their horses had passed, for all the world like knights in a joust.

Reins still loose, Johnson swayed in his saddle, couldn't lift his left arm and stop his horse. The Arkansas men were running away now, some of the Colorado boys pursuing down the lane after them. Not many. It had been a vicious tussle. Nobody was much in the mood for more. A last flurry of shots over on his left. The Union battery was blasting away, just as belligerently as before.

Johnson got his revolver jammed into his belt, groped for the reins with his right hand.

Jennison rode up from that side, all grin.

"Well done, Captain! You played that hand mighty fine, mighty fine!" He clapped a hand on Johnson's shoulder, almost dislodging him from the saddle. The congratulatory hand now gripped the shoulder in concern.

"Johnson, you're hit!"

8:45 A.M.

WITH THE CALL OF THE BUGLE, Slayback's Missourians were on their feet racing toward the thick woods on the right of the lane.

Over on the other side, some men were falling back. Where was their commander? Then General Jeff Thompson saw Moses Smith rising from the ground, shouting at them. The colonel's horse had been shot out from under him. Thompson had seen it before. A commander goes down, the spirit leaves the men like smoke. Over there, Frank Gordon was trying to steady his Fifth Missouri, pinned down under a galling fire coming from another of those damn fences to the left of the lane. That stone row had to be cleared! Who's going to do it? Jackman looked to have his hands full over on the far left.

Thompson ran to Slayback, minié balls making the corn stalks rustle around him.

"We're going to take that wall!" he yelled, as the opposing batteries crashed as one. He sensed something ominous pass over his hat. The guillotine. "Get Johnson's companies, too. Let's see what those recruits are good for!"

The struggle was bitter, but they rooted the Yankees out — "inch by inch and foot by foot," as Shelby would report — from behind the fences and pushed them back to the thick belt of trees, where the Federals were still laying a fairly heavy fire. Slayback took advantage of the confusion to send some companies farther to the right, into the woods on the east side of the road. The Federal battery was limbering up, its position suddenly threatened. Slayback had turned their flank. Bravo! Now, some of Thompson's men were penetrating the trees ahead, their figures wraith-like in the smoke. A horse trotted near, dragging a badly wounded Yankee with a foot in the stirrup. Thompson motioned for a man to grab the horse's reins and disentangle the moaning man. By the shouts, the brigade already was well down the slope in the pursuit when Shelby rode up.

"Hold 'em here, Jeff. You must be low on cartridges after a fight like this. We need to bring up some wagons before you push into town."

Thompson did not think this was a good idea.

"General, we've got them running now. I hate to let a Yankee stop and catch his breath. Look, Jackman's out of sight already, chasing a bunch. To the east there, in that timber, Elliot's doing the Lord's work. And then there's your toddy."

Shelby shook his head. "It will have to wait just a bit longer. We've broken the Yankees, Jeff. Once you fill your cartridge boxes, you will break them again."

Thompson believed Jo Shelby had never given a single poor order in this whole march. But this felt wrong. Shelby had been the one advocating this attack the night before, saying the Kansans needed to be whipped good. After Shelby trotted away, Thompson called over some of his officers and told them to bring the men back and rest. They were exasperated by the news, Slayback especially.

"The ammunition wagons must be miles away," he said. "Let's rest in Westport and use Yankee cartridges."

Thompson just shook his head and sat down on the stone wall, making sure to miss some puddled blood. A fallen tree created a gap through which he could see some of the high ground sloping from Brush Creek up to Westport. The firing had died almost completely away. The enemy batteries probably were setting up new positions. He could hear shouting over there, Yankee voices. No making out what was being said, but he detected no panic. Surely these were Blunt's devils, not home guard. Didn't drive worth a damn.

One of Thompson's men came out of the woods, waving a carbine he'd found or captured. Looks like a Sharps, he thought, good, we can use those, not like the Spencers or Henrys. They were amazing weapons, but the shells were all new-fangled metal. The South couldn't make that kind of ammunition yet, and it was hard to capture enough to be practical.

He realized some people were on top of buildings to the north in Westport, some Union signal corps, waving flags. He noted it to Slayback.

"That's the Harris House," the lieutenant colonel said. "If it helps, it's just across the street from where old Boone had his place before he lit out for Colorado."

"It would help if we were up there right now. How're casualties in your battalion?"

"Not so bad," Slayback shrugged.

Some men were filtering back up from the creek and settling on the south side of the fences, gulping from canteens. Jackman rode up. "Why are we holding up here? I could have been at the mission by now."

"I know, colonel, I'm not overjoyed, either. Shelby's worried about our ammunition. He's back with Price if you want to talk to him. Pretty hot on your end?"

"Seen worse." Jackman pointed back west from where he had come. "Occurs to me that there's a lot of Kansas over that way. I've put part of a company in those farm buildings, anchor the end of our line."

"Bent's place," offered Slayback.

"Bent? The old boy who blew up his own fort out in south Colorado?"

"Same one. Ornery as they come. My pa and me came by here once when he was home, and you know, he took a squaw, and she wouldn't live in the house like a white woman. Stayed out in the yard in a tipi."

Slayback knew this area. His wife was the daughter of William Waddell, a partner in the Russell, Majors and Waddell Freighting Company. Thompson was very familiar with those men, having made speeches — as St. Joseph mayor — with them on the day the first skinny Pony Express rider galloped away to the west with the mail.

They heard a rumble well away to their right and somewhat to their rear.

"That would be Marmaduke getting busy," said Jackman. As Thompson understood it, the Confederate lines now resembled a miles-long "7," with Shelby's brigades running less than a mile across the top, Fagan at the turn, and Marmaduke's division making up much of the stalk. Hold 'em, my friend, he thought.

As Jackman offered good luck and rode back west, Union batteries across the creek began firing, a booming concert. Blunt's people pretty much were just shooting at trees from what Thompson could tell, but he warned his men to stay low. Now and then a shell tore through the limbs, sending splinters into the fields. No axes needed for this winter's wood ricks, just come up the hill here and pick it up.

"Here comes Captain Dick," Slayback observed.

Collins's battery had moved up the lane for a talk back with Billy Yank. Postlewait, the tame black bear that the battery kept as a mascot, was nowhere in sight, probably back in an ammunition wagon somewhere. Thompson watched as the gunners sighted the Parrotts, wondered whether they actually had a target or were guessing where to put their rounds. A crew stepped back and the lanyard …. Lord, what happened! Had they been hit just as they fired? The smoke blew away, and Thompson divined the answer. A gun had burst. He could see that Collins seemed to be all right, but at least two men were on the ground. The iron Parrotts had a bad habit for that, especially if the tube cooled between bouts of firing.

An officer came riding up from the east, his face a storm. He didn't get off his horse, or salute.

"Murdered, sir. They've been murdered!"

"Who's been murdered?" Thompson stood.

"Those that made the charge."

"McGehee's boys, you mean? Murdered, are you sure? They got cut up bad in the fight."

"Sure enough, road's corduroyed with 'em, but this pile is head shot, most of 'em."

There will be hell to pay for this. Thompson thought, hell to pay.

9 A.M.

CAPTAIN HENRY PALMER AGAIN PICTURED BEING made a prisoner, and making the long walk to Texas, in his stockings.

After joining the dawn attack south of Westport, his Union regiment was being forced back north toward the Shawnee Mission. He called for his A Company to form another line.

He snapped off a shot at a group of Johnnies who seemed to be thinking of charging his way. It had no noticeable effect. His whole company appeared to be having no effect. He still had Edwards' carbine and a borrowed cartridge box, from which he dug out another paper-wrapped load. He looked for a close target. No shortage; the butternut-clad men flowed around Bent's farmhouse like water around a pink boulder.

Blunt's attack had started well. Moonlight's 11th had gotten well south of the Bent spread, but as more southerners appeared on the field, fortunes changed. The Federal line had to abandon its stone fences and take cover in the deep timber south of Brush Creek. Now the rebels were in the trees, too. In the center of the line, Jennison's 15th fell back too quickly and left Moonlight's flank exposed.

Major Ross was screaming, pointing toward their left. My God, the brush was full of Johnnies, where did *they* come from? Palmer's A Company along with I Company were ordered to wheel left. Somehow two of the regiment's howitzers made it through the tangle of brush and men and began spraying grape into the trees to the east. One of his troopers, Leander Hull, dropped his Gallagher carbine, his right arm hanging uselessly. Palmer jumped down from his horse, grabbed the weapon from the weeds and remounted. He placed it across the saddle in front of the 18-year-old. "Go to the rear," he shouted.

Now, Palmer worried that the 11th would be cut off from its division, pushed away from Bettie back in Westport. Her father had refused to leave, insisted that some thin blood link to Robert E. Lee would save the family, as if Jackman or some of those other rebel murderers would give a damn. Stubborn old man, too tough for his own good.

A horse went down, one of his best scouts senselessly cursing the unfortunate animal.

Palmer encouraged his men to shift down the slope to the creek. He tried to keep the largest sycamore trees between him and the reb rifles. Where did it end? Was that Leander over there, trying to use his carbine and hold the reins at the same time? As Palmer watched, the weapon tumbled to the ground once more. Damned fool. Brave fool. Once more he jumped down to retrieve the blood-smeared weapon, ramming it this time behind the boy, between the blanket and saddle. Then he turned the horse toward the creek and slapped its rump. "Now get to the rear, Hull, and see to those arms," Palmer shouted.

Remounted again, Palmer found himself next to a man with whom he had a bone to pick. On Friday, the fellow had raced back to Westport to tell Bettie that Palmer was slain at the Little Blue. Palmer was still furious at the coward for terrifying her; she could have lost the baby. The imbecile had been dodging him ever since. Now they were side by side for a moment, their horses forced together by thick stands of creek-bottom saplings.

"Captain," the man shouted. "I'm awful sorr…." Crimson spurted from his jacket, and he tumbled off his horse.

Palmer despaired. Surely he'd worn out his luck at the Little Blue. Seized by a panic of leaving a widow and orphan, his best hope seemed a non-fatal wound; let them have an arm. He was right-handed; his left was the obvious answer. A ball snipped a cottonwood branch beside him. He saw a flash of blue overcoat, now hidden but still heard crashing through the brush. One of ours? He thought not. Squeezing off a one-handed shot toward where the reb might be, Palmer then switched the carbine to his left hand, which he held high.

He lowered the arm again. As a sacrifice to the gods of war, it seemed a cheap gesture. And perhaps more cowardly than the trooper lying back there in the brown leaves.

Across the creek now, Palmer dismounted his scouts, organized a fresh line. Reloading again, his shaking fingers made a fast exploration of his cartridge box; eight rounds remained. But his ears were at work, too. The sputter of long arms was lessening. Were the men out of ammunition? The old Shawnee Mission was not far behind them. Perhaps they could use its buildings as a fort. Yes, shooting definitely was slackening. On both sides, thank the Lord.

"The rebs are pulling back," one trooper shouted.

Palmer sensed a weight lifted from his shoulders. He wasn't hit yet, might still see Bettie again.

And damned if the Leander kid wasn't still on the line.

10:20 A.M.

Byram's Ford, Big Blue River

PLEASONTON WAS TRYING TO GET HIM killed!

Lieutenant Combs had taken one in the guts. Another lieutenant, Dale, had been screaming at the men to take the ridge when a minié snapped his head back. Christian, Vansickle, Hamilton, Barclay, all down. And Blair — Christ, Blair! — was gone, his brains splattered.

"I came upon the body of Captain Blair, the top of his head blown off by a cannonball," Colonel John Finis Philips would write afterward. "I stooped over him and took from his breast pocket a photograph of Miss Eliz. Wilson, of Marshall, Missouri, to whom he was engaged...." The mustachioed Fourth Missouri Cavalry officer was uncommonly handsome, resembling the actor John Wilkes Booth.

At least, Philips thought, Tom is still on his feet.

Now in charge of the Seventh Regiment, his friend Tom Crittenden had got the men across the Blue, amid the shelling and sniping. The abatis had not been the problem Philips had thought. Once abandoned by the rebs, the downed trees had been provided some cover from the Confederate cannon fire from the hill.

Coming down the road to the Big Blue River crossing, the Missourians had been completely exposed, pinned down on the east bank. Finally, a few hundred yards to the north of the ford, the battalion of Fourth Iowa under Captain Edward Dee had sneaked down a gully unobserved. The rebs were so busy riddling Philips' men that the flanking movement wasn't spotted until the Iowans were across and it was too late. The rebs fell back into the fields between the river and the higher ground to the west.

The Fourth Iowa soldiers later would give Philips' Missourians few laurels. "His regiments were dismounted and in line, half a mile in front of the guns and quite as far from the rebels lines, doing nothing," recalled Sergeant Major William Forse Scott. "Near the river, (they) stopped and threw themselves upon the ground. They had lost a few men, and found the rebel fire too severe. Winslow rode down the hill to the water, and again ordered them to charge across…."

Colonel Edward Winslow, the Fourth Brigade commander, also complained: "The enemy were at once driven back upon his main line, half a mile farther back. Almost three companies, being partially surrounded, would have been captured from the enemy but for the awkwardness or negligence on the part of some militia officers."

But rebel artillery was not zeroed in on Winslow as it was on Philips, as he exhorted his brigade to get across the stream. A shell hitting the water behind "exploded, blowing horse and man to bits," Philips recalled later. "The sight sickened me."

Waiting for them on the west bank were the Confederate skirmishers of Colonel Thomas Freeman's Brigade and Colonel John Burbridge's Fourth Missouri Cavalry, who fell back and escaped the pocket created by the curve of the river and the flanking Iowans. The main line of General Marmaduke's division, however, was high on the hill with its artillery. To reach it, the Federals had to cross the fields and scramble up a 15-foot wall of crumbling limestone. Viperish fire was coming from a pair of log cabins up there; more sharpshooters were spotted in the limbs of trees at the hill crest. Very determined people up there.

The most obvious way to attack was to charge up the road that climbed the little bluff, but that led right into a thousand gun barrels. Twice Philips had sent Lieutenant Colonel Bazel Lazear and the First Regiment up the road in mounted charges, both mistakes. Even crossing the ford mounted — making bigger targets — had played hell on the Fourth Regiment.

As General John Clark would write in his report, the rebels contended manfully for the crossing, "but was forced back after having repulsed the enemy several times. (While they were) falling back through my brigade the enemy came upon me with the full enthusiasm of pursuit, and … my brigade contended nobly with the foe for two hours and strewed the open field with his dead…."

Winslow's report noted how he was directing the attack "when the whole line gave way under the fire of the enemy and retreated in disorder to the reserve where I succeeded in reforming the broken detachments. I again ordered an advance with the Third and Fourth Iowa Regiments closely supporting."

A ball clipped bark off the young hickory tree Philips was behind, stinging his face. He reached for a splinter, and realized his forehead was bleeding. He was expected to charge the hill again, but had little hope for a better result. It would not be on horse, he knew that for sure.

Crittenden was up ahead trying to work up closer to the hill. His troopers used tree stumps as cover, Philips would recall. "Behind one of them you could see as many as five or six men strung out on their hands and knees one behind the other in a straight line. They would rest there a minute and then break for another stump ahead." The regular cavalry regiments to his right, however, had almost no cover once they left the river.

Suddenly little Private Barnes, soaked to the neck from the wade, mud all over his face, appeared at the next tree.

"Where have you been? Where is your rifle?" called Philips, his throat ripped by the effort of shouting.

"I don't know. Guess I've lost another one." Barnes seemed a little dazed. "They going to dock me again."

"Well, there's one just over there. He won't be needing it."

Barnes started to walk toward the downed trooper, heedless of the lead tempest.

"Damn, Barnes! Hurry!"

Barnes seemed to come to a bit and scurried back with the rifle, an Austrian Lorenz muzzle-loader. Reaching into his cartridge box, he brought out clearly soaked loads. Another run to the body, much quicker this time. "These are good," he yelled to Philips.

"Then use them," his colonel replied.

Just across the road to his right was the Fourth Iowa, cranking their Spencers, those marvels of Yankee know-how. Beyond them were more of Winslow's people, the Third Iowa with their Gallaghers and Sharps, then the 10th Missouri, firing Halls. Many of Philips' regiment, originally designated mounted infantry, had to make do with the old Lorenz muzzle-loaders, although troopers often made private investments in something better. In their usual line of work, they fought with a brace of pistols, useless in a fight like this.

On the far right of the Federal line were more companies of the Fourth Iowa. Some of them were pushing hard, getting close to that little cliff. Time for his brigade to try again. Philips yelled to Lazear and Crittenden to get their people ready for another push. Was the rebel fire slacking? Hard to tell. The smoke at the hill seemed just as thick, maybe they're directing more fire at Winslow. Yes, time to get in on it.

This time they succeeded. "The enemy's lines were stubbornly held until the troops met, and the contest became hand to hand," according to one later account. "Across the field, for one hundred and sixty yards, our troops pushed steadily. They literally moved in a shower of lead."

Philips made a rasping yell to those who could hear him, motioned to Barnes, and they both broke from their trees and ran forward. The Iowans rose up almost as one, yelling the charge. Up ahead, others of Crittenden's Seventh Regiment were racing at the hill, stopping to aim their carbines at the moving forms in the smoke above.

"The colonel's down!" he heard. It's Tom!

"Keep going, Missouri! Keep going, First Brigade!" Philips yelled.

His men stumbled forward, firing, loading, running, firing again. Philips worried about his ammunition again. Some of the Iowans were at the base of the little cliff now. He looked north. Yes, the blue uniforms were almost home. Winslow's people were clawing up eroded spots in the limestone wall. "Col. Winslow was wounded badly in the leg," Fourth Iowa Sergeant Samuel O. Bereman would write, "but did not leave the field till the rebels were all driven off." Hit just as his men got up to the rebel-infested timber, Winslow considered commanding from an ambulance, but gave up and turned command of the Fourth Brigade over to Lieutenant Colonel Frederick Benteen, a hard-headed Missourian.

Now Philips' brigade swarmed over the crumbling rock as well. Ahead of them still was the brow of the hill and the main rebel line. Rebs fled from the cabins, behind which some of the Missourians huddled. Again, Philips had to exhort and curse and kick his men to continue the attack.

Men were swinging rifles, grappling. Only a sputtering fire was coming from the trees. Philips didn't hear the batteries now. Some of the Iowa men cheered, gathering around a captured flag.

In a matter of minutes, the Yankees owned the ridge.

Philips would describe it this way: "The timber was gained and the enemy driven in confusion, leaving his dead and wounded and a large number of prisoners in our hands, the large number of these showing the stubbornness with which the enemy resisted and the desperation with which our men fought."

The Confederates made a half-hearted attempt to form a second line on the next ridge, but melted away before the Federals could reorganize for a fresh attack.

As the Confederates' Clark explained: "… Our ammunition exhausted, we were forced to leave the field to the enemy, our dead in his hands…At this point I was directed by General Marmaduke to pass the train and protect its left flank."

Philips gave instructions to junior officers to pull the Missourians together and wait for ammunition. Then, nearly tripping on his scabbard, he ran back down the road to the field. Don't be shot in the bowels! Don't be like Combs, Philips prayed.

Barnes was turning Crittenden over when the colonel reached him. Philips knelt beside his friend. Where was the blood? He didn't see any blood. Crittenden moved a hand to his belly. He's alive, then. But gut shot?

Philips looked up, checking the aftermath of the fight. He should be up front, but just scattered shots came now. Nobody wanted more fight until the ammunition came up. Tom groaned, opened his eyes.

"Finny, is it bad?"

"Don't know, no blood that I see."

"It's my stomach."

Philips opened his friend's tunic, pulled out the tail of his grubby linen shirt and even worse undershirt, exposing pale skin. The belly had an ugly little bruise on one side. Philips went back to the tunic, held it up and saw the hole in the pocket. He stuck his hand in the pocket and brought out Crittenden's fat wallet.

The ball had struck a leather pocketbook filled with "shinplaster" money — low-denomination paper currency. He waved it in front of Crittenden, who was up on his elbows and looking at his midriff, confused. Barnes laughed.

"It never hurts to be rich!" Philips said. "Tom, the bullet didn't penetrate! You're going to be all right." Barnes helped the grimacing officer sit up. Philips forced him to a take a slug of his peach brandy, then passed the flask to the private. As he affectionately brushed clumps of mud from his friend's chin whiskers, he heard teamsters shouting, "Yah, mules, yah mules!" from the river.

"Help me up, private," Crittenden said. Barnes gave him a hand and then stooped and picked up the officer's revolver. He looked at the barrel to check for mud, saw none and handed it over. Crittenden detached the drop-in cylinder, put it in a pocket and dug out a fully loaded one.

The little river bottom was busy now, the artillery coming over at last, and the holders were trotting up with the regiments' horses. Men were coming back off the hill to check on comrades, bring them water.

Philips looked nervously west. "I must be moving, Tom. Are you going to be all right?"

"Yeah, let's get up there." Crittenden said. "Old Pleasonton is sure to have us arrested if we don't get kilt soon enough."

11:45 A.M.

South of Westport

"FOLLOW HIM," CURTIS YELLED. THE UNION general's gloved hand was pointing not at some brave color-bearer or officer with his hat on the tip of his sword, but at the back of a farmer hopping from rock to rock across Brush Creek.

The farmer grabbed some tree roots and pulled himself up the south bank. Curtis looked at the officers beside him. Major Henry Hopkins stared back. Captain G. L. Gove was coughing into his glove again. He should have been in bed somewhere but wouldn't leave the fight. Then the general shrugged. Dismounting, they plunged down the north bank, soaked their boots in the frigid water and made their way to the waiting farmer's side.

"Vee go dere," called the civilian, a German immigrant who farmed land southeast of Westport. He pointed at a place in the heavily wooded bluff where water flowed silently out of a tangle of logs and vines into the creek. It was obvious that erosion had widened a break in the rock face, leaving a ravine disguised by brush and flanked by tilting slabs of rock the size of pianos. Hopkins pulled his sword and began hacking at some gooseberry canes, sending the shriveled berries flying. The Ninth Wisconsin artillery captain, James Dodge, was there now. He scanned the damp vegetation and gray outcroppings of limestone doubtfully.

"Sir, you mean to get guns up that?"

Curtis looked back. The crews had found an eroded place in the stream bank and were urging the horses down into the gravel. The sweating Hopkins stepped back, to get his breath.

"Yes, damn it," Hopkins snapped. "Get at it, captain!"

"Sir, I don't know. We need more men, for sure."

"There's plenty of militia rifles around," Curtis said, "more on the way."

"Yessir, that's good, only I meant to get a Parrott up through this would be one hell of a haul. We'd have much better luck trying with Lieutenant Gill's howitzers."

"Well, get at it, then," Hopkins repeated. Henry was being aggressive, Curtis noticed. The seasoned Second Kansas veteran had shared in General Blunt's victories in Arkansas, but just a month ago had been badly shaken in the Cherokee Nation. It was his escort that had been whipped by General Stand Watie at Cabin Creek, who then got away with the huge Union wagon train.

Dodge turned to his officers. Gove assigned most of Curtis's escort, G Company of the 11th Cavalry, to help the battery crew. Then Hopkins and the farmer started picking their way up the gully. Curtis fell in behind and heard Gove bringing up the rear. Behind them a couple of artillery men with axes already were flattening thick saplings. Once above some particularly steep rocks at the gully's mouth, they climbed over a fallen tree. Hopkins slowed, peering ahead as the timber began to thin and weak sunlight filtered in. Closer to the field ahead and crouching now, the major pointed to the east. Curtis saw a brick house and watched as a reb, then two, moved from a back door to an outbuilding. One reb was in a tree in the orchard. Sniping? No, trying to find an apple that wasn't too wormy. Hopkins scuttled back to his chief.

"This seems to be the end of their line," he said. "Did you see the stone fence running east, a hundred yards from the house? A mile of rebs are behind it. If we can get our guns just a little ways past here without being spotted I think we can shoot down their line, enfilade em."

Curtis turned to the cavalrymen coming up and cautioned them against getting too close. He heard sounds below, men chopping at the toppled tree, others trying to coax a horse over an obstacle. It all seemed very loud. Hopkins had gone back to his scouting position with Gove. Curtis, excited, wanting to be everywhere at once, decided to join them. Yes, there it was, the reb line hunkered behind a low wall, waiting for the word to attack. He saw one Confederate take a handful of cartridges from a fellow limping back to the rear. A southern officer rode up to another officer on foot to gesture toward the southeast.

Price is over there somewhere. Curtis had beaten him at Pea Ridge, now he would whip him again this day, he told himself.

He noticed a patch of jewelweed — rather late for *impatiens capensis*, thought Curtis, a collector of wildflowers.

Suddenly, he was slipping backward down the ravine on the wet leaves, knocking his knee on a rock. Curtis swore softly and took the shoulder of the farmer, who was following "*Herr* General" everywhere like a dog.

This was George Thoman, the German immigrant. Somewhat oblivious to the battle, Thoman had wandered looking for his mare. It had been appropriated by southern troops despite his entreaties that the animal was with foal.

The farmer had marched up to Curtis unnoticed and loudly stated something the general could not understand, something about "revels." Curtis had just attempted another drive up the south bank on the creek only to watch his men melt away in the galling fire. He had been peering through the smoke, trying to get a feeling of what was going on up across the creek, when the fellow yelled, "*Herr* General! Der revels tuck *mein stute*!" Curtis had looked again at the farmer, still puzzled.

"He's lost a horse to the rebels," Gove had translated, and then offered the obvious, "He's Dutch."

Grabbing at a sapling to steady his limping descent, Curtis checked on the progress of the guns. Men were being very rough with a balky horse pulling one of Lieutenant Edward Gill's mountain howitzers on its half-sized carriage, a gun made for just such terrain.

The Parrotts, usually requiring six horses, would be hell to get up here, just as Dodge had warned. Another horse pawed for better footing farther below. It carried a pack, ammunition. Rounding a curve and finding much of the fallen trees chopped away, Curtis had a good view of Dodge's gun crews, which had unharnessed one of their teams and unhitched a Parrott from its limber. He was still going to try, eh? The men had roped three horses so they could haul single-file up the ravine. Within minutes, militiamen were pitching in, grabbing the gun's spokes and shifting rocks and heavy branches behind its wheels to keep the piece from rolling back. Those were Blair's militia people. Colonel Charles Blair had done a good job, sensing the emptiness on the right flank and moving quickly to fill it. The men were cursing the slippery rocks.

"Hush," he called softly. "Unless you want to bring down those rebs up there. They're not so far away."

With the second howitzer making good progress but the Parrott still doubtful, Curtis decided to ignore his throbbing knee and start up again. Panting and sweating in his wool coat, he arrived at the assembly point to find a company of 14th Kansas Cavalry, sent over by Blair, lying quiet in the leaves. The first howitzer was tethered to a tree so it couldn't retreat down the slope on its own. The ammunition horse was not tied, but it was not going anywhere. The beast's ears drooped in fatigue.

The Federal artillery back at Westport seemed louder, more guns on the line now. General Blunt was readying for a third run up the hill. Curtis moved up and found Hopkins kneeling behind a milkweed patch. Curtis and his faithful German crept up to him.

"We will have to clear that house, sir," Hopkins said. "They will make it hard on the gunners, if it's not done."

The general nodded. As Hopkins waved over a militia officer came. It was Col. A. C. Hogan of the 19th Kansas Militia. Hogan agreed to lead the attack on the brick farmstead after Curtis promised him the help of the 14th cavalrymen. Curtis heard Gove ask whether anyone had seen where Moonlight had gone. After the Scot's Second Brigade had been pushed back across the creek earlier in the morning, Curtis had decided to send them around to guard the Kansas border toward the south. A mistake? Now his best regiment was out of sight and, it seemed, out of the fight.

The second gun was up, and its huffing crew seemed ready. The Parrott was still far behind. Checking the howitzers' supply of canister, Gill assured the officers there was plenty and more coming up. Curtis asked about the Parrott, and Dodge grimaced. Curtis could not contain himself. To hell with the Parrott.

"Forward," he shouted, and the mixed band of dismounted cavalry, militia and gunners burst from the timber.

The little guns, bumping easily over the friendlier terrain, quickly came in view of the house, but could not be seen by the rebels at the long stone wall beyond. A puff of smoke came from a window, and an officer fell. Within seconds, heavy fire from Hogan's Leavenworth men chipped at the brick near the windows. Three men lunged ahead to empty their Wessons through broken panes on another side of the house.

Dodge signaled for the guns to swing to the left, up a gentle rise. Curtis suddenly had a wide view of the battlefield, even better than from the roof of the Harris House earlier in the morning. Slightly south and west of the main rebel line, Curtis and his band were still unnoticed. The hundreds of Confederates were focused on the threat developing to their fore: regiment after regiment of Union militia and cavalry thrusting out of the timber south of Westport. Blunt had finally gotten his people across the creek and up into the fields again, across which smoke was rolling as from a prairie fire.

Two butternuts burst from the farm house, only to be picked off by the Kansans. Curtis hobbled the last steps to the guns. The charges already were rammed home, the vent hole covered and lanyard attached. Dodge was ready, too.

Curtis nodded. One of the howitzers went off first. Shock registered on the southern faces turning their way.

"*Arschlöcher!*" the excited farmer yelled at the rebs. Curtis had spent enough time among the Teutonic population in St. Louis to recognize this bit of German. "Assholes." And then something else, but the second blast drowned it out.

11:50 A.M.

Russell's Ford, Big Blue River
Jackson County

CAPTAIN LEVI UTT LOWERED THE FIELD glasses.

"I'm telling you, I don't think most of them have rifles!"

Lieutenant Sanders took another study of the longest line of wagons either had ever seen. They and the other Seventh Kansas Cavalry officers sitting on the high ground were working on a powerful riddle:

Why was their brigade not slashing through the rebel column, cutting traces, shooting mules and men, creating the kind of mayhem that God had in mind when He designed cavalry?

"Is McNeil going to do *anything?*" muttered Utt.

The Seventh, along with the 13th Missouri, 17th Illinois regulars and some smaller units, had been attached to General John McNeil's Missouri militia regiments. From what they'd understood, Pleasonton had ordered them to circle south toward New Santa Fe, following the Blue as it turned toward Kansas. The Confederates had to cross it again on their way back home, and cutting off the road to Fort Scott seemed like a good plan. The brigade was thin, but had enough carbines to wreck a supply train. And here it was, trundling by under their noses.

It was true that every one of them felt worn to the bloody nub, man and beast. Many of the troopers had been in their saddles for 19 hours *before* Pleasonton put them on their midnight march. So the move from Independence along the Blue had been slow and cautious. Badly strung out, the column had skirted one large Confederate camp across the river on the west bank.

At daybreak, McNeil had stopped to let the horses graze, but as it grew light, heavy firing from a battle to the north seemed to wake the commander. The pace had picked up, and before long, Levi Utt's company, which was at the front of the march, was atop a piece of high ground with an excellent view of the ford being churned by the endless enemy train. The major chose to send word back to McNeil, rather than to barrel on in. But it was an hour before the general reached the hill. By the time he sent orders to charge, the train's escort spotted them and formed a firing line. With only about 300 troopers, the Kansans felt the odds shift against them rather dramatically. Not content to just sit and wait, the rebels aggressively sent skirmishers out. With the element of surprise lost, the cavalry fell well back, and a fairly long-distance fire was exchanged.

As the rest of the brigade came up, McNeil reorganized and assigned the Seventh the center of the line. Once supported by some rifled guns, he pressed back. But when rebel crews unlimbered their own pieces, the general seemed content to take off the pressure and watch the artillerists duel. The troopers in the audience got a good laugh when a wayward piece of shell stunned one of their horses right in the forehead. It abruptly sat and toppled backward, mashing a cursing Jim Campbell.

Utt watched some Illinois companies disappear into the heavy brush along the river to probe for a way to hit the foe's flank. Malone yelled for the Kansans to get ready. With the regiment down to a third of its original mustering roll he did not have to shout too loud. Canteens got a last pass around, the men juggling reins as they unslung their five-shot revolver Colt rifles. Utt's people still had their Sharps; he wondered whether they would ever get the Spencers they were promised. But when the rebels drew up a second heavy line of men, maybe 2,000, maybe more, McNeil had the buglers call back the frustrated Illinois officers.

In fact, the extra Confederates were mostly for show. Colonel Charles Tyler's brigade consisted of a few thousand unarmed recruits — how many will be debated forever — who were formed into heavy lines. Tyler's column was attached to Shelby on paper, but useless to him in battle. Some accounts would say that the arraying of the unarmed recruits was the idea of Price, who had scurried to the rear the moment a threat to the train was known. At any rate, the recruits served their purpose well.

Tyler and his unarmed men were attached to Brigadier General William Cabell, whom McNeil had beaten handily the day before in Independence. Nevertheless McNeil was intimidated, faced by three ranks of the enemy and believing more were nearly surrounding him. As his report would later exaggerate, "I found myself in contact with the entire force of the enemy."

"My skirmishers (Seventh Kansas and Merrill's Horse) most gallantly pressed up to the main line of the enemy's centre," McNeil would write. "In the meantime he placed batteries in three different locations, and opened a well-directed cross-fire…. I was consequently compelled to … recall my skirmish line, and occupy the new position, I determined to hold this position at all hazards, in hope that the remaining brigades would come up. Towards night the enemy retired…." He added that the rebels left about 40 bodies on the field, a fairly obvious lie.

Marmaduke's Confederate division, having been pushed off Byram's Ford, pitched in to protect the train as well, according to the diary of Lieutenant

William Ballard: "At 2 o'clock they attempted to capture our train by a flank movement on our left. We was whisked into position and after some skirmishing drove them back and held them in check until the command passed."

Walking his horse over, Pitts called to Utt, "What are your ghost toes telling you?"

"That McNeil doesn't seem of any mind to mess with Price. Letting them absquatulate." It was the whimsical slang of the day for "leave in a hurry."

"I suspect he has his own haunts, not in his boot, but on his shoulder," said Pitts.

"What haunts would those be?"

"The ones from Palmyra; they're whispering in his ear," said Pitts, drawing Sanders' skeptical stare.

"If it would not trouble you too much, please make sense," Utt said.

"Old story, you've probably forgotten," Pitts said, watching a southern refugee urge a balky buggy horse down into the stream. "Back in '62, McNeil was up in northeast Missouri, in Palmyra."

Palmyra. Utt now recalled the story. The town, about 12 miles out of Hannibal, had been raided by Confederate partisans recruiting in that corner of the state. Andrew Allman, a Union sympathizer and informant against southern neighbors, had gone missing.

McNeil — a Novia-Scotia-born Bostonian who'd found success in St. Louis as a hatter, insurance salesman and state legislator — led his forces into the town in October 1862. Unless Allman were returned, he declared, 10 southern prisoners — apparently of varying degrees of innocence — would be shot. But Allman was certainly dead in the brush somewhere; a skull later found near Troublesome Creek was probably his. McNeil already had been executing recaptured men, sometimes because they had been paroled and broken their oaths.

This would be a large step beyond that.

"The grave with its terrors is near me," wrote Thomas Sidenor, who was one of the 10. Engaged to a Ralls County girl, Sidenor determined to die in the black broadcloth suit and white satin vest that were to have been his wedding garb. "I have not had a trial & they won't give me any chance for my life," he said. "Oh, is this justice?"

When the deadline for Allman's return passed, the 10 men sat on their coffins, waiting for a firing squad of Second Missouri Militia. The account of the pro-Union Palmyra *Courier* soon was being read in outrage as far away as the capitals of Europe:

"A few minutes after 1 o'clock, Colonel Strachan, provost-marshal-general, and Reverend Rhodes shook hands with the prisoners, two of them accepting bandages for their eyes. All the rest refused. A hundred spectators had gathered around the amphitheater to witness the impressive scene. The stillness of death pervaded the place. The officer in command now stepped forward, and gave the word of command, 'Ready, aim, fire.'

"The discharges, however, were not made simultaneously, probably through want of a perfect previous understanding of the orders and of the time at which to fire. Two of the rebels fell backward upon their coffins and died instantly. Captain Sidner sprang forward and fell with his head toward the soldiers, his face upward, his hands clasped upon his breast and the left leg drawn half way up. He did not move again, but died immediately. He had requested the soldiers to aim at his heart, and they obeyed but too implicitly. The other seven were not killed outright, so the reserves were called in, who dispatched them with their revolvers." The family of one testified to the sloppiness; his body, they said, had 18 bullet holes.

Utt rubbed his chin. "The Butcher of Palmyra. That was McNeil, was it? So they would be the ghosts? There's lots of ghosts out of this war. What makes them so frightening?"

"Because they're reminding him what the rebels have in mind should they get their hands on him. As I recall, a woman got violated in the deal, too."

One of those executed was a 22-year-old man brought in to replace William T. Humphrey, whose wife, Mary Humphrey, got off him the death list by raising $500 to bribe Colonel William R. Strachan. The provost agreed to the deal, but he had more than money on his mind. As the *Quincy Herald* would report across the river in Illinois: "The money was raised; Strachan pocketed it; compelled the poor, heartbroken, afflicted woman to submit to his hellish lust...." He was caught because other soldiers saw Humphrey's little girl crying outside in the hall outside the provost office while Strachan had his way with her mother. Strachan was acquitted of the rape but convicted of using his office for immoral purposed and financial misdealings.

Now Sanders jumped in with a couple of words that would not make his mother proud. "I don't see it. You're telling us that McNeil has lost his nerve? He did all right yesterday in the Independence fracas."

"He did, didn't he?" Pitts nodded. "But then Pleasonton was there with his damned whip, pushing us along, wasn't he?"

"Do you think Smith's infantry is waiting for them down there, that's why McNeil is letting them go?" Sanders mused. Utt thought about the possibility. Nine thousand infantrymen definitely could knock the wheels off Price's escape plans. Surely, they hadn't marched all the way over here to do nothing.

Now Utt watched columns of riders, these clearly armed, joining the rear of the column, which now had a portion of gigs driven by civilians who, good riddance, had thrown in their lot with the traitors. It was not the most orderly military procession Utt had ever seen. Looked whipped, in fact.

After the lines of soldiers and horsemen had followed the vehicles south over the Blue, McNeil began a cautious advance again.

Before long, the wind in their face told them the Confederates had set fire to the prairie grass. The blaze would mean another detour.

Their last chance to catch Price seemed to be going up in smoke.

12:15 P.M.

Wornall farm, south of Westport

THE LEFT WAS FALLING BACK.

Something was wrong on that flank. Thompson turned his horse that direction and cleared a low row of stones before seeing Frank Gordon waving at him.

"Guns shooting down our line, General! We can't stay here!"

Artillery smoke to the west. One, no, two mountain howitzers, just below that house, Bent's place. Where did they come from?

Thompson told the colonel to gather his Fifth Missouri about a quarter-mile back, then galloped toward the Fort Scott Road to pull those units back into the new line. After being forced back from the timber above the creek, the Confederates' front had seesawed for a while, but then things began to unravel very fast. Shelby had ordered a counterattack that was broken up almost as it started.

Word had come from Price that the train was under threat, and General Fagan left the north-facing line to back up Marmaduke, who was having a hard day on the east line. Dobbin's and Slemon's brigades went with Fagan. So much for reserves. Then Shelby called Jackman away to assist Fagan. Captain Collins went along, taking a Parrott.

That left only Thompson's brigade on the shell-whipped Westport front, and it was not enough. He sent word to alert Jacob Connor, his two tubes the last facing north, that Federal artillery had now appeared on the left, knowing the lieutenant could not be everywhere.

At that moment, Connor may have been the most overworked artillerist in the Confederate army, facing up to 29 Federal field pieces. "Line after line poured out of the town, and battery after battery galloped to the front and opened at a half-range," Major Edwards would write. "...Shelby's old brigade seemed resolved to perish where it stood."

Yankee horsemen, now clearly confident, made impetuous saber and pistol charges at Thompson's line, scattering his skirmishers. A section of Parrotts crewed by shouting Negroes emerged from the drifting walls of smoke and unlimbered behind a fence Slayback had abandoned just minutes ago. He wasn't sure but it looked like the guns had a colored officer. Remarkable. He rode to Slayback, who held his right flank east of the fort road.

"They have got us in a proper twist, Alonzo. Bring your boys back, but slowly. Keep the line."

Suddenly, Major Robert Woods was there, shouting: "General Shelby requests that Colonel Slayback bring his regiment about a mile and face it to the east. Our rear could be in danger."

"Where is Marmaduke?" Slayback asked.

"Don't know." Woods shook his head ruefully. "We've received no messages."

Now Slayback is being taken, too? Thompson couldn't believe it. He should be getting more men to stem the tide from the north, not watch them drain away. Slayback shrugged, began to salute Thompson, who grabbed his arm.

"Alonzo, you've got to make Shelby understand the situation here. We can't hold them. Let him know that we're facing two dozen guns at least."

"Without a doubt, Jeff, without a doubt. He shall know."

Thompson issued orders for his regiments to carefully shift companies to the east to fill the vacuum around the road, their most vulnerable section. The line was thin now. Some of Rector Johnson's companies settled in around a brick farmhouse just off the road, where some bodies lay in the yard.

Men trickled to the rear, and horse handlers trotted their charges yet farther back. A shell burst near one group, and a roan shied, dragging a private off his feet. Thompson watched as the panicked horse trampled the trooper's legs before he regained his feet. He was screaming at the horses, not making them any more calm. He would feel that in the morning, Thompson sympathized. I think we're all going to feel this in the morning.

Moses Smith and Johnson had settled their regiments behind some fences and were keeping up a good rate of fire, but the Yanks appeared to be massing for another push. Thompson figured his brigade had been pushed back a good mile so far, but every rod had been contested.

Here was Erwin, clearly wanting to hear that it was time to pull out. But it was not.

"William, your Jackson County boys are going to have to hold these fellows in check," Thompson told him. "Price is still in the rear, some Yankees are threatening the train. No word on what's happening on the Blue, but Shelby keeps drawing off our people and sending them that way."

"As you say, general, but we're running out of fences."

Although Lieutenant Colonel William Erwin had revealed nothing his commander wasn't already worrying about, Thompson instinctively glanced to the south. Fairly flat and distinctly barren. One might as well look for cover on a billiard table.

Erwin turned his attention back to his 12th Missouri, then thought to ask, "General, have you seen Vivian?"

"No, I haven't. He probably pulled back when Fagan did," Thompson said.

Major H. J. Vivian, part of Erwin's regiment, had been sent by Shelby that morning to watch a ford to the east of Westport, apparently the one for the Harrisonville Road. He had seen some Federal troopers but none that seemed to want to contest his position on the south bank of the creek. He listened to the fighting all morning and finally decided he had been left behind. Leaving the creek, he would recall:

"The Federals were on every side of us, with the exception of one small space on the south. Just when we reached the top of the hill about a half a mile east of the Wornall homestead the Federal regiment mounted their horses and rode parallel with us, thinking we were Federals, I suppose; in the distance I recognized General Shelby by the horse he rode. I started for him, and it was then that the Federals realized their mistake and started firing, but General Shelby, seeing the situation, soon covered my retreat…."

"At his chance of conversation with me, (Shelby) shouted, 'Where in hell have you been all this time?'" A courier had been sent to retrieve him, but Vivian had never seen him. "Well, I suppose the Federals killed him," Shelby said, "If they didn't, I will have him court-martialed and shot."

Now Moses Smith decided to come up to Thompson and state the obvious. "Not good, General, not good at all," he observed.

"Can't git up and git just yet, Moses. Your men are holding up well."

Smith open his mouth to say something then pointed over Thompson's shoulder. The general turned his horse to see Bob Duffy. Oh, no. Now Shelby wants Gordon or Smith. The major was pointing back the way he had come, and Thompson didn't catch his first words for an exploding shell, but got enough.

"… move by the flank, and come in a trot."

Thompson ordered bugles to sound the call, "To Horse," sent two officers down the line to make sure everyone knew the drill and went to join Elliot at the right end of his line. Calm as if on a parade ground and not in an artillery turkey shoot, Elliot shouted to form ranks of four, acknowledged Thompson's gesture and began turning his men south down the Fort Scott Road. Keeping an eye on the crowding Yankees, Thompson checked that his other regiments were readying to fall into the column.

Come in a trot, the man says. Perhaps, Thompson thought, but only perhaps, we can hold it to just a trot.

12:30 P.M.

South of Westport

THE MEN FRANTICALLY WORKING THE LITTLE howitzer from the farm yard were just shy of being overwhelmed. Rebs gathered in different clumps of timber readying to rush it.

James Blunt sized up the situation in a second, spurred his horse forward, waving his heavy Army revolver. He and his escort got to the yard just before the Confederates gained its south fence, a rock toss away. For a long minute, both sides blasted away, and then the foe melted back again, some into the creek timber to the left and others to the main body of Shelby's men.

For it was Jo Shelby who was up ahead now, some captives had proudly revealed, and Blunt rejoiced with the news. The best of the Confederate's western army was in Blunt's hand, and he intended to crush it like a rose in a virgin's Bible. Oh, old Curtis probably would strive to take credit for flanking Shelby with those damned guns. But Blunt had known it all along, felt it in his bones as he took his men up to the prairie for the third try that morning. This advance, driving like an iron wedge down the road, would not be stopped.

Captain Richard Hinton, his stubby aide, gave an odd yelp of excitement and the howitzer crew cheered. Blunt gave them a grin, but cautioned them against operating so far up without support. Find some militia to hook up with, he told them. Two of his escort, Company E men from the 14th Kansas, were down, one with a chest wound. One of the cannoneers was dead. Looked like four or five rebs were heaped on the other side of the fence. The farm house, belonging to a family named Simpson, was well on its way to ruin after five hours of cannon fire.

Blunt hadn't been scratched. Hadn't expected to be. It was his destiny to win this battle. Shelby had been thrown back from the high ground overlooking Brush Creek, had been pushed back from stone fence after stone fence. Giving way.

Doc Jennison was there on the road again with a clot of other colonels — the Coloradan James Ford, the Red Leg George Hoyt — the lot of them calling for permission to make another charge. They felt it, too, Blunt thought. We're thumping the sonsabitches.

"Hold them up, Colonel!" he yelled. "I haven't got all the guns where I want them."

The day hadn't started so promising. He had sent Jennison and Ford over the creek at sunup, and they'd quickly found the enemy. His boys pushed hard for a while, and then Shelby pushed harder. After an hour or two of fighting, all his forces had found themselves back on the north side of Brush creek, first Jennison's brigade, then Thomas Moonlight's. Once the rebs got into the trees around the left flank, they had squeezed out Ford and his miners, too. Without support, the batteries had to be pulled back. The situation, as he would report, had been "severe and unequal."

"We fought them all day," Sergeant D. C. Nettleton of the Second Colorado would recall. "Sometimes we were forced back and at other times we advanced."

Then Charlie Blair had showed up with several regiments, mostly militia, but he'd handled his "Tads" like they were "old" troops. Blair, normally based at Fort Scott with the 14th Kansas Cavalry, was a shrewd soldier. He had seen how the Federal right flank did not extend as far west as the rebel lines. He had started shifting people that way, not waiting for permission from anyone.

When Blunt had ordered his general advance, the weight of Blair's half-dozen regiments made a big difference, especially after Curtis had sent Moonlight's brigade, his best men, off to watch the state line. All of the Union regiments, volunteers and 30-day men, had waded the creek and flushed the rebs out of the timber. Then Blunt had hustled up nearly all of the available artillery. That had been his mistake earlier; not enough field pieces had arrived from Kansas City in time for the dawn action on the prairie. But now he controlled the road and was taking back the fields and pastures.

Blunt studied the situation ahead. Shelby wasn't giving up; his men still showed admirable discipline. Blunt waved to a battery to hurry up to a new position. A small swarm of officers were picking their way from the west through the fields. It was Major General Curtis. Well, the old man cannot bugger this up, Blunt thought. It's too clearly a victory.

Curtis was all smiles, looked 20 years younger than the previous evening. He graciously congratulated Blunt and his officers. Blunt managed to say something cheerful in return. He had wished Curtis had stayed at the hotel on the levee in Kansas City but no, once the old man got to Westport, he was everywhere, placing militia, dragging cannon around after him. He said he had already sent a telegram to Rosecrans that the enemy appeared to be retiring and now would have to send another, even more favorable.

Hinton pointed ahead. Blunt caught it, too. Well ahead, rebel officers were gesturing, trying to rally their men for a counterattack. Blunt looked around. Lieutenant Henry Hicks with his Second Kansas battery was the closest with a section of the Wisconsin guns. His captain, James Dodge, was still over to the west, working his other section back closer to the Fort Scott Road. Blunt cantered over to the lieutenant.

"They're forming up, Hicks, they're forming up. Hit them quick, man, give them some hell."

Blunt watched with satisfaction as shells ripped at the rebels, breaking up their line again. More of his batteries were there now, pushing ahead of Hicks and the cavalry. Now Bill McLain's guns were rattling up to take a place on the new line with Colorado troopers in support, some mounted, some taking positions behind fences. The general laughed aloud, realizing there was a contest between the gun crews over which could get closer to the rebs. Already he heard Dodge yelling for his horses to be hooked up to leap ahead of McLain.

Blunt and the other officers now had a good view of a handsome brick house just east of the road. It gave no sign of its inmates. Dead rebs in the yard indicated it had done duty as a hospital.

"When the battle was nearing its close," then-little Frank Wornall would recall years later, "the Confederates took our house for a hospital and the floors were covered with them. While the surgeons worked, mother boiled water to wash the wounds and helped with the bandages. I remember one man who was terribly wounded in the face. Our house was so full he could not come in and he sat on the curb of the cistern and I drew water to wash his wound, then he got up and walked away."

"That's Wornall's place," said Jennison. "I used it as a headquarters a couple years back."

"And it's still standing?"

The rogue laughed. Hoyt, naturally, joined in.

"Sir, you wound me. By nature, I am a gentle man. Why, a little sprout lived there who loved me."

Blunt raised an eyebrow. A Jennison-loving Missourian was a rare item.

"We traded knives. He got the better of me, a fine boy."

Well, you old tender heart, Blunt thought. And here I was suspecting the boy's love stemmed from the fact you forgot to hang his daddy.

The little boy was young Frank Wornall. When Jennison commandeered his home, it terrified his family, who feared the Kansans would kill John B. Wornall, who was neutral in the conflict but had owned slaves. It was when the jayhawker chief generously swapped "a beautiful knife with several blades" for the boy's "old barley knife of no value," the younger Wornall said, that the family breathed a sigh of relief.

During the Westport battle, Frank's father had fled to the little town, assuming he was a marked man one way or the other on his farm. According to family lore, bushwhackers once tried to hang John from his own porch, but were interrupted by the arrival of some troopers. Wornall's wife, Eliza, and children were left to huddle through the battle that raged around their home. It is said that when Eliza left the safety of her brick home, a minié ball passed through her hair bun.

"He paid them quite handsomely, too," Hoyt joined in. Jennison reportedly left $2,800 in compensation to the Wornalls. This was another pleasant surprise. As Frank said: "They were with us for eight days, and destroyed every fence on the place, and burned every stick of wood, killed all the hogs and beasts, as well as those on neighboring places."

Now he'd heard of *two* good deeds done by this rascal. Blunt thought he might faint. Surely the world would come to an end soon. But not before he had got through whipping these whoreson traitors. A company or two of them were insolently firing mounted from a small rise. Blunt had been a doctor before the war like Jennison. The idea of being the man's patient was revolting, really, but he was in such good humor that he tossed out a joke.

"Johnny says that's his hill, Doctor. Perhaps you should make an examination of his guts?"

Jennison laughed, looked around, shouted to organize a column. Some of the Colorado men begged to go along. Doc said something like, the more the merrier, and then they were howling away in sloppy formation, waving sabers and pistols. The rebels watched them come for a minute, then casually turned their horses and disappeared back behind the rebs' main line, where a sputtering burst of firing kept Jennison well off. Blunt's attention was caught by movement up ahead. He stood in his stirrups. Yes, the Confederates' mounts were being brought up all down the line, hundreds of rebs were quickly taking to saddle. For a general charge? No, their regimental colors were turning south on the road, others, in fairly orderly ranks, preparing to do the same. Shelby was withdrawing!

At that moment, a round shot splattered into one of the stone walls, the rock chips stinging the horses and making them rear. Blunt was nearly thrown. Where did that come from? He heard an anguished curse. It was Major R. J. Hunt, Curtis's chief of artillery, holding his head, fingers dripping crimson. Apparently a fragment nearly had brained him. Curtis was talking to the major as staff officers helped Hunt to the ground.

A Parrott rolled by, its team steered by Negroes, that Leavenworth battery. Captain Dodge came up, dismounted and began discussing things with a light-skinned Negro lieutenant, who was pointing at a feverishly reloading rebel gun crew. Blunt expected another shell winging their way again. He had little fear of it. But no, the enemy fieldpiece was now swinging toward Jennison's band, who saw it and treated it a bit too respectfully for Blunt's taste. It fired at the moving troopers, but Blunt saw no one fall. Now Dodge was sighting down the barrel. He nodded to the Negro, who called the order to fire. The Parrott jumped back. Blunt could see little through the smoke, but some of the black men started to cheer. Hinton was shouting excitedly. Now Blunt understood the sounds of triumph. Their first shot had wrecked the carriage of the southern gun. Amazing!

"We'll make a goddamned artilleryman out of you, yet, Captain," Blunt called as Dodge and the black lieutenant grinned at each other like boys who had just brained a rabbit with the first rock.

Curtis was calling for one more hard push.

Blunt issued orders for all his cavalry companies to mount. Most of the militia would have to go back farther for their horses, but no matter. In the saddle they were nearly worthless. He called for a brief halt to let his people form up and find a place on the road, then ordered his division into a careful trot toward open prairie. Blunt reached the rise where the rebel riders had watched him and swore an excited and especially purple oath. Across the plain was a good part of the Confederate army, some riding in disciplined order, some forming lines for the next fight, some clearly running for their lives.

"Who's that to the east, more rebs?"

Hinton would recall the scene this way:

"A heavy column of cavalry could be seen emerging from the timber, and deploying about a mile to the east, and advancing toward the rebel right. Some doubts were felt as to its character, but as the line deployed, the Union guidons plainly visible, were hailed with thundering cheers."

Blunt did not cheer. Curtis he could undercut and elbow aside, but it would not work with that fellow over there. Blunt could not claim this victory as his alone, and shared glory had a bland taste.

"Prepare yourself to meet a bigger son-of-a-bitch than me," Blunt said. "That is Pleasonton."

XV

Running south

"I believe I am not to be killed by a rebel bullet."

— Major General James Blunt

eɔeɔeɔeɔeɔ

Prairie east of State Line
Jackson County

IT WAS A SEA OF BLUE, dark Yankee wool blue.

Thompson had mounted his lonesome brigade and swung out in column away from the punishing artillery and cavalry that had flooded out of Westport. But he could see no improvement to the south, and from the east … well, the east hardly bore speaking of. More and more of a new foe, forming for an attack.

There was Slayback's battalion with Shelby. But Thompson looked in vain for signs of Fagan or Jackman. And any of the rest of Price's army.

"Are we surrounded? " yelled Elliott.

"If not, damned close to it, Benjamin."

"Shelby's waving at us."

Their commander, who had lost his plumed hat, was not just waving but gesturing wildly toward the threat that was cutting across their path, the Fort Scott Road.

"General, break that line, or the army is lost," he yelled.

Thompson looked back at his brigade. Some of his regiments were too far back to lend their weight to any immediate effort. He looked at Elliott, and the colonel nodded grimly and shouted for a charge. Then both spurred their horses and headed for the center of the Union line.

It was an ugly place to be, this rebel right flank.

Ammunition exhausted and facing the rapid fire of Union carbines, Major General Marmaduke, with General Clark, had grudgingly given up "Bloody Hill" overlooking Byram's Ford a couple hours earlier. Marmaduke had tried to form a second line but it was no use, the pressure was too great. While the first Federal brigades over the Big Blue stopped to reorganize and replenish their ammunition, Major General Pleasonton sent General Sanborn's relatively fresh regiments straight across the prairie, pushing the rebels back west to the Harrisonville Road and "the ragged edge of panic."

Shelby had received no couriers from Marmaduke, but could read into Price's worry over his precious train that Shelby's rear, as well as the right flank, could be in danger. He ordered Colonel Sidney Jackman's brigade back south to the same place where it had captured the 24-pounder howitzer the day before, near the Mockbee place, a bit more than two miles south of Thompson's evershakier line.

Jackman came upon a desperate General Fagan just in time to dismount, form a line and face Federal cavalry who "came on in a swing trot, and when within eighty yards ... a destructive fire was poured into them, killing and wounding a large number of men and horse and causing their line to reel and break."

The longer Federal line lapped around Jackman's right, but he broke it up as well, helped by Collins' Parrott. By now the open prairie felt crowded with Yankees, and it seemed to Jackman that he was taking fire from every point on the compass. It was time to remount. Forming defensive positions several times, he made his way back to the southern ford to take his place at the rear of Price's retreating column.

For Shelby, still back to the north a couple miles, "the prospect was dark and desperate."

"I fell back as rapidly as I could after the retiring army... reaching the road, the prairie in my rear was covered almost by a long line of troops, which at first I supposed to be our own men. This illusion was soon dispelled...."

So it was Thompson's turn to face Pleasonton's brigades, at this moment Sanborn's column. Most of these Missouri State Militia cavalrymen had spent their enlistments chasing elusive bushwhackers. Now, instead of running for cover, these rebel Missourians ignored the smattering of carbine fire and drove deep into the militia cavalry.

In the colored recounting of Yankee historian Richard Hinton, Thompson's rush on Sanborn's brigade caused it "to yield a little." Pleasonton was more generous to the rebs, saying they "shook it considerably." Broken and scattered was more the truth. As one Iowa trooper said later, "As Shelby had to get out, he was ugly...."

"Run, you bastards, run!" Thompson heard Elliot scream. The general slowed his mount, a pretty good horse for a change. Appropriated near Lexington, this big bay could actually see where it was going. The sergeant who had exulted over his luck while throwing his saddle over the beast wouldn't need him anymore. He had been shot through the hips at the Little Blue. A few more horses were running free right now, mostly with U. S. brands on them.

Time to round up the boys. They were too spread out now, needed to regroup. Thompson looked for Elliott's bugler — and heard the trills of several horns, none of them Confederate.

After the fight at the Big Blue River, Winslow's tired veterans, now commanded by Lieutenant Colonel Frederick Benteen, had let their mounts feed in a cornfield. But hearing the clash to the west, recalled Fourth Iowa Sergeant William Forse Scott, "Benteen did not wait for news or orders. His trumpeter sounded 'To horse!'

"And quickly the brigade was out of the field, formed in column of companies on the open prairie. Half a mile in front, along a low swell in the prairie, was the enemy's line ... Nothing between but the tall light grass.

" 'Forward!' Rang out from a score of bugles, followed by 'Trot!' And then 'Gallop!'"

At this point, too, Captain Thurber's Second Missouri guns rushed up, throwing double canister into the rebel horsemen, causing, as one Federal recalled, "almost instant demoralization." Colonel Philips noted in his diary that night how Pleasonton thundered up and began haranguing the hurrying artillerists, as if they were blind to the giant turkey shoot ahead. "Rebels, rebels, rebels! Fire. Fire, you damn asses!," he cried, "Fire!"

"The enemy could not stand it," Scott said. "Before they were reached they broke and fled in the utmost precipitation, scattering widely toward the south, fighting more or less as individuals, but mostly trying to escape only."

Thompson could only watch helplessly as Elliott's regiment was thrown back, thrown to the winds. His men were racing back by him, some taking shots over their shoulders, others just lighting out. No chance to rally them. Thompson unholstered his Adams pistol. He had never personally shot at anyone so far in this war, but now seemed the perfect time to begin.

In the melee, the shoulder tabs of a Federal lieutenant colonel flashed into view. A worthy opponent. Thompson aimed, squeezed the trigger … and felt the weapons jam at half cock. He tried again. No result.

The Adams was an English design. Double action, self-cocking, it did not need a hammer to draw back. The trigger mechanism did it all, which in theory meant fast shooting.

In reality, a ball whizzed angrily past Thompson's long nose. The offended lieutenant colonel was not waiting for the Adams to sort itself out. Thompson heard another slug pass and leaned over the side of his horse Indian-style. It was time to be someplace else!

He saw some prairie ahead that did not appear particularly Yankee-infested and pointed the bay at it. Another report behind him. Thompson realized with some disgust that the Federal's murderous intentions would not be satisfied until his own revolver — perfectly functioning, Yankee-made —had been emptied at Thompson's back.

<hr>

2 :15 P.M.

AS A CHILD, SOMETIME BEFORE MARSE Jo's stepdaddy bought him, Billy Hunter had been set to toting rocks brung up by the plow and stacking them on the edges.

He had hated them finger-mashing rocks. But he did not hate this here long pile of limestone at all.

The east-west running fence was the only thing between him and a Yankee bullet, a whole lot of Yankee bullets that were chipping away at the other side.

It could not be denied that it was a hot place, but not as hot as 'twas for the soldiers just a half hour ago.

As Marse Jo Shelby would describe it: "In attempting to reform my lines an enfilading battery of six guns swept the whole line, and another in front opened to terrific effect. At the same time the column (Blunt's) which followed me from Westport came down at the charge, and nothing was left, but to run for it, which was now commenced. The Federals seeing the confusion pressed on furiously, yelling, shouting, and shooting, and my own men fighting everyone on his own hook would turn and fire and gallop away again."

On his own hook was not where Hunter wanted to be. He had stayed close to the gen'l as they galloped this way and that, his escort and Colonel Slayback's people trying to keep the pack of Federal hounds at pistol's distance. But one by one they had done reached the bottoms of their revolvers. Marse Jo had emptied one "maybe," and Hunter had his reserve pistol pulled out of a saddlebag before it could be requested.

Hunter heard the familiar and sickening sound of a lead plowing into flesh. A lieutenant to his right grunted, lost his reins to his lathered mount and slipped out of the saddle. A noise occurred just under his hip that Hunter did not recognize for a minute, then realized it had come from his frying pan. It had done stopped a slug. Hunter wished he could hang that iron off his back. It was this damn Yankee prairie, wasn't nothin' on it for a man to get behind, take a stand. Then he heard the major, the genr'l's writing man, hollering. And they all saw it.

"Up from the green sward of the waving grass two miles off a string of stone fences grew up and groped across the plain…," Major John Edwards recalled. "The men reached it. Some are over; others are coming up, and Slayback and Gordon and Blackwell and Elliott are rallying the men, who make a stand here and turn like lions at bay. The fences are lines of fire, and the bullets sputter and rain thicker upon the chasing enemy. They halt, face about, and withdraw out of range."

The wall began to fill as men of the Iron Brigade found the rallying point, dismounted and began reloading their rifles. Somehow, Lieutenant J. D. Connor got there to skillfully use his two cannon to discourage any Yankee rushes down the road.

"Strategy and skill had been expended at Westport — there was no place for either here," Edwards wrote in his book after the war. "A grim, sullen, steadfast, unconquerable, decimated division of desperate men held the wall and they meant to die there."

Two ammunition wagons found them. No one was more surprised than the teamsters themselves that they hadn't been bagged by the bluebellies. Hailed as heroes by the soldiers passing around the fresh cartridges, they picked up rifles and moved up to the wall.

The Federals continued to make runs at the thin line, but did not break it. In one telling, Jennison arrived and sent out his skirmish line, but when the rebel artillery opened fire, the jayhawkers decided there were better places to be.

Been a long day for them, too, Hunter figured, as he reloaded Marse Jo's pistol again. He looked again to the west, trying to will the sun to go down. Even if they can't whip us here, them Yankees know they done come out on top today.

They's thinking, no point in getting drilled now, tonight's camp whiskey might leak out the holes.

XVI

Dead and dying

"Why need he dread death? Is not the grave the common receptacle of the young, the beautiful, the beloved? Let not the brave then fear to die."

—Chaplain John J. Hight, in his 1895 history
of the 58th Indiana Volunteers

e/3e/3e/3e/3e/3

OCTOBER 23 — 9 P.M.

Kansas City

"SHE HAD THREE SILK DRESSES, TRYING to keep them out of the mud, but they kept sliding and making a mess of it. I was trying so hard not to laugh, Henry."

Elizabeth Millett's husband grinned and puffed smoke around his pipe stem.

What a vain girl their neighbor was, so worried about her gowns as the Union men went to shed blood down at Westport.

"The rebels are going to burn us out," the woman had warned from the sidewalk. Then she fled across the Kaw.

Millet had never even thought of leaving. It had been the most exciting Sunday she could remember. She had awakened to cannon fire and church bells. Henry, who had spent years newspapering before going into his own printing business, kept her supplied with news of the battle through the day, assuring her that the rebs were being pushed farther and farther south.

Now Henry was telling her a little story about a friend, but her attention was being diverted to Wyandotte Street outside. It was filling with wagons. Henry rose and went to the window.

"They've got lamps burning in the church," he said.

"The Southern Methodist?"

"Yes, wait, those are wounded men! They're taking the wounded from the fighting into the church!"

She glanced at the crib to confirm that her six-month-old son had not awakened, then rose with a rustle of blue silk to join her husband at the window. It was true. They could make out a string of mules and wagons waiting their turns to unload.

"My heavens, Henry, I can't see the end of them!"

"Here comes someone."

A man was striding to their door, an officer. A gentle knock on the door, promptly opened. The officer entered, swept off his hat, and got to the point without pleasantries.

"I am Doctor Joshua Thorne. I will be setting up one of our hospitals across the street. We've got more than 200 wounded that I know of, maybe twice that many still out there."

The Confederates at Westport had no time to take their wounded with them. A report to the Leavenworth *Times* said Dr. W. Booth Smith went to the battlefield about 2 p.m. and found the dead "strewn and scattered along the blood-stained track of the enemy's route and retreat, lay buried in hollows and ravines, or concealed in the brush and timber. Seven rebels lay dead in one ghastly heap; others, whose moaning attracted his ear as his step approached, kept silent, as if to escape observation. Confusion and tumult everywhere prevailed; arms and equipments covered the ground, abandoned in flight or surrendered in death. The steed and his rider lay side by side in one gory bed, where they had been stricken by the fatal shot or shell, while the maimed and wounded horse and soldier put forth their crippled strength to erect themselves, or to creep along the earth, seeking relief from their suffering in change of position, or to assure themselves of life by the exercise of will or instinct. The red flow of life-blood, the face begrimed with powder, the shattered and the disemboweled forms of men, the piercing outcries of tortured nature, the shudder, the gasp, the last convulsions of the dying, the dead still warm with life, but whom, 'No sound can awake to glory again.'"

Thorne continued in his slight English accent: "We're going to need help. A lot of it. I would consider it a great kindness if you could serve as a nurse until we get things sorted out."

Henry started to protest, but Elizabeth cut across his words. "I'll do what I can, sir, but I alone cannot do very much."

"Of course not. We're canvassing the neighborhood trying to enlist more volunteers. It is very gracious of you, but I must warn you, perhaps I should have at the beginning, it will be a very long night, and you will have to be very strong."

Glancing at her husband, the doctor conceded, "It is perhaps wrong of me to subject a woman to what is over there, but my experience has taught me that the wounded often respond much better to a woman when they are hurt."

"Of course," she replied. "Henry, could you find my heavy shawl? I think I left it in the kitchen. I'll be across the street immediately, sir, please do not let me delay you."

Henry came back from the kitchen, a frown bending around his pipe.

"Beth, I don't think this is proper. What if little Van needs you?"

"He's perfectly fine, Henry, and they want me over there." She pecked him on the cheek. "I'm sure I'll be back fairly soon."

She stepped into the wet and mushy street, and realized she was wearing a fairly good dress herself. Well, she would not be silly about it.

Squeezing into the church door after two men who were supporting an officer hopping on his one good foot, she heard the screech of wood on wood. Pews were being dragged around to make more accessible resting places for the wounded. And another screech, dreadful, from high in the throat of a mere boy. They were laying him on the floor. He thrashed a bit, hitting the face of a gray-headed man prone next to him. The older man's eyes were open, but he did not flinch at the blows. Lord, was he dead? The boy's movements pulled the blanket off his neighbor. His shirt was bloody, torn at the stomach. Elizabeth's gorge rose. She quickly jerked her head at the sight of intestine.

She walked a few steps away, unsteady, reaching for the back of a pew, noticing then that a man in a gray uniform was lying there.

"Ma'am? Ma'am? Could I trouble you for a little water? Don't believe I've had a drop all day."

Elizabeth collected herself. The rebel's arm hung off the pew, blood dripping on the oak flooring.

"Yes," she said, "Yes, I'll go find some right now."

Bedlam was fast overtaking the sanctuary. More men were carried in, some on litters, some on doors. The concert of moans was growing. A man was gagging nearby. She tugged at the sleeve of a bearded orderly. It was filthy.

"Where is the water, please?"

"Where is the pump, ma'am? I don't know myself."

There was Doctor Thorne over there. His hat and coat were gone. Perhaps he could help. As she approached, he plunged an instrument into a chest wound. A sharp odor wafted her way, some chemical. She swallowed hard twice and turned to the door: I cannot do this. But coming in was Adela Van Horn. Thank goodness, her friend was here, a woman with a sharp tongue but a mind to match.

"Beth! You're here, too, thank Heaven. Darling, you're pale! Are you all right?"

Elizabeth looked past her, saw the soft glow of light in the windows of her home. Then she gazed at a straw-haired young trooper being guided in with a scarlet neck wrap. He looked like her younger brother, she noticed, same nose and mouth. The hair was all wrong, of course. Her gaze went back to the street. At least two more wagons were looming out of the dark.

"Elizabeth, are you all right?"

She looked at her friend.

"I'm fine, Adela. We need your help desperately. Please run across the street and tell Henry to fill two buckets of water and bring them immediately."

Earlier in the day, the two women had ventured down to what had been Milton McGee's hotel on Grand at 16th Street. A number of local enrolled militiamen — everyone still called them the Home Guard — were halted in the street among the horse apples. A gentleman in a top hat was carrying a bucket up the line, giving each man a dipper of water, she thought.

Adela had been the wiser. "No, my dear, that is whiskey."

Elizabeth wondered whether any of those men were lying before her now. There were very few uniforms, and most of those seemed to be rebel garb.

The dipper. She called to her friend: "Also, we'll need the dipper."

Adela already had hitched her skirts and was dodging a four-mule team. She waved acknowledgment. In places other than Kansas City, with its small, rough-edged society, a printer's wife might not give an order to the spouse of the town's most important man, at times mayor, newspaper publisher, local guard commander or provost. But Adela Van Horn had turned at once to her task, perhaps grateful to be spared the dread of the church for a little longer.

"Mrs. Millett! Could you give me a hand over here!"

It was dawn before the situation seemed under control at last. Several other townswomen were ministering to the men, many of whom seemed to be more settled, either from the exhaustion that she felt herself, or perhaps the loss of blood. It was less crowded, too, now that some of the Confederates with minor wounds had been seen to and sent off to a stockade somewhere. She understood that some of the injured had been taken to other locations, such as the Lockridge Ballroom nearby on Fifth Street.

Many of the wounded Kansans had been taken no farther than Westport. The steamer *Tom Morgan* picked up 86 and carried them to the Leavenworth army hospital. The Harris House in Westport was converted into a hospital. The Leavenworth *Daily Times* would report that "the ladies of Westport supplied lint and bandages, and contributed, by their kind attentions, much to the assistance of the Surgeons, and the relief of suffering."

At the Southern Methodist Church, the men were laid head to foot on the benches, all covered with white bedclothes from Kansas City homes. Edward Scarritt went to the church with his mother, who was one of the volunteer nurses. He would recall that the patients looked like "an army of ghosts," and Union sentries walked the aisles.

"Some of the soldiers were mortally wounded and were sending dying messages through the dear women to their loved ones at home," Scarritt would remember. "Some were bitterly bemoaning their fate and all were hushed into stillness when it was announced that a comrade had closed his eyes to earthly scenes and is 'slipping o'er the brink.'"

Elizabeth pulled a rag from a bucket, wrung it out and wiped the fevered face of a man named Homer, who kept wanting to know where the surgeon had taken his foot. "Don't fret so. It will be all right," she reassured him. "Rest easy, now."

Adela, having quietly assumed the role of head nurse, came by, conferring with the doctor. Elizabeth was distracted by the orderlies removing the body of a big Indian. A shell fragment had ripped across this face, taking out both eyes and leaving the tip of his nose hanging lopsidedly. She was sure he had been conscious when brought in, but he had never uttered a sound. The white man next to him had been much less dangerously wounded, but he had cried and whined enough for both men.

She had given the Indian some water shortly before he passed on. It seemed that she had the talent to seek out the men who would die.

She had asked one young reb from Arkansas what she could do for him.

"Well, miss, if I had my druthers, I'd druther have some pork and turnips than airy other time." Elizabeth had patted him. Her short but intense course in battle wounds indicated he was unlikely to survive the wound over his ear that made a gory mat of his dark curls. Adela glanced down at the angel-faced reb and nodded.

Elizabeth had gone home to nurse her little Van while she waited for the meal to cook, then put him down and returned with a cloth-covered dish. She knew the smell of food would be noticed and worried that other men, who must be starving, would begin placing orders, but they did not.

The rebel barely raised his destroyed head upon her return, looked at her and then laid it down again, a slight movement that spoke of tides of weariness and regret.

"I don't believe I can eat it, but God bless you, ma'am, for bringing it to me." And moments later, he began violently convulsing and was gone.

Now she again dipped the rag— it was scrap ripped from the hem of her dress, long ruined — and dabbed at blood leaking from a bandage.

She straightened, her back stiff. Her hand slipped into an apron pocket to check on if the little twist of brown paper with its lock of hair. It had been handed to her by a young Confederate officer, who had earlier asked her name.

"Take it, ma'am," he had implored. "Someday someone will come asking for George Lucas. It will be my wife. You can give her that."

Elizabeth smiled to him, said she certainly would, he needn't concern himself. And then she wept as death reached the lieutenant before the surgeon.

OCTOBER 24 — 9:35 A.M.

Ray County

THE HALF DOZEN MEN IN UNION uniforms sat their horses casually, reins slack, letting the animals drink from the muddy little stream where it crossed the road.

They watched another blue-garbed rider approach from the south, then pull up at a safe distance.

One of those waiting raised his forage cap, which showed a strip of red over the bill, and held it high. The rider took off his own hat with its red band, but held it horizontal. "Lyon," he shouted.

"Reno" came the answering code word. Thus reassured, the Federal courier spurred his chestnut back into a trot and moved toward them.

When he joined the cluster, the men conversed. The courier gestured back toward the southwest. A few more words, he laughed, then began to move along on his mission. One of the group, it was Archie Clement, naturally, let the Fed get about six feet away before whipping out a Navy and plunking him between the shoulder blades.

The Federal collapsed off the horse, tried to get a grip of weeds to crawl away. Archie put another into him.

Ike Berry sniggered at something Jesse muttered and then both kneed their horses and broke from the autumn vegetation. Riley Crawford joined about 35 men walking their horses out of the heavy brush. They emerged onto a field gone to weeds, probably evidence of an owner gunned down by one side or the other.

Archie was inserting paper cartridges into his Navy when they rode up. Bill Anderson asked, "Wha'd 'e say?"

"He was a pretty happy feller. Said Price got hisself bottled up outside Westport and whipped on. Now he's running south with the whole Yankee army tight as a tick on his ass."

Anderson digested this for a moment. "I don't believe it." Thought some more and then spat, "Shit! The old tub of guts got 20,000 men, and he's pulling out?"

No one else spoke for a while. Bill was often at turns morose, even weepy, then raging. It was as tiring as it was unnerving. Riley was missing the quietly sullen George Todd more and more. He must be heading south with Price, Riley thought.

Then John Rains ventured: "Well, guess he's going to need them fancy pistols you gave 'im."

A couple of laughs.

"Pap shoulda given 'em to some of his new boys," Berry said. "Some of 'em didn't have guns, ya know."

Anderson decided to display his wisdom at this point.

"See, boys, this is why we fight on our own hook. Had we gone along like Todd, we'd be in hot water, too. Hell, Pap was just too damned slow. I heard Shelby was besides hisself about that wagon train. Said infantry could move faster than Pap's idea of cavalry."

"So we didn't make any difference?" asked Clell Miller, one of the new boys who had been excited about the Army of Missouri and its promise to save the state. Miller, who seemed a bit of a clown to several of the men, had gone along on the Danville run to mess with the Missouri Northern, a task for which Riley had seen little sense.

Anderson just looked at him, then spurred his big gray toward the east.

"We're the *only* ones that make *any* difference," Archie snorted. Buck James said Archie was the "brains" of this outfit. That hadn't settled Riley's mind any. He nudged Folly with his right foot, the good one. The other one ached. The air was cold, but he was sweating.

Earlier, the guerrillas had run into another milish troop and dispersed for a while, rendezvousing back near the James place for a quick raid on Haynesville. Now here they were, a few miles from Albany, according to ol' Eisenhour, the

Dutch farmer they forced into guiding them.

Rains eased up beside him. "You look like you've got Dick Yager's toothache."

It was another of those stories that grew with every telling. Yager had taken a couple dozen men far into Kansas on a raid spring of last year, but had been suffering mightily from a rotten tooth. The story was that he had lined up his men on a rise overlooking Council Grove and just sat there until the townspeople discovered them. When it was clear the riders were waiting, a small delegation had come out. Yager rode down alone and after some palavering, trotted his horse on into the town.

An hour later, he had ridden out again, leaving his misery behind in some dentist office. Still spitting blood, he had smiled and ordered his men back on the trail. Council Grove had struck a fortunate bargain. Diamond Springs and some other folks hit by Yager's bunch later could not say the same. That Yager had gotten to Council Grove, 130 miles west of the state line, and back had emboldened Quantrill that Lawrence — Yankeetown — was not out of range. Dick was a fine fellow, had told good stories from his freighting days out west. He'd gone under the dirt three months ago.

"How's the foot, then?" asked Rains.

"Purty good, John."

Riley lied. The wound would not heal.

He didn't look at Rains. He felt so bad about everything, he was afraid he might start bawling and that wouldn't do. Buck had dropped out of the band to hole up at the James place for a while. Riley would have liked to stay with him, but hadn't been asked. And he was pretty sure of the reason. That goddamned Jesse. He and the little brother had been getting along less and less, and the tension had finally erupted into a fistfight night afore last over Jesse's latest freak. He'd found a half-rotted cat and hid it under Riley's blankets, damn his eyes. Buck had scolded Jesse, but Riley could tell Buck had wearied of the fuss. And blood was thicker than water.

"Well, you better keep washing that heel. Don't wanna get mortification in there. Lose your foot, then you can't dance or bring Yankees back to life."

That got a laugh from some of the riders who had been at Baxter Springs or at least knew how Riley had gotten drunk on captured whiskey and had been dancing around the bodies of the Yankees scattered around the fort road. Ordering the dead to get up and dance with him had gotten a big laugh out of the older men, so he'd kept it up. He'd been kicking them and whacking them with the flat side of a sword and yelled, "Get up, you Federal son of a bitch" or something like that, when damn if one of 'em didn't do just that.

The possum-player had sprinted away, so startling Riley that he missed him with his first shot, but the next somehow found his brain pan. He'd been pretty proud of that shot. One less damn skulking jayhawker. But other killings troubled Riley some, such as at Yankeetown.

Lately, he had been thinking of two men at a gunsmith shop there in Lawrence, both wounded by pistol fire. The raiders had tied them together, tossed them into the shop and set it on fire. The men struggled through the flames to the door, but were shoved back by the Missourians. The ropes burned through, one raised his hands above his head.

"The red, fierce flames wrapped him in a sheet of unutterable agony," according to one account. "One cry to the All Merciful — 'O God save us!' — pierced the roar of the fire and the tumult without, and he sank into the embers as upon a bed."

Riley remembered how the bushwhackers, these were the drunken stragglers, cheered. He remembered Old Skaggs had cheered the loudest before wandering off. That was the last they had seen of him.

So when was the debt ever paid? When did a feller get to move on? With ol' Price running back south, Riley was having a hard time believing that the Federals weren't going to come out on top and not just in Missouri. The whole war seemed barren of result. Maybe it was time for it to be over. He had been silently shocked to hear Bill say that it was soon going to come to killing Yankee women. Riley couldn't believe it, but then there were many things he was having trouble believing right now.

Like Eisenhour, in whose white-tuffed ear Archie had just burnt powder. The old fellow would be feeding the woods hogs tonight. That was the thing that terrified Riley: that hogs would eat his body. Riley had been knocked down in the pen when just a tad, and pa had heard his screams and leapt in just as the Goddamned boar had been biting on his arm. He thought of old Bill Bledsoe. They'd tried to take his body with them from Baxter Springs to Texas in a wagon, but his stink got to be overpowering. Nobody'd brung a damned shovel, so wagon boards and knives were employed to scrape a shallow grave in the hard soil. When some had come back up from Texas, though, the hole was found dug up with some scattered bones bleaching on the prairie. It wasn't Christian. Riley shivered.

Archie apparently wasn't satisfied with just sending the old man to his maker. Riley watched as the little fiend got off his horse and pulled his Bowie. With three savage strokes, he hacked the Dutchman's head off. The body was pulled around and the hands folded across the bloodied shirt. The head he set on the hands.

Maybe it was some kind of message. But all it was telling Riley was that Archie and Bill were going mad.

7:30 P.M.

Kansas City

THE SERGEANT CHEWED ON HIS PENCIL, thinking about that morning on the Big Blue River, then began the chore.

"Dear Sister: It is with great sorrow that I have to find myself in communicating to you the sad news of the Death of Poor James....between Independence and Westport. We were formed in a line..."

The Seventh hadn't even gotten down the road on the east side of that river before the shells were crashing into the Missourians.

".... We had not advanced ten steps toward the rebels when he was shot through the bowels. I was standing by his side when he fell. I picked him up and carried him back out of the lines and laid him down..."

Colonel Philips had come hustling down the road and hesitated a moment. He'd looked into James's eyes and then at the stricken brother, had shaken his head, and then kept trotting down the hill. James yelled after him, "Colonel, I'm shot to death!"

"... and he said he would like to see you, but he new that he never would..."

Sergeant George W. Combs decided not to say anything in his letter about the baby. He remembered when James had confided that he was going to be a father next year.

".... he said he was willing to die. He lived until dark that evening. He suffered very much through the day...."

Why write that? Shouldn't he have said he died instantly? A lot of the fellows from Henry County saw, though, how parts of him showed that shouldn't never be seen. Sarah would find out sooner or later, Lord preserve her. Combs' mind numb, his brother's blood still under his fingernails, the pencil seemed to move on its own across the paper.

"... put in a metallick coffin and nicely buried. When times get a little better I will have him brought home..."

When times get better. Just when will that be? It seems as if we have been killing folks forever.

"...You know the trouble I have seen. Our men pushed on after the rebels and I was left on the Battlefield among strangers and had no one to help me much about taking care of my Dear brother..."

He had tried to get the surgeons to stop, but they could tell from 10 paces that it was no good for James.

"...I am going to start to the command to morrow..."

Combs was letting the regiment go on south without him. They'd probably think he was hit, too. Made him a straggler, he guessed, or worse. As soon as he got James in the ground, though, he would get down there, too. Good thing James was an officer. They're tender toward their own. If James had been a private, he'd have been ordered to push on, to leave his brother behind. But he couldn't face mother or Sarah, tell them that he'd allowed James to be buried by folks he didn't know, in a grave that might never be found. They could bust him to private, he didn't care.

"... *Price is on the run. There has bin a great many killed and wounded. Richard Jones is wounded in the leg. You must excuse my letter, my trouble is so great that I cannot write so good....*"

Price was indeed on the run, but it was not a fast run. He was hardly pushed on the evening of Sunday the 23rd. After the rebel column had cleared out of Jackson County to the south, the three Federal major-generals suspended pursuit. They and Senator Lane and the Kansas Militia commander, George Deitzler, met at the Thomas farmhouse about five miles south of Westport. There, they agreed Deitzler could send some of his regiments home, the ones from counties north of where Price was now. The others would melt away to the south as the march passed their homes.

Even for the fire-breathing major generals Pleasonton and Blunt, the intermission was understandable; their troops had been fighting fairly steadily, many without much or even any food, for two or three days.

Given a head start with his lumbering wagons, Price made 38 miles on Monday, but he could have done better, according to General Jeff Thompson: "On the morning of the 24th, we lost several hours in getting the train untangled in forming the brigades ... in the confusion of the night before, men and wagons, artillery and refugees, were so mixed that it was nearly impossible to untangle them."

Colonel Philips' diary entry for the 24th: "Marched at daylight, reached Little Santa Fe at sunrise. Got to half wash my face, water scarce. Rations of hard bread came up. Men half starved. Moved out again at 10, crossed fork of Grand River, marched all day on old military road without halting. Men almost exhausted with fatigue. Passed through Finneyville and West Point, towns only that were. Overtook Pleasonton and Curtis at a branch in the night, enjoying a sumptuous supper. It made my hungry palate dilate, but got nothing to eat. Marched on until 2½ a.m."

That second night the rebel column made Trading Post having followed the road back across the line into Kansas. This made sense; the Missouri side had been desolated by a year of Order No. 11 and a much longer period of jayhawking. But once on the Kansas side of the line, the angry rebels found homes that were more than just a blackened chimney. Here were working farms with livestock, haystacks and crops in the fields.

"The rebels sustained their well-earned reputation for savage brutality, which had previously secured for them an infamous place in history," Captain Hinton, Blunt's aide, would say. "Seven or eight men, aged and unarmed, were murdered near Trading Post. In an extent of six miles wide through which the army passed in Linn County, every house was plundered of all kinds of provisions, blankets, clothing and all articles, valuable or worthless, that could be carried off. Even the flannel was taken from infants, in two instances that have come to my knowledge; and two young ladies were stripped of every article of clothing except one under-garment to each...."

In the rationalization of Major Edwards, Shelby's adjutant and biographer, it was simply "soothing the wounds of Missouri by stabbing the breast of Kansas. (Shelby) was fighting the devil with fire and smoking him to death. Haystacks, houses, barns, produce, crops, and farming implements were consumed before the march of his squadrons, and what the flames spared the bullet finished."

What Union Major General Philip Sheridan's army delivered out East that fall was now received by his Yankee supporters in Kansas, Edwards reasoned:

"If the crows could not fly over the valley of the Shenandoah without carrying rations, the buzzards of the prairies had no need of haversacks."

XVII

Backs against a wall

"I could see the cannons a mile away belch out their flames and smoke but could not hear them for the noise of the small arms all around me."

—Barbara Dolson, whose cabin was just south of Mine Creek

e/3e/3e/3e/3e/3

OCTOBER 25 — 10:45 A.M.

Mine Creek
Linn County, eastern Kansas

THE WHEEL HORSE WAS ON ITS foreknees, struggling and failing to regain its footing.

Even more hard-pressed now, the rest of the team, which had been nearly half way up the creek's south bank, began back-stepping, surrendering to gravity and slippery wet clay. The men behind, who put their shoulders to the overloaded wagon, shouted warnings and leapt clear, some into a chest-high current. The driver threw himself against the brake, but it made no difference. The dripping wagon slid backward into water well over its hubs. Behind, men shouted curses from a buggy that had lost momentum and was threatening to float away. Two soldiers put down rifles and came sliding down from the grass above to try to help get the horse on its feet. The teamster, furious or terrified, stood in the box and laid the whip on the droop-eared animal, barely missing the volunteers.

Major General Marmaduke was appalled.

Why wasn't the crossing cleared by this time?

He had promised Clark, who was making holding actions behind him, that the division would have a strong defensive position on the south side of the stream. But here was a line of maybe 60 wagons, many belonging to civilians. Two women, taking the opportunity to escape to Texas, were in line with their overloaded landau, pleading for help.

His adjutant, Captain Moore, writing decades later would describe "the teamsters dismounted and lying in the grass or talking with each other and about one wagon crossing the creek every five minutes."

"Sir, there comes General Cabell," said Captain Stallard. Marmaduke had sent word that the pressure from the Federal pursuit would require help from Fagan's division. The two generals and their escorts saluted the other.

"What's happening here, Bill?" Marmaduke asked Cabell. "I thought everyone would be on the south side."

"Some of us were, but General Fagan thought we'd do you more good on the north side. Moses himself could not deal with this mess. All the traffic this morning has ruined that side of the crossing. Takes forever to get a wagon up, mules slip and tangle their harness. One wagon tipped over, and it was hell getting it out of the way, took maybe 20 minutes. As you can see, my brigade is anchored to the road; it extends a ways to the northwest. That's Slemon in line here, and over there, where you can't see them for the trees is Dobbin and

Anderson, keeping an eye on that other crossing...."

"Other crossing? Can we use it?" Marmaduke trotted his horse near the main ford, a squalid mess, chewed to mud soup by wagons, cattle and whatever else Pap was trying to drag home to prove this wasn't all one giant disaster. And that south bank was truly steep, too, easy for a horse to slip on it.

"Riders probably, but this place here, bad as it is, seems the only one with a rock bottom. Just there, downstream, is another spot where you can get up and down the banks, but it's a mud bottom and deep, too." Marmaduke looked that way, didn't like what he saw. Good in dry weather only. Harris and Hynson's guns have to cross here with the wagons — whenever they can try it.

He and Cabell conferred a bit more about troop placements and then parted. Marmaduke was glad the Arkansan was on his flank. The man was destitute of fear. He wondered where Fagan was.

"Colonel Freeman, strike a line straddling the road. Overlap Cabell over there. He is to withdraw over the creek before us when the time comes."

Freeman looked toward the stream. Some of Cabell's regiments were almost backed up to it. Marmaduke's men would have a little more room behind them, but not much.

"Dismount, sir?"

Marmaduke was already trying to answer that question for himself. If this was a trap, every man would need his horse to get across that creek. But because most of their arms were Enfields, they wouldn't be able to reload them on horseback. Then it would be pistols, for whoever had them, against Yankee carbines and sabers. Cabell's men were still in their saddles.

Stroking his beard in thought, Marmaduke decided. "Stay mounted."

Freeman's relief was obvious as he went to set his men.

"It is contrary to all military precedent to fight a battle with an impassable stream in the rear," Colonel John C. Wright, who was in Fagan's division, would write later. "In this case, however, Marmaduke ... had no choice. To have crossed the stream would have involved the loss of a large part of the train and he had reason to believe he could whip the enemy."

Marmaduke noticed a cabin just off the road on the other side of the creek. A young woman was there, holding a baby. He wondered what she thought of all this.

"What is this place, Moore, the Little Osage?"

"I have no idea."

Stallard spoke up. "Mine Creek, I'm told, sir."

"And what was the one this morning?" asked Marmaduke.

"Not sure, sir, some French name."

"Mary Somebody," suggested Moore.

That will be good to write up in the official report — some French name. The town was Trading Post, Marmaduke knew. That would do.

Marmaduke decided to place Hynson's Battery on the far end of his flank. Just two now. One had been captured earlier in the day; Fagan had lost two six-pounders, as well. A ravine running south to the creek seemed like it would provide them some protection from being flanked.

Riding past his line, he kept his eye on the top of the slope. He didn't know how many Federal brigades were out there, but it was too damned many. It had been a while since he'd been shelled at 4 o'clock in the morning. Those boys back there — Blunt, Rosecrans, Pleasonton, whoever — are in an unpleasant hurry. He wished Price was. Him and his damned wagons.

Some of the men were muttering as the hooves of their stamping horses made sucking sounds in the mud. They didn't like being stuck waiting on this side, either. Harris was positioning his guns at the road. Marmaduke looked at the ford again. Some progress, but hardly enough. Why weren't there extra teams on the south side to help pull the wagons up that bank? Was anybody in charge there?

His eye caught movement on the gentle grass cloaked slope to the north. Horsemen! Marmaduke stiffened. But no, that was Clark, his brigade coming in, falling back.

Clark's horse was blowing hard when he reached Marmaduke.

"John, as you can see, we have problems here…."

"General, we have problems there." Clark pointed behind. Blue uniforms, at least a thousand, were coming into view not that far behind Colton Greene's fleeing troops, the very tail of Marmaduke's rear guard. The Yankees were stopping, however, their lines spreading out.

Cabell had mentioned Moses a little while ago. Well, here is Pharaoh's army.

Marmaduke looked toward Cabell and his colonels, who were pointing at the Federals and discussing a charge against them — until another mass of Union cavalry materialized to the right of the first. Marmaduke still mulled the idea of an attack. It would push the Yankees back, disorganize them, buy a little time. But it would disorganize his own men, too. Better that they stay in line for now.

"Cabell's on the west side of the road," he told Clark. "Form your men on Freeman. There's Burbridge over there, supporting Hynson's guns. He will be to your right. Double your lines, triple them if practical. Set Greene back as a reserve. At this point, John, I think it's best to keep the men mounted."

"I heartily agree, sir," Clark said, moving off to position his men.

Marmaduke noticed a good-sized gap between the two enemy brigades. Perhaps that could be exploited. Giving orders for his artillery to open fire, he began to feel that he might just bluff those fellows over there. After all, there must be twice as many of us down here.

Some of the Yankees were dismounting, firing rifles at long range. Some horses in Freeman's ranks squealed in pain, two went down thrashing. Smoke erupted from Freeman people in return, mostly wasted shots. Now their rifles were emptied, nearly useless. As Marmaduke watched, he could tell the men were unsure. Perhaps, he thought, he should head over that way, buck them up some.

Then an odd sound, no, an old sound, filtered through the firing. Marmaduke instinctively tilted his head at the honk of geese, saw long, undulating "V's" of geese not so high above. Kindred spirits up there, he thought. Everyone wants to get south, but it's easier for some than others. Geese don't … wait, that was it.

"Captain Stallard, I believe that last river was called Marais des Cygnes."

"Sir?"The captain responded, concentrating on the Yankees. "Mary De-Zane?"

"No, not 'Mary.' 'Marais.' The old French named it. Marais des Cygnes. Marsh of the Swans. Beautiful name, don't you think?"

Then they both heard the shouting of the enemy officers and the bugles. The first line of Federal troops began walking their steeds down the slope. When several yards of space was created between it and the second rank, the bugles spoke again and the enemy ranks broke into a trot. To the west, the other Federal brigade was picking up speed. Yelling from the foe, confident sounds.

Marmaduke looked at Clark's ranks. They looked solid, good men. There was Jeffers, his stalwart oak. A thought struck him. He should have put Jeffers in the center, instead of Freeman's green men. Well, it was too late now. He decided to keep his sword sheathed and drew out his Savage, hoping the loads were still dry.

"I believe it will be a long day, Captain Stallard."

No sooner had the general uttered the prophecy, than it began to come to pass. Freeman's men had turned their horses and were fleeing — spreading panic like a contagion — toward the crossing.

11:35 A.M.

WHAT THE DEVIL WAS BENTEEN ABOUT?

Sergeant Samuel Bereman's Fourth Iowa, in the second rank of Benteen's brigade, had been thundering at full tilt down the gentle slope toward the Confederates … when suddenly they realized that the horsemen in front, the 10th Missouri, had pulled up.

But the shouting, cursing Iowans could not, would not be stopped.

Half the reb army was in their front. Anybody could see what was happening. They were having trouble getting their wagons over, some riflemen were formed on the other side of the water, but most were just down the slope, uneasily sitting their horses, waiting for what came next. Spread out along a mile of the full creek, their asses practically in it.

"They had ten pieces of artillery which they opened on us before we got within range of muskets," recalled Bereman's diary. "'Charge!' was heard. It was repeated by field & line officers and then we started on the gallop. We had orders not to fire until within close range. Every one could see that there could be no drawn battle there. There was no skulking, no hiding behind trees. Every movement — every man could be seen. The rebels had more than twice our number — besides the artillery of which we had none with us there. But we were better armed than them."

The First Brigade of Missouri militia cavalry, on the Federal right, had gotten there first. Lieutenant Colonel Bazel Lazear, commanding the First Missouri State Militia Regiment, had the advance on that wing. He had dismounted his men in the high prairie grass, losing a few to the rebel artillery fire. His commander, Colonel John Philips, came up with the bulk of the brigade, and Smiley's battery unlimbered and begun to toss shells into the butternut ranks below. Then the brigade now commanded by Lieutenant Colonel Frederick Benteen appeared on their left. As quickly as Lazear's men could remount, the Federal attack commenced.

Then, within 300 yards of the rebel line, the 10th Missouri on the left froze. A puzzled Philips also halted, thinking that perhaps the plan had changed to a fight on foot. Embarrassed and furious, the round-faced Benteen cursed his men, although part of the blame lay with his own decision to ride at the right of his line, not out in the lead where his troops could see him.

Trying to get the attack underway again, "he rode directly in front of his men, within pistol shot of his enemy, hatless, white with passion, waving his sword and shouting the order to charge," Fourth Iowa Sergeant Major William Forse Scott would recall. "His trumpeters repeated it, and all the trumpets answered with the same piercing notes… the two opposing lines of men simply stood, glaring at each other."

Led by the gallant Major Abial Pierce, however, the Iowans were not to be deterred. Most managed to veer around to the left; others, like Sergeant Bereman, blasted through gaps between the frozen Missourians. His stirrups thudded into horses and men on either side, but he squeezed through.

Seeing the Iowans barreling toward the rebels' right flank, Philips again ordered the charge. By this time, the 10th Missouri had come out of its trance and bolted forward. The gap between the two Federal brigades closed just before they slammed into the rebel center.

Benteen would say he came up beside Philip's regiment, saw that the rebel artillery was vulnerable, sent "a request for him to charge with me, for God's sake…. The line of the brigade was soon passed, but it did not charge with us." Philips, for his part, would report that "Benteen's brigades came upon my left, and as soon as his advance regiment got into position I began the attack." Whose report would be true? Perhaps Benteen would let it slip when he wrote,

"The fire of the enemy was so hot that for a moment it staggered even my own gallant regiment." That might cover up the embarrassing episode of his own 10th Missouri Regiment's freezing.

"Come on, Iowa! Come on! We've got em!" Bereman yelled, watching the southerners trying to control their nervous horses while taking aim from their saddles. An officer's sword flashed down, and the rifles erupted in smoke. The young sergeant did not look back, heard the grunt of men and screams of horses as the balls found targets, but instinctively knew the damage was light.

"Commenced firing before we had got within good range, but we never faltered," Bereman would say in describing the event. "Kept on like an avalanche when within two hundred yards of them we opened on them with our Spencer carbins & revolvers. Every man had a dozzen shots without reloading. It must be terrifying to see 4 or 5 thousand horsemen coming with almost the speed of the wind yelling firing rushing like a tempest. Before we had reached their line they began to break (melt away) — a gap here — another there — yonder on the left the line is bent back — now they give way all along the line & begin to run — attempt to get their guns away, they are shot down, we are within their line, we mingle."

Over to the right, Philips' Missourians plunged in, too, accompanied by one company of the 11th Kansas cavalry that had been assigned as Pleasonton's escort since Westport. This was Captain Henry Palmer's Company A, where Private Sam Worthington was having trouble with his mount, "so hard mouthed, I could do nothing with him. I had emptied my revolvers before I got to the line of battle and, with three other horses, charged clear through the lines."

Bereman saw Pierce plunge into a clot of rebel horsemen, chop frenziedly with his saber, emptying two, no, three saddles. One reb came up from behind to try to club the bladesman, but slumped from a bullet before a blow could be delivered. Pierce cut down one more Confederate before they turned from the fight. He pursued, dispatching them one by one. "In that charge we crushed the enemy's right completely. We pressed them so close that I cut eight rebels from their horses," Pierce would report.

"Suddenly the first and second lines gave way," recalled Confederate Colonel Colton Greene, "and rushing in great disorder ran over and broke the eight right companies of my regiment. The same wild panic seemed to seize everything. I wheeled my only remaining company to the right and opened on the flank of the enemy's column until two of the guns were born to the rear."

Benteen would call it "a fierce hand-to-hand fight, one that surpassed anything for the time it lasted I have ever witnessed." To Colonel Charles W. Blair of the 14th Kansas Cavalry: "…the fire was incessant and terrific. Both lines seemed like walls of adamant — one could not advance; the other would not recede. The crash of musketry, the scream of shell, the hissing sound of canister and balls, mingled with the shouts of the soldiers and the cries of the wounded

… formed a scene more easily remembered than described."

Bereman chanced a glance to the right. The First Brigade Missourians were driving their foes in confusion, as well. A pistol round sang from his left, he swung his Spencer at the rider now nearly beside him, but his finger relaxed at the sight of the Union overcoat. Wait, no Union man would wear that hat! The treacherous reb veered away into the melee.

Many Johnnies were giving up, others trying to break away to the west. A shell burst in the horse-churned mud, splattering the Iowans. Bereman looked over the creek trying to spot a rebel battery, but saw nothing but fleeing men. Another burst, and the men were shouting that they were being targeted by Federal batteries. What? Bereman looked north and saw that horribly it was true. Smoke erupted from two howitzers that seemed directed straight at Bereman. He jerked his reins and sent his mount back the way he had come.

"We advanced so far into the enemy ranks that Major-General Pleasonton ordered our own battery to shell us, thinking we were the retreating enemy, and my men were obliged to scatter to avoid being cut to pieces by our own shells," Pierce would recall.

Over on the Confederates' left flank, Colonel John C. Wright was fighting off a weak Federal force that "gave way with but little resistance. My sole attention was now called to the confusion on our right. Facing the regiment about, I moved rapidly to the rear and in a few minutes was in the midst of a disorganized mass of fleeing men, pursued by and mixed up with the Federal cavalry. Many plunged into the boggy stream and floundered across…. All sense of order and discipline was at an end. It was 'save who can!'"

"The stream was everywhere full of men and horses," recalled Confederate Private James Darr, of Cabell's brigade. "The Confederates trying to make their escape and the Federals trying just as hard to capture or kill them."

Another private, James Campbell, had put up his six-shooter but had no intention of giving up yet. He spurred his little mule hard, and "forty of us simply ran over a solid line of Union Cavalry who tried to halt us. Just as we struck the edge of the prairie we were cornered (by) a new stake and rider fence, but the leaders threw the fence down to knee high and as we jumped over, I heard the command: 'Scatter, boys, or they will kill every one of us!'"

Wright and hundreds of others galloped toward the fence gap, but it quickly became blocked in the panic. The colonel thought to give up, "but I saw men shot down while holding up their hands in token surrender."

He then determined to run the gantlet of Union cavalrymen, who now were as disorganized as the rebels. With some calling for him to halt and sending carbine rounds at him, Wright circled his black mare, dug in the spurs and sailed her over the fence. He quickly reached a smaller and now well-mucked ford and passed Lieutenant Zimmerman's guns stuck in the mire.

The whole prairie, Wright saw, seemed covered with fleeing soldiers, whom he could not get to stop. His mare had bottom, though, and galloping ahead of the mob, he found a rider with a flag and ordered him to slow his gait. Then he began to gather other riders and called them to form on the flag. Before long, Wright had a fighting unit again, although one not as well armed as before. Greene reported that more than two-thirds of his surviving men had lost their weapons — most tossing them aside for better escape.

To Bereman, the rout at Mine Creek was Shakespearean.

"They rush pell mell, like a drove of cattle across the creek & away, away across the prairie —we follow on until our horses tired and jaded can run no farther," the Iowa sergeant wrote. "Oh! 'a kingdom' for a fresh horse! Tis too bad to see so many of them slipping away from us & to have no power to hinder them...."

12:30 P.M.

PHILIPS SHOUTED THAT REBS WERE ESCAPING across the creek. Then in his peripheral vision, a flash. Suddenly vision in his right eye exploded into blazing yellows and whirling reds.

He slumped, grabbed his face with a gloved hand. Pulled it away, looked dizzily at the glove with his good eye. What, no blood? God, but it hurt! Was he shot? Was he blinded? God, it hurt!

"The colonel is hit!" he heard. An officer grabbed his reins. Philips straightened on his horse and almost vomited from the agony.

He took his glove down. "Is my eye still there?"

It seemed intact, his aides said, best as could be told. Philips probably was hit by the wad from a round fired close by, a round that passed over his head. Through the throb of pain, he squinted his left eye and scanned the aftermath of a sharp, savage fight. Wagons abandoned, some burning, weapons in the grass everywhere.

A man named Henry Trinkle, who lived in the vicinity of the battlefield, would recount it this way:

"Fully three hundred horses horribly mangled were wild, running, and snorting, and trampling the dead and wounded men. Their blood drenching all around them and added to the ghastliness of it all."

At the ford over Mine Creek, a little dam was created by the bogged-down wagons and dead horses and mules. The body of a man in a red shirt pulled by the current bumped off a wheel and continued its voyage downstream. An officer told Philips that they'd captured eight enemy guns. The Federals now possessed a great many rifles, too, tossed down in the crushed grass and horse-churned mud. At first observation, one could assume that the Union men had suffered most. But that was deceiving, he realized. Most of the prone men were actually rebs wearing blue.

Some scattered shooting still could be heard to the west along the creek, but many of his men had their carbines or pistols leveled at captives on foot. There were more than a couple hundred of them, many in blue overcoats, and that was just Philips' captives. The other brigades were busy in the aftermath, too. Here came perhaps three dozen more prisoners into the group, some limping, some supported by comrades. One was trying to bandage a hand that was missing fingers, probably caused by trying to ward off a saber slash; next to him was a fellow who sank to his knees, holding his side.

A wave of pain flashed from Philips' eye to his temple. His good eye closed and he emitted a low grunt-groan between gritted teeth.

Tom Crittenden spurred his horse over. "Christ, John, what got you? That eye looks like hell. Can you go on? Rebs are reforming on the other side, and we're supposed to hit 'em again."

Philips heard a great splashing and looked back at the stream. The movement of his head caused another lightning bolt to strike the back of his eyeball. He jerked and lightning struck twice. Benteen's people were crossing the creek to pick another fight on the south side. He turned his head slowly toward his friend.

"Start forming the men. We'll cross as soon as that bunch clears. Tell Lazear to follow up as soon as he can get his First reorganized."

He looked back down at the prisoners. Some were insisting they had been conscripted, that Price had forced them to join his column. Philips did not doubt it. Dozens of them — no, hundreds? — wore Union blue overcoats or jackets. How many times had Anderson and Quantrill and the other murderers worn the Federal uniform to get close to their victims? The practice had infuriated the militia officers, another indication of how the cowards had no honor, followed no rules in their godless war. Rosecrans had issued an order that rebs caught this way "be dealt with accordingly." Pleasonton hanged three rebs in Union garb at Lexington a few days ago.

These were fellow Missourians, but what kind of Missourians? Philips had no love for Kansans, but he'd seen what these Missourians had done to the settlers in the path of their retreat south. Jackman's men were probably here. He was little better than Quantrill, had killed prisoners up at Westport. Was Jackman here himself, was Quantrill or Anderson? No decency resided in such men, who lurked in the woods, only coming out to murder the Union men who were once their neighbors. They deserved no clemency.

"'Lo, Petersen," he heard one blue-overcoated prisoner say to a trooper recognized as a neighbor from Tipton. "Have any water on you? This prisoner bid'ness is mighty dry work." The trooper tossed his canteen and got a nodded thanks in return. Philips waited until the canteen had been returned.

"Separate out the ones in our uniforms," Philips quietly ordered, turning his horse toward the creek. The eye throbbed so.

"And shoot them."

1 P.M.

"I AM OBLIGED TO YOU," MARMADUKE told the young soldier who waved a biscuit of hardtack toward him. The general suddenly realized he was famished.

He bit off a piece, taking care to chew just on one side of his mouth. A back tooth was acting up, and he did not need a larger ration of misery just now.

The bread was hard, but facts were harder. His division was gone. He was a prisoner. His war was over.

It had happened so fast — had it taken more than 30 minutes? — he was still grappling with the events.

Such a rush of Yankee cavalry he had never experienced in four years of war, thousands of them, lapping around his right flank, swallowing up his guns in a blink. Some were behind his line so fast that at first he thought they must be Fagan's reinforcements wearing those Yankee overcoats. And then the rest slammed into his line, leaving his men to fend off sabers with empty rifles. Panic had raced through his lines as fast as the Iowans' horses. Some of his command had fled west to hide behind Cabell. Some had tried to swim their mounts to safety, although Yankee carbines had made that an expensive undertaking.

He remembered a staff officer grabbing his sleeve, shouting, "Sir, you need to fall back!"

"Fall back?" He'd shouted back furiously. "Fall back to where?!"

A major, hatless and blond hair wild, screaming "Re-form! Re-form, here!" One of his ears, nearly torn off, had flopped back and forth spreading a light shower of blood. Suddenly a young rider had appeared, blasting away at the sabered major. Furious, Marmaduke had shouted at the imbecile:

"He's one of ours, you damned fool! Stop firing."

The youth had looked oddly at him, lowered his pistol. Marmaduke's horse was becoming harder to control, pivoting in a full circle. When the youth had come back into his view, his revolver was leveled at Mamaduke's chest. With a jolt, Marmaduke realized that he had grown so accustomed to seeing his own men wearing the captured woolens that he'd committed a fatal error.

"You are my prisoner!" the corporal — for now Marmaduke saw the chevrons — had screamed. "Get off that horse! Now!"

Marmaduke had still gripped his own revolver, but lowered it to his thigh while wrestling with his mount. He calculated the chances of getting a shot off.

"Get off that horse! Get off or I'll shoot you off!" The boy's voice was yet more shrill.

Suddenly as weary as he'd ever felt in his life, Marmaduke shrugged, dropped his weapon and dismounted. He stood waiting when suddenly his big gray reared, jerked the reins away, and galloped away.

"You are my prisoner," the boy again had shouted.

The conflicting currents of blue uniforms had confused many. After the battle, Andrew Jackson "Buck" McManus would recount the story of Confederate

Colonel William Jeffers of the Eighth Missouri Cavalry: "Jeffers galloped up to a battery that had been supported by our men, but the Yanks had captured it unknown to the Colonel. He waved his sword and ordered them to get away or they would be captured in five minutes…. As he stopped his horse, one grabbed his sword, one his bridle, and some his legs. Then he saw his mistake. He looked back at me and said, 'Oh, hell!'"

Marmaduke had seen the blood dripping from his captor's hand. A Union officer cantered by, and the corporal had asked whether he could turn his prisoner over to him. The officer seemed uninterested and began to ride away. Suddenly it occurred to Marmaduke that no rank showed on his overcoat, that neither Yankee knew who he was.

"Sir," he'd called to the older man, "you are an officer. I claim protection at your hands. I am Major-General John Sappington Marmaduke."

That got the attention of both men.

"I am Colonel Charles Blair. I take responsibility for your person until I can present you to General Curtis."

The corporal had looked alarmed.

"Colonel, remember, I took him prisoner. I am Dunlavy, Company D, Third Iowa." James Dunlavy was one of two Union soldiers who for his action that day would receive the Medal of Honor and an eight-month furlough that got him through the end of his enlistment. The other was Sergeant Cavalry N. Young, who captured General William Cabell.

Blair had smiled and suggested that they both take Marmaduke back. The corporal would get credit and also attention for his wounded wrist.

Now, gnawing at the biscuit in the yard of a house, Marmaduke realized that he shared his humiliation with at least eight colonels. All looked exhausted. Slemon was covered with mud. Apparently, his Arkansas line had been handled as roughly as Marmaduke's Missourians. There was Enoch Wolf, but the major would not look at him. Ashamed perhaps of how his people behaved in the center, but he apparently had not run, too, or he would not be here. Marmaduke would say something to him. But where was Clark? He called over to Jeffers, who sat with his face in his hands, but got nothing definite. Marmaduke worried about that, hoped John was not lying in the grass down there by that damned creek.

Those in the left wing of the Confederate line had much more luck in getting away, but Clark had managed to fight his way out of the pocket.

"Both flanks gave way in hopeless confusion," the general would report. "Every effort was made by appeals and threats to relieve the route to no avail. Gallant spirits, however, were seen here and there in sad contrast to those who had thrown away their arms. I succeeded in forming about 500 men and retired in some order to the main column."

Marmaduke noticed a little commotion in the yard; it was Cabell's delivery into their company. Seeing Marmaduke, a fellow West Pointer, the general rushed over.

"They shot my men, John, shot them as they surrendered," he moaned. "It was butchery. I got them to stop, but it was too late for many. Sons o' bitches. Shot them for wearing those goddamned overcoats."

"I called Colonel Cloud's attention to the outrageous conduct of the Kansas Militia," Cabell would say later. "He tried to excuse their conduct by saying … they only killed our men who had on Federal uniforms…. I replied that four-fifths of our men were without uniforms of any kind. He then stated that he would put a stop to their killing my wounded men. Being a prisoner I could do no more."

Cabell had barely escaped execution himself. A "deserter," as he later recalled, probably a Union soldier in Colonel Phelps' Second Arkansas (USA), approached and said, "Old Tige, we have got you now, and I intend to kill you." The would-be executioner raised his carbine, but a Union sergeant intervened.

He had been captured three times, Cabell told them, the first after he tried to jump his horse over the stream, a prodigious leap but its back legs had not carried to the south bank. The poor beast had toppled backward on him. He had kicked free of his stirrups and surfaced gasping in the freezing water. He had tried to swim away, but Federals fired a round in front of him and yelled for him to come back. Once on the north bank, however, he was allowed to wander off into the trees to make another try — and to be caught again. Once more he slipped away in the confusion. But his third capture had stuck, and here he was.

Teams of horses were approaching, pulling some Parrotts and caissons to the rear.

"Any of your guns get over?" Cabell asked Slemon, who had been bagged while trying to get a field piece across the creek. He shook his head. They did the math. Eight 12-pounders lost here, three smaller ones earlier in the day. That left just the three of Shelby. Marmaduke shrugged. Those lost guns would be irreplaceable, but it was nothing against the losses at Vicksburg, where 260 cannon were captured by the Federals.

Before long, Marmaduke and Cabell were presented to the major-generals Pleasonton and Curtis, who were perhaps more gracious to the captives than to each other. Reporting back to his superiors, Pleasonton, as was his wont, would claim responsibility for the charge by Benteen and Philips and would be brutal on the senior general on the field: "I regret to add that Major General Curtis gave me no support whatever this day (25th), but, to the benefits of the rebels his troops were kept back and did not participate in any of the engagements; otherwise I should have captured Price's whole force. After the fight was over General Curtis moved his forces up, and with the most exemplary modesty laid claims to the prisoners … that had been captured; but which I could not recognize, since he had waived his right to command at the time…."

Captain Richard Hinton would take Pleasonton's side when he wrote his account immediately after the war: "Curtis came up and ordered his own provost-marshal to take charge of the prisoners, captured artillery, and property, and when he got to Fort Scott that night directed that these trophies of the campaign be sent to Fort Leavenworth. He thus proposed to deprive the Missouri troops of their justly won trophies and to bestow them upon the Kansas troops, who were not entitled to them, nor to the prestige...."

Colonel John Ritchie, an aide to Curtis, took possession of the "trophies," even arresting a hotly protesting officer on the staff of Pleasonton, who then had Ritchie himself placed under arrest.

Trying to smooth things over, Curtis would write to Pleasonton regretting that "fuss and feeling was got up." The two commanders would reach a compromise that both Missouri and Kansas troops would have the honor of marching the rebels to Fort Leavenworth, from where they would be shipped to wherever necessary. Rosecrans, however, would break the agreement, getting wind of a plan — it smelled a lot like an idea of Senator Lane — to parade the captured generals in Kansas towns for political reasons. Instead, he would have Pleasonton transport the prisoners to Warrensburg, where they would be placed on a train to St. Louis.

As the generals squabbled over this batch of "trophy" Confederates, a few hundred more of lower rank lay where they had crawled or fallen all through that awful battle. Most probably were shot in the body, their diminishing moans and cries for water haunting the freezing darkness. No one came to gather up them up until the next morning.

"As soon as the firing ceased mother and I went out to see what we could do for the wounded," Barbara Dolson would recall. "We showed the men with the ambulance where the wounded were. They had fallen all about the house and crawled away to fence corners or brush.... When we got home we found two wounded men in our house, one a Union man and one a Rebel."

A few cabins in the area were designated as field hospitals, but surgeons were in short supply; many had stayed behind to clean up after Westport. Sixty-two of the wounded eventually made it to a makeshift hospital at Mound City, Kansas, and then when they could be moved were sent to Fort Leavenworth for care. Exactly half recovered and were shown on prisoner-of-war lists.

Marmaduke found himself beside Wolf, who still had trouble meeting his eyes. He had been in Barney Ford's battalion that had a high proportion of men, some more or less weaponless, whom Shelby had conscripted at the beginning of the campaign.

"I am so sorry, General. They would not stick, you know? I tried to hold them in line, but they would not stick. I am so sorry. I am the unluckiest man in the world."

Marmaduke assured him that he was not, that he had done what he could, that they all had. It nagged the general that he had left these men in his center. But, he told himself, it was his right that had failed most disastrously, and those were his best men. Ah, well.

He remembered how Jeff Thompson, when they had shared a stove in Hermann, had talked of his tour of the Yankee prison camps. Thompson had said many of the high-ranking officers got sent to Johnson's Island up on the lake above Ohio. Desperately cold, terrible winds, Jeff said.

It would be a long winter.

6 P.M.

North of Dry Wood Creek
Vernon County, western Missouri

HIS MOUTH WAS COTTON, HIS THROAT constricted, his skull pounding. He lifted his head from his weaving trot just in time to avoid smacking into a horse's ass.

Private Guilford Gage and the others in the rank of prisoners had been running for hours. Just ahead on the road were four rebel horsemen riding abreast down the road south. Just behind him were another four. Behind them yet another rank of exhausted Federal captives, another line of cavalry and so on.

Gasping for air, the miserable Kansans had to keep up to avoid being trampled by the horses trotting behind. Desperate for water. The afternoon before it rained lightly off and on. Skin was numbed by cold; he'd sucked moisture off his mustache. Today, no rain. Only crossing little streams could they scoop up water in their palms as they ran on. Water thousands of horses had churned. Gage wanted to curse his tormentors, but no breath, could not concentrate on the words, could only comprehend that he was dying of thirst. And he ran on.

The only things keeping his mind off his thirst were his feet, which felt like pounded meat. His boots were yanked off not long after the artilleryman was captured with the 24-pound howitzer. His captors left Gage his socks, but the bottoms had worn away long ago. His feet were raw, toenails broken and bleeding from stubbing rocks and frozen ruts. He could not bear to imagine how the soles of his feet looked. And he ran on.

Two days before, as the armies had slugged it out around Westport, the prisoners were moved south across the Blue to join the baggage and supply train. The wagons sat there for a couple of hours and then began moving. The rebels shouted at the prisoners to fall in.

"We kept this rapid gait all that day and far into the night, and the train was galloping or trotting all the time," Gage would write, "we halted late that (Sunday) night and had made at least sixty miles… and when we did stop at last it was only for long enough to get forage for their horses, and then we went on again. …far into the night, every night, and we started again before daylight every morning. Halting and rest came seldom.…"

Certainly, it must have felt like 60, but it was only about 10, a shockingly small distance considering that Price had an aggressive Union army just behind him. The rebels shared some stolen beef with the prisoners at night, but water always was in short supply when on the run. When the column stopped Monday night at Trading Post, Captain Andrew J. Huntoon, a physician captured with the Second Kansas Militia, noted an "acute mania" among the men. One was Gage, who in a daze began to dig a two-foot "well" with his hands even though they sat on the banks of a dry stream. One of the Germans in the group went mad. They led him on a rope like a stumbling child to keep him from running and being gunned down by the guards. That night it rained heavily. The men were able to relish the clean water falling into their mouths, but once sated, they shivered in misery.

"…Their feet were frost-bitten and bleeding, they were without coats, hats, or blankets, and almost famished and worn out," Doc Jennison would report of prisoners his 15th Kansas Cavalry came across later in the week. "They had been driven like cattle at the rate of forty and fifty miles a day, had been starved and stripped of all clothing except such as would barely suffice to cover their nakedness, and when they could walk no further, were paroled and left on the road without food, or clothing, or shelter, or fire. Such pitiable objects I hope I may never see again. They ate hard tack (of which our commissary alone consisted) with the eagerness of famishing animals, and hugged the fire as closely as it was their last chance. These men live in our midst now. Ask them if the picture is overdrawn."

Now the staggering prisoners overheard that a stop was planned for Dry Wood Creek. Gage resolved that he would run no more. Two other men, First Sergeant J. A. Polley and Private Nelson Young, signaled that they were game. When the prisoners were halted for the night, Gage looked around and saw a copse of black jack oaks that might serve as an escape route. But then they were kicked to their feet to shamble another mile. No timber here, but a small waterway 100 yards away.

While most of the Kansans gratefully slumped to the ground, Gage got a quick bead on where the guards were posting themselves. Gage gave a little jerk of his head and the others followed to the edge of the invisible boundary before collapsing. They lay roughly equal distances between two of the weary Confederate watchers. One of the fires where other rebels huddled was a little too close, Gage thought, but it couldn't be helped.

Huntoon stood up, began wandering between the prisoners, talking to them or crouching to offer his negligible medical help. As an officer and physician, he got more leeway than the other captives, who were not allowed to rise. In a few moments, Huntoon was squatting next to the three escapees, whispering.

"So it's tonight, is it? I think you're right. Seems to be more confusion than usual. I think there's been a fight, and they got whipped again."

Gage was not sure how Huntoon had divined that they wanted either to escape or die. Both of his companions, however, were members of Huntoon's B Company.

"Will you come with us, sir?" asked Polley.

"No, I can't. Have to stay with the men. But don't worry about me." Then he began speaking louder and handling one of Gage's ruined feet for effect. One of the guards had shifted their way, stamping his feet.

"Yes, Guilford, it's certainly frostbite, but keep rubbing the toes and you'll probably save them." The guard, thinking of his own toes, stamped away. Huntoon resumed whispering.

"Keep your eyes on me. Choose your moment well, and once you go, keep going west. You know which way that it is? Yes. Well, good luck."

The captain rose stiffly and wandered to another huddle of miserable Kansans. The guard was stamping back. Huntoon rose and addressed him, jokingly complaining of the wet chill. The guard stopped and turned to offer his own opinion on the weather. Huntoon laughed and said something, at which the rebel laughed, too. As the captain moved a little closer to continue the conversation, he angled slightly to pull the reb's peripheral vision away from the tensed Kansans. Gage looked over his shoulder toward the next guard on duty. He was impersonating a turtle, trying to pull his head deep into the collar in his overcoat.

Gage tapped Young's leg, then began belly-crawling through the grass as quickly and silently as he could. They would have to pass near one of the sentries who was taking the most of his turn to sleep. Gage heard snoring, which was a good. Under his blanket, the Confederate truly was tight in the arms of Morpheus, and his sounds might cover noise the escapees made. One of Gage's lacerated heels wound up in Young's face, but the soft thud did not interrupt the snores. Huntoon laughed loudly at some joke the guard made. Gage detected a recession in the ground and turned slightly to follow it. He could hear Polley wheezing behind him, hoped that the guards couldn't. The low place became a little eroded gully, better and better.

They slipped into the brush of a creek. Before starting off west toward Fort Scott, Gage knelt and put his face to the cold water sliding over a gravel bar. He gulped and gulped, raising his face only enough to breathe. And he drank on.

OCTOBER 26 — 2 A.M.

Shiloh Creek
Vernon County

A WHINNY BROKE LEVI UTT'S FEVERED sleep on the frozen ground. The horse itself nearly dislocated the captain's shoulder. Utt had wrapped the reins of the animal around his wrist to keep it from wandering off in search of forage. Now he and his troopers sat up and heard what had spooked the animals. Explosions. Artillery?

Utt got his right boot under him and stood, aching but alert to a battle that he should perhaps be attending.

Then the southern sky grew light. A big burning down there. Something flaming went flying high into the sky after a burst of sound. Then another. The glow brightened. Utt broke into a laugh that became wheezing.

"They're burning their train," he exulted when he could make words. "All those wagons we let get away are going up in smoke. That's their ammunition."

Old Ellsworth, a private about 70 years old and the pride of F Company, grunted and lay back on his chill rubber blanket, muttering about his bones. Others around him, Utt's little regiment and the men of McNeil's brigade, gave a little cheer. It wasn't much. They were still famished, still freezing.

General John McNeil's bad case of the slows had not been cured, and his brigade had missed the scrap at Mine Creek. Showing up fresher and better organized than the units that had smashed into the rebs at Mine Creek, they were sent to take the lead in the pursuit. But then Major General Pleasonton had left them out here with Benteen's bunch to maintain contact with the rebs. Everyone else had gone to Fort Scott. Supply wagons, once they caught up with the column, were supposed to have been sent, but apparently got lost. The last grub issued to them was two pieces of hardtack — three days ago.

It had been that kind of a day.

For General Jeff Thompson, as well.

Price had sent him to capture the supplies stacked at Fort Scott and burn the weakly manned installation if possible. It would be a prize, just as a nervous Federal Captain M. N. Insley had warned the commanders in Kansas City. "It seems to be you are leaving this post an easy conquest for the enemy," Isley wrote. "I know the situation here and speak advisedly. There are $4,000,000 worth of public property to be protected or lost...."

Thompson and the Iron Brigade had barely gotten underway, however, before new orders came galloping after it.

Scouts had spotted Colonel Thomas Moonlight's shadowing Federal cavalry force not many miles to the west of Price's train, so he diverted Thompson to a blocking position against a possible flanking attack. Once the two brigades saw each other, men began to spread out for an engagement. Thompson considered the ground and decided to place his thin regiments along some high ground. The pickets had begun a desultory fire when Thompson got yet another countermanding order. Jo Shelby wanted the brigade to return to him at Little Osage River.

Like everyone else south of Mine Creek, Shelby had had no clue about the disaster unfolding behind him. "A courier came rushing to the front, saying that Marmaduke had been seriously wounded and that General Shelby was ordered to the back," Major Harry Vivian would recall. "This so angered old Joe that he had nothing to do all the way to the rear but stand up in his stirrups and swear with every step of his horse."

Nor had Thompson been particularly alarmed by the recall. Because Colonel Jackman's brigade had been placed at the head of the train early that day, Thompson's men were the only reserve. He passed word to his colonels to pull back the pickets and bring their men off the line as discreetly as they could, one regiment at a time. As the Confederates re-formed out of eyesight of the Yankees, Thompson sent them back the way they had come.

He stayed at the ridge with his staff to keep an eye on the Federals, who did not appear all that pugnacious, who in fact were retracing their own steps. Moonlight had had no thought of attacking Price's column. His objective was purely defensive, trying to protect Kansas towns from raiding Confederates. His column had fought off one attack on Mound City and was headed to Fort Scott to do the same. Moonlight's priority now was to reach the supply depot before the hungry rebels.

Satisfied that his brigade would not be hit in the rear, Thompson and his staff officers began trotting back east to rejoin the rest of the army.

"To my astonishment, the Army was gone," he wrote later. He was not speaking geographically, but existentially.

The disaster at Mine Creek astonished everyone. Price got on his horse to ride back to restore order, but "met the divisions of Maj. Gens. Fagan and Marmaduke retreating in utter and indescribable confusion, many of them having thrown away their arms. They were deaf to all entreaties or commands and in vain were all efforts to rally them."

As Thompson's regiments returned, Shelby drew up them up in three lines as a holding position on the south side of the Little Osage. Now they were about six miles southeast of the Mine Creek crossing. Arriving, Thompson saw that no pickets had been deployed out front, so he ordered his staff officers to do the dangerous duty.

Around 2 p.m., McNeil's long line of dark blue, ready to take another bite out of the Confederate army, filled the road to the north.

"In a few minutes the Carbines commenced throwing their long range balls about us," Thompson would write, "and an occasional hit or frightened horse began to shake our line. A few of our men answered them, but the single shot arms were held quiet. When they approached to within two hundred fifty yards of us, the command was given (to the Federal troopers) to prepare to charge. Carbines were thrown back, and the revolvers and Sabres were drawn, it seems that some preferred one and some the other! We now blazed away with our volley and wheeled to retreat. They came after us like the wind…."

Supported by General Sanborn's Third Brigade, McNeil charged through the cornfield after Thompson, who retreated through the rebels' second line. Unnerved, however, these rebels fired their volley even before Thompson could get his first rank past them, causing panic among both groups and angry cursing among their officers.

A third line, made up in part of Slayback's battalion and positioned behind a creek held, however, and McNeil's advance petered out. When Pleasanton's other two brigades under Benteen and Philips came up, the third line, too, was swept away.

The Federal point of view would be described somewhat excitedly by Colonel Charles Blair. "The General (Sanborn) formed his brigade in close column of companies & made them a little speech while forming to the effect that it made no difference where there was 1,000 or 10,000 men in the field, he wanted them to RIDE RIGHT OVER THEM! The men responded with a YELL, the dismounted skirmishers tore down the fence in the face of a GALLING FIRE & the COLUMN SWEPT THROUGH IT LIKE A TORNADO! In the rear of the cornfield another line was formed on the prairie, the right resting on a skirt of timber fringing a small stream, while the advance of the brigade rapidly deploying into line, charged and broke them at the first onset.

"A third line of battle was formed still farther to the rear on a low basin, where there had been an evident intention to encamp, which was surrounded by semicircle of hills, where they held us at bay under a severe fire for about twenty minutes or more & until the whole brigade formed in line & charged. Before this impetuous charge they were again broken & as I passed through their temporary halting place there was an abundant evidence of the haste they were in, in the broken wagons, dismounted forges, fragmentary mess-chests & smashed crockery with which the ground was strewn."

Over the next hours, Thompson made several desperate stands, started prairie fires, organized his men two lines deep to discourage the Union charge, feinted forward with yells to keep the Federal horse on their toes, but noted later that the Yanks "did not scare worth a cuss."

Sergeant Bereman's diary recorded a tense moment when his Iowans ran out of ammunition: "We had been firing more or less all day without being supplied at all. Some had half a dozzen rounds others none… A messenger was sent to the rear after some but it was no doubt miles & miles away. The rebels began to advance again. (they were now within long musket range and began to fire.) We did not return the fire. Our orders were that if they made a charge on us that we must meet them half-way…. 'Where are your sabers?' 'We were ordered to leave them in camp.' 'Club your guns then….'" Fortunately for Bereman, reinforcements arrived.

Although the fight was nearly full tilt for a while, the horses, underfed and jaded from the relentless march, had begun to wilt. Bugles blew the charge, but Utt's troopers cursed and kicked and buried their spurs into the stark ribs of their mounts in vain.

As Sanborn would report, "the powers of nature both of men & horses had failed & not even the excitement of battle could keep them up longer."

The now slow-motion steeplechase continued to just south of Shiloh Creek. This stream was just a couple of miles north of the Marmaton River, where another wagon train bottleneck was crimping the retreat. Once in the river, the thirsty teams of horses and mules all stopped to drink, ignoring their frantic teamsters.

Shelby organized the defense on Charlot's farm, which would lend the little battle its name. By this time, some of the soldiers under Fagan and Clark, who had assumed command of what was left of Marmaduke's division, had been reorganized. Jackman had returned from the van of the train as well. When McNeil came up, he faced several thousand men.

"Oh but it was grand sight — (sublime!) Ten thousand men in battle array, on the open plain their arms glittering in the declining sun, such a sight is not seen often in ones life," Bereman would write, again exaggerating the numbers.

Both armies tried some proven tricks, but with less success.

Once more, Confederate Colonel Charles Tyler's brigade of nearly weapon-less volunteers, normally plodding along with the wagon train, took its place on the field. This time, it was not just for a bluff. As Tyler reported later, he was directed to support the rear guard "morally by an ostentatious display and physically" by his enlistees, many of whom had not so much as a shotgun. Then came the order to charge.

"This they did and very gallantly, considering that they were unarmed recruits and had the example of so many armed fugitive veterans to demoralize them," Tyler wrote. Their charge, an act of incredible bravery, got 11 recruits killed and two dozen wounded.

Then the Fourth Iowa's Major Abial Pierce tried another of his flanking attacks. But the maneuver that had paid huge dividends at Mine Creek that morning was foiled by spent horses — his "charge" was performed at a walk. Jackman made a countercharge with somewhat more momentum, and Pierce took away a shot-up foot that would bother him for the rest of his days.

"Their line began to give way," Bereman wrote, "not in confusion, or flight — but retired regularly & in good order. We followed them but did not risk another charge…. Night shut them out of our view."

And the exhausted armies called it a draw. Major General Pleasonton took two of his brigades to get provisions and rest at Fort Scott, about six miles away. Major General Curtis rode up to argue, correctly, that the rebels had to be in worse shape. Although he was the senior officer, he did not force Pleasonton to stay for a night attack or at least an early start on the next morning's chase.

Worse, when Major General Blunt came down the road with his brigades, he saw Pleasonton moving off to the west and followed along. His troops, Jennison's Kansans and Ford's Coloradans, were the freshest on the field, having not fought since Westport. Some accounts say Blunt was sulking because the cautious Curtis had not agreed to his ideas of a flanking attack on Price; others that it was just a mix-up. In any event, Curtis did not even try to stop his clear subordinate from going into Fort Scott, either.

This left Utt and the others alone on the line north of the Marmaton.

"Not many times during the War was such a call made upon the powers of men and horses that was made upon our brigade during these two days," wrote Sergeant Major William Forse Scott of the Fourth Iowa. "The distance of march was 108 miles. We had but two feeds for our horses and only twice were we able to make coffee. We laid down in the open prairie with horses tied to our wrists without food, without fire, cold, hungry and very tired…."

"How many wagons they burning?" Utt wondered, teeth chattering now with a chill. "Dozens for sure."

"Wish we had one of 'em burning here," remarked old Ellsworth. "Can't feel my nose."

XVIII

Final shots

*"If I cared for my life I would have lost it long ago;
wanting to lose it, I cannot throw it away."*

—"Bloody Bill" Anderson

e/se/se/se/se/s

South of the Marmaton River
Vernon County

JEFF THOMPSON HAD BROUGHT NEXT TO nothing to this festival of fools, had less now. His saddlebags contained but a comb, a bottle of fresh cider and two boxes of cartridges. He had two blankets but no opportunity to deploy them. The general had holes in the soles of both soggy boots, and his pants were worn through in embarrassing places.

So the blazing wagons meant nothing to him but a hope for more speed on the retreat. He wanted nothing more to do with the damned things, although many others in the column were greatly troubled, lamenting their lost loot.

The general had a headache throbbing at his temples, a horse had mashed the little toe of his left foot, and in between those two poles, he felt as near dead as you could get without having dirt shoveled into your face. Yesterday had been the longest of days, one thin defense after another formed to keep the Yankees back, to keep the brigade from melting away.

And then at the crossing at the Marmaton the damned wagons, of course, had jammed up again. Part of it was the stock that was desperate for water; part of it was men who wandered around like they had left their common sense back up on the road somewhere. Thompson had become so frustrated he had knocked men down in the dark and pressed them into squads to help haul the wagons up the steep south bank.

A good part of what had been the last reserves of his energy had been wasted at the ford, for Old Pap finally absorbed the lesson that his train was a ball and chain. On a good road, not cut up by rains and heavy traffic as he was following, a wagon averaged less than three miles an hour; on a good day, the pursuing Yankee cavalry made four.

So Major General Price ordered Colonel Jackman and Colonel Greene to burn part, perhaps a third, of what Reynolds called "the petted but detested train." The always disgruntled governor recalled how "numerous wagons which the soldiers believed to contain untold wealth of plunder by staff officers and dead-heads, had dangerously augmented his train, so that it numbered over five hundred vehicles, and shockingly controlled and conducted, often stretched out eight or ten miles in length."

Its burning, said Private James Campbell, was "a sight never to be forgotten by anyone who saw it…. Flashes of powder go up in the air like lightning and the constant bursting of the shells was terrific."

Two more shells in an ammunition wagon burst with a terrific bang, but

Thompson's weary mount didn't even twitch. In the light of the fires, Thompson could see stock stumbling around untended. Some were the remnants of the cattle herd, some were the horses and mules released from the traces. Some of them would have been candidates for a bullet in the brain box in a kinder time, but no one had the inclination. Over to the west, he saw perhaps a dozen mules being ridden to the north. Deserters? Then he heard one of the riders laugh and knew it was some slaves taking advantage of the confusion to head back to the Yankees on the other side of the river. Thompson hoped they would all leave. What had Price been thinking to allow them in the army wagons? The starved soldiers were furious over the Negroes' presence, convinced they must be eating up the provisions.

Pretty wishful thinking for those bringing the blacks out of Missouri or perhaps stealing them out. They would not bring much, even in Texas. The bottom was out of the slave market, bottom appeared just about out of the Confederacy, too. Reminded him of his pants.

Thompson waved at McPheeters slumped on the seat of an ambulance rumbling by. No wave was returned, but Thompson thought nothing of it. The good doctor had been tending the last of the day's wounded, including three of Thompson's boys. He started. Slayback was at his side, suggesting a change in the brigade's order of march.

When the rest of the divisions had resumed their sad, southerly trudge, Lieutenant William Ballard would write, "Three brigades was marching side by side though the night was very dark… You could continually hear the cries — 'Where is Clark's Brigade? Where is Freeman's Brigade — Where is McCray's Brigade?' or this or some other regiment."

Well, Thompson knew where the Iron Brigade was. Right here, covering the rear for the rest of the march. They had the last three pieces of artillery, were the best armed, had the most spirit in the army, although that was faint praise indeed.

"I believe you are right, Alonzo. Switch with Moses. Tell him to sweep for stragglers." A series of especially loud blasts erupted from the wagons that were receding into the dismal drizzle. Slayback whistled.

"In a few minutes, the sleepyheads and the stragglers came rushing by with terrible descriptions of the terrific battle going on and their narrow escape…" Thompson would later write. It was hard to believe. These men had been sleeping so deeply that they had been unaware of the army's leaving and the wagons' destruction. But then, if he had had a chance to sleep, what would have awakened him?

But then the now-wide-eyed men were describing imaginary hand-to-hand conflicts with phantom Yankees. One fellow swore he shot one of the cannoneers before he ran.

Thompson and Slayback could stand it no longer and began laughing at the men.

"You are liars and very bad liars at that," Slayback roared. "Go find your regiments."

9:30 A.M.

Old Albany
Ray County

THE SMELL OF HAM FRYING WAS almost enough to make Riley stir from his blanket cocoon. Almost.

Feeling a nudge from a boot, he opened his eyes to find Rains smoking a little twisted cheroot beside him.

"Nigh time to be mounting up, Crawford. Brought you some grits and bread with jam. Believe it's gooseberry."

Riley sat up, put on his hat. Foot didn't feel so bad right now. He reached for the plate.

"Much obliged, John. Where'd you get it?"

"Oh, the good folks of Albany are always looking for ways to hep their dashing, brave cavaliers of the brush."

"You forgot 'handsome.'"

"Didn't forget. Talking to you, ain't I?"

"Oh, right. Where's Bill at?"

"Still in that little cabin over there. That's where these grits came from. Bill's in a fine mood. You know what I saw him do? He was looking in a mirror and talking to himself, said: 'Good morning, Captain Anderson, how are you this morning?' And then he answered himself: 'Damn well, thank you.' Oh, he's full of the beans today!"

"Thanks for the warning," Riley said, wiping a little gob of jam off the plate and sticking it in his mouth. "I'll make sure I ride well back of him today."

Rains laughed. "Don't forget to wash that before you give it back!"

"You certainly are a demanding sumbitch." Riley smiled. "Thanks for fetchin' me sumthing."

John Rains was a fine fellow. How the son of a general, who had fought at Wilson's Creek and Pea Ridge, ended up with this bunch, Riley wasn't sure. The general had come up a ways with Price, but John had learned at Boonville that his pa had been assigned to escort the Fort Davidson wounded back to Arkansas, so they hadn't had any reunion.

Some were still coming from the mill, with the ground corn for the horses. Riley had gotten in line the night before, had a nice bag full for down the road. He hobbled to Folly, who nickered at him, cocking her pretty ears to ask what might be in that good-smelling sack.

"Later, sister, later," he murmured to her. He looked around for a well so he could clean the plate. But there was Anderson striding through the horses toward his big gray mare, putting on that hat with its black plume. Went nicely with his finely embroidered black shirt. Riley thought he might need such a shirt himself. The boys were adjusting girths, putting rolled blankets on the mounts. Riley quickly decided the dish would have to wait. He jammed it in the saddle bag, where it clanked against a pistol Frank James had lent him since the Crooked River mess. It was a .38 caliber, unlike his other pieces, and he wanted to get rid of it as soon as he could.

He was doing a sloppy job with his blanket roll when the commotion began. Some pickets sent out early past the settlement's few houses were hauling back in, shouting, "Blue-bellies ahead! Not many!"

Then everyone saw them at once. A squad, maybe 20, galloped around a bend in the road, pulled up hard at the sight of the big guerrilla band. They wheeled and raced back out of sight.

Go get 'em! Bill roared, and the chase was on. Riley found himself in the rear of the column eating dust and urging Folly for a little more speed. The fleeing milish were in sight again, racing down the lane that led through some woods. Suddenly the southerners were taking fire from the tree line. Ahead, John Pringle, the shy, red-headed giant, pitched to the ground, sprawled face-down, not moving. Lines of men with rifles. Dismounted. Another Centralia? Smoke was rolling out of the timber on both sides. Riflemen in the lane, too. A horse collapsed on its side, another went to its knees, blowing blood. Some were pulling up, turning their horses; others, though, were still racing ahead.

Riley aimed two rounds at muzzle flashes in the smoke-filled timber, but Clell Miller got in his line of fire. He was trying to control his bay. It had a third hole in its nose. Then, *thugg*, and Clell was out of the saddle.

Riley sensed what was happening. It was a trap, executed exactly the way the partisans had done to the milish again and again. Dangle a few fleeing riders as bait and draw the quarry in for the kill.

He pulled a second Colt, but before he could aim it, a bullet nipped the top of his thumb. Shit! That hurts all to hell. The pistol was on the ground under the mare's hooves. He reached into a saddle bag for the little Remington, tried to pull the hammer back. Oh, shit! The thumb! Despite the rapid fire of a hundred pistols, the line of gunmen in the trees did not give way. No Centralia this! More like kicking over a beehive! Jasper Moody dropped his reins to grab his throat. Tarkington got it, too!

Two of the band raced straight down the lane, waving their pistols and yelling. It was Anderson and Rains, seemingly untouchable in their frenzied charge. Suddenly they were though the wall of Union men and across a little bridge. But the Yankees in the lane sent a shower of lead after the escapees.

"Our lines held their position without a break," reported Lieutenant Colonel Samual "Cobb" Cox, who was leading about 300 men of the lowly 33rd and

290 • Final shots

51st Enlisted Missouri Militia. A tough former wagon master and Indian scout, Cox had left active army service because of illness, but, determined to hunt down Anderson, he had returned to duty. His report continued: "The notorious bushwhacker, Anderson, and one of his men, supposed to be Captain Rains, son of General Rains, charged through our lines."

Riley saw Archie start to follow Bill, then rein up. Like Riley, he must have sensed that only Bill could pull it off. But wait, had he? Both bold riders veered a little to the left. One, then the other, fell from the saddle. It was Rains that got up, staggered into the brush despite a fresh volley. Weasel yelled that Bill was down, and the men who still could began to turn their horses away.

"Anderson was killed and fell some 50 steps in our rear receiving two balls in the side of his head," Cox would exult that day. He would not be aware of his success, however, until a search of Anderson's body revealed orders from Price to attack the Missouri Northern and, improbably, to report on his operations every two days. The militiamen also would find $600 in gold, letters from Anderson's wife back in Texas and a "brace of six pistols."

"Their forces retreated in full speed," Cox would report, "being completely routed; our cavalry pursued them some 10 miles, finding the road strewn with blood for miles."

Thumb throbbing and dripping, Riley risked rising in his stirrups for a better view of Rains' fate. Then he dropped into his saddle and jerked Folly's head around to join the others back down the road. Bending low over her neck, he gave her his good heel, hard as he could.

Time to ride, time to hide.

OCTOBER 28

Newtonia

Newton County, southwest Missouri

"IS THE DANGER PAST?" THOMPSON ASKED breathlessly, with flourishes that the Bard surely would borrow were he among the boys lounging on the blankets.

"Oh, yes," the audience chorused. "Long past, long past!"

The officers had been "discussing" a canteen of whiskey. Thompson was encouraged to join their circle. He had stayed dry for nearly two years, believed he was a better soldier for it. "We had captured thousands of gallons of whiskey and wines," Thompson would recall, "and I had not touched a single glass."

But after this campaign, well, maybe a little one might be in order to celebrate its end. Naturally, something so momentous required a bit of speechmaking. The boys would be disappointed if their bombastic general failed to make a production of it.

"O God, that men should put an enemy in their mouths to steal away their brains! Have I not sipped enough, drunk on the blue flow of Yankees?" he hammed, cracking the fellows up anew. Who better to break the ban with? These men of his beloved brigade, all his friends now. Tattered brothers under a ragged flag, they had faced the worst together. Brothers.

Shelby was a little ways over, paroling the prisoners. Letting them go, the poor bastards. Don't know why they were kept so long, anyway. It was a good day for all.

The Federal outpost and its supplies had been easily captured, most of its defenders having performed tall traveling to the timber. Most. The men had been excited about catching somebody called "Old Grisly" and killing him on the spot.

This was Lieutenant Robert H. Christian, alleged by many southerners to have used his 76th Enlisted Missouri Militia as a Federal bushwhacking gang that burned out families.

According to one story, the ill-named Christian killed four men who were hiding in the hills nearby. "The men were all shot in the right eye and the top of their heads blown off. Their brains were taken out and put in their hats which were set beside their bodies." A Confederate officer, Joseph Peevy, wrote, "This man Christian also tried to hire two ladies, with sugar, coffee, &c., to poison Southern men lying in the brush."

It is fair to say Christian was one of the most hated men in the district. Samuel Moore, legend says, slew the villain and Moore's son told this tale: "Father scalped him while he was still alive and hollering. Afterwards he took the scalp, washed it in the creek, rolled it up and put it in his pocket. Sitting before the fire that evening with Mother sitting on his right, he pulled the rolled up scalp from his pocket and tossed the roll into her lap. She drew back and the scalp fell to the hearth and partially unrolled. In the light of the fire, she saw it, and she said, 'That's Bob Christian's scalp!'"

Price had decided that the column could lay up at Newtonia after passing through the Order 11 counties. "The Border of Missouri, through which both armies were passing, was entirely desolate," noted Federal Captain Hinton, "not with the grand monotony of nature, but with the ruin of civilization and cultivation."

The men needed to find provisions and forage for the poor beasts that somehow got them this far. Some wanted to keep moving south, but Shelby had argued, "It is better to lose an army in battle than to starve the men and kill the horses."

Shelby was enjoying these few waking hours out of the saddle, and Thompson heard him wheedle a cook about whether just a little sugar wasn't left in a provision wagon. Reckon he felt the need for a real toddy.

"Think thou I require this physic?" Thompson asked in his best theatrical voice.

"More than anybody," laughed Moses Smith, "well, except me."

"Well," Thompson held the canteen aloft, "maybe just one swig."

"Here they come," somebody yelled.

A glance to the north revealed a mass of blue uniforms, streaming past the Forsyth place with its huge stone barn. The officers scrambled to their feet, yelling for hairy-faced battalion majors and smooth-chinned company lieutenants.

Lips still dry, Thompson handed the canteen back to its owner.

"Throw physic to the dogs then, I guess," he remarked. "I'll have none for a while longer."

A rich variety of curses accompanied the forming of the tattered ranks. Federals had been reported a few hours earlier, a false alarm, and Thompson had found reluctance to go out on the prairie. Now, here the Yankees were, practically on top of the camp. The terrain that Thompson scanned showed two small fields with a lane running east and west between them. The bluecoats were taking position along the northernmost fence.

Sweet tooth forgotten, Shelby came up with brow furrowed. "Go and fight them," was all he said.

"The whole brigade from Genl. Shelby down to the cooks," Thompson would recall, "had been heartily tired of this running without fighting for several days and had determined to take a stand somewhere and redeem their credit." Quickly crossing himself, he ordered his "iron" men to occupy the southernmost fence and have at it. Slayback took his bunch to the west, set up on the lane so he could fire down the little 10-foot alley between the corn and cut up any Federal attempt to cross it.

"No chance for science, no occasion for skill," Thompson said of his brigade that day. "The only thing they needed was just what the men each had, and that was *pluck*."

Each line began pouring lead into the other. The first volley hit Thompson's horse in the head, not fatally, but messily. It blew and snorted blood, shaking its head in pain and splattering its rider. More than one man ran up to Thompson to ask where he was wounded. Not hit, he shouted, keep your mind on those fellows! Smoke hid the enemy except for the muzzle flashes. The southerners, not content with their own fence, began climbing over it and heading for the enemy's. Thompson exhorted them, managed to spur his fearsome-looking beast over a low place in the rails.

The Federals were falling back from their line. Moses was there, standing on the foe's abandoned rails screaming for his regiment, his pitiful few, to give it to them, give it to them! And he was knocked from his perch. Slayback, too, went down with a grunt, writhing amid the pale stalks. Thompson went to the belly-hit colonel. Turned out, a private reported cheerfully, the ball struck the sword belt buckle, knocked out his breath. Thompson passed the gasping man to join his brigade in driving the Yanks back.

"Captain Dick" could not be kept out of this fight; his crews pushed up to fling canister. Another Collins, George, was well up front, madly waving the colors and hollering. Thompson had replaced a former color-bearer, who'd lost his nerve and tried to keep the flag furled as much as possible so as to not draw fire on himself. Assigning it to Collins, the officers admonished him not to be shy. Well, young George was giving them their money's worth, Thompson laughed.

Across those fields was Major General James Blunt, nervously watching his lines bend backward. Nearly a month later, a writer for the Leavenworth *Daily Times* would dish purple, pro-Union prose to its readers, recalling that, "With the impetuosity of a tiger and the unflinching firmness of a Cour de Lion, Blunt charged the rebel lines with barely six hundred men…

"Behind the rebel skirmish lines and reaching to the woods, rank after rank, mottled and ragged, unfolded itself, until it seemed a huge snake which might envelope and crush us in its coils. Night was drawing on apace, and in the shadow of the woods we could see the rebel officers preparing their lines for a charge, as if determined to wrest victory from defeat and turn the pursuers into the pursued. Blunt was everywhere along the lines, inspiring the men with his own hope, his own reckless courage, his determination to hold the position until the other Brigades arrived."

To translate, Blunt, in his eagerness for a victory solely his own, had bitten off more than his men could chew.

"Their superiority of numbers enabling them to press upon my flanks with a large force compelled me to fall back about 500 yards from my first line," the general would acknowledge. "The enemy pressed forward their center, but were promptly checked by the canister from the First Colorado Battery. It was now near sundown, and my command had been engaged near two hours…."

For Blunt, this was the second battle fought at this hamlet. He had been here on September 30, 1862, and, rightly or wrongly, did not miss a chance to criticize another Federal commander. General John Schofield, he said, had failed to arrive in time or the Federals would have captured many Confederates.

This time Blunt could blame no one but himself. About to be driven from the field, he was saved by the arrival of Sanborn's brigade.

"Along our lines a shout of thankfulness went up to the placid Heavens," the *Times* correspondent would write.

The Confederates probably were saved by the falling darkness.

Both sides claimed victory.

Blunt would report that the Confederates "now retreated rapidly under the cover of night … leaving their dead and wounded in our hands." The rebels considered Blunt to have been duly whipped.

"Night closed the contest, and another beautiful victory had crowned the

Confederate arms," declared Shelby's report.

Thompson, too, considered it "a brilliant day in the history of 'Shelby's Brigade,' for we had led the advance on the morning and defended the rear in the evening, when all else were demoralized."

It was the last of the fighting for the raid in Missouri, but it would not be the end of the march or the misery that attended it.

On this day, Samuel Curtis, the Union commander, confidently wrote: "Everything now promised complete success in view of our close proximity to the enemy, his exhausted condition, and his disastrous defeat. He was still in a fruitful section of Missouri, but by pressing him another day or two, he would have not time to collect supplies, and would reach the devastated, destitute region of Arkansas without provisions, and must surrender or starve...."

Curtis underestimated the peevishness of Pleasonton, however. Not for nothing had the commanders in the East cast him out. Without bothering to tell Curtis, who was the senior general on the field, he sent the Department of Missouri commander, William Rosecrans, a message suggesting that his depleted Missouri regiments be sent home. When Rosecrans did not agree, Pleasonton pled illness for himself — although he seemed unencumbered retracing his steps to St. Louis.

Finding a telegraph office, Curtis appealed directly to Ulysses S. Grant, who agreed with him that Price should be run down and wiped out. Pleasonton's brigade commanders, however, blamed distance, bad country and broken-down horses for not returning to the chase. Only Benteen, already at Springfield, turned around to join colonels Moonlight, Jennison and Ford. As soon as he got there, on November 1, the Federals resumed the role of the hounds. They had given the exhausted hare most of a four-day lead.

OCTOBER 29

St. Louis

When McKim came to baptize them, Asa Ladd knew it was all up.

He had better things to do. He'd committed his soul to the Lord long ago. His time was better spent adding a few more lines to his last letter to his wife. He and the others held in the Gratiot Street Prison had been told nothing until now. But Phillip McKim had quietly confirmed it.

They were to die today.

His hand shook enough to rattle the chains on his wrist. He took one hand and steadied the other. He prayed she would be able to read his handwriting.

"Dear wife don't grieve after me. I want you to meet me in Heaven. I want you

to teach the children piety, so that they may meet me at the right hand of God. I can't tell you my feelings but YOU can form some idea of my feeling when you hear of my fate.

"I don't want you to let this bear on your mind anymore than you can help, for you are now left to take care of my dear children. Tell them to remember their dear father. I want you to go back to the old place and try to make a support for you and the children. I want you to tell all my friends that I have gone home to rest...."

He instructed her to go to Conner to get help to settle their affairs, suggested that she could make a crop before leaving their farm to go back to the old place. He sent his love, asked her to kiss the children for him.

"You need have no uneasiness about my future state, for my faith is well founded and I fear no evil. God is my refuge and hiding place. Good-by Amy."

Down the hall of Gratiot Street Prison, doors were scraping open. He signed it "Asey."

McKim came in, and Ladd stood. He entrusted the minister with the letter, then followed the guards out. A covered wagon was waiting, and the men helped hoist each other in under the canvas. They looked out the back upon the activity in the street, observed the passing of women and children, who paid no attention to them. A wagon stacked with barrels trundled by, pulled by giant Belgians. The words on the casks were German. Steamboat whistles told of departures from the levee. At a cross street, a buggy with two young sports dashed in front of the wagon, making the driver cuss. When the fine houses had thinned appreciably and more gardens and small fields appeared, they heard the driver say something about a Fort Number 4. He and the men riding behind the wagons with their rifles were all 10th Kansas fellows, Ladd had learned. Seemed all right. Two small boys, watched over by a matted collie, tossed walnuts into a gunny sack. Their hands were dark with the hulls' stain.

The wagon hit a deep hole and Ladd lurched against George Nichols, who was weeping. Ladd looked away. He would not weep, would not give that to the Yanks. The procession stopped, and the Kansans swung off their horses. The men sat in the wagon, no one making a move to get out. A lieutenant with an unsheathed sword ordered them to get down. No one responded. The officer looked away. Please get down, he said. Ladd rose and did what he was asked. The others followed.

What the men saw was described by the next day's issue of the Saint Louis *Daily Democrat*:

"On the west side of the fort six posts had been set in the ground, each with a seat attached, and each tied with a strip of white cotton cloth, afterward used in bandaging the eyes of the prisoners. Fifty-four men were selected as the executioners. Forty-four belonged to the 10th Kansas and ten to the 41st Missouri. Thirty-six of these comprised the front firing party, eighteen being reserved in case they should not do this work effectually."

More than a thousand people, largely soldiers, had showed up. Ladd was pretty sure that this Yankee Major Wilson and his men, who folks said Colonel Reeves had shot after Fort Davidson, did not have that many friends. They were here for the spectacle of watching him die. As Ladd was led to his post, he saw that his killers were only about a dozen paces away. He saw the row of open coffins. He looked closely at the plainly painted box where they would install his earthly remains. The words he had used to close his letters to his wife and father leapt from his throat.

"I fear no evil, God is my refuge and hiding place."

First out of the wagon, Ladd had been led to the far post. He sat as he was told. A rope went around him, securing him to the rough wood behind him. His eyes welled up, and he blinked a few uncontrollable tears. Retrieve yourself, he told himself fiercely. Make no sound! He snuffled hard, inhaling the moisture filling his nostrils. Well, all right, the Yanks might see his tears, but they shall not hear any sobs. He focused on the ground at his feet.

McKim and another man were speaking to them.

"Put your trust in God, my son," the other fellow was saying.

"Certainly better than putting my faith in Ol' Pap," George Bunch muttered. "I done that, and where did it get me? Roped to this damned post like a steer to be butchered."

Nichols was next to Ladd. Then it was Harvey Blackburn, Bunch, Charlie Minnekin, and Jim Gates. He glanced down the line and then back at the ground.

"I notice the major is not here," remarked Blackburn dryly. "I wonder what might be detaining him?"

But now Nichols was weeping loudly, asking a man with a doctor's bag whether there were any hope of a postponement for the poor enlisted men, too.

"Lord, have mercy on my poor soul!" Nichols exclaimed. "Oh, think of the news that will go to father and mother!"

Ladd felt no different about his father, hoped the letter would help.

As a colonel read the sentence — in so many official words, that they were to die for the sins of others — he thought of Amy. He'd warned her in the letter not to try to cross the St. Francis if the water was up. They had drowned a yoke of oxen doing that once. But she wouldn't; she was a good wife. He wondered how John, her brother in the Union army, was faring. Better than him, certainly.

"May I have a few words, colonel?" called out Minnekin, interrupting Ladd's thoughts. The colonel assented.

"Soldiers, and all of you who hear me, take warning from me. I have been a Confederate soldier four years, and have served my country faithfully. I am now to be shot for what other men have done, that I had no hand in, and know nothing about," Minnekin stated. "I never was a guerrilla, and I am sorry to be shot for what I had nothing to do with, and what I am not guilty of. When I took a prisoner, I always treated him kindly and never harmed a man after he surrendered. I hope God will take me to his bosom when I am dead. O, Lord, be with me!"

When he had finished, a sad-faced sergeant stepped up to bandage his eyes.

"Sergeant, I don't blame you," Minnekin murmured. Then he again spoke louder, addressing the line of fellow condemned. "I hope we will all meet in heaven, boys. Farewell to you all. Lord have mercy on our poor souls!"

Ladd's face, too, was quickly wrapped. He thought he detected some muttering among the Kansas men. Somebody said it wasn't right. He heard their captain respond. No threats or officer bluster, just quiet words about how it was their duty, that they had never shirked their duty before. They should have no hesitation, he said. The rebels here had not hesitated to take the life of Union men, who were no less innocent. Well, that was the long view of it, certainly, but Ladd had never shot at an unarmed man, never assumed he was some sort of avenging angel.

He could hear the Kansans loading their shoulder weapons. Three dozen of them, he had noticed, for six of us. Taking no chances, he thought.

I fear no evil, God is my refuge and hiding place.

The command came for the squad to ready. Thirty-six and six.

I fear no evil, God is my refuge and hiding place.

The command came to aim. Six bullets were his.

I fear no evil, God is my refuge and hiding place.

The command came ....

XIX

Closure

"Men are greatly demoralized and we present a pitiable forlorn aspect. God damn Old Price."

—Unnamed Confederate soldier after return to Texas

❧❧❧❧❧❧

NOVEMBER 2

Boonsborough

Washington County, northwest Arkansas

MacLean heard the low groan from the next room. The old man had hoped to catch a little rest before dinner, but it didn't sound like he was getting much. The adjutant bent back to his papers. First, his journal must be caught up. He noted that this was Camp No. 60 of the campaign, reached yesterday. What else happened on that foul Tuesday, the first of November? Yesterday was Tuesday, wasn't it? Yes. The pen began scratching across the sheet.

"Marched to Boonsborough; raining all day; roads bad and hilly; stock worn out; much of it abandoned. Reports from Colonel Brooks, who was investing Fayetteville; asks aid…."

His fingers found the string, wrapped around his penknife, and he measured. Seventeen miles. On the next line, he wrote in the current date and decided to kill two entries at one sitting. Whatever this day would bring, he was fairly sure, had already been delivered — largely in buckets.

"In camp all day. General Fagan with re-enforcement went to Fayetteville. Colonel McCray order to go on the 3rd and Colonel Dobbin on the 4th, to report south of Arkansas River on December 15, 20, and 25…"

A flash of lightning quickly followed by a loud clap. Just as quickly, a startled "Goddamn!" and through the door came Captain T. J. Mackey, flinging slush off his hat and repeating his blasphemy.

"… raining hard."

MacLean closed his journal and opened another sheet where he had made some notes.

"The general is trying to sleep, you know?"

"Ah, I didn't, sorry. But, who could sleep through all that outside?" Mackey pulled up a chair and thrust toward the hissing and popping fire his soaked boots — on the left one, a side seam had given way, exposing the fact that the captain had worn out his last pair of socks about 250 miles ago, almost at the exact time he remembered an intact pair had been forgotten and left in a fired wagon. "Well, Fagan's people are finally off for Fayetteville. Got two of Shelby's guns with him, but I will bet you a barrel of hams they will not capture much."

"Speaking of imaginary food, did you get anything to eat?"

"Hardly anything to be had, except…" Mackey reached into his coat pockets to produce some shriveled apples, "there seems to a bounty of these poor things. What I didn't offer my poor horse, I give to you." He tossed two to MacLean, who nodded his thanks and offered hope in return.

"I believe the quartermaster still has some flour or meal, at least. We'll get our ration tonight or tomorrow morning. A little dodger to go with our rump of mule, of which, I admit, I have quickly grown weary."

"Not so bad, if we just had salt," Mackey reasoned. "Without, I tell you, the meat will not stick. Rushes rudely right through, with hardly a tip of the hat to my stomach. What are you working on?"

It was an outline for the report that Price would have to present to Kirby Smith when they finally got back to Texas. Some of it was beginning to blur in MacLean's memory, some of it he wished he could forget.

Good men lost, the path to their graves marked by the wolf-gnawed bones of horses. Many of the living were so sick or weary that they had toppled from saw-boned mounts to crawl to refuge in barns or caves. Scouts were saying that that devil Blunt, who had nearly caught them at Newtonia, was still coming. Would he follow them to Texas?

A creaking of wood, a phlegmy cough from the next room, and then Price filled the door. His hair was frowsy, the darkness of the bags under his eyes alarming. The man had developed a habit of nodding off during conversations, but was having trouble sleeping on his back.

"How does it go there, Lauchlan?"

"Only middling, sir."

"With what aspect are we having difficulty?"

With what aspect are we not? thought the aide, but he said only, "I'm just trying to get a start on your report of the campaign."

"Ah," said the general, pulling his own chair closer to the hearth and sitting heavily with a murmured greeting to Mackey, followed by a query about Fagan's adventure to Fayetteville. The captain responded to both and scraped his own seat a respectable distance away, but his feet, the leather steaming now, did not give up their stake on the hearth.

"Well, accent the achievements, of course. Kirby will want it to be positive."

The younger man considered that. It wouldn't make much of a hurrah, would it? Two generals captured, perhaps a dozen colonels dead or missing, all but Shelby's artillery gone....

His silence irritated Price.

"Really, Colonel. Think about it. It was a most gratifying campaign. Think how far we marched. You will have to put a string to the map, but I wager it was around 1,400 miles. Who else could have done that, but our gallant Missourians? How many battles did we fight? Where is the whiskey?"

MacLean got up to prepare the man his toddy. That done, he also poured two fingers of liquor into thin cups for himself and a still chilled and pitifully grateful Mackey. MacLean felt a little light-headed even before sipping the bourbon. Here he had been thinking of Napoleon's retreat from Moscow — he was sure it was cold enough to snow again — and the old man's mind was full of Austerlitz.

"I'm obliged," said Price, taking the sugared liquor to his badly chapped lips. "Ah, that is the medicine!" Then he picked up the thread. "At least two dozen, won just about every one. Jove! Shelby certainly broke Blunt up in business at the last one!"

MacLean knew they would be looking over their shoulders until they got over the Arkansas River. Curtis and Blunt were reported still on the hunt. The Confederates could not stay here long.

"How many stand of colors did we capture?"

"Not sure, sir, at least, a half dozen…"

"Oh, it had to be more than that!" Another sip. "Think of the miles and miles of railroads we destroyed, was it a hundred?"

"Probably not a hundred, sir," interjected Mackey.

True, they had destroyed some line, burned several bridges, but everything probably was being rebuilt as they sat there. They had destroyed some rolling stock, but wrecked no locomotives.

"I do not think," Price waved his glass, "I do not think I venture beyond the truth to state that my army destroyed $5 million in Missouri property!"

"Five million, sir?"

"No, that is too conservative, surely. Make it $10 million. You should be writing this down."

MacLean picked up his pen, dipped it, wrote "ten million" in his careful school-teacher hand.

"Get a reckoning of how many prisoners we took and paroled. We captured two hundred wagons…"

And burned twice as many. He understood why the old man had clung to his wagons, the only tangible success of the campaign, other than the recruits. But they had been his yoke. Until they become kindling. On that cold night south of the Marmaton, the line of flaming vehicles created a false dawn and warmed MacLean's face from 100 feet.

"And what shall we say about our lost artillery, sir?"

"Let me consider, hm-m-m. We gave up ten guns but captured, hm-m-m, 16, no, 18, I think."

Ah, he's counting the big cannon the Yankees spiked at Fort Davidson. MacLean wrote those numbers down. Yes, this was getting easier.

"We must have taken at least 3,000 stand of small arms," Mackey volunteered.

And probably that many were lost or thrown away in the panic at Mine Creek, MacLean knew. Smith would miss those rifles.

But General Kirby Smith, who had much staked on the expedition, also would try to put the best face he could on it. He emphasized that, as planned, the invasion had drawn Federal divisions away from the hard-pressed Confederate armies to the east in Tennessee and Alabama. It was all, as they said at the time, "much cry and little wool."

But it was not only the top generals. In his official report in December, Shelby said Price "stamped his expedition as one of the most brilliant of the war," and blamed many of the problems on "elements in his command so weak, so helpless, so incongruous that no human hand could control them." He closed his report by saying, "Time will vindicate the greatness of the scheme, history crown it with the laurel wreath of fame."

Colonel Jackman's report also would look on the bright side: "I moved into the State with about 500 armed men and 1,500 unarmed and, after the deduction of all losses, I came out with about the same number almost entirely armed."

It would be Governor Reynolds who would hammer Price mercilessly once they got back to Texas.

Price pointed his finger at MacLean. "Don't forget all those overcoats and shoes the men got."

Och, those cursed cloaks of death, yes, those should be mentioned.

"And the recruits, of course. That is the great thing for Kirby. He wanted men, and we'll give them to him. I'd say at least 5,000 joined us, wouldn't you? Remember Boonville?"

"Very well, general," MacLean said, scratching away, not looking the old man in his fevered eyes. How many veterans did we sacrifice for those recruits? More than half of whom had melted away before the Missouri line. The other half are starving outside in the rain.

Inside the fat man, the toddy was doing its work, warming him to his task.

"Get this down. This is important. Smith, Davis, all of them, they must know this about Missouri. Are you ready?" Price waited until the pen was dipped again and poised above a fresh sheet of paper. He pushed himself out of the chair, deciding to dictate while pacing.

"The people thronged around us and welcomed us with open hearts and hands. Recruits flocked to our flag in such numbers as to threaten to become a burden instead of a benefit, as they were mostly unarmed. In some counties the question was not who should go to the army, but who should stay at home...."

He waved his glass, spotting the thirsty oaken floorboards. Price stopped walking, looked into the fire. A deeper sip.

"I am satisfied that could I have remained in Missouri this winter the army would have been increased 50,000 men."

And I am confident that if you had remained in Missouri this winter, my blanket would be a few feet of dirt, McLean thought. I have felt death on my track for weeks, yet I seem to have eluded old Davy. He shivered a little, knocked gently on the table and went on scribbling notes about the imaginary glories of Price's campaign. Lord knew that it was his last. No one would trust the old man with an army again.

Price, who had grown quiet now, seemed to be thinking along the same lines. He shrugged to himself, let a little more whiskey slide over his tongue and stared through the embers at the ashes of the South.

"Did you know, Lauchlan, that the ladies of Memphis serenaded me when I landed there back in '62? Because of my victory at Elkhorn Tavern. I wish you had been there, lad, it was a lovely time."

The tune to be sung in Texas, both men knew, would not be as sweet.

NOVEMBER 3

Odessa

Lafayette County, western Missouri

THE WHITE NIGHTGOWN SEWN WITH THE scarlet ribbon at the throat. Only it would do for tonight.

Red was the rebel color, and now she was a rebel wife. She slipped the garment over her head, tied the ribbon in a bow and began pulling pins from her hair. From the parlor below came the sounds of men relaxing after a good meal and decent whiskey. Elizabeth Hook Gregg heard snatches of their voices. McCorkle was laughing at something Papa said. She heard the preacher, a Methodist named Murphy, join in, even more thick-tongued than during the ceremony.

The men certainly had tucked into the wedding supper. If McCorkle hadn't come across those sleeping geese and shot two, they surely would not have had enough food.

Normally there would have been plenty, it being butchering time. Papa had penned 30 fattening hogs for next year's meat, but before he could do any slaughtering, the Yankee infantry tramped in and did it for him. Shot every shoat, cut the pieces they wanted off the carcasses and left the rest to rot. Meanness. The brushing of her hair became almost savage with the memory. Just Yankee meanness. One of the horrid officers had said it was done to keep the beasts from falling into Price's hands, but everyone knew the general wasn't coming back this way. Thank God for the cold or all that meat would have gone to waste. Papa had managed to save a little. Thank God again for the cold, or the stink would have driven us out.

Elizabeth put down the brush and looked into the mirror, the ribbon primly at her throat. It seemed too tight, so she loosened it, letting the strings hang down. A roar from the parlor. The soldier/witnesses were getting a little boisterous. She heard her mother's steps on the stairs, a soft knock.

"Do you need anything, Lizzie?"

"No, Mama, I'm fine."

"Well, I hope you're patient, too, because they show no signs of abating.

Your father is being no help at all."

At that moment, a roar came from the parlor and her Papa shouted, "I hear you saying it!"

Lizzie was used to being patient with Will Gregg. They had been engaged for nearly two years, but in secret. Not much courting, either. Mama did not consider the Greggs of Cass County to be quite of their station, but even she admitted the war had interrupted the order of things and sadly reduced the number of suitable beaus. Will *was* a bit crude at times, but look at the company he had been keeping. The partisans included some of the best stock from the farm aristocracy, but also a fair amount of riffraff.

And there was the fact that Lizzie was not getting any younger. She had reached the age of 20 just the day before, but still....She nervously fiddled with the ribbon, deciding to tie it again.

If the Federals had heard of her betrothal — Will's face had been recognized at Lawrence — they surely would have hauled her off to prison. Many of her girlhood chums had been arrested and sent to St. Louis. They would have come for her, too, sooner or later. The wedding would have to stay secret, as well. Her father could be shot and the house burnt for their feeding those men downstairs.

Besides, she had no wish to be made fun of by the Yankee press. She had seen one remark on a rebel wedding and it had been so rude. The bride was described as "a short, fat and brown-skinned lass, who has been strutting about for some time with several revolvers girdled about her, and a bowie knife stuck in her belt." Lizzie wondered what they would print about her if they knew? Whatever, Papa would probably try to shoot the editor for it.

Truth was, the young woman was trying to think about just anything but the womanly duties soon to be called upon. It all was to be endured, of course, but she wasn't sure how she would take it. She understood the natural process. The animals on the farms all went about it rather matter-of-factly, though the yowlings of the female cats were a little disturbing.

Absentmindedly, she put down her brush, wound a ribbon around her finger and the knot pulled loose once more.

Will did look dashing in his captain's uniform, even if the braid was somewhat worn. After dark, he had come trotting in at the head of a dozen men, some picked from the recruits gathered north of the river, others old friends from his days with Quantrill. They all had done their best for the occasion, some finding clean shirts, brushing their hats, cleaning the mud off their boots and combing their wild hair.

"It was a strange scene, that wedding ceremony," McCorkle would recall fondly, "a beautiful black-eyed, black-haired Southern girl, with her little hand placed on the arm of a stalwart soldier with four Navy revolvers buckled around his waist and with 12 long-haired, heavily-armed soldiers standing as witnesses...."

What kind of man was Will? A good soldier, she was sure. One of the men said he could clip the bill off a plover at 30 yards. Destitute of fear, too. Bud Younger told her once that Will was "one of the bravest men that ever faced powder." But a good husband? Well, she hoped. He'd been running pretty much wild for three years. He'd have to get between the trace poles one of these days. She intended to do something about his hair, which was far too long. Would he let her trim it before they embarked?

The ribbon bow now seemed too tight. She pulled the strings and looked into the little mirror. It seemed untidy that way, so she decided to try a more elaborate knot.

She hadn't seen much of Will since he left Quantrill. When he hadn't come back with them in the spring, he'd sent a secret letter to her explaining why, that George Todd had tried to have him shot in the back. Knowing that Todd never forgot a grudge, Will had slipped away to General Shelby's camp, where his talents were more appreciated. Todd, as her father would say, was a son-of-a-bitch *on wheels*, but he was safely dead now. Today, Will had assured her that McCorkle and the other men below held nothing but good feelings toward him.

She had fretted for her beau when he did not appear as the Confederates marched by not far to the north. Then, days after Price had gone, Will came riding in. Her relief was followed by surprise when he proposed taking her off to Texas. She hadn't had to think on it long. She had been begging Papa to leave for months. The Yankees kept throwing him in jail, the last time was for feeding some unfortunates from Jackson County. But he was hard-headed, wanted to stay put.

"Heard a man say once if he owned both hell and Texas, he'd reside in hell and rent out Texas," Papa snorted. Will insisted it was fine enough down there; a lot of Missourians were already in Sherman. Lizzie needed little convincing. She was desperate to get out of Missouri.

Her heart stopped. A horse had whinnied out on the lane. Was it Yankees? Will had put out a picket but that hardly ensured safety against those snakes. Oh, God. Yankees would kill Papa. And Will, too, of course. She listened for the sound of pistols cocking in the trees. The noise below was undiminished. Those men would not hear a cannon fired in the summer kitchen.

She reached the window, flung aside the drapes, heedless of her lamp drawing fire. Through the falling snow, she saw the rumps of three horses being led away into the shadows next to the house.

While trying to sort this out, she heard boots stomping off snow on the porch and cheers from the parlor. A woman's voice, loud and coarse, returned the greetings. Lizzie breathed again.

Apparently, Dick Maddox and his wife had decided to come in tonight. They and Will's sister and brother-in-law also would be making the trek to Texas. Lizzie hoped the company of the other, older women would be pleasant.

It would be a long trip. She had noticed that the third horse was a pack animal. It had better be bearing some provisions, she thought, because they would have none too many.

Will had secured an ambulance for the women. Lizzie had taken one look at the rickety vehicle and decided her trousseau would include a side saddle and riding clothes for just in case. She believed she could make it to Texas on the back of a horse if necessary. She'd had horses forever, used to ride with Papa to look over the stock.

It sounded as if the party below was breaking up. "We all stayed to a fine supper and we 12, at a late hour, left the house and stood as guards for the bride and groom," McCorkle would write.

Lizzie took another look into the mirror; the cursed ribbon still was not right! She tugged at it impatiently, forgetting that it was no longer a bow, pulled the thin strings into a tight little knot. Oh, bother! Her fingers tried to unlock it, no success. She wished she could get her teeth at it. Hang it! Growing frustrated, she decided the ribbon had to be cut. Nothing else for it. She searched around for her sewing scissors but remembered they were downstairs. Boots on the stairs. She recognized her father's tread as he passed unsteadily past the door. She looked around, spotted the little knife with which she had picked out pecan meats the night before.

So the knife was under her chin with the scarlet ribbon streaming down her white gown when the door swung open, silhouetting the weaving figure of her husband. The confusion on his face changed to shock.

"Oh Lizzie! Don't! God, please don't!" he whispered. "It'll be all right. I'll be the best husband ever. I promise. Put it down! Please!"

Lizzie's countenance changed, too, but from confusion to humor. She laughed and sliced the ribbon with a little flourish and held out her arms. This marriage business might be all right after all.

NOVEMBER 4

Cooper County
Central Missouri

SURPRISED, BUT PLEASED, ALLIE WOULD STAND demurely on the porch as Riley tipped his hat and gave a slight bow from the saddle. Or he would get off Folly and remark how he'd kindly love a drink of well water but only if she brought him the dipper her own self.

Of all his daydreams, Riley Crawford's favorite probably was the one involving a long lane leading up to the farm house. Allie would spot him coming and run to meet him. She'd hold on to his stirrup and turn her face up to his smile. And he'd listen to that excited chatter, chatter, chatter.

Riley had this idea to suggest to her that they go to California together. And she'd think it was the Missouri town just down the road from Tipton, and he'd say, no, I'm talking about the real thing.

He had gotten the idea from Captain Gregg, who had said on the Boonville ferry he wanted to surprise his sweetheart and sweep her off to Texas. Riley thought nothing of it until after Glasgow. Since then he had thought of little other than Allie. About the marrying stuff, Riley was honest enough with himself to know he might have to lie about his age. He was just shy of 17, but figured he would tell Allie's folks that he was 19.

Hadn't decided whether to tell his ma about all this. He wasn't sure how she'd take him leaving the war before the war was done. But after the ambush where Bill Anderson got his, the war was plenty done for Riley. It was like them Osage orange trees over there, their trunks bristling with wicked thorns. He got one stuck in the palm of his hand once. Swelled up a dark knot that throbbed and throbbed until he'd dug the poison tip out with his knife. Well, he was plucking out the war now.

He wondered whether Buck James had left for Kentucky yet, but he didn't much care anymore, just knew he hadn't wanted to ride another day with that little bastard Jesse. Just as Buck had tossed him aside, Riley had discarded all his tell-tale Union gear. He wanted no evidence of his past if stopped on this trip. He kept only a single Navy in his belt, so as not to draw attention. Another Navy and the .38 caliber were secreted in his saddle bags, though, because you never could have enough guns in these parts. He had been cautious, too, about picking the roads leading back to central Missouri, 'cause folks knew him in these parts. He'd run into no milish scouts, and at the ferry his lucky streak continued. The two fellows keeping an eye on it were too busy bubbling the bottle and playing sweet cloth, a gambling game involving the guessing the sums of three dice thrown on a cloth.

His heel was not hurting today, and the thumb was scabbed over and healing well. It was bright and cloudless, the best the season had to offer, and he was mostly dried out from the wet snow of the night before.

Folly's ears twitched. A bluejay screamed about something, probably a fox up in the weeds of that fence corner, where the farmer could not easily get his mule and plow. Riley remembered his Pa used to rag him, but not too hard, about leaving too much ground unturned in the tight spots back in their own fields.

Somebody else could work them fields now. Farming didn't appeal no more. That's why going west was the plan. New country, new enterprises. He figured Allie would talk his ear off all the way across the prairies and over the mountains, and he couldn't wait. She'd fret about the wild Indians, and he would pat his Navys and say, never fear. They'd hook up with a caravan or something. He might have enough money for an ox cart and team — not the best, probably, but enough to get them there. He'd heard that Bud, his cousin, was out in California with some kin. And any relatives of a Younger pretty much had to be kin to a Crawford. Maybe he and Bud could start up something together.

A metallic click in the timber off to the left of the road snapped Riley eyes in that direction. His Navy was out and ready now. He cocked it two-handed, taking care not to rip off the thumb scab. Squinting into the brush for any foe lying in covert, he kicked Folly into a gallop. Intent on the trees, he only half saw the milish rise from the opposite side of the lane, from the weeds in the field's corner. Folly screamed as a piece of her ear went flying in the first blast. Having taken the brunt of the flying lead straight-on, the mare staggered, about to go down. Riley was hit as well, not mortally, but the wound hampered him from getting his pistol to where it needed to be. From about a dozen feet away, he got off a bad shot at the man, and then the shotgun's second barrel roared.

The buck and ball load took Riley in the stomach. He was flung back in his saddle but did not topple. Folly was doing plenty of toppling for the both of them. She fell on her side with an expiring sigh. Riley's shoulder and then head slammed against the stiffening road clay.

The revolver flew out of his hand, but it didn't matter now. The milish had cut the bark this time, had nigh cut him in half, he reckoned. A groan escaped from deep in his desperately dry throat, then a thin gasp.

He'd kindly love a drink of well water.

Epilogue

*"There are no bygones in the world, and
the past is not dead and cannot die."*

— Frederick Douglass

⋵⋰⋶⋰⋶⋰⋶⋰⋶⋰⋶⋰⋶

WHILE STERLING PRICE AND KIRBY SMITH declared victory, many in the tattered remnant of the Army of Missouri were having none of it. John Newman Edwards was the most colorful, calling the campaign, "The stupidest, wildest, wantonest, wickedest march ever made by a general who had a voice like a lion and a spring like a guinea pig." Most would have agreed with the later verdict by historian Thomas Goodrich, who wrote that, far from "liberating" Missouri, Price was lucky to have escaped it.

Price's loudest detractor was Governor Thomas Reynolds, whose bitter and public accusations of gross incompetence spurred the general to demand his own court martial to clear his name. Testimony was heard, but the Confederate surrender interrupted proceedings, making the issue moot.

"The long retreat from Westport was over," historian Howard Monnett declared. "The final Confederate invasion of Missouri was history. Peace, at long last, had come to the Kansas-Missouri border."

Well, not quite. It was true that George Todd and Bill Anderson were dead, that some of the bushwhackers had left for Texas and that on New Year's Day William Quantrill would cross over the Mississippi into Kentucky, never to return. Yet, quantities of blood were still to be spilled in Missouri.

As late as April 27, 1865, Bates County Sheriff John Atkinson was bemoaning in a letter to Jefferson City: "The Bushwhackers are numerous in this County. They are passing almost everyday in bands of six to thirty, robbing as they go...."

The sheriff might have been referring to Dave Pool, Archie Clement, Jesse James and Bloody Bill's brother, Jim. Back up from Texas, they robbed the stores of Holden and killed a civilian, then went to ransack and burn Kingsville, where they slew eight more. At some point, they captured a lone militia man near the Osage River. It was Clement, of course, who slit his throat and scalped him, while James and others sat on him.

On the other side, Colonel John Philips and the militia cavalry were still snuffing out guerrillas and their benefactors. "Have had heavy scouts through La Fayette for five days. They killed N. B. Mitchell and wounded 4 or 5 others, captured 8 of their horses, equipments, and 2 Sharps carbines and 1 revolver," he reported. "Families who harbored bushmen were discovered."

The Trans-Mississippi did not fly the white flag until more than a month after Robert E. Lee signed documents on April 9 at Appomattox Courthouse in Virginia. Jo Shelby supposedly threatened to place General Kirby Smith under arrest if he tried to surrender. The fateful day came, nevertheless, on May 26 when Lieutenant General Simon B. Buckner submitted in New Orleans. Smith, wearing a calico shirt and slinging a shotgun across his saddle, would cross into Mexico.

Shelby, with Price, Reynolds, Edwards and perhaps 2,000 others also refused to give the Federals satisfaction. At the Rio Grande, they paused in the middle to sink their flag into its shallow waters, keeping it from Yankee hands. Once more on the wrong side of history, they offered their services to Emperor Maximilian.

With the army's surrender, many bushwhackers began asking about terms. General Grenville Dodge, now commander of Missouri, replied that if they laid down their arms they would not be subject to military law, although he could not speak for the civil justice system. The guerrillas were relieved simply to hear they would not be hanged without a trial.

Over the four years of the war, the population of Missouri had dropped by 300,000 people, roughly 25 percent. Some were killed, some were banished. Many, white and black, had fled for their lives. Those Missourians who had worn the Union blue suffered 14,000 fatalities from combat, disease and accidents. The number of military dead on the southern side is placed at 6,500. Add to those the unknown hundreds of unmarked graves of guerrillas and more than 5,000 civilian casualties. It is clear that a state that had begun the war hoping for neutrality ended up paying a very dear price, and much of Missouri could only be described as exhausted.

Next door, Kansas — where 2,600 soldiers had been lost, and perhaps 400 more civilians killed — was beginning to flourish. The stunting two-year drought was long past, the business of supplying Federal forts and Colorado miners lucrative and the railroad boom about to begin.

It took another generation to bury most of the bitterness in Missouri, longer to erase the angry memories along the state line. Harry Truman's grandmother did not like his wearing the uniform of a U. S. officer in her home. In Kansas City, the northerners lived on Quality Hill on the edges of the old foundations of Fort Union; the southern families preferred avenues farther east. It was not easy to return to live next to neighbors, who had once married their daughters but ended up killing their sons.

Yet nearly all put the war behind them and began rebuilding and resettling, reclaiming farmsteads and expanding cities. Survivors, such as generals Curtis and Thompson, went on to lay railroads and drain swamps. Some, like the James brothers, followed less constructive pursuits.

What awaited many of the main figures in this book:

GEORGE CALEB BINGHAM: Filed a futile claim against the government demanding $5,000 for damages to his Grand Avenue building. Finishing his famous painting, "Order No. 11," he sent prints to Ohio to try to undercut Thomas Ewing's political ambitions. Appointed Missouri's adjutant general in 1875, Bingham evaluated ex-soldiers' claims against the government. In early 1876, he lobbied Congress for funds to pay its enrolled state militia for war service. After his second wife died, he married Mattie Lykins, the widow of a Kansas City mayor, in 1878. The secessionist cousin of "Stonewall" Jackson had been banished, but upon her return, opened the Widows and Orphans Home for Confederate Survivors. In 1879, Binghan succumbed to cholera — while composing yet another indictment of Ewing. Mattie had herself buried between her two husbands in Union Cemetery in 1890.

MAJOR GENERAL JAMES BLUNT: His version of his war record written for the Kansas Historical Society labeled just about every general in his theater as incompetent or worse. Not surprisingly, he would complain that if the Federal garrison at nearby Fort Smith had tried to delay the exhausted Confederates at the Arkansas River, they could have been trapped and destroyed. As it was, the campaign was over, and the Federal troopers returned north for their own grueling, mount-killing march. The 1864 campaign, however, restored Blunt's reputation, and he was to command a cavalry division in a planned invasion of Texas. When the end of the hostilities intervened, he resumed his medical practice in Leavenworth, waiting for a political post that did not come. He moved to Washington, where in 1873 he faced federal charges, eventually dismissed, of fraud against the government and some North Carolina Cherokees. Diagnosed with "softening of the brain" in 1879, Blunt went into St. Elizabeth's Insane Asylum in Washington, where he died two years later.

COLONEL SEYMOUR CARPENTER: Leaving medicine, he failed in an Iowa railroad venture, but ultimately prospered from building gas works in various Midwestern cities and setting up a toll bridge across the Des Moines River. Contracts to construct railroad bridges in the swamps of Louisiana led to a flourishing lumber and shingle business. He died in 1912.

ARCHIE CLEMENT: Took over Anderson's gang and, once the war ended, went back to Texas to let things to cool off. On his return, he tried his hand at peacetime robberies of banks, many of which were owned by Union men. State authorities considered him involved in the nation's first daylight heist (since the war at least) at the Clay County Savings Association in Liberty. The James brothers possibly were among the dozen or so accomplices on that day. In the 1866 elections, Clement tried to intimidate Republicans, which led to a fatal foray into Lexington. He was drinking in the City Hotel when authorities tried to arrest him on a warrant for the Liberty robbery. Gunshots rang out, Clement was hit in the chest, but made it to his horse, only to be riddled by a volley from militiamen near the courthouse. Lying in the street, still trying to cock his revolver with his teeth, he gasped, "I've done what I always said I would do ... die before I'd surrender." The scene led a militia major to say: "I've never met better 'grit' on the face of the earth."

LIEUTENANT COLONEL THOMAS T. CRITTENDEN: Appointed Missouri attorney general before the war ended, he later practiced law with Francis

Cockrell, the famed Confederate general of the Missouri Brigade that fought from Vicksburg to Mobile. As a Democrat, he won a Congressional seat that was taken next term by John Philips, his former commander. Crittenden got the seat back, then ran successfully for governor. He directed the breaking up of several criminal bands rampaging across the state, but is best known for the demise of the James gang. It was his offer of a $10,000 reward for their capture and conviction that led to Jesse's killing by Robert Ford in 1882 and Frank's surrender. Crittenden also appointed Philips to the state court of appeals. He was watching a baseball game at Association Park in Kansas City in 1909 when he suffered a "stroke of apoplexy." His son, T. T. Crittenden became a Kansas City mayor; another son, H. H., tried in vain to establish a Gettysburg-style battlefield park where Loose Park is today.

MAJOR GENERAL SAMUEL CURTIS: Sent to clean up the end of the Sioux uprisings in Minnesota and the Dakota Territory. With peace, he returned to Iowa, where he had been mayor of Keokuk. He became a government consultant on the Union Pacific Railroad. His death came in December 1866 while he inspected track near Council Bluffs, Iowa.

MAJOR JOHN EDWARDS: Following Shelby across the Rio Grande, he co-published *The Mexican Times*, a "weekly English Confederate newspaper." Back in Missouri, he wrote *Shelby and his Men or The War in the West* and *Noted Guerrillas, or the Warfare of the Border* and served as an editor of *The Kansas City Times* with former Captain John C. Moore. In 1872, three men, including possibly Jesse James, robbed a ticket booth of $900 at the Second Annual Kansas City Industrial Exposition, accidentally shooting a little girl. Edwards was moved to pen an editorial entitled, "The Chivalry of Crime." Moving on to St. Louis newspapering, he fought a bloodless duel in Illinois with another paper's editor and continued as a one-man public relations organ for the James gang. When Jesse was gunned down, Edwards wrote: "Tear the two bears from the flag of Missouri. Put thereon, in place of them, as more appropriate, a thief blowing out the brains of an unarmed victim, and a brazened harlot, naked to the waist and splashed to the brows in blood." He returned to Kansas City and *The Times*, but died in 1889 while visiting Jefferson City, at age 50.

GENERAL THOMAS EWING: Promoted to brevet major general for his actions at Fort Davidson, he had made one last effort to become a U. S. senator from Kansas, but Lane had it sewn up. He went to Washington to personally resign before his friend, Lincoln, and start a law practice — just in time to take over the defense of Dr. Samuel Mudd and two others accused as conspirators in the president's assassination. Athough they were convicted, he managed to save them from the noose. He served as an adviser to President Andrew Johnson, whose policy of Reconstruction of the South was too gentle for the Radicals.

Returning to Ohio, Ewing failed three times to win the governor's office as a Democrat. In those campaigns, Bingham and his son flogged him with critical publicity and prints of "Order No. 11." Having been tough on southerners was not really a political handicap in Ohio, however, and it is hard to judge whether Bingham's attacks had any real effect. Ironically, after the war, Shelby said Ewing's "wise" action was justified. Ewing did succeed in serving in the U. S. House from Ohio, but eventually moved to New York to practice law. He was killed by a cable car there in 1896.

ELIZABETH HOOK GREGG: Came home to a Jackson County farm after the war. Her husband, William Gregg, tried numerous occupations, including deputy sheriff and jailer. Taking the role of "the unofficial historian of the Quantrill band," he later would insist that, "At the time of the Lawrence raid, the entire male populace of Kansas were soldiers, minute men, organized and equipped by the government. I tell these facts to show the world that Quantrill and his men only killed soldiers in Kansas." Both died in the spring of 1916.

MARGARET HAYS: Remained in Jackson County, Missouri, until 1872 when she and her children left for the west coast to finally join her mother and brothers in Mariposa, California. In 1873, she homesteaded a farm in Tulare County (later Kings County), California. Four years later, she married William B. Overstreet, an acquaintance from Missouri. He recovered the battlefield remains of Margaret's first husband, Upton, and placed them in Forest Hills Cemetery in Kansas City near those of Shelby and their kinsman Dick Yager. Margaret died in 1923.

BILLY HUNTER: Stayed with the Shelby's wife and children in Texas until the family went to Mexico to join the general. Taking his freedom, Hunter apparently traveled around the country. He was in Indianapolis when he learned Shelby was back in Kansas City as a U. S. marshal. He had someone write a letter to him, and soon a train ticket arrived from his old master. "I hadn't seen old Mars Jo for thirty years," the old man told a reporter for *The Kansas City Star*. "He tole me he would always give me a home and would bury me when I died, but I'm afraid he won't live to do it. I followed that child through thick and thin. I nursed him and stayed up nights to watch him in the camps and the hospitals and on the battlefields. I've seen a lot of hard knocks." At this point, the reporter said, tears rolled down Hunter's furrowed cheeks, and he bent his gray head. "Dat chile's allus been good to me and I hate to see him layin' thar sick and don't know nobody. (The old slave drew his sleeve across his eyes and added): "An' he's as brave as b'ar." In Shelby's funeral procession, a weeping Hunter led the general's horse behind the hearse.

FRANK JAMES: Accompanied Quantrill east into Kentucky, where he gave up and was paroled and allowed to go home to Missouri. After building an impressive resume as bank and train robber, Frank surrendered in 1882 once his brother was killed. Most of his crimes were erased by the statute of limitations or the death of witnesses, but in 1883 he faced a murder trial in Gallatin, Missouri. He was acquitted by a jury of southern sympathizers. Two other attempts to bring him to justice failed. He did odd jobs in Kansas City and St. Louis, including being a burlesque house doorman, then moved to an Oklahoma farm. Joining the "Cole Younger and Frank James Historical Wild West Show," his role was passenger in a stagecoach being robbed. Back at the old Clay County farm, he charged visiting tourists 50 cents. After his death in 1915, he was cremated and for decades his ashes were stored — in a bank.

JESSE JAMES: Went with Quantrill as far as the Mississippi River in January 1865, but decided to join Archie Clement in Texas. At the end of the war, he took a bullet through the lung near Lexington. Nursed to health by a cousin, who became his wife, he picked up his revolvers and rejoined Clement, this time as a bank robber. The rest is history.

COLONEL CHARLES "DOC" JENNISON: Arrested December 11, 1864, for the conduct of the 15th Kansas Cavalry in Missouri as it returned from the pursuit of Price. He blamed the depredations on other units, but was dismissed. After the war, Jennison settled in Leavenworth, running saloons, gambling houses, farms and — according to his divorced wife — a house of ill fame. Representing a constituency of "the blood tubs, the blacklegs, the shoulder-hitters and the pimps" who got him elected, according to the *Kansas State Record* of Topeka, he served on the city council and was sent to Topeka for three terms in the state legislature. He died in 1884.

SENATOR JAMES LANE: Re-elected January 12 by the Kansas legislature by an 82-16 vote, he watched his power evaporate with Lincoln's death. He infuriated the Radical Republicans by siding with President Johnson and was implicated in fraud involving government Indian contracts. The "Grim Chieftain" grew despondent and shot himself in the mouth with a derringer on July 1, 1866. He lingered 10 painful days before dying.

MAJOR GENERAL JOHN SAPPINGTON MARMADUKE: Imprisoned at Boston's Fort Warren, where his promotion finally became official in March 1865. He went into the life insurance business in St. Louis, became involved in journalism, and was elected railroad commissioner. In 1880, he ran for governor, but was defeated by Thomas T. Crittenden, who had railroad backing. Marmaduke went on to be elected in 1884 but died in office December 28, 1887. His tombstone reads: "He was fearless and incorruptible."

LIEUTENANT PATRICK HENRY MINOR: Died March 26, 1865, possibly succumbing to dysentery contracted during the campaign. Two days later, the battery's black soldiers formed a funeral procession through the streets, headed by a band and followed by carriages. Daniel Anthony's *Evening Bulletin* reported that "it seemed as if the entire colored population of Leavenworth, with no small sprinkling of the white, lined the streets."

JOHN McCORKLE: Followed Quantrill into Kentucky, where he surrendered after the renegade's death. He returned home to work on the farm of a relative and in 1914 dictated *Three Years with Quantrill*. He died in 1918 at age 79 and is buried on a bluff overlooking the Missouri River.

LIEUTENANT COLONEL LAUCHLAN MACLEAN: Back in Arkansas, got into an argument over a furlough for Lieutenant Colonel Robert Wood of M. Jeff Thompson's command. MacLean may have thrown a glass of whiskey in the face of Wood, who reacted by pulling his Bowie knife. MacLean died three days later of multiple stab wounds. Wood was sentenced to death, but because of the shortage of officers was allowed to continue serving in the army.

CAPTAIN HENRY E. PALMER: Lost his beloved Bettie and their first baby in childbirth in February 1865. He turned down a post-war cavalry commission, tried being a trader in the Little Big Horn region, but Indian wars forced him out. He wandered as far as Virginia City, Nevada, before turning back east to Nebraska and prominence in the insurance business and Omaha civic affairs. He died in 1911.

COLONEL JOHN F. PHILIPS: Later served as Sedalia mayor and Democratic congressman and set up a law practice with a former Confederate Senator George G. Vest. Called the "Silver Fox" for the color of his hair and the glibness of his tongue, Philips was one of the several prominent lawyers who defended Frank James. He also delivered the oration at Shelby's funeral. He presided on the federal bench in Kansas City for 22 years, stepping down to practice law in 1910. He died nine years later.

MAJOR GENERAL ALFRED PLEASONTON: Stayed for three years after the war in the regular Army, where he had powerful enemies. Dissatisfied with the colonel's rank offered him, he resigned to work as a commissioner of Internal Revenue and as president of a railroad. His personality led to his leaving those posts, too. He spent some time lobbying for the repeal of the income tax. The town of Pleasanton near Mine Creek is named for him, never mind the misspelling. He died in 1897.

MAJOR GENERAL STERLING PRICE: Went to Mexico, where he led a Confederate-exile colony in Veracruz named Carlota after the Empress of Mexico. He returned to his beloved Missouri, where his admirers took up a subscription to buy him a house on 16th Street in St. Louis. Hearing of it, Shelby complained: "They had better damn sight appropriate that fifty thousand dollars to the orphans and widows that were made by his damn blunders." Price soon died in the 1867 cholera epidemic.

GOVERNOR THOMAS REYNOLDS: Also removed to Mexico, where he served the emperor as railroad commissioner. He prepared the better part of a book indicting Price, not always fairly, but suspended his work when news of the general's death reached him. Upon his homecoming in 1869, he presented the Great Seal of Missouri to Governor McClurg. He practiced law in St. Louis, where he took a role in establishing Forest Park. He served in the state legislature and eventually become a trade commissioner to South America for President Cleveland. Fearing he was losing his mind, he leapt into an elevator shaft at the St. Louis Customs House in 1887.

GENERAL JOSEPH ORVILLE SHELBY: An effort to promote him to major-general came too late to take effect. Shelby tried farming at the Confederate colony at Carlota, but the area became unsafe and he returned home. He testified — roaring drunk — as a character witness for Frank James at his Gallatin trial. When Democrats finally came to power in Washington, he was appointed U. S. marshal for Western Missouri. After Shelby's death in 1897, his body was viewed in state in a federal courtroom; his funeral procession is thought to be the largest in Kansas City history. His grave is in Forest Hills Cemetery, a few feet north of the Confederate monument that was erected in 1902 by the Daughters of the Confederacy. Historians calculate Shelby was in the saddle at least 5,000 miles in all his campaigns, probably more than any other Civil War commander.

GENERAL M. JEFF THOMPSON: With his luck with horses unchanged — his last mount was stolen at the Arkansas River — he more or less walked into Texas. "Thus ended the year 1864," Thompson would write later in his memoirs, "of which I spent seven months in prison and five months in the saddle." He was appointed commander of the Northern Sub-District of Arkansas, and, unlike many of the Missourians, surrendered his troops on May 11, 1865. Clement Evans, in his 1962 *Confederate Military History*, wrote: "A combination of sense and bombast, of military shrewdness and personal buffoonery … gave his campaigns a decided opera bouffe aspect." Thompson tried unsuccessful business ventures in Memphis and New Orleans but ended up as chief engineer of a levee commission. Working in the Louisiana swamps may have undermined his health. In 1876, he traveled home for a family visit in St. Joseph and died there of tuberculosis, likely contracted as a Federal prisoner of war. Mark Twain and Charles Dudley Warner referred to Thompson in their quasi-historical satire, *The Gilded Age*. "You ought to know Jeff; he's one of the most enthusiastic engineers in this Western country, and one of the best fellows that ever looked through the bottom of a glass… there was nothing that Jeff wouldn't do to accommodate a friend."

CAPTAIN LEVI UTT: Promoted to major not long after the Price raid, he and his troopers were sent to St. Louis, assigned to guarding bridges and then chasing bushwhackers in southeast Missouri. Stephen Starr, in his history of the jayhawkers, noted one last episode that revealed the Seventh Kansas Cavalry's everlasting scorn toward orders and its fierceness toward Missouri rebels: When two prisoners in their stockade expressed delight over the death of Lincoln, the officers voted 25-5 to shoot them, but asked for permission from headquarters in St. Louis. When the answer was no to a public execution, the rebels were killed anyway, the story being that they had attempted to escape. Utt died in 1895 in San Diego County, California.

Notes

With photographs and maps

Notes for Chapter 1 — Homecoming

SEPTEMBER 20, 1864 — SOUTH OF POPLAR BLUFF, *BUTLER COUNTY*

What did General Price ride on his invasion of Missouri? In *Action before Westport*, Howard Monnett wrote: "His great weight prohibited his using a horse for any length of time and compelled him to lead his troops in a 4-mule carriage driven by a Negro boy." Toward the end of the campaign, U. S. Major General Samuel Curtis would report seeing Price's abandoned carriage. What one would describe as a "plush-upholstered coach," others called a wagon fitted with cushioning. That Governor Thomas Reynolds, Price's most severe critic, made no reference to the general's transportation argues for its modesty. Major John Edwards, a great exaggerator, later wrote that Price never left his ambulance.

In the minds of pro-Southern Missourians like Price, the state needed plenty of redeeming. "Missouri is completely subjugated — has no more power than a chained and muzzled dog while the swine are rooting up everything," wrote a dejected Confederate Captain Griffin Frost from his Gratiot Street Prison cell in St. Louis the previous year.

The number of Confederate soldiers was given by Price, whose divisions were woefully short of men. According to Deryl P. Sellmeyer in his *Jo Shelby's Iron Brigade*, among the 1,455 cavalry troopers of the "Iron Brigade" were 278 men who were not armed and 48 who had no mounts. Jackman's Brigade, the other half of Shelby's small division, had it even worse; of nearly 1,600 men, only about one in four was armed and 133 needed horses. The other two divisions of Price's "Army of Missouri" were in no better shape. Before the war was over, Missouri would send 150,000 men, well more than a tenth of its population, to the battlefields. Of those, at least 40,000 went to the Confederate flag, a fuzzy estimate that included the guerrillas who were on no regiment roll and some Missourians who fought in the units of other states.

The 1860 census showed St. Louis half again as big as Chicago. "St. Louis more than doubled in population during the 1850s to 166,773 persons of whom 60 percent were foreign-born, the highest percentage of foreign-born in any American City. They included 39,000 Irish and nearly 60,000 Germans. The existence of this powerful new city, peopled with so many immigrants, made St. Louis very strange indeed to the southern white, Anglo-Saxon, Protestant farmers of the vast Missouri countryside," wrote Michael Fellman in *Inside War*. In comparison, Kansas City had about 4,400, about half the size of both St. Joseph and Leavenworth. Westport had declined to about 1,200.

Concerning the military readiness of Price's force, John W. Halliburton, one of the fellows who came to join Price, said: "All were mounted on untrained horses, with equipment of every kind that the country afford. Probably one-third had not any kind of arms, and two-thirds carried muzzle-loading shotguns, squirrel rifles, and revolvers of various kinds and makes." His was a .32 caliber Smith & Wesson with a six-inch barrel.

Major General Kirby Smith's opinion of Price was detailed in Monnett's *Action Before Westport*. The author detailed how Smith wished to be rid of Price, writing at one point that he needed "boldness, energy and activity, with prudence" for the Department of Arkansas, and "Price is not equal to the command." Price had performed well enough at Wilson's Creek and Lexington in 1861, and despite ultimate Federal victory at Pea Ridge, Arkansas, he and his Missourians marched away unbeaten. In Mississippi, however, they were whipped at Iuka and Corinth. Back on the west side of the river in 1863, Price had captured his objective, Graveyard Hill, at Helena, but the battle was a bloody Confederate defeat, as was Jenkin's Ferry the next year.

General Nathaniel Lyon was truly bloodthirsty. Stationed in California during the Gold Rush, he wiped out two tribes, at least 400 Indians, as punishment for the deaths of three whites.

Earlier in his life, Price had cut a dashing figure. Still handsome in a (very) plump English country gentleman sort of way, Price in 1864 was past his prime. At 55, however, he was still two years younger than Robert E. Lee. Some have suggested his Bucephalus (named for Alexander the Great's steed) was probably pretty heavy-hocked.

SEPTEMBER 21 — CAMP GAMBLE, *ST. LOUIS*

Captain Levi Utt calls Private Charles Thompson a "coffee cooler." The phrase referred to a soldier who lagged behind — "be with you in a minute, boys, just letting my coffee cool" — and "playing old soldier" was a term for malingering. The author apologizes for maligning the reputation of Private Daniel Newman for the purposes of this story. History records that he died of wounds the next April at Cape Girardeau and that poor Private John Tefft succumbed to chronic diarrhea in the coming December. Thompson deserted four days later.

At one point, Major General William Rosecrans was considered to lead the Army of the Potomac and even to join the 1864 Republican ticket with Abraham Lincoln. But a bad whipping at Chickamauga left him, in Lincoln's words, "confused and stunned like a duck hit in the head." The duck had been put in the smaller, out-of-the-way pond of Missouri. Even there, he continued to irritate his superiors. Major General Henry Halleck, chief of staff back in Washington, considered Rosecrans' pleas for reinforcements overwrought. So did General-in-Chief Ulysses S. Grant, who complained Rosecrans would want more troops even if "stationed in Maine."

The quip about Colonel Charles "Doc" Jennison's taking Missouri horses is based on horseman lingo for equine bloodline, in which one says "out of (the name of the mare) by (the name of the stud).

While it was Jennison's name that was feared, it was his second-in-command, Lieutenant Colonel Daniel Read Anthony, who often called the shots in the regiment. Jennison, although a doctor, was "in reality unfit … on account of his poor education," Anthony said, and the regiment's officers were "very careful not to permit him to write or do anything unless done under the supervision of some of his friends who have good judgment." As Anthony wrote: "Col. Jennison has been Col of his regiment six months and has yet to give the first command to them. I have always commanded them." Anthony exaggerated, but there was no doubt that the burning of Columbus and Dayton and the execution of nine men in Kingsville occurred on his watch. When Anthony left the army and became mayor of Leavenworth, he promptly burned the homes of southerners around the city.

Like Jennison, Anthony had a taste for Missouri horseflesh, writing to his brother-in-law: "I have taken a Secesh Stallion worth $1,000, and a grey horse worth 200. I now have three tip top horses — Don't you want a captaincy or a majorship in the army?"

D. W. "Webb" Wilder, editor of the Leavenworth *Conservative*, on September 20, 1861, defended the Kansans' actions: "Jayhawking was got up in Kansas. It's one of our things. It works well; we believe in it, we are going to have it. It don't make any difference whether the authorities, civil or military, believe in it or not. Kansas don't care much for authorities; never did, never will." Private Webster Moses of the Seventh wrote home about it: "About 10 of us went out jayhawking … before breakfast," he wrote about a typical foray near Lone Jack. "... Caught their horses and took the best ones... Found some silver ware... I got the cupps, two silver Ladles and two sets spoons...." John Ingalls wrote his brother on January 2, 1862, after visiting the Kansans' camp: "If there was ever a band of destroying angels in one congregation, I saw them there. They take no prisoners and are not troubled with red tape or sentimentalism in any form."

After walking away from the Seventh in '62, Jennison later asked Senator Lane for command of a colored regiment being raised. Lane said no for reasons of his own probably, but some doubted the wisdom of turning over 1,000 black infantrymen to the jayhawker. Colonel James Montgomery, who led his own black troops out east, wrote to the Kansas governor, "I cannot imagine any greater calamity that could befall the blacks than the appointment of Jennison to command them...I have been solicited by the honorable portion of our Citizens — Those who wish to see the Negro elevated instead of being made a thief and a pest to society."

America would later know Private William Frederick Cody, the lowly teamster in the Seventh, as "Buffalo Bill." If Cody wasn't a liar during the St. Louis encampment, the showman's autobiography certainly would make him out to be one later. He was never a Pony Express rider, although he may have worked at one of the route stations; neither was he a scout and dispatch rider who slipped through Price's army numerous times. Cody probably came closest to telling the truth about his Civil War military experiences when he recounted getting drunk and waking up enlisted in the Seventh. After this campaign, the regiment would return to St. Louis, where he performed duties such as hospital orderly and messenger for the Freedmen's Relief Society. He met and married his wife, Louisa Frederici, while stationed there. Cody's military career was more distinguished in the Indian wars, when Major General Phil Sheridan made him, at 22, the chief scout of the Fifth U. S. Cavalry.

SEPTEMBER 22 — NEAR PATTERSON, *WAYNE COUNTY, CENTRAL MISSOURI*

Sam Hildebrand was a notorious guerrilla of southeast Missouri. After Union men killed his relatives, he led what could be seen as a "death squad," coming up from Arkansas to hunt down and kill men marked on his list. He briefly joined the Price expedition, but did not follow it out of his territory. He survived the war, but was gunned down in 1872 in Pinckneyville, Illinois, resisting arrest.

The early March 1862 Battle of Pea Ridge in the northwest corner of Arkansas was known in the south as Elkhorn Tavern. This was for the establishment in the thick of the battle on the Confederate left wing, where Sterling Price commanded. Similarly, Wilson's Creek, fought the year before south of Springfield, was called Oak Hills by the rebels.

This chapter is based on a February 12, 1897, article in *The Kansas City Star* in which "Uncle Billy" Hunter was interviewed while Shelby, his old owner and friend, lay dying. He described the rebel yell, saying, "Lots of times in the last thirty years I have jumped out of bed with that yell a ringing in my ears. It always meant fight. When ever that yip, yip, yip! started, the horses got scared and begin to prance and pitch. Then the troops begin to shoot off their pistols and first thing you knew, off went the whole brigade and you couldn't see nothing but a big cloud of dust. That's what a cavalry charge looks like and it sounds like a storm tearin' through pine timber. I've heard people tell all about what they did in battles, but I never could recollect much about what I did. Dust and smoke and fire and cussin' and hollerin' was about all I could ever recollect when I found myself laid out under a pile of rails and hosses and men running over me."

Among generals killed soon after the start of the Pea Ridge fight were Ben McCulloch and James McIntosh. Another brigade commander on the Confederates' right flank also was captured, effectively wiping out the command structure there.

The story of the frying pan comes from the author's imagination, but Hunter did remark that he had been hit by a skillet himself during the war.

Notes for Chapter II — Partisan rangers

SEPTEMBER 23 — IN THE BRUSH, *HOWARD COUNTY, CENTRAL MISSOURI*

Several historians write that William Anderson — not given his sobriquet "Bloody Bill" until after the war — led the attack at Goslin's Lane in south Boone County. John McCorkle and Frank James, who recalled being at the fight, said, no, it was George Todd. The 1882 *History of Boone County* emphatically said it was Todd and that Anderson had not arrived yet. Dave Pool, whose name many spell with an "e," often rode with Todd. Crawford is said to have ridden with both.

The future outlaw's shooting by George Heisenger, a German farmer, was hardly heroic enough for his son, Jesse James Jr., a Kansas City lawyer. "My father was badly wounded and almost killed August 13, 1864, at Flat Rock Ford (leading the charge against) three hundred militia and one hundred and fifty Kansas Red Legs…," he declared in *Jesse James My Father*. "The first wound made him reel in his saddle and his pistol dropped from his right hand. He recovered himself and drew another pistol with his left hand and fired several shots. But a Spencer rifle ball struck him in the right breast, tore a great hole through the lung and came out his back near the spine. No man could bear up under such a wound as that. My father fell." This fight is not found in the war's *Official Records*. Judge Thomas R. Shouse, an old friend and neighbor, said James told him of the saddle-theft-shooting after the war, quoting him as recalling the wagon ride to safety as so rough that, "I was suffering so intensely that I wished every minute the soldiers would overtake and kill me."

In St. Louis, Captain John Thrailkill had experienced the full menu of Federal imprisonment before being sent to Alton. First he was confined at the Myrtle Street Prison, which was actually under the sidewalk. Freezing in winter, it held perhaps 150 men. He was transferred to the famous Gratiot Street Prison, a large domed building that had been a medical school before it was seized. Thrailkill's letter to his sister is from *Forgotten Rebels*, a book about John Thrailkill by James and John Farley.

Some say it was John Lobb who spied on Lawrence for Quantrill before the big raid, others that it was John Noland. Like Henry Wilson, a third African-American member of the constantly changing band, they were freedmen, not slaves. Noland would attend Quantrill reunions after the war, had all white pallbearers at his funeral and was considered "a man among men" by his guerrilla peers.

Among the passengers killed on the ill-fated train at the Platte River bridge was Barclay Coppock, who had been with his brother at John Brown's raid on Harper's Ferry. Barclay got away to Canada and escaped the government noose; Edwin Coppock did not.

Many knew Quantrill's paramour, Sarah Catherine King, as Kate Clarke, after one of Quantrill's aliases; later she would call herself Sarah Head to avoid trouble. Fletch Taylor said she kept "a fancy house in St. Louis," perhaps from money Quantrill left her. Some historians discount the bordello tale, noting Taylor had a grudge, and say the young widow found a rich man to wed. If so, she ended up destitute back in Kansas City at the Jackson County Home for the Aged, from which she ran away with an old fellow to be married one more time.

The consultation among guerrilla chieftains, according to some accounts, occurred during a meeting on the road the next morning. Frank James, who was with Todd, recalled Anderson joined them that night, making no mention of Quantrill. McCorkle indicated Anderson and Quantrill came into camp at the John R. White farm. Some accounts have Todd enthusiastic about the Fayette attack, others not. All agree that Anderson wanted it, and Quantrill did not.

SEPTEMBER 24 — 9 A.M. — WILLIAMSBURG, *CALLAWAY COUNTY*

Margaret Hays, an enduring and endearing woman, created a large and fascinating collection of Civil War communications. It can be found at wattshaysletters.com. Her letters to her mother include everything from war passion to a deformed child, a widow's grief over her lost husband to a mother's frustrations about how photographs of her girls came out. This chapter largely uses her letter of September 7, 1864. The story of Dick Yager (often seen as Yeager) was a noted guerrilla, who, relying on his Santa Fe Trail experience, struck 200 miles into Kansas in May 1863.

Upton Hays had government contracts to supply U. S. troops in Utah before the war. One of his young teamsters may have been William Clarke Quantrill. Area Federal officers considered Hays little more than a guerrilla chieftain; he played major roles in two Confederate victories in Jackson County, the first Battle of Independence and the Battle of Lone Jack. By the time of his death on September 13, 1862, he had joined Sterling Price and was colonel of a cavalry regiment, the 12th Missouri. The fight referred to here was probably with the Seventh Kansas Cavalry on the Little Blue River.

"Reason" was a male slave who once belonged to Hays' mother and was sold to kin. Another letter speaks of a slave named Diann, who refused to leave the Yagers after their house was burned by Federals: "They told her that she had to pretty Children that ought to be free and that she should be as free as her Master and Mistres. She told them that she was as free as they were, that her Master and Mistress had treated her more like a father and a mother than anything else. She cursed them all the time the house as burning, they then robbed her of all her clothing."

Among Hays' many, many kin from her Kentucky heritage was Abraham Lincoln, a second cousin of her mother. One of the few things Hays was able to save was her mother's wooden yardstick, a plain round stick marked off at foot intervals with the initials "N H" carved at the end, a gift from Nancy Hanks, the president's mother. Hays' descendents still have it.

10 A.M. — FAYETTE, *HOWARD COUNTY*

Some accounts of the fighting at Fayette omit the shots fired by the provost guard soldiers from the courthouse. John McCorkle's accurate memory of Lee McMurtry's being hit in the face there is found in his book, *Three Years with Quantrill.* Published in 1914, four years before McCorkle died at age 79, it illustrates the lopsidedness of the information from this era. His story, like those of other bushwhackers, found print long after the war when animosities — and memories — had dimmed. Living in the brush and being often on the move, the guerrillas left very few contemporaneous records while the Federal and Confederate armies were producing bushels of official reports and communications. In Kansas and even Missouri, the newspapers also were almost uniformly pro-Union. There is one constant, however. Both sides constantly exaggerated the number of foes shot out of the saddle. Indeed, if official report and lore were true, hardly a man would have been left standing for hundreds of square miles.

Other than McCorkle, the guerrillas had little use for rifles, instead carrying as many pistols as they could. "Major Leonard killed 6 of Anderson's gang, taking from their dead bodies 30 revolvers and capturing 7 horses," wrote Union General Clinton Fisk on September 24. The guerrillas' charge was usually effective at short range because they could empty a revolver between shots taken by a Missouri militiaman equipped with a muzzle-loading rifle. The repeating carbine adopted by Federal cavalry forces neutralized this advantage in rapid fire power.

Historians accept that 13 bushwhackers perished as a result of the Fayette action, and perhaps 30 were wounded, some of whom probably died soon after. If only 75 or so of the assembled guerrillas made the charges, as some sources say, that would mean a casualty rate of at least 50 percent. The militia suffered either one or three killed. General Fisk was delighted, writing to the Fayette commander: "You will congratulate (your men) for me and tell them I do not believe they are the 'bread-consuming, cowardly pack of jayhawkers' that some of their old friends represent them to be."

McCorkle missed the slaughter. "When I reached the pasture I there found Colonel Quantrill with Jim Little, who had received a bad wound in the right arm. I left McMurtry with Quantrill and started up north for the town where I could hear a great deal of firing. Quantrill called to me and asked where I was going, to which I replied, 'To help the boys.' He said, 'Come on back, there's no use trying to shoot through brick walls and logs with pistols.' I then turned my horse and rode back to where he was."

Notes for Chapter III — The gathering storm

SEPTEMBER 24 — 6 P.M. — FREDERICKTOWN, *MADISON COUNTY*

Assessments, the tax levied by the authorities on Missourians believed to be disloyal to the Union, originally went to pay for the operations of the Enrolled Missouri Militia units and the costs of Unionists displaced from their farms and villages by the violence of their southern neighbors.

Dr. McPheeter's wife, who already had lost her cook stove and rosewood piano to Federal confiscation, would lose her freedom in four months. Trying to get a letter through to her husband, Sallie wrote to a Federal officer acquaintance, "hoping the war has not changed you as it has many others from gentlemen to fiends." She then closed with: "You will have the thanks of a Rebel 'though she be.'" That tore it for the St. Louis authorities, who were always infuriated by the southern women who reigned in the city's society. The Federals even banned the wearing of red — considered the rebel color — in bonnet ribbons, silk linings of capes or even in petticoats. Sallie was arrested January 17, held for two days, then placed penniless on the steamer *Romeo*, which dumped her and her two daughters on a landing in southeast Arkansas. The same boat was carrying the surviving sisters of Bill Anderson and, according to one story, Mrs. Ulysses S. Grant, who ordered soldiers to give the women assistance.

After Sterling Price's contentious meeting with Jefferson Davis, the general's 4,000 Missourians were "sold to the Dutch" an expression meaning to be chewed up in fighting against foreigner-filled Federal ranks. The use of "Dutch" came from "Deutsch," or German immigrants. Captured at the fall of Vicksburg, they were exchanged and reorganized into just one brigade of about 1,500 and sent east. When General M. Jeff Thompson found them outside Atlanta, they were under Confederate General Francis Cockrell. "In the trenches they held a division's front," Thompson reported, "and each small regiment was a host in itself." Estimates of how many in the original ranks survived run in the few hundreds.

In 1861, Price had taken a steamer out of Boonville as General Nathaniel Lyon and his Federal regulars moved upriver from Jefferson City. The 28-year-old Colonel John Marmaduke was left with 500 green, under-armed State Guard enlistees. The result was the "Boonville races" and Yankee jokes about the Guard choosing its officers by who could run the fastest through the brush. A humiliated Marmaduke resigned and left for Richmond, Virginia, to obtain a regular commission. The young West Pointer was soon a colonel leading a regiment into the Hornets' Nest at Shiloh, where he was wounded. Fate put him back across the Mississippi under Price's command.

The general with whom Marmaduke dueled was Lucius M. "Marsh" Walker, his commander in the debacle at Helena, Arkansas. Afterward, Marmaduke wrote him, "I have not pronounced you a coward, but I desire to inform you that your conduct as commander of the cavalry was such that I determined no longer to serve you." To no one's surprise, Walker took offense. They dueled with revolvers at 10 paces, their first shots simultaneous, but going wide. Quicker with his second round, Marmaduke got his opponent to spit out the insufferable toothpick he was always chewing by ruining his right kidney and spine. Always the gentleman, Marmaduke offered the use of his ambulance. Price had him arrested, but most of the officers argued for Marmaduke's release, saying he was too valuable to lose. It helped some that Walker forgave his subordinate before dying, although Walker's men did not.

SEPTEMBER 25 — 5:15 A.M. — SOUTHBOUND FROM ST. LOUIS

In Civil War army organization, the company was the smallest unit. It would muster at 100 men and immediately begin shrinking — from disease, desertions and casualties — to a fraction of that. Ten companies made up a Federal infantry regiment, 12 in the cavalry. A battalion usually was four companies. A brigade could consist of two to six regiments. A division was made up of three or four brigades, theoretically 12,000 men, but usually many fewer. Three divisions made up a corps, which were assembled to make an army. The Confederate army was organized nearly the same way.

Lincoln's fingerprints were all over Ewing's promotion to brigadier general and command of the Department of the Border. Even his father, Thomas Ewing Sr., a former Whig senator whose other two sons had gone to West Point and wore general's stars, was surprised. He wrote the president: "What did you appoint the brat a Brigadier General for?" After the 1864 events in Missouri, says Ronald D. Smith in his Ewing biography, Lincoln spotted the father at a social function and displayed his amazing recall, asking, "What do you think of your brat now?"

Missouri was one of the places where General Sherman had been dogged by newspaper reports of his insanity. It began in 1861 when an incredulous Kentucky reporter picked up on Sherman's hard-nosed and far-seeing prediction that it would take 200,000 men to win in the Western theater. Fighting the press and his own depression, Sherman was transferred to Missouri, There, he did not help himself by becoming alarmed in Sedalia at false reports of Price's return and calling for reinforcements. His commander, Major General Henry Halleck, wrote "confidentially" that Sherman was "stampeded" and "entirely unfit for duty …in his present condition it would be dangerous to give him a command here." The letter was leaked to the newspapers, and an embarrassed Halleck dropped his request for a new brigadier. Sherman took some time off in Ohio, where even his wife complained of "that melancholy insanity to which your family is subject." Returning to St. Louis, he quietly assembled regiments at Benton Barracks to send south to the fighting. Eventually, he managed to join Ulysses S. Grant at the front and redeem his reputation at Shiloh.

Major General Frank Blair's brother had served in Lincoln's cabinet, and his father had advised presidents from Jackson to Lincoln. As congressman, Blair had held huge sway in St. Louis, where he had organized the mostly German secret militias, the "Wide Awakes," to keep the city from falling under southern control. He left his seat in Congress and ended up leading Sherman's XVII Corps in the famous — or infamous, depending on where you live— "March to the Sea," in which the army left supply lines behind and lived off the land.

The July 19, 1863, entry in Fourth Iowa Cavalry Sergeant Samuel O. Bereman's diary: "All the Gen. Officers met at Blair's Hd. Qrs. and had a 'big drunk.' Blair himself was dead-drunk, & Gen. Ewing, Brother-in-law to Sherman, was so drunk that he vomited all over the floor. It is enough to disgust a decent soldier." Once, Blair's men were delighted when his personal wagon tipped over crossing a creek in Mississippi and spilled out whiskey bottles and barrels of beer, which they retrieved for themselves.

Ewing's little bit of engineering with shovels around Fort Davidson would pay large dividends.

Captain Campbell's question was on point. General Shelby, was indeed, circling behind the Union force.

6 P.M. — WARRENSBURG, *JOHNSON COUNTY, WESTERN MISSOURI*

Although some Missouri towns on the border, such as West Point, never recovered, Pleasant Hill would survive, in part because it was a Federal outpost and thus exempted from Order No. 11. Also, it was revived by the smoky breath of the Missouri Pacific Railroad.

The performance of the Enrolled Missouri Militia units "ran the gamut from laughable to laudable," according to Bruce Nichols in his exhaustive volumes, *Guerrilla Warfare in Civil War Missouri.* By this point, authorities had concluded the part-time, unpaid soldiers were inadequate to the task and so came up with yet another organization, the Provisional Enrolled Missouri Militia, made up of the best men picked from the Enrolled Militia. Eleven of these Provisional units were scattered around the state.

An example of the mettle of the Missouri State Militia is found in an 1863 report of First Regiment Lieutenant Colonel Bazel Lazear: "I must also call your attention to Corpl. Andrew J. Fuller, of Company I, who seized a bushwhacker, after they had emptied their revolvers, and beat his brains out with his pistol. This is the same man who a short time since attacked 3 bushwhackers, killing 2 and running the third. His bravery is certainly worthy of reward."

At an 1863 bushwhacker wedding at Chapel Hill in southwest Lafayette County, Si Parker and his bride exchanged vows, each holding a pistol at the altar, according to Nichols.

"Shelby," wrote one biographer, Daniel O'Flaherty, "fought like a man who invented fighting."

SEPTEMBER 26 — 10:35 A.M. — ON THE ROAD TO IRONTON
IRON COUNTY, SOUTHEAST MISSOURI

"Our soldiers were poorly clad and most of the time my company presented a motley appearance," wrote Lieutenant George Washington Grayson, who fought in Arkansas. "The Confederacy being very hard run had very little in the way of clothing to issue to the men of this part of the country, and we were never very presentable. So when we caught a prisoner…we generally stripped him clean of such of the wearing apparel as we desired, they being always better than our own, and place upon him instead such of our old duds as he could wear."

Loggy Bayou is a feature of far southeast Arkansas, where R. E. Holley and two other Holleys, S. J. and W. H., enlisted May 12, 1862, at Monticello, joining Monroe's Arkansas Cavalry.

The story of Cyrus Russell and his family was told later by Mrs. C. J. Pitkin, his sister-in-law who was there. Her account ended this way: "'Well,' sighed my sister, 'we will go over to William's and see how they have fared.'" It was no better there.

SEPTEMBER 27 — 8 A.M. — PILOT KNOB, *IRON COUNTY*

The experiences of Colonel Carpenter are drawn from his letter written to General Ewing's wife a few days after the fight, as well as autobiographical material he left, published in the *Genealogical Notes of the Carpenter Family*.

The last train out of Arcadia Valley was a story all in itself. Its crew could see Ewing's forces falling back to the fort as it pulled out. It stopped to pick up the now-isolated pickets Ewing had placed at the stations and bridges, with Shelby's Confederate cavalry never far away and sometimes seen in pursuit on the roadbed. At one point, under fire, the men aboard had to climb down to replace a rail pulled off by the rebels and, as one wrote, "went fleeing on, urged by hands that feared the avengers of blood." Soon after the Big River bridge was crossed, the trestle was fired by the enemy. The few Union troops at Mineral Point — Major General A. J. Smith had decided against marching his men that far south — supposedly got their artillery on the train in just three minutes, while the townsmen also scrambled on board. Shelby was shelling the village as the train pulled away, but it arrived safely in DeSoto.

The building Carpenter originally picked for his hospital, St. Mary's Catholic Church, no longer exists. He scattered the wounded in several buildings in the town, including the still-standing German Lutheran Evangelical Church of the Unaltered Augsburg Confession nearly a half mile away.

Notes for Chapter IV — Hell fire

SEPTEMBER 27 — 10 A.M. — CENTRALIA, *BOONE COUNTY*

The author here used a rather outdated newspaper story about Bill Anderson's depredations, the July 22, 1864, edition of the *Missouri Statesman* of Columbia.

Sergeant Thomas Goodman described his captivity in his little 1868 book, *A Thrilling Record*, including the drunken antics of the guerrillas. "By night nearly the whole command, Anderson and Todd included, were drunk even to madness. God help me, I never witnessed so much profanity in the same space of time before, nor since; and it is my earnest desire, I never may again. They whooped, ran, jumped and yelled like so many savages. Once, Anderson, leaping on a horse, rode wildly through the crowd; firing his revolvers indiscriminately, and yelling like one possessed."

Some accounts of the Centralia massacre have Anderson making a speech in which he told the doomed prisoners that from then on he would give no quarter to "Federal soldiers (who) have just killed six of my soldiers (Bissett and his men), scalped them and left them on the prairie." Had the speech occurred, Goodman's book surely would have mentioned it, but it did not.

Euphemisms for executions such as "Parole them" were common. Union reports routinely noted captured bushwhackers "mustered out." Walking over the ground with Centralia journalists 33 years later, Frank James said he had been back in camp with Todd and was not part of the massacre of train passengers. Edward E. Leslie in *The Devil Knows How to Ride* places him with Anderson going through the express and baggage cars, where they found perhaps $13,000.

The locomotive that was sent on its way toward Sturgeon ran out of steam and was found by its engineer, who walked down the track with some passengers. He got it fired back up, and they made the rest of the trip with riders hanging off the engine. Before leaving Centralia, Anderson's men apparently bagged another train, this one carrying gravel, by tossing a body across the tracks to make it halt.

1:15 P.M.

The "barbarisms" of Centralia seemed to nearly unhinge General Clinton Fisk. The next day, he suggested another Order 11 was needed, this time north of the river. "Nearly every family in this infernal region has a representative either with Price's invading column or with Anderson in the brush.... We have in these counties not only the resident rebels, but in addition a large proportion of those who, by General Ewing's order, were last year expelled from Johnson, Jackson and the other border counties. Depopulation and devastation are extreme measures, but if this infernal warfare continues it will be humane and economic of human life to adopt and rigorously enforce such measures wherever the bushwhackers have more friends than the Government."

In May 1863 — before Lawrence — Nevada citizens watched Union troops from Fort Scott, angry about being shot at, burn 75 buildings, including the Vernon County Courthouse.

Sneed's Boone House hotel would survive the bushwhackers and the angry Federals, but not the wrath of hungry Germans. To protect the North Missouri cars after the massacre, Union commanders put on guards in the form of the St. Charles German Home Guard. When the trains stopped in Centralia for dinner, the soldiers would race to the hotel to eat, crowding out paying passengers. Thomas Sneed finally had enough and said the Germans could not eat at his establishment, to which they responded by setting fire to his hotel. The blaze reportedly was extinguished, but the Germans lit it again and stood around with their rifles ready to shoot anyone who might try to put it out. Their commander watched, contentedly smoking his pipe. After the war, the Sneeds returned to Centralia and built the Phoenix Hotel. Alas, it, too, burned in 1872. Ten years later, all of the Sneeds were still there when a Boone County history recounted their tales.

Another account has Major Andrew Vern Emen Johnston saying, "We will go out and feel of them." The author thought the closing quote from a 1924 account by M. F. Hicks, who was a 10-year-old boy with big eyes and big ears when Anderson came to Centralia, was too good to pass up. Hicks also said he saw a Yankee soldier from the train escape on a rebel horse, a highly unlikely memory.

1:40 P.M. — YOUNG'S CREEK, *SOUTH OF CENTRALIA*

Major Johnston was a former school teacher near Hannibal who had written the previous day: "I have mounted nearly all of my men & have broken up the rebel bands of this county to 'Skulking Squads.'" Frank James claimed his little brother, Jesse, was the one who killed Johnston. It's possible he was. Bill Anderson himself is said to have praised Jesse: "Not to have any beard, he is the keenest and cleanest fighter in the command." Frank James later got a little carried away, saying the only battles that surpassed Centralia were Thermopylae and the Alamo.

Pro-Confederate tribes in the Indian lands often reverted to scalping during battles, and a tribesman in Lawrence dealt similarly with a bushwhacker too drunk to get out of town with his fellow raiders. The practice, however, may have originated in Jackson County, Missouri. In October 1863, guerrillas found Ab Haller, one of their own, missing his hair on the Texas Prairie on the east edge of Jackson County. Viewing the corpse, Andy Blunt supposedly reflected: "We have something to learn yet, boys. Scalp for scalp hereafter."Another version of this tale is that Blunt found the bodies of bushwhacker Jim Bledsoe and two Confederate recruits, who had been wounded at Lawrence, tracked down and executed. Supposedly a Delaware Indian in the pursuing party named White Turkey took their scalps and ears. T. J. Stiles, author of a Jesse James biography, wrote that "Missouri's war was small scale, intensely personal, intensely vicious. Its signature were the revolver and the scalping knife, close-range arms that required the killer to look his victim in the eyes...."

Perhaps trying to sell more copies of his memoirs, Sergeant Goodman went on to claim: "Men's heads were severed from their lifeless bodies." He also said the heads were switched between bodies or stuck on fence poles. But Federal officers soon on the scene did not report that level of atrocities. Besides scalpings, at least one genital mutilation did happen, however.

Although families claimed some bodies, most of the 22 soldiers from the train and the perhaps 124 Missouri infantry killed this day were buried in a trench near the railroad tracks. For years, train passengers peered at a monument marking this "bivouac of the dead." In 1873, officials moved 79 bodies to a National Cemetery in Jefferson City, where a stone obelisk memorializes that fatal day. Every skull bore a bullet hole, according to accounts.

Notes for Chapter V — Assault

SEPTEMBER 27 — 2 P.M. — PILOT KNOB, *IRON COUNTY*

While many Civil War soldiers did consider the surgeons to be "butchers" when it came to saving or discarding wounded limbs, the Butcher in this case is a hacksaw-like device, with a special blade-turning capability designed by English doctor Richard Butcher. Later calculations would find that amputations were involved in 75 percent of all battlefield operations. Three-fourths of Federal amputees survived. Civil War surgeons preferred to perform amputations on patients who were sitting up if possible. The use of chloroform was prevalent on both sides; another "wonder drug" of the time was bromine, which, injected around the wound, nipped gangrene in the bud. For pneumonia, the treatment was often a mixture of opium, quinine and brandy.

Before the war, David Murphy, an immigrant worked his way west as a carpenter with the railroads. Wounded in the knee at Wilson's Creek, he rose to major and commanded batteries in Mississippi. He resigned his commission to teach in St. Louis, but when the 47th Missouri was being raised, he enlisted again, apparently happy enough as a junior officer. After the war, he would become a judge in St. Louis.

Seymour Carpenter took charge of the medical department in Kansas City when Ewing was in command there. Headquarters, he said, was in "a new brick building on the top of the bluff, which had been a Hotel, and was large enough to accommodate the entire staff." This was the Pacific House, part of which still stands on Delaware Street.

2:30 P.M.

All four attacking brigades were supposed to begin at 2 p.m., but Major General Price's plan did not take into account the differences in terrain. As a result, the brigades advanced on the fort one at a time, allowing the Federals to shift much of their defensive fire to the newest threat. General Marmaduke's forces came down off Shepherd Mountain, but most hunkered down in a creek bed that passed to the west of the fort. General Fagan's attack came off Pilot Knob from the southeast, with General Cabell's brigade getting the closest to the fort. General Clark of Marmaduke's division next tried to renew the attack from the creek, but was easily repelled. Fagan and Marmaduke had both recommended the assault, Fagan predicting he'd take the fort in 20 minutes. When some of his division "broke in a most disgraceful manner," the embarrassed Fagan asked to make another charge. The chief of engineers, Captain T. J. Mackey, recalled that Fagan suggested that Price's personal guard, a company of Shelby's men, go in, too, but "Price said no; Cabell remarked to General Price that it was a damned wise decision." Cabell had not wanted even the first assault.

The Confederates ran into the fire of four 32-pound siege guns, three howitzers, a few newly mounted field pieces, two or three mortars and rapid rifle fire. Shelby had wanted to bypass the stronghold and race on to St. Louis. "If we attacked Pilot Knob," he noted later, "…it would only cripple and retard our movements, and I knew too well that good infantry, well entrenched, would give us Hell, and Hell we did get…"

The Enfield rifle weighed just under 10 pounds.

Mackey later testified that the army had not attempted to shell Fort Davidson from the surrounding heights because of a report that General Ewing had herded southern civilians into the fort to serve as shields against bombardment. Although civilians were in the fort, they were volunteers. Getting more guns up the rugged hills — one private recalled each one sent up required 20 span of mules — was thought to be too time-consuming. Mackey said he had climbed Shepherd's Mountain to reconnoiter, but cannon smoke obscured his view, and Federal sharp-shooters discouraged a long stay. He reported a "slight ditch" around the fort, not enough to be an obstacle. Mackey testified that a measurement of the moat after the battle found it to be six feet, four inches deep. Perhaps trying to minimize his part in the disaster, he insisted that he easily scaled the slope of the fort's wall, which was nine feet above ground level. Of course, no one was shooting at him during the experiment.

The explosive device that landed near Private Holley was probably a Ketchum hand grenade. The bulbous dart-like object had cardboard or wooden fins to cause it to fall on its nose, pushing in a front plunger to ignite the gunpowder inside. The author has no way of knowing whether Holley made it to the moat, although his unit may have. Records show him wounded in the left side and right hand. He was one of the estimated 1,400 casualties suffered by Price's army here, perhaps 400 of whom died. Ewing lost only 28 killed and less than 100 wounded. Like nearly all of the seriously wounded rebels on this campaign, Holley was left behind for the Federals to deal with. He died of his wounds December 15, 1864, in the military prison at Alton, Illinois.

10 P.M.

Being hit more than once was common. One genteel Southerner, Colonel Mathias Martin of the 23rd Tennessee, when asked at Shiloh about his injuries, replied: "My son, I am wounded in the arm, in the leg, in the head, in the body, and in another place which I have a delicacy in mentioning." — Larry J. Daniel, *Shiloh: The Battle That Changed the Civil War.*

In the November polling in Missouri, Thomas C. Fletcher would be elected governor — the first actually born in the state. Had he been captured by Price's army, it would have made for interesting headlines, in part because the Confederate Governor-in-exile Thomas Reynolds would have been among his captors.

"Captain Jim," who died of his wounds the day after the battle, was James Farrar (or Farmer). Townspeople hid him from the rebels under a concealed trap door in the floor of the parsonage part of the Lutheran church. Bloodstains can be seen on the floorboards of the little wooden church today, and recent archeology revealed a bullet with scalpel marks.

"The Rebels did not come in until the next morning, when they pillaged the town indiscriminately. I was treated moderately well. They said the General was the best fighter they had met in a long time. I stayed two days, and came up under a flag of truce." — Carpenter's letter to Mrs. Ewing. The surgeon would report back to Jefferson Barracks bringing a wounded Confederate major named Surridge.

SEPTEMBER 28

Seymour Carpenter had gone to an empty hotel in Pilot Knob to rest. As he recalled: "I threw myself upon a bed, thoroughly exhausted, and instantly fell asleep. I could not have slept long, when I was aroused by a shower of glass, and the window frame, which was in front of the bed. It was intensely dark, and the air was filled with sulphurous fumes. In my confusion, and in trying to pull myself together, it flashed through my mind that I had been killed, and had come to consciousness, in the place where good people are not supposed to go. Presently I realized that it was only the explosion of the magazine, and that mercifully I was given another chance."

The fort's defenders did not bother to dig graves for dead comrades, but just placed the bodies so the explosion would bury them. Carpenter had protested that the blast would harm the many wounded Confederates lying just outside the walls, but General Ewing brushed off his concerns. War was not a "benevolent institution," he said, and he would not leave the powder and ammunition behind to be captured. A good-sized crater has dominated the interior of the earthworks ever since.

Lieutenant Colonel Lauchlan MacLean, the Scottish or Irish-born adjutant to General Price, may have been the one to carry the white flag and forward Price's call to Fort Davidson to surrender. The story goes that he was a strong advocate of attacking once he learned that Ewing was in the fort. MacLean had left his school teacher post in Missouri to become chief clerk in John Calhoun's office of the Surveyor-General of Kansas during the "Bleeding Kansas" years. Calhoun, although a friend of Abraham Lincoln and a strong supporter of Stephan Douglas, led the rigging of the 1857 election to pass the pro-slavery Lecompton constitution. MacLean may have been the one to hide incriminating fraudulent ballots in a candle box under a woodpile near their Lecompton office. Finding the proof of pro-slavery election fraud, the story goes, Ewing confronted MacLean. When a sheriff arrived later with an arrest warrant, MacLean, like his boss earlier, had disappeared.

Some of Shelby's far-flung troopers apparently showed up in a store that served as a post/telegraph office in what was then the outskirts of St. Louis.

SEPTEMBER 29 — PAWNEE FORK OF THE ARKANSAS RIVER

The aptly named William S. Tough was chief of scouts with a reputation for slaying or capturing more than his share of guerrillas — and he killed at least one more on this day as he cut his way to Fort Blair. Some identify Tough as a former Red Leg, which organization General Blunt at one point condemned and ordered disbanded. The general assured superiors that Tough was "kept under my immediate supervision," but when Blunt was reassigned, the scout apparently reverted to his old activities.

Immediately after the disaster, an angry Blunt wrote: "I will follow the hounds through the entire southern confederacy, as long as there is a prospect of overtaking them. And I will have it well understood, that any man of my command who again breaks from the line and deserts his post shall be shot on the spot…"

Years later, it was reported from a regiment reunion at Baraboo that one of the Third Wisconsin survivors, "F. Arnold carried a piece of his scull in his vest pocket as a reminder" of Baxter Springs.

According to Leslie's biography of Quantrill, after Lawrence and Baxter Springs newspaper articles, diaries and even "cold Federal military reports (referred) to the bushwhackers as 'demons,' 'devils from hell,' and 'fiends incarnate.'" Andy Walker, recalling in 1910 his bushwhacker days for the Weatherford Texas *Weekly Herald*, said the murderous spree continued. "… We entered the Cherokee nation, and Quantrill placed a detachment of twenty-five—wearing Federal uniforms and carrying a Federal flag—a quarter of a mile ahead of the main body. Each day, ten to twenty Pin Indians (Federal) would join us and each night we would shoot the recruits of the day."

At Baxter Springs, besides his escort, his whiskey and his reputation, Blunt also lost his flag. "It was the finest I ever saw, inscribed 'Presented to Maj. Gen. James G. Blunt by the ladies of Leavenworth Oct. 2d, 1863,'" later wrote bushwhacker William Gregg. "Quantrill sent the flag to Gen. Price." The flag, in pieces, was recovered by the 4th Iowa Cavalry, which pursued Price after the Battle of Westport the next year.

A reorganization of the Kansas military districts had moved Blunt's headquarters to Fort Smith, Arkansas, in part to break his grip on the many government contracts funneled through Fort Leavenworth and to end "irregularities and abuses." In late '63, Major General John Schofield wrote how he had become convinced "that Sodom was a pure city compared to the Kansas border." Blunt resisted, reinforcing the belief he was losing a source of graft (likely shared with his protector, Senator Lane). He threatened duels and blasted back that no "baser traitors" existed than the quartermaster and commissary at Fort Leavenworth. Of the Kansas governor, he wrote the president that "A greater thief and Corrupt Villain than Thomas Carney does not live … And all that he lacks to make him a finished Scoundrel is his Stupidity — and want of brains to enable him to Carry out his Corrupt Schemes Successfully." President Lincoln had replied coolly: "I regret to find you denouncing so many persons as liars, scoundrels, fools, thieves, and persecutors of yourself."

Notes for Chapter VI — Flesh and blood

OCTOBER 1 — PARIS, *MONROE COUNTY, NORTHEAST MISSOURI*

Ann is the only true character in this book not identified by last name. Not all slaves had the surnames of their current owners. She was one of nearly 115,000 slaves counted in Missouri in 1860, and while she may be lost to history, her spirit lives on in her letter to her soldier-husband published in *Free at Last: A Documentary History of Slavery, Freedom and the Civil War*. Her letter actually was written January 19, 1864, dictated to a sympathetic white neighbor, possibly James A. Carney, who added his own note that Hogsett had forbidden Ann to visit him so Carney could read Andy's letters to her privately.

Mama Jo is imaginary, but Private Flavius Shortridge of Paris, Missouri, was the author's great-granduncle, who joined Colonel Joseph C. Porter's First Northeast Missouri Cavalry. Captured in 1862, Shortridge was sentenced to hard labor at the Alton, Illinois, prison, where after two years he died of typhoid fever.

The shooting of the slave Alfred occurred in October 1863 near Louisiana, Missouri.

The first black regiment recruited from Missouri slaves originally was called the Third Arkansas Infantry so as not to offend or frighten Missouri whites.

Farmer Joseph Hickam, a couple of counties away, apparently tried to keep slavery going. Upon his death, 24 years after the war, his black domestic, Eda, sued his heirs, alleging she had never been told that slavery had been abolished when she was a 16-year-old girl. In 1893, she filed suit for $1,400 against his estate for lost wages at $5 a month. A probate court in Boonville decided to split the difference at $785. But the family appealed. Four *Hickam v. Hickam* civil trials later, in which no one could prove whether the woman had been deceived, jurors denied Eda any back pay.

PRICE'S 1864 MARCH INTO MISSOURI

Sterling Price's invasion/raid began Aug. 30 in southwest Arkansas with the capture of St. Louis as his ultimate goal. Within a week of crossing into Missouri, that idea was abandoned as Union forces reinforced St. Louis and Jefferson City. All that was left of his mission was to raise new recruits along the Missouri River, bring out supplies and to raid Kansas on his way back south.

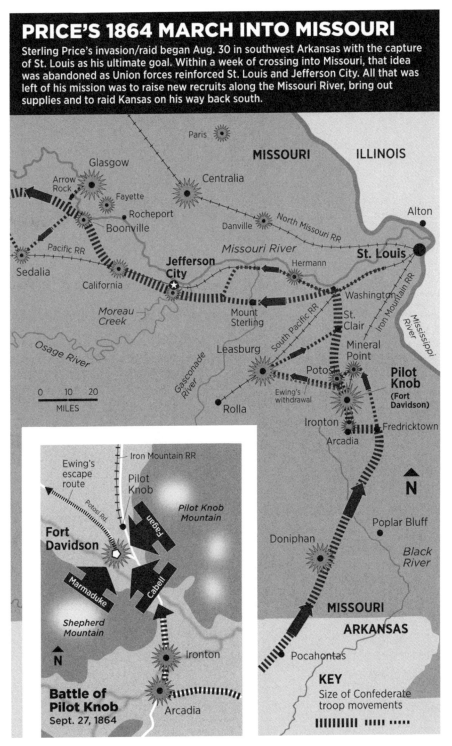

Dave Eames, Kansas City Star

Archie Clements, left, David Pool, center, and fellow guerrilla
State Historical Society of Missouri

Bill Anderson
State Historical Society of Missouri

George Maddox
Courtesy of Wilson's Creek National Battlefield,
National Park Service

John McCorkle, left, and fellow guerrilla
Jackson County Historical Society

Frank James
Jackson County Historical Society

Jesse James
Kansas City Star files

William C. Quantrill
Kansas City Star files

George Todd
Missouri Valley Special Collections, Kansas City
Public Library

Egbert Brown
Courtesy of Wilson's Creek National Battlefield,
National Park Service

Seymour Carpenter
Missouri Department of Natural Resources, Division of State Parks

Thomas Crittenden
Missouri Valley Special Collections, Kansas City
Public Library

Samuel R. Curtis
Courtesy of Wilson's Creek National Battlefield,
National Park Service

Henry Curtis
Courtesy of Wilson's Creek National Battlefield,
National Park Service

Thomas Ewing
Courtesy of Wilson's Creek National Battlefield,
National Park Service

Charles "Doc" Jennison
Courtesy of Wilson's Creek National Battlefield,
National Park Service

A. V. E. Johnston
State Historical Society of Missouri

John Philips
Courtesy of Wilson's Creek National Battlefield,
National Park Service

James Blunt
Courtesy of Wilson's Creek National Battlefield,
National Park Service

Troopers, Seventh Kansas Cavalry
Kansas State Historical Society

Andrew Jackson Smith
State Historical Society of Missouri

James Fagan
Courtesy of Wilson's Creek National Battlefield,
National Park Service

Margaret Watts Hays
Courtesy of Marian Franklin www. Wattshaysletters.com

John S. Marmaduke
Courtesy of Wilson's Creek National Battlefield,
National Park Service

Sterling Price
Courtesy of Wilson's Creek National Battlefield,
National Park Service

Jo Shelby
Courtesy of Wilson's Creek National Battlefield,
National Park Service

Jeff Thompson
Courtesy of Wilson's Creek National Battlefield,
National Park Service

Lauchlan MacLean
From *Doniphan's Expedition and the Conquest of
New Mexico and California* by John Taylor Hughes.

Marmaduke Flag
Missouri Department of Natural Resources,
Division of State Parks

A guerrilla raid as envisioned by artist Thomas Nast
Kansas State Historical Society

Centralia, Missouri, in the 1860s
State Historical Society of Missouri

Notes for Chapter VII — Up the Missouri

OCTOBER 2 — BOLTON'S FORD, OSAGE RIVER *COLE COUNTY*

How important was coffee to the Federal soldier? One model of the Sharps rifle was produced with a little coffee mill built into its stock. According to one soldier, the troops preferred their brew "strong enough to float an iron wedge."

Trying to discern the enemy's intentions and whereabouts was always iffy. One Union commander noted the intelligence-gathering process with a captured Confederate engineering officer. "This lieutenant is not very communicative, but my staff got him drunk last night…"

As busy as the one-armed paper hanger — literally — General Egbert Brown pressed the men of Jefferson City into service, even emptying the penitentiary, to dig trenches, cut trees for fields of fire and build strong points around the state capital. On October 4, he wrote Major General Rosecrans: "We have a long line to defend and few troops and but little artillery. A range of hills about three-fourths of a mile in front of us, overlooks the town; makes it a bad place to defend; yet I have no doubt I can hold the place longer than the enemy can stay to fight us if it is less than a month." The next day, he sent another telegram to St. Louis, complaining how from Kansas "Major-General Curtis telegraphs me encouraging words, but does not send any battalions."

Rosecrans had his own problems. Besides the Price invasion, he had to contend with the aftermath of the Centralia disaster, a possible strike of terrified railroad employees and trains on the Hannibal & St. Joseph railroad, also being robbed and burned, and wild rumors of an attack by 500 Confederate Indians at St. Clair. In the middle of all this, Major General "Fighting Joe" Hooker had telegraphed for disposition of Rosecran's forces in case they were required in Ohio to suppress draft riots. An exasperated Rosecrans shot back: "I will send you a map of Missouri. We are now having a rather lively time…."

While ruthless, Lieutenant Colonel Lazear was not heartless. After the Lawrence raid he recommended that "every citizen, man, woman and child, in Texas Prairie (around Lone Jack), and near it, be sent out of the country…." Weeks later, when Order 11 did just that, he wrote his wife one of the area history's most often repeated quotes: "It is heart sickening to see what I have seen since I have been back here. A desolated country and women & children, some of them almost naked. Some on foot and some in old wagons. Oh, God. What a sight to see in this once happy and peaceable country."

Colonel Philips' own regiment resembled a death squad at times. His second-in-command, Crittenden, had ruffled feathers among Jefferson City lawmakers by ordering the execution of two men on reports of horse theft. In the coming December, Philips reported that one of his scouts, or patrols, heard Quantrill had been in Saline County, and that "One McReynolds, near Miami, confessed to have fed and aided him all he could voluntarily. The scout shot him." The patrol had pretended to be bushwhackers to trick the man into feeding them and giving them information about Federal movements. The killing of Allen McReynolds, a wealthy farmer, prompted commanders in St. Louis to rein in their militias somewhat.

OCTOBER 3 — THE ROAD TO MOUNT STERLING *FRANKLIN COUNTY*

The Franklin that Lieutenant Colonel Lauchlan MacLean mentions in the beginning of his account is not the one near Boonville. Today the town is called Pacific.

Price's invasion of Missouri did not incite the hoped-for mass uprising, but he did pick up some thousands of would-be soldiers in the heart of the state's slave belt along the Missouri River. The diary of Doctor William McPheeters, Price's medical director, recorded the new blood, 700 at Jonesborough alone: "Recruits in large number are all the time joining us. The people of Missouri are thoroughly aroused and it is evident that the great heart of the people are thoroughly with us if they will only act in accordance to their principles — Now is the time for their deliverance."

While the rebels assembled in southern Arkansas, McPheeters wrote how he "attended and joined a secret order, having reference to military and political affairs, and took two degrees in the order. Enough said of that subject." In the end, all the secret meetings produced little. The Copperheads, who wanted the war over, the draft ended, the South allowed to leave the Union and Lincoln and the Radical Republicans shoved out of office, proved no stronger than the shadows they inhabited.

It was in the hours in which the guerrillas held Platte City, apparently, that Jesse James visited a photography studio to make his famous bushwhacker image. The face under the little curled brim-hat seems to register some uncertainly despite the threat of his props, two revolvers in his belt and a third heavy Colt in his lap. Over white linen is his guerrilla shirt with its deep pocket for ammunition. A silk bow tie, as askew as his soul, wraps up the package.

As others marched on to win battles at Veracruz and Chaultepec during the Mexican War, Price, then a nobody former congressman, was assigned the boring task of holding the just-seized New Mexico Territory. The place had erupted in revolt in January 1847, and some would accuse Price of being inattentive to warning signs. Resentment of imposed American rule was the prime motivator, but the arrogance of the Second Missouri Mounted Volunteers toward the Hispanics and Indians had not helped. In Taos, Charles Bent, the appointed U. S. governor, was slaughtered along with several others. Price, pushing out from Santa Fe with a small force, beat back more than 1,500 poorly armed rebels. After his artillery failed to break the thick walls of the Taos pueblo, he sent his volunteers in to root out the insurgents. The chiefs got trials and were hanged. Perhaps his appetite was whetted for real glory, or he believed he needed to offset the uprising's effect on his reputation, for the next year saw Price marching 300 Missourians out of his backwater to El Paso. Mexico City had been captured months earlier, no threatening enemy forces were to be seen, and his orders were to stay in Texas. Instead, he crossed the Rio Grande and headed south. They met Mexican couriers with the news of a peace treaty signed the month before. Not trustworthy, Price declared and marched on. Eventually, on March 16, 1848, he forced a reluctant Mexican commander into the Battle of Santa Cruz de Rosales — 10 days after the U. S. Senate approved the treaty. Price defeated a force three times larger than his own; The fight left fewer than 50 men dead all told. Small price for glory —some might call it small potatoes, too —but enough to make him a hero back in Missouri. Secretary of War William Marcy reprimanded Price, but the Missourian had a powerful patron in the U. S. Senate, Thomas Hart Benton, and no fuss was made. Price went home to become a slave-holding tobacco grower at Keytesville and eventually a popular governor in the mid-1850s.

OCTOBER 4 — HERMANN, *GASCONADE COUNTY, EASTERN MISSOURI*

Captured near Pilot Knob, the unlucky Major James Wilson and five soldiers of the Third Missouri State Militia Cavalry were executed by order of Colonel Timothy Reeves, commander of the 15th Missouri southern cavalry and an old foe of Wilson. Southerners alleged a "massacre" of dozens of Reeves' 15th Missouri troopers and civilians had occurred at a Christmas Day dinner in 1863. One Federal report notes that Wilson killed and wounded 35 in an attack that day, capturing 115 and rescuing men of Company C of his regiment who had been captured. Union atrocities against the towns of Doniphan and Martinsburg also were attributed to Wilson and his Company C. Writing later, Major Edwards viewed Wilson's death as "eminent justice." The Federals saw it as something else. On October 25, after the bodies were found, an angry General Thomas Ewing recommended "that fourteen privates of Price's command be executed in retaliation," eight for Wilson alone. Major General Rosecrans settled for six, total. Jeff Thompson later blamed Price for not stepping in, "but responsibilities of this kind were not to our commander's liking, and they were turned over to Reeves to guard, with a pretty full knowledge that they would be shot." Ewing reportedly later got a letter describing Wilson's execution, which said that Reeves had declared: "Major, you are a brave man — but you never showed my men quarter, neither will I give you quarter." Supposedly the condemned major, himself, gave the order to the firing squad.

There was no one to keen over Wilson. Because of his loyalty to the Union, his father and brother would not speak to him, and his wife had left him, taking their children back to Virginia. After the war, Reeves returned to his vocation as a preacher.

To "see the elephant" was a 19th century term for experiencing danger, generally in combat, but immigrants on the western trails would refer to the experience as well.

The lost Cortez Kitchen was picked up by Federal cavalry and released after the invasion was past.

OCTOBER 5 — IN THE BRUSH, *BOONE COUNTY*

Newton "Plunk" Murray survived the war and later became a sergeant in the Texas Rangers.

Different versions exist of the Union patrols that tried to hang Jesse James' stepfather, Reuben Samuel. Lieutenant James Rodgers said the old Baptist minister cracked after "one good swing" and directed them to a bushwhacker camp a short distance from the house. Some versions have Jesse cutting Samuel down, others say it was his mother, Zerelda. Her attitude toward Yankees was pretty well summed up when she had a baby girl in October 1863 and named it Fannie Quantrell Samuel, as she later said, "just to have a Quantrell in the family."

The two most notorious guerrillas fabricated stories about Federals killing family members. Quantrill said jayhawkers killed his older brother when they stopped their wagon near Lawrence on the way to Pike's Peak, but both of his brothers were living after the war. Anderson's father, belligerent and threatening in an incident growing out of Bill's horse stealing, was shot-gunned in self defense by an area man. According to one Quantrill biographer, Anderson said his papa had been tortured and killed by Yankees, and, "As time went by and he became increasingly cruel and violent, he actually seems to have come to believe the lie himself."

Colonel W. R. Penick saw traitors everywhere, especially in the Independence girls' school run by Mrs. Bettie Tillery. During the 1862 battle in the town, Tillery brought a mortally wounded Confederate officer into her house to die. "One of the worst rebel women in the state," Penick had declared, and he ordered her to sew death shrouds for Union soldiers killed by guerrillas. Her retort? She would be delighted to sew the shrouds for his whole regiment.

The man after whom Lee's Summit may be named, Doctor Pleasant Lea, was going to a nearby home in late summer 1862 to borrow a newspaper when "the Hounds of Old Pennock," as some called the Fifth Missouri State Militia, stopped him on the road. Supposedly, they broke his arms to gain information before delivering the fatal bullet and burning his large house. The officer who murdered Henry Younger was Captain Irvin Walley.

Little history is available about Riley Crawford, but this tale of being given to Quantrill is the most repeated fragment. One or two accounts say the widow Crawford also brought Riley's older brothers, William, Marshall and Marion, but they do not show up on the guerrillas' rolls or in any fighting. How old was Riley? Family records offer no birth date. Many have written he was 14 when turned over to Quantrill. The census listed Crawford at 13 in 1860 so 15 is more likely. In fall 1864, the period covered by this book, he probably was 16.

The guerrilla hideouts weren't always the place where roughhousing boys played. In an abandoned bushwhacker camp in the deep woods in October 1863, Kansas troops found a dog keeping company with a Union soldier long ripe from hanging. They cut him down and found a note that said the man "was hung in revenge for the death of Ab Haller. He says that his name is Thomas and that he belongs to the Kansas 7th." Considering the condition of the corpse, the note was helpful. Company H First Sergeant Sherman Bodwell noted how the camps were "always hidden where hardly more than a horse track points the way, in heavy timber and creek bottoms, offal lying about, cooking utensils, cast off clothing… the very air seems thick with the clime with which so lately they seethed."

OCTOBER 7 — ALONG THE MOREAU RIVER, *COLE COUNTY*

When war broke out, M. Jeff Thompson had been headed east to fight back in Virginia, but stayed in the state after taking a colonelcy in the Missouri State Guard. Frustrated by the lack of clear answers from Governor Claiborne Jackson, Thompson had declared: "Governor, before I leave, I wish to tell you the two qualities of a soldier. One he must have, but he needs both. One of them is common sense and the other is courage — and By God! You have neither." Despite the insult, Thompson received command of Missouri's southeast quarter, a very active sector at the war's start, where his battalion became known as the "swamp rats."

One part of General Jo Shelby's after-action report, clearly written by his adjutant, Major John Edwards, dealt with the fight at the Osage River: "The swift and beautiful water was torn into foam-flakes that hurried and danced away to the sea..." To translate from Edwardsese: The river was high. "Chivalry was his religion," wrote Daniel O'Flaherty, who in his Shelby biography called Edwards a "Bombastes Furioso." "He could scarcely think, much less write, except in hyperbole." It also was said of him that more horses were shot from under him than any man in Shelby's command.

Lying in his blood after the sharp Osage River fight, Colonel Shanks expressed his opinion that the Yankees "would not drive worth a cent." He would recover in captivity.

It was somewhat unusual to place a State Guard officer over regular Confederate units, but Thompson's reputation appears to have satisfied everyone on this march.

Once a prisoner taken to St. Louis, Thompson checked into a hotel after being released on his promise not to escape. There he was interviewed by newspaper reporters and held a dinner for friends, leaving the bill to his Federal captors.

OCTOBER 8 — JEFFERSON CITY

Civil War correspondents fancied themselves the "Bohemian Brigade."The mastheads of the St. Louis newspapers gave little clue as to their politics: *The Daily Missouri Republican* espoused the beliefs of Democrats, while the *Missouri Democrat* was a Republican sheet.

The words of the fictitious reporter actually are those of Kansas Governor Samuel J. Crawford, who was a colonel at least 100 miles away, at the time. In his 1911 book, *Kansas in the Sixties*, he mocked Price with the words for bypassing Jefferson City. Unhappily, Jay Monaghan seemed to pick up much of this nonsense in his often-cited 1955 book, *Civil War on the Western Border 1854-1865*: "Against the lowering sky, majestic Price — a shining knight — rode to and fro on Bucephalus. Time and again curious citizens saw the flash of a thousand blades drawn for a charge, but no horsemen came. Throughout the night sentries watched and waited in the rain. At dawn the russet hills, the shining roads and lanes were empty. Price had gone." For the record, Price was at the front, but observing as Fagan occupied positions on the heights outside the city. The Confederates would not have used swords or horses to attack entrenchments; they had few swords anyway. Some men were bloodied in skirmishing on the afternoon of the seventh and the morning of the eighth before the army marched away in broad daylight under clear skies.

The newly installed Major General Albert Pleasonton found himself in what has been called the "personnel junk yard of the Union army," the Department of Missouri, along with his commander, Major General Rosecrans. The sense that the Trans-Mississippi got the castoffs also was felt down south. In August 1863, a Confederate army chaplain wrote to Jefferson Davis "that every disorder that has befallen us in the West has grown out of the fact of weak and inefficient men have been kept in power... I beseech of you to relieve us of these drones and pigmies (sic)."

Many alleged that George Caleb Bingham's building at 14th Street and Grand Avenue was ramshackle. However, it was not even 10 years old. When the property, called the Thomas Building, had come into Bingham's hands from his late father-in-law, he'd added the third floor, thinking it would serve as his studio in Kansas City. The building, having only been used as a prison for about a month, fell August 13, 1863. As late as 1910, Kansas historian William E. Connelley was still writing that the girls brought their deaths upon themselves by digging through the foundation. He also threw in rooting hogs and high wind.

On this day in Kansas City, poorly armed civilians were called out to begin preparing for the invasion. During the war, the city had been protected by a variety of cavalry units from various states, the state militia cavalry, the enrolled militia and a little-known citizen unit, the Kansas City Station Guards. Formed by General Ewing after the Lawrence raid, members of the Guards are recorded in pension records as "digging trenches and throwing up breastworks." A sister unit just to the south was the Westport Police Guard.

The painting Bingham had in mind to defame General Ewing became "Order No. 11," which the artist originally thought to title as "Civil War." It was not completed until three years after the conflict — in a rough cabin/studio on the front yard of what is now the Bingham-Waggoner Home in Independence — but the State Historical Society of Missouri says it was begun in Jefferson City. Perhaps not great art, but excellent anti-Ewing propaganda, it is the best known image from the Civil War in the West. Two versions were painted, the second being slightly larger. This 1870 painting is displayed at the State Historical Society in Columbia. As Frank James reportedly said after a viewing: "This is a picture that talks!"

OCTOBER 9 — THE BOONVILLE ROAD, *MONITEAU COUNTY*

Largely forgotten are rumors that the Northwest — then the states around the western Great Lakes, which were less concerned about slavery than the more abolitionist New England — might break off and form its own confederacy. This appealed to some Missourians who always feared Richmond would sacrifice them in any negotiated settlement with Washington. Today, it seems ridiculous, but the Southerners and the Copperheads in the north clutched at such phantasms.

A letter from Congressman Thomas Snead, General Price's previous adjutant, confidante and biggest supporter, seems to contradict a theory that they hoped to install and isolate Thomas Reynolds in the governor's chair up in Jefferson City. Price, supposedly, would return south to headquarters where the real power was. But unless an election were held, according to Snead's letter, noted in Albert Castel's 1996 Price biography, Reynolds would hold on to office, and "continue to exercise, after the expiration of his present term of office, what will then be an autocratic, despotic, and illegal authority… Don't understand me as advocating Governor Reynolds' re-election."

After the campaign, the fiery Reynolds accused Price of many things, including lying on a carpet to sip toddies as his troops rode by. He did not, however, indicate that Price came with personal comforts out of the norm for a 19th century army commander. Earlier in the war, supposedly, Price and his huge staff once entertained his commander, General Earl Van Dorn, with "the luxuries of large wall tents carpeted with thick buffalo robes, a breakfast of kidneys stewed in sherry served in a silver chalice and the music of his regimental band," according to an earlier Price profile by Robert E. Shalhope.

OCTOBER 10 — GASCONADE RIVER, *GASCONADE COUNTY*

This chapter is taken from Sergeant Samuel Bereman's excellent diary. The place and time are not clear, but it was shortly before his unit reached Jefferson City. After arriving at the Missouri capital, Bereman and the other veteran horsemen under Colonel Edward Winslow joined Major General Pleasonton's all-cavalry division. Bereman, from near Mount Pleasant, Iowa, was one of six brothers and two brothers-in-law to join the Union Army. His father went into the "grey beard" regiment and his mother served as an army nurse, according to family history.

If Bereman could get another Spencer for $25, he was getting a deal. Carbine replacements are listed at $30, a revolver at $24. A saber was worth just $7.

Although the Confederates often had superiority in numbers in Price's campaign, too few had the fast-firing carbines they faced from Federal cavalry regiments. In practiced hands, the longer-range Enfield perhaps could get off three rounds in a minute, but that was dismounted. The Spencer, loaded through a magazine tube in its buttstock, could expend its seven metal, rim-fire .52-caliber rounds in less than 20 seconds, all from horseback. One Confederate soldier recalled an attack on Federals equipped with Spencers. "The head of the column, as it was pushed on by those behind, appeared to melt away, or sink into the earth. For although continuously moving, it got no nearer."

Perhaps the worst thing that could be said for the Spencer was that a hard knock on the stock could set off the cartridges in the magazine, a nasty surprise for the trooper. "The advantage of Spencer Carbines is that they are capable of being fired very rapidly," Bereman noted. "The disadvantage is that you soon get out of amunition," which would happen to him later in this campaign. As in future wars, the army brass grumped that such fast-firing weapons resulted in reduced marksmanship and wasted ammunition. That philosophy led in part to the Seventh U. S. Cavalry fighting with single-shot Springfields twelve years later at Little Big Horn, while some Sioux and Cheyenne warriors carried Spencers and 15-shot Henrys.

Even a single-shot, paper-cartridge breech-loader carbine, such as the Sharps, could pump out a rate of fire three times that of a muzzleloader. Northern factories supplied a surprising variety of these handy weapons for Union horsemen — Sharps, Joslyns, Ballards, Merrills, Starrs, Burnsides, Smiths, Halls, Maynards and Gallaghers. The French, supposedly, first created the weapon, but apparently not to universal approval in their ranks. The root of "carbine" is "escar-rabin," translating roughly to dung beetle or corpse-bearer.

"We started westward in the vain attempt to out-travel and overtake a mounted enemy," summed up the regimental history of the 119th Illinois Infantry, which was part of this pursuit.

"We forded the rivers on all occasions, all bridges being destroyed, which was no pleasant occupation for October."

Notes for Chapter VIII — Regulars and irregulars

OCTOBER 11, 10 A.M. — BOONVILLE, *COOPER COUNTY*

Major General Samuel Curtis allegedly sent William Hickok, Dave Tutt and a third man as spies to infiltrate Price's column. One story has Hickok staying with the Confederates until their retreat from Westport, while Tutt became a double agent and the third man was killed. True or not, it was Tutt whom Hickok killed in Springfield the next year, more likely over a gambling debt than a war grudge. The face-off on the town square quickly enhanced the future reputation of "Wild Bill" as a gunman — and later inspired the many fast-draw duel-in-the-street scenes Hollywood loved.

Actually, Cole Younger would later write that one female had been murdered, but by accident. "One Negro woman leaned out of a window and shouted: "You —— of ——." She toppled out dead before it was seen she was a woman." One Miss Mary Wiederman came close to collecting a bullet, according to her recounting. She had run to the family barn to shoo out the horses before the guerrillas got to them. She'd cut the bridles with a butcher knife, but one horse had blundered into the garden and considered itself stuck. Mary was smacking it with a bean pole when bushwhackers yelled for her to desist scaring off the horses. "The air was blue with curses as they stopped their horses before me," she would recall. "'We told you to let those horses alone,' one of them shouted, fingering his pistol very freely. When the other said (to him), 'Don't you do that, don't do it….' They chased them all over Mt. Oread, but did not get them…."

Josephine Anderson, who was only 15, is buried in Union Cemetery, about 100 feet south of the grave of the owner of the collapsed building, George Caleb Bingham. The bodies of the Crawford siblings and McCorkle's sister were taken to the small Davis-Smith cemetery beyond the village of Raytown. Eliza Harris would later write: "I was a girl of eleven at the time as I remember that the Union men sent three caskets containing my cousins to Little Blue. With the caskets was the satchel of trinkets and dry goods that my sister and Charity had gone to town to buy." Their resting place, which is between the lanes of Missouri 350 east of Westridge Road, is covered by weeds in 2011, although local historians hoped to mark it in some way.

Not surprisingly, the Anderson sisters were disliked by their guards in Kansas City. One fellow prisoner who was released sometime before the collapse was Venetia Colcord Page. Her sister, Mary Hall, had written her a cautionary letter, advising: "Don't say a word before any. That will only make your case worse. Remember you are a lady and act accordingly. The guards say they like you and Miss Parrish. They say very hard things of the others. The officers told me this." The Anderson girls, Mary, 18, and Martha, 13, would be arrested again a year later. A newspaper noted their arrival in St. Louis by train, remarking: "They are said to be very genteel and modest young ladies but decidedly rebellious in their sentiments." The article went on to say they were accompanied by one Imogen E. Brumfield, who although a widow of a member of Anderson's band, "does not appear inconsolable for his loss, as she remarked that there were 'Plenty more men left.'"

A "Mrs. Wilson" was injured in the collapse and later died of her injuries. Some have suggested she was a Union spy placed among the women in the Kansas City lockup; a Mrs. Wilson tried to warn Federal officials right before the Battle of Independence in 1862. Women spies were not unusual in the war. Federal records indicate Elizabeth W. Stiles, widowed in George Todd's October 1862 raid on Shawneetown, was employed "as a Spy & Secret Agent on this border." Todd's own spy, a Miss Eliza Brown, was quickly caught in Independence and confessed she had been assigned to determine Union troops strength "with a promise if she did so, he would make her a present of some fine dresses."

According to Kansas historian John E. Connelley, one young woman, Alice Van Ness, who was not hurt in the jail collapse, became a favorite among Union officers for her singing voice. Lieutenant Cyrus Leland, Jr., was such a friend that he arranged to have her banished so she could leave town with a theatrical company and start her career. She used the stage name Alice Vane.

Edward Leslie in his 1996 Quantrill book called the theory of the prostitutes "as natural as a sudden gust of wind." But Paul Petersen in *Quantrill of Missouri* contends the Union soldiers purposely brought the building down on the women and that General Thomas Ewing was aware of the dangerous situation, but did nothing about it. His book refers to Mattie Lykins quoting Doctor Thorne at the scene as saying: "Not a blue coat will be found (in the debris); every man who has been detailed to stand guard at this prison for the last few days and weeks knew the house to be unsafe and have kept themselves at a safe distance from the trembling walls. I knew the building to be unsafe and notified the military authorities of the fact, and suggested the removal of the women prisoners, but my suggestion was not heeded and before you is the result." Even if true, the quote does not prove that the Federals weakened the building to kill anyone. Mrs. Lykins, who was in Lawrence nursing a stepson when the raiders came in a few days later, would soon be banished from Kansas City for her southern views.

Petersen was perhaps the first to spot Riley Crawford's presence at Lawrence. Many assumed this recollection, found in the files of the Kansas State Historical Society, referred to the better-known Bill Anderson. The reference to two sisters arrested, however, and two killed clearly points to Crawford. Another good clue comes from William Bullene, who was a boy in this house that the guerrillas decided not to burn. He said the Wisconsin woman said the young fellow requesting food was "of gentler aspect than the rest, and of fine personal appearance...." While the bushwhackers generally were young, and Anderson was handsome, no one would have accused him of "a gentler aspect" in Lawrence. As Cole Younger wrote of that day: "Bill Anderson claimed to have killed fourteen and the count was allowed."

Thespian Hall, finished in 1857, is still there today, the oldest operating theater west of the Alleghenies.

11 A.M.

_____

Different historians have different versions of what bushwhacker leaders showed up for the Boonville meeting with General Price. The only one for sure is Bill Anderson. While newspapers said John Thrailkill was there, most histories ignore him while contending George Todd was present. But sources put Todd in southern Lafayette County slaughtering German militiamen with Dave Pool the day before. When Todd brought Price some prisoners on October 18, the general reportedly did not know who he was. Some of those who believe Todd was at Boonville say he was sent south to break up the Missouri Pacific Railroad around Sedalia. Todd did botch the job of burning a bridge over the Lamine River on October 9, two days before the Boonville meeting, but there seems no record of any official orders to do so.

All Confederate generals had the same insignia, so one could not tell their ranks by that. A better indicator seemed to be the rows of buttons on their coat, although that didn't seem foolproof, either. Colonels also wore stars on their collars, although not wreathed. Lieutenant General Robert E. Lee's simple coat consistently bore a colonel's three stars. Yankee generals did then as they do today: one star on the shoulder for a brigadier, two for a major general and three only for Lieutenant General U. S. Grant.

After Price's death a few years after the war, Governor Reynolds acknowledged that he had been disappointed and unduly bitter when he made his accusations of the general's incompetence. The one about drunkenness in Price's headquarters is probably pretty close to the truth.

Many have assumed from Price's written orders that Quantrill was at Boonville, but the best accounts indicate the deposed guerrilla chief never got his instructions to attack the Hannibal & St. Joseph Railroad far to the north — not that he would have attempted it. The railroad, however, had been disrupted, already. On October 4, another guerrilla/bandit band had burned two freights near Hunnewell and robbed a passenger train.

"As to clothing, arms, ammunition, horses, they want nothing, and indeed they are totally indifferent as to pay," Price wrote after Quantrill's men arrived in Texas in late 1863. "They desire to serve with me as partisans, and in this they are adept, and could be made very valuable as such to the army; but for reasons which they hold good they will not … be attached to any brigade, but are willing and anxious to serve if allowed to do so as above." As Anderson himself wrote in July 1864, "I have killed many. I am a guerrilla. I have never belonged to the Confederate Army, nor do my men."

Guerrilla Andy Walker recalled "one glorious lark" when Anderson's men came into Sherman, Texas, and stole a demijohn of whiskey from a drugstore. The next morning, he claimed, "after a riotous breakfast, Anderson muttering heavily formed his men in platoons, and they made a systematic circuit of the streets and public square shattering with bullets, amid mighty peals of laughter, every door knob in the district covered. The merriment was no less when they rode into the lobby of old man Christian's hotel. To begin with, the clock was perforated with quite a number of bullet holes. Then two troopers at once urged their steeds over a lounge on which Dick Maddox lay. They succeeded in reducing the couch to kindling wood.…'

Insult of insults, Anderson's men later tried but failed to sneak into Quantrill's camp and steal his horse, Old Charley, Leslie writes in his Quantrill biography.

OCTOBER 12 — 9 A.M.

Some historians say Anderson's band was ferried across the Missouri river to do General Price's bidding and destroy a Northern Missouri Railroad bridge far to the east; McCorkle, riding with Todd's separate group, said decades later, however, that Anderson got all the way to Jackson County on the south side before turning back east. This seems unlikely. On October 14, some of Anderson's men, probably led by Archie Clement, sacked and burned much of Danville, as well as the depots at Florence and High Hill, three counties east of Boonville and roughly halfway to St. Louis. They did not venture on to the St. Charles County line, where their objective, the bridge, was situated. Most sightings of Anderson after Boonville seem to have him on the north side of the river.

Sergeant Thomas Goodman did not return to military service other than to be discharged the next summer in St. Louis. He returned to blacksmithing in Iowa, until enticed to Santa Rosa, California, where he died in 1886.

The southern women did their best for their men. In Platte County a few miles from Weston, Major Robert H. Hunt of Jennison's 15th Kansas recalled treating an old man "pretty roughly" for refusing to reveal local guerrillas. "A daughter of Fulton made her appearance, and aimed a revolver at Sergeant Gill and David Causort, our scout; the latter, however, disarmed the fair damsel; he also took from her a bowie-knife and flask of powder, all of which said scout has in his possession as a love token." The girl and her father survived, although he was taken out "and hung a little…" After the Lawrence raid in August 1863, First Missouri State Militia Lieutenant Colonel Bazel Lazear reported: "We had a number of skirmishes this day, killing 3 (no doubt wounding several) and capturing a number of horses, and some prisoners, who were unarmed, and a female, by the name of Miss Hutchins, of this place, who was standing picket while 2 bushwhackers were eating their dinner, and … giving them timely notice of the approach of troops." At another point that summer, Lazear wrote a (teasing?) letter to his wife: "I now have two very pretty rebel girls on my hands as prisoners and what the devil to do with I don't know, as I don't like to put them in the guard house. I expect I will have to take them into my room and let them sleep with me."

Notes for Chapter IX — Marching orders

OCTOBER 13 — GRAND AVENUE, KANSAS CITY, *JACKSON COUNTY*

This chapter is drawn from *Three Years and a Half in the Army: A History of the Second Colorado*, written in 1885 by Ellen Williams, who followed her husband, bugler Charles Williams, in his campaigns in New Mexico and Missouri. While she was not present during the fighting, Williams certainly heard all the stories in Camp Smith.

The war often was hard on women and children of both sides. Records show Federal officers in Westport and Kansas City requesting army rations for the widow Wilhelmina Hedding, as well as Nancy Jane McGuire, Amanda Dresser, Margaret Gilman and Susan Barnard, all married to soldiers in the Sixth Kansas and "destitute and in need of assistance."

The monument to the fallen Colorado troopers that stands today in the northeast part of Woodlawn Cemetery in Independence could be the first such memorial to Union Civil War dead in the country, being dedicated in 1864, the year before one was put up at the Manassas battlefield in Virginia.

The guerrillas were losing men, too. Captain J. H. Little told his commander, Colonel James McFerran of the First Missouri State Militia, about the execution of Benton Gann and two other guerrillas in Lafayette County: "They refused to give any useful information; said their trial had been fair and that they were not afraid to die, which boast they made good. They calmly walked to their graves, looked contemptuously on the detail assembled, said they were ready, quietly folded their arms, kneeled down, and met death with a dauntlessness worthy of a better cause."

When word came that guerrillas, Pawpaws and Confederates recruiters had overrun Platte County in July, the Colorado troopers were in a mood to bite back. Pushing ahead of Doc Jennison's 15th Kansas and some Missouri militia, they attacked a large rebel picnic at Camden Point. Many of the more hardened and long-headed guerrillas, aware that the Federal hive had been kicked over in the county, already had moved on, but Calhoun "Coon" Thornton had not taken the hint. As the Federals advanced, the remaining, poorly armed recruits formed a battle line under John Thrailkill's direction. Thornton, on the other hand, ruined his reputation forever by making tracks. Before the rebels scattered, at least six were stretched out, four of them having been captured and executed on the spot. The Colorado regiment lost four killed and eleven wounded.

OCTOBER 15 — SEDALIA, *PETTIS COUNTY, WESTERN MISSOURI*

This is a true story, although what silver item the looter had isn't known. The author made it a basket simply because of Colonel John Philips' unhappy October 18 entry in his diary after learning that his possessions left at Sedalia were lost. "Heaps of news about capture of train, my saber, etc., wife's fine silver basket. Wrote to wife." No indication of how Fleecie Philips took the news. Forty years after the war, Paul Jenkins wrote in his history of the Westport battle, "Eye-witnesses of that day tell of seeing them, riding through the streets, their feet bare in their stirrups, carrying their boots full of whiskey, for lack of other facilities for its transportation."

Many of the men were just plain hungry. General James Fagan would write to Major General Price, on October 18:"I beg leave to call to your attention to a want of breadstuffs for my division. My men are much dissatisfied and complain a good deal. They deem it strange that in such a plentiful country as the one in which we are now operating breadstuffs cannot be supplied at least while we are moving so leisurely." It was even worse for the Federal cavalry following in the wake of the rebel locust tribe. "We have to live off of the country and this is poor living for a large body of troops," wrote Bazel Lazear of the First Missouri State Militia on October 17.

In a letter for his four-year-old daughter Martha to read after growing up, he had tried to explain that her father, "... has done many terrible things in the line of duty, yet no blackened chimney standing amid the ruins of the homestead, no solitary grave by the roadside of the murdered citizen, no blood upon the threshold or hearthstone mark his line of march. This will be a matter of pride to you someday, my dear...." Thompson's record was good, but not perfect. When he commanded rebel forces in southeast Missouri, his men rampaged through a German settlement, leaving several murdered civilians that the general rationalized away as enemy militia.

New York Times correspondent Franc Bangs Wilkie would have been first to agree. Passing through Sedalia in 1861, he found "a God-forsaken kennel of filth and all possible mean things ... the centre of a region accursed as if blasted by the simoon of death. The women were intensely secession, one of whom I heard say that she had a husband and two brothers in the Federal army, and that she 'hoped to God the Southern troops would kill every one of them.'"

The Thompsons' St. Joseph home had been vandalized, and when Emma Hayes Thompson had fled to St. Louis, she was briefly held as a spy. It was too much for her; she suffered spells of insanity. In late 1872, Thompson allowed his youngest daughter to be adopted by his sister and her husband because Emma had "relapsed and is now in an asylum," according to Doris Land Mueller in her 2007 biography of Thompson. After that, her fate seems unknown.

7:45 P.M. — WESTPORT, *JACKSON COUNTY*

In his various reminiscences, Captain Henry Palmer made mistakes that cause historians headaches. In one of his tellings of the feats of his A Company of the 11th Kansas Cavalry, he was ordered east to find Shelby on the October 10 and stayed in contact with the foe continuously until the fight reached Lexington. In another account, however, he tells of visiting his wife on this Sunday, the 16th. This version is probably correct because reports by his commanders verify that he was not sent out until the 17th. Some of the 15th Kansas rode out the night before, recalled E Company Captain Curtis Johnson, with a touch of humor: "We left Hickman's Mills on the 16th, previous to which the Division was reduced to light marching order, with only such supplies as could be carried by the men on horseback. All extra blankets and clothing was left at the Mills to follow with the train, and as far as I am aware they are following yet, as I do not know that anything has been seen since."

Sterling Price was enjoying his domestic interlude as well this evening, catching up with Kittie, the wife of his son, Edwin. She joined the major general for Sunday dinner in camp west of Marshall.

The war was never very far away from Westport. In June of 1863, Ninth Kansas Cavalry Captain Henry Flesher had been called from Paola because Kansas City was said to be threatened by guerrilla bands. Believing they had reached a safe zone, his troopers of E and K companies had sheathed their carbines and trotted straight into one of George Todd's best ambushes. "Just before sundown last night, my advance was fired on by from 200 to 300 rebels at the edge of timber this side of Westport," reads Flesher's report. "They were strongly posted behind a stone wall. I was compelled to retreat through a long lane. They followed so closely that I could not form my command until we got to the end of it." As guerrilla John McCorkle recalled it: "When we reached this lane, we formed in platoons of eight and waited for them. They came riding very leisurely over the hill, the captain in front, with his leg thrown over his horse's neck. He asked who we were when Captain Todd yelled, 'Charge, kill 'em, boys, kill 'em,' which we immediately proceeded to do." Hemmed in and panicked, the Federals were driven back south along the Fort Scott Road (today's Wornall south of Brush Creek).Before the evening of June 17 was over, 16 troopers were dead or dying with perhaps ten more wounded. Three guerrillas were killed, including Fernando Scott, a Clay County partisan and early leader of Frank James, who also was a participant in the skirmish.

Palmer tried to infiltrate Todd's band, sending in brave Henry Starr. It had seemed to be going well until Todd came up behind Starr and delivered a bullet to the back of his head, pitching him into the campfire by which he had been sitting and joking.

Palmer family legend says this Westport House was the place where, the year before, General Thomas Ewing dictated the words of Order No. 11. This seems apocryphal.

OCTOBER 16, 3:30 P.M. — HICKMAN'S MILL, *JACKSON COUNTY*

Playing the peacemaker, Major General Samuel Curtis had General H. M. Fishback released to his command but kept Lieutenant Colonel James Snoddy a prisoner in Paola until the Confederate army moved south. "Motives, measures, and men were all distrusted," Curtis would write. "The Senators, Governor, and the people commanding, composing, and controlling this militia reserve were all fiercely engaged in this political strife."

Major General James Blunt and Senator James Lane probably had cut Governor Thomas Carney out of some lucrative government contracts, but it was not all about patronage and petty graft. Blunt and Lane also foiled Carney's efforts to exercise the normal perogative of a governor — commissioning officers of state-raised regiments. Carney had named R. C. Anderson to lead the First Kansas Colored Infantry. Lane and Blunt wanted their own man, James Williams. They slipped supporters into the regiment's lower officer ranks, who in turn threatened to shoot Anderson if he tried to take command, according to Albert Castel in his *Civil War Kansas*.

The fortunes of Doc Jennison and George Hoyt had emerged from the ashes of Lawrence. Carney had clasped them to him, finally getting to raise a new regiment, the 15th, which was not in Lane's pocket.

Daniel Read Anthony had been a founder of the ultra-radical Leavenworth *Conservative* in early 1861 and killed a rival newspaper's editor in a street shootout. His short stint with the Seventh Kansas Cavalry ended in August 1862 to the relief of his commanders. Given the patronage plum of postmaster for Leavenworth, Anthony became mayor in April 1863. It was no secret that, under Anthony, it was a place to make serious money from Missouri plunder. Apparently, by 1863, the odors emitted by Leavenworth's stables grew too rank for General Thomas Ewing, as well. "There are very many men in Kansas who are stealing themselves rich in the name of Liberty. These men must find some other mode of giving effect to their patriotic zeal. As they want to kill rebels, let them join any old regiment." He placed the town under martial law, warning Anthony he would not allow "any town in my district to become a city of refuge within whose precincts the pirates of the border may escape the swift process of martial law." Anthony was not re-elected so he dabbled in journalism again and apparently cattle stealing. It was not until later that the Anthony name would become respectable and synonymous with newspapering with the

Leavenworth *Times*, his vocal opponent in the turbulent war years.

One story about the origins of the red leggings stemmed from Colonel Jennison's 1861 foray into Independence where Joe Swain, Hoyt's future Red Leg lieutenant, had taken a fancy to the red-dyed sheepskins on some shelves and appropriated them from the cobbler. Apologists contend that Red Leg outrages were committed by criminals who later stole their good name with their distinctive fashion of leggings. In an 1863 letter to Illinois newspapers, C. M. Chase agreed that the Red Leg was a distinct species of the border, describing one as "more purely an indiscriminate thief and murderer than a Jayhawker." In 1915, Ed Blair, in his *History of Johnson County, Kansas*, wrote that Hoyt's men performed legitimate and official Federal duties of scouting and dispatch carrying. "No company of better fighting material was ever organized. The men were all young, inured to western life, splendid horsemen, thoroughly accomplished in the use of weapons, rashly reckless and fearless, and, as an old Missouri lady once remarked, 'As full of the devil as a mackerel of salt.'" As Blair continued, he began digging a hole. "It was charged they were robbers of the worst class, but this accusation was unjustly applied. It is true they did a good deal of confiscating in the enemies' country, but it was always in the face of the enemy, and from known enemies. No quiet citizens were ever molested...." Apparently, he did not read Leverett Spring in his 1885 history of Kansas, who said, "The gang contained men of the most desperate and hardened character, and a full recital of their deeds would sound like the biography of devils." William Cody said he was with the Red Legs, "the biggest gang of thieves on record," although his autobiography gets the dates wrong. William Hickock probably was a Red Leg.

Private Albert Greene, Ninth Kansas Cavalry, had observed Hoyt speaking at Paola in the summer of 1863, "dressed in a suit of black velvet, red sheepskin leggins reaching to the knees, a red silk handkerchief carelessly thrown around his neck, and a military hat with a flowing black plume. At his waist was an embossed morocco belt carrying a pair of ivory-mounted revolvers." How anyone could be an undercover "detective" while wearing red leggings over their boots and a brace of silver shooters is hard to grasp.

A Federal detective had the broad power to arrest the deserter and the disloyal, and seize "property found in improper hands." For many, the only pay was that property, which was an embossed government invitation to plunder. One provost marshal officer who moved up to be the Kansas congressman received an 1865 letter from Fannie Wright who was writing for her friend "Beauregard," that is, John Bridges, the Red Leg. "The sum of my request is this — that 'detective papers' be given him under you, you undoubtedly are aware of the gain pecuniary to be realized from such papers exercising jurisdiction over country south of this, he expecting to share liberally with his friends." This comes from Matt Matthews and Kip Lindberg, in their May 2002 *North & South* magazine article, "'Better Off In Hell' The Evolution of the Kansas Red Legs."

OCTOBER 17 — UNION HOTEL, KANSAS CITY

This statement beginning "All my troubles..." actually was made by Mary Vaughn on February 11, 1865, after her arrest for supplying food to Sterling Price's soldiers when they reached Jackson County. She insisted that it couldn't be avoided: "I never willingly furnished the rebels anything last year except my own sons and son-in-law who belonged to Price's army, whom I willingly fed when at my house.... Price's men took the only horse I had and ate the flour, cornmeal and meat."

The nickel would not be minted until 1866.

Uncle Jim was something of a bushwhacker martyr. He'd taken off his guns and was sitting in a barber's chair in Wyandotte City when the Yankees rushed in on him. Jim Vaughn's hanging on

May 29, 1863, infuriated the guerrillas. John McCorkle quoted the doomed man on the gallows as saying: "You may kill me, but you'll never conquer me, and taking my life today will cost you a hundred lives and this debt my friends will pay in a short time." He also may have said: "This is my last look. Let her slide." In response, Confederate Benjamin Parker killed four captives from the Second Kansas Battery at Fort Scott. The next month McCorkle was with Todd's band when it cut up the Ninth Kansas cavalry on "Bloody Lane" just south of Westport. McCorkle said a note was placed between a Yankee's teeth reminding the Federals of Vaughn's last words.

Dan Vaughn, who reportedly had ridden in Todd's band before the battle, apparently let the two captives go. Colorado State Archives show Bay and Fox mustered out of the regiment January 2, 1865, at Fort Leavenworth.

The Vaughn women were released in November, but their troubles hardly were over. In January, Nancy Vaughn was at the home of a neighbor woman named Taylor when two Federal soldiers were killed nearby. One Colorado trooper described a Miss Virginia Taylor as "a notorious Rebel, and one of the worst young women I ever knew." The homes of both women were burned, so Vaughn moved to Westport, where she was arrested the next month. The Taylors would be among those banished that spring.

While the world knows about Order No. 11 and the largely emptied border counties, most are unaware of Order No. 10, also issued by General Thomas Ewing. This allowed the Federals to arrest and banish women and families thought to be aiding southern fighters or considered too outspoken in their disloyal views. The records of the Gratiot Street and Myrtle Street prisons in St. Louis show hundreds funneled into them. Such treatment of Southern womankind infuriated their men. Confederate Captain Griffin Frost, held himself at Gratiot Street, wrote in his diary on February 7, 1864: "Great Heavens, my blood boils — women in this hole of filth and blasphemy! I could scarcely believe it until I saw with my own eyes, Mrs. Mitchell, who is here with a little daughter five or six years old. She is charged with smuggling goods through to the Confederates. The Northern armies move making deserts in their tracks, and a loving woman is imprisoned for stretching out her hand to the needy…" Bill Anderson threatened Federal officers with retaliation: "I do not like the idea of warring with women and children, but if you do not release all the women you have captured in LaFayette County, I will hold then Union Ladies in the county as hostages for them. I will tie them in the brush and starve them…." It was an empty threat.

Nancy, with her children, Susan and Mary Vaughn, were sent in March to St. Louis, where Nancy died within hours, possibly of cholera. Sadder still is how her in-laws, Mary and Susan, then testified against the dead woman to try to gain their own release. Mary said her daughter-in-law had often fed guerrillas at her home. Before dying, Nancy had informed on nine young men, the widow Henry and Susie Rule as "bad rebels."

On May 11, 1865, an officer wrote to Colonel J. H. Barker, provost-marshal general in St. Louis: "… the son from the first marriage of Nancy Vaughn who died the 17th of March 1865, the day after her arrival at the female prison, is at Gratiot St. Prison, and wishes to be sent to his Uncle William Whitehouse, who resides at Raytown near Independence, Mo. The boy is very good and it would spoil him for all his life if he remains longer with the prisoners."

Notes for Chapter X — Preliminaries / Skirmishes

OCTOBER 18 — LEXINGTON, *LAFAYETTE COUNTY, WESTERN MISSOURI*

No doubt many honorable soldiers were in the 15th Kansas, but the regiment had a shockingly high number of scoundrels. To jump ahead in time, all but George Hoyt and Curtis Johnson of those at this fictional poker table would end up court-martialed for behavior against civilians in southwest Missouri. Major Laing would be accused by other officers of cowardice and cashiered for his conduct, including dancing around in a stolen quilt and allowing looting by his men. As mentioned, Captain Swain was sentenced to hang — another punishment not carried out — for murders. Colonel Jennison would lose his command after reports like the following: "Jennison has just passed through this vicinity on his return or the Arkansas river. The night of the 19th he staid at Newtonia, the 20th at Sarcoxie and the 21sts at Dry Fork," wrote Captain G. C. Stotts to General John Sanborn. "Where he passed the people are almost ruined, as their houses were robbed of the beds & clothing... All the horses, stock, cattle, sheep, oxen and wagons were driven off... There were cases where the men tore the clothing off of the women in search of money & threatening to burn houses in order to get money is common practice. THEY ACTED WORSE THAN GUERRILLAS...(Stotts' emphasis)" Arrested December 11 for the conduct of his troopers, Jennison blamed the depredations on other units, but was dismissed from the service.

The story of the Lawrence farm robbery comes from Captain Henry Palmer of the 11th Kansas Cavalry, which considered itself above the 15th. All of Palmer's stories must be taken with a few gains of salt, but including his account seems fair; Swain later was convicted of murdering civilians in another situation.

Four distinct waves of Kansans looted West Missouri. The first was the invasion of Lane's Brigade in September 1861, which climaxed in the burning of Osceola. The second was the jayhawking raids of the Seventh Kansas Cavalry under Jennison and Lieutenant Colonel Anthony that lasted from November 1861 through January 1862. The third, the Red Leg activity under Hoyt, occurred from summer 1862 into spring 1863. The last occurred under Jennison and Hoyt after they organized the 15th Kansas in late summer 1863. During it all, however, free-lance brigands on both sides were taking advantage of the chaos on the border.

"Parties from Kansas, both civilian and soldiers, have during the past year entered the nation and driven out herds of stock," wrote Captain H. S. Anderson of the Third Indian Regiment. "Captain Johnson, Fifteenth Kansas Cavalry, with men of his command, proceeded across Arkansas River and drove a large herd last summer. I think he went several times, but one case can be clearly proven." Just on September 28, General George Sykes had written to Major General Curtis of the problem: "In regard, General, to the cattle business, I see but one way to control it and that is to seize all cattle coming from the Indian territory into the state and hold them for the benefit of the government. Two thirds of them are stolen and the Government has a far better right to them than (do the) thieves.... Anthony, Osborn, Durfee, Eldridge & Co., are all in the business and it is my firm belief they do not purchase one-half of the cattle they procure. It is beyond question that persons in the military service have been offered bribes to assist in this business." Just how far the bandit rings stretched is hard to say. The Anthony mentioned above was probably the former Seventh Kansas commander and Leavenworth mayor. In a jab at James Lane, the Leavenworth *Times* on September 6 sniffed that the senator was in town "fresh from the cattle stealing zone."

By that November, the *Times* picked up a report from *The Oskaloosa Independent* lamenting that "a number of men have been in that vicinity stealing horses, and claiming to be members of the 15th." The next month the *Times* reported: "About nine o'clock on the evening of the 10th inst., three soldiers, partially disguised, entered the house of William Bates, two miles below Delaware, called him a d——d traitor, presented their revolvers to his head, and threatened to blow his brains out unless he gave up his money. Bates remonstrated, and his wife begged, when the soldiers struck them both on their heads, inflicting seven cuts.... Two of the men Bates says he knows, and that they belong to the Fifteenth regiment...."

The 15th Kansas report of the action on October 19,written later probably by Hoyt, noted that Orren Curtis in his forward position had been surrounded. "The action of Captain Curtis in cutting his way through and joining his command should entitle him to something better than a cell in the Missouri penitentiary and zebra pants." An odd remark, until it is learned that after the campaign, Curtis was sent to the Missouri penitentiary for mistreating civilians. Earlier in the year he had been reprimanded for burning some homes around Harrisonville. The captain appealed to Republican Governor Thomas Fletcher: "If I had of stoal anything or of murdered a single man I would have said that it was right for me to be punished for it but I don't think it wrong to cill bushwhackers but I hav to suffer for it." A bald lie, but he got his pardon and went home to his three-quarter-Indian wife. He also went down in history as the father of Congressman Charles R. Curtis, who became the first Native American vice-president under Herbert Hoover.

OCTOBER 19 — ON THE DOVER ROAD, *LAFAYETTE COUNTY*

Graybacks were also the soldiers' term for body lice. Southerners also employed the term.

This chapter mixes the memoirs of Captain Palmer and Captain George Grover, both written decades later. Palmer indicated he had A and F companies of the 11th and 65 men of a Missouri cavalry regiment, probably Grover's bunch. Palmer incorrectly recalled having a company of Colorado men, but they were still in Independence. Grover remembered that he was attached to the 15th and also was sent out to the Dover Road, where he fought all afternoon beside men of the 11th led by a Lieutenant Joseph L. Thornton. Colonel Thomas Moonlight's report made special mention of how long the companies held up the Confederates on the Dover Road.

"Scyugle" was a utility verb employed by soldiers for anything from "gobble up" to "run for it." In a dispatch sent to the *New York Tribune*, correspondent Charles A. Page humorously recounted a conversation with an officer in Grant's army in 1864. "He informed me that he had been sent out on a general 'scyugle,' that he had 'scyugled' along the front, where the Johnnies 'scyugled' a bullet through his clothes; that on his return he 'scyugled' an ice house; that he should 'scyugle' his servant — who, by the way, had just 'scyugled' three fat chickens — for a supply of ice; that after he had 'scyugled' his dinner he proposed to 'scyugle' a nap, and closed by asking how I 'scyugled.'" — *A Bohemian Brigade* by James M. Perry.

As for the Federal's weaponry, the author is guessing. Different companies in the same regiment might have different makes of carbines, although all were of the same caliber. Company I of the 11th carried Smiths; other companies had Gallaghers and Starrs.

"Up the spout" was the Civil War expression that translated to "SNAFU" a few wars later.

Both Palmer and Grover said they escaped through the streets of rebel-held Lexington. Grover recalled losing one man in light fighting. Palmer told how his column rode unnoticed practically to the center of the town, shot an inquiring rebel major and, blasting away on all sides, roared out of town untouched.

That night Jo Shelby shared his belief that the army had run into General Blunt. Two years earlier in Arkansas battles, his command had been beaten by the Federal general, with Shelby nearly being captured. Others disagreed, according to Paul Jenkins' 1906 history, *Battle of Westport*, but Shelby simply answered: "Well gentlemen, all I have to say is that it was either Blunt or the devil!"

Back down the road in a few hours, the aggressive Colonel John E. Phelps of the Second (U.S.) Arkansas Cavalry, part of Pleasonton's force, burst into Dover with a "furious pistol fusillade upon everything in sight," capturing shocked Confederate soldiers who couldn't get to their horses. A Captain Redd later rued spending too much time with the town's Southern ladies that day, writing his friends from the Johnson Island prison:

"My only books,
Were woman's looks,
And folly all they taught me."

OCTOBER 20 — 7 A.M. — ROCKY FORK RIVER, *RAY COUNTY*

Although they had been invented, the metal cartridges we equate with the revolver today were still a few years from becoming commonplace. When he had them, the guerrilla loaded his Colt's Revolving Belt Pistol of Naval Caliber, 1851 model, with rounds of bullet and gunpowder wrapped in combustible paper. Jams, misfires — sometimes "chain" fire would erupt with multiple chambers erupting almost at once — and the often laborious loading process were major reasons the bushwhackers carried so many pistols.

This chapter comes in part from Enrolled Missouri Militia Lieutenant Thomas Hankins, whose diary was recast as a narrative in the *Richmond Missourian* in June 1938 and uses his date and location. After learning that James Crowley had been captured, three companies approached the rebels from as many directions. After the guerrillas scrambled off the hill, Hankins said, came "a fierce running fight, across an open glade, where the bushwhackers ran into a detachment of the militia from the east. Several guerrillas were killed or wounded." Other bushwhacker tales of a surprise attack on Anderson's camp near Flat Rock Ford on Crooked River or Sambo Slough place it in late summer. Those versions add 150 Red Legs to the 300 militia foes and give Jesse James his first chest wound here. As that tale goes, Jesse's brother, Frank, Bill Anderson, Archie Clement and Cave Wyatt all were wounded and others killed.

A captured bushwhacker often measured the rest of his life in minutes. As General Clinton Fisk told a militia major: "Take no prisoners. We have enough of that sort on hand now. Pursue and Kill!" So the October 1863 entry in the diary of Sergeant Sherman Bodwell, 11th Kansas, was not unusual: "Lt. asked Maj., Are you through with him? Maj. nodded assent. Lt. said to men standing about 'mount your horses' & as they drew off aimed & fired the revolver, ball striking just back of the eye." Back in 1862, Major General Henry Halleck had issued Special Order No. 2: "All persons are hereby warned that if they join any guerrilla band they will not, if captured, be treated as ordinary prisoners of war, but will be hung as robbers and murderers." Two months later, Major General John Schofield ordered captured guerrillas "shot on the spot." Schofield's order did not catch the attention of the bushwhackers immediately, so eight soldiers captured five days later in a Liberty gun battle were paroled. Quantrill, however, soon dropped such niceties, perhaps starting at the Blue River bridge where his band caught a sergeant — was he assigned to guard it alone? — and killed him immediately. Then a quick trial was held for the civilian tolltaker, who ended up shot as a spy in front of his young son. The bridge, which crossed the Blue around what is now 27th Street, was burned. It all pretty much went downhill from there. By 1864, few prisoners were being taken on either side.

Anderson kept his word and let Crowley go, according to Hankins.

Union soldiers complained bitterly about the bushwhackers' usual decision to scatter to fight another day, but when a guerrilla did make a stand, he could be a handful. Colonel Charles Blair told of one stay-behind killed not far from Fort Scott. "Yesterday about ten men of my outposts ran into five bushwhackers in the Clear Creek timber and fired on them, killing 2. The rest scrambled off except one, who dismounted, got behind a tree, and deliberately went to work emptying two revolvers and firing several shots with his carbine, wounding 2 of our men, shooting 1 through the breast and 1 through the thigh. Our men shot him fifteen times before he fell."

Notes for Chapter XI — Opening fire

OCTOBER 20 — 11 A.M. — LITTLE BLUE RIVER, *JACKSON COUNTY*

The abatis was an age-old defensive ploy of felling trees in the direction of the enemy and sharpening their branches to slow him down.

When introduced to his first mountain howitzer, one wit said it was too small to be a cannon and too large to fit in a holster. The whole outfit weighed less than the barrel of a conventional field piece, but threw the standard 12-pounder shell. It could fire at a higher trajectory, and thus over obstacles, but in range was out matched by the larger Parrotts or Napoleons. Designed to be broken down and carried in pieces on the backs of mules, these howitzers probably were drawn behind a special small, wheeled cart called a "prairie carriage."

"If at the proper time, Gen. Curtis had arrested a half dozen politicians in the Militia camps and sent them to Fort Leavenworth in irons, and at the same time shot one of two Militia brigadiers from a cannon's mouth, he could have an invincible army," then-Colonel Samuel J. Crawford would write later.

After the Lawrence raid, recalled Ninth Kansas Private Albert Greene, Lane delivered a harangue at Paola that, "was wild, incoherent and bloodthirsty; a Niagara torrent of invective, profanity and bad grammar. Gamble, Schofield and Ewing were rebel sympathizers… (Here he pulled off his long linen duster.) The remedy was in the people's hands. The way to kill wolves was to hunt them in their dens; the way to exterminate snakes was to crush them in their nests; the way to punish Quantrill and his friends was to make a burning hell of Missouri! (Here went the cravat.) Throwing his bony arms upward to their fullest extent he yelled in the frenzied tones of a Comanche Indian, 'Missourians are wolves, snakes, devils, and d—n their souls, I want to see them cast into a burning hell!' (Here he tore open his shirt front and exposed a wide expanse of hairy jungle.) Men and women jumped on the benches and fairly yelled their delight and approval…""He was immoral and brave, cunning and eloquent, audacious and resourceful," Albert Beveridge wrote of Lane In his *Abraham Lincoln, 1809-1858.* "His skill in intrigue was uncanny and his power over audiences like magic. In short Lane was endowed with a kind of mad genius."

On this day, the opposing newspapers backing Lane and Governor Carney were broadsiding one another on the question of just where the Confederate army was and where it was going. Carney's *Times* railed against the martial law imposed by Major General Curtis, contending that grass was growing in city streets, "when no foe can be found, even in the state of Missouri, and Price is said to have gone into Arkansas… *The Conservative* of yesterday issued a bogus dispatch stating that Blunt had corralled Price at Lexington. The imposture is too shallow to deceive anybody. It was got up for the purpose of keeping the militia in the field…" The pro-Lane *Conservative* thundered back: "*The Times* appears to have discovered the astounding fact that Price and his forces are south of the Arkansas River, and that Jim Lane is perpetrating a great humbug upon the volunteers of Kansas… The howl of petty politicians that the General of a Department is intriguing with Lane for political purposes is absurd." Alarmed at the *Times*' reasoning, Major H. H. North, the Federal provost marshal at Leavenworth, telegraphed Curtis in Kansas City to say: "Am of the opinion that the paper should be temporarily suspended, and editors and writers arrested as enemies to the public and cause…. Please instruct. Course of paper is highly treasonous at this time."

3:30 P.M. — THE ROAD TO INDEPENDENCE, *JACKSON COUNTY*

The Chief, published in White Cloud, was a bit more cynical: "The Kansas office-seekers now in Washington, have formed themselves into a military company, called the 'Frontier Guards,' for the defense of the Capital. Pretty good idea, as they will thus have their board paid by the Government, besides advancing their chances for office by a show of spunk and patriotism." C. S. Pomeroy, the other brand-new Kansas senator, played the part of a private, or perhaps Falstaff. He was given a sword, but a belt could not be found to fit his rotund figure.

Osceola probably was larger and certainly more far completely burned than Lawrence two years later, although far more civilians died in the Kansas burg. "Three thousand people were left homeless when Osceola was burned, and perhaps the fairest city in Missouri had been utterly wiped from the face of the earth," wrote Thomas Goodrich in *Black Flag*. "Fairest city" might be stretching it. Bryce Benedict, in his *Jayhawkers, the Civil War Brigade of James Henry Lane*, thinks other things were stretched, including the tales of mass intoxication and the senator's taking of dresses and a piano. Benedict also refers to the 1860 census that shows only 267 "free inhabitants," but others say that only counted the original few blocks of the town plat and ignored at least 2,000 residents in the town's additions.

As an Indiana congressman and ally of Illinois Senator Stephen Douglas, Lane had voted for the Kansas-Nebraska Compromise, giving slavery a chance to expand north of the Mason-Dixon Line. Voters promptly booted Lane out of office, so the Democrat moved to Kansas, where the troubles of the '50s offered a perfect place to employ his skills. Lane had been prepared to let Kansas become a slave state if the climate proved right for hemp growing. "I look upon this nigger question just as I look upon the horse or the jackass question. It is merely a question of dollars and cents," he once said, but soon conformed to the abolitionist landscape of the Kansas prairie.

Quantrill probably had about 450 men when he raided Lawrence on August 21, 1863. The number of Kansans killed is often estimated at 150, but Edward Leslie in his Quantrill biography calculates as many as 200

Kansas towns closer to the border already had suffered from bushwhacker raids. When Aubry was hit in March 1862, at least three unarmed civilians were ridden down, and Abraham "Bullet Hole" Ellis got his nickname from a very noticeable indentation square in his forehead. He had looked out a second-story window, prompting a shot by Quantrill. The guerrilla, who had known Ellis before the war, apologized and helped mop the blood off his face. In September, Olathe was sacked to retaliate for the Federals' hanging of a guerrilla. More than a dozen victims were left dead, although again Quantrill spared more than 100 militia who had surrendered. The next month his men burned much of Shawnee, creating perhaps 10 more grave-ready Kansans.

Lawrence had fretted about the rumors of an attack that summer. General Thomas Ewing had heard them, too, and sent enough troops there that the *Western Journal of Commerce* opined that July: "Lawrence is probably the best defended place now in the west." But no attack came. Ewing pulled the soldiers out for other duties. Just two small camps of recruits, one white, one black, remained, and their weapons were not nearby.

Several Federal units followed the dropped plunder well into Missouri. Red Leg chief George Hoyt would brag of summarily executing any Jackson County man wearing a new coat. Ninth Kansas Private Albert Greene mentioned this: "We came bump against a drunken bushwhacker in the middle of the trail... exercising (a) calf by making it run in a circle after the manner of the prize horse at a country fair... His red-topped boots befitted a stage villain; his coat was turned wrong side out and thereby displayed the flamboyant linings; around his swarthy neck flowed a red handkerchief, and on his shaggy head perched a stack of felt hats as high as a joint of stovepipe. As we came up he uttered a hiccough and a watery smile, and in attempting a bow he lost his balance and fell headlong. Then he let out a wild shriek which proved to be his last. For on looking back I saw a grinning soldier putting a smoking revolver in his holster..." Most agree two or three wounded raiders were found in a hidden buggy and dispatched on the spot. One account has this done by Hoyt. Finding that one's loot consisted of "marbles, jew-harps, mouth organs, toys, shoestrings (and) cheap buttons," Hoyt put a bullet into his brain "for being a damn fool."

A few days after the raid, according to the April 2008 *Blue & Gray Chronicle*, J. H. Shimmons interviewed former slaves in Lawrence who might have recognized any raiders. On his list of suspects was William Johnson, "Son of Preacher Johnson that formerly preached at the Mission..." Johnson County, Kansas, is named for "Preacher Johnson."

Lane supposedly threatened Ewing that, "You are a dead dog, if you fail to issue that order." Following that theme, Daniel Anthony, the mayor of Leavenworth, called the general "a liar, a puppy, a cur, a dog, and a coward."

OCTOBER 21 — 9:30 A.M. — WEST OF THE LITTLE BLUE RIVER

The bridge that was burned was just a stone's throw to the south of where U. S. 24 crosses the stream today.

Some versions put Colonel Moonlight's shouting trick later in the day. It was not the only bluff on the battlefield. Colonel Colton Greene's Third Missouri of Marmaduke's division found itself hard pressed as it stretched across the Independence Road. With a field piece on each flank, Greene said he "ordered rapid volleys of blank cartridges to be fired (the position of my men prevented the use of missiles). It produced the desired effect. The enemy fell back and was charged by us."

The estimate that Sterling Price had 25,000 men — 20,000 troops and the rest unarmed recruits — was still being used by James Blunt in 1866 in a report to the Kansas Adjutant General. By Blunt's own count, his force on the field did not exceed 3,000 men and it may have been somewhat less. Cavalry regiments were organized with 12 companies, supposedly of about 100 men each. But sickness, casualties, leaves and desertions quickly riddled every call of the roll. Jennison reported bringing only 600 men to this fight. Nor did Ford have all of his companies; the Second Colorado and the 16th Kansas together may have had only 800. Moonlight's 11th Kansas, reorganized and refitted the previous year, had the broadest shoulders, missing just one company still out in central Kansas. But it may have totaled only 600 at the bridge because two companies were guarding other fords. Another company served as escort for Major General Curtis, but he had come up to the front, so it fought here with the others. A few hundred in the Third Wisconsin, some other scraped-up detachments and the crews for 15 guns rounded out Blunt's command. Even these numbers exaggerated the firepower of cavalry on the ground. Every fifth or sixth trooper was held back from the line to hold the horses.

Some accounts are blurred by decades. George Grover, leader of the Warrensburg provisionals, recalling the fight for the *Missouri Historical Review* in 1912, said his unit had "Martin-Henry breech loading rifles, so we could fire sixteen shots before reloading ... (and) frequently break their advancing lines and hold them in check for a long time, with a small force..." Because the British army's Martin-Henry rifles would not appear for more than 10 years, he meant the Henry rifle, the precursor to the familiar Winchester lever-action rifle "that won the West." It was not a breech-loader at all, but was fed by a tube of bullets under the barrel. Army quartermasters did not stock Henrys, in part because the rifle had little more punch than a pistol. The Henrys carried by Grover's men (and some in the Fourth Missouri State Militia cavalry) were private purchases, and they must have come to the fight well-stocked with their own special ammunition. Nor was a Henry cheap: $42 without the sling. Sales records show that Blunt owned No. 2,378, gold-plated with a rosewood stock.

The Third Wisconsin had been in the region for a good while, and Lieutenant Colonel Elias Calkins had little good to say about the "poor white trash" Missourians. "Not one in a hundred could write. They were seldom married to the mothers of their children, which grow up around them in savage filth and squalor. They are usually of a yellow sandy complexion with a sandy beard straggling over their faces, and they had uniformly bad teeth. They talked with a whine and snuffle, or listlessly… They were ignorant, uncombed, unwashed…" All of which made such poor specimens of the species easier to kill.

After the war, Blunt would complain how "Gen'l Curtis came up, and by interfering with the disposition of my troops without conveying his orders through me, threw the command into confusion that might have been avoided. He soon after left the field and gave me no further trouble during the day, except on his return to Independence, he ordered back my ammunition wagons which I had ordered to the front, which circumstances came near proving disastrous…"

Major Edmund Ross, E Company, who had two horses shot beneath him in this fight, re-layed to Moonlight the danger to the guns. Four years later, Ross would be at a much more crucial tipping point in history, the impeachment of President Andrew Johnson. Appointed to the U. S. Senate after Jim Lane's suicide, Ross became the deciding vote in the trial. Expected to be a safe vote with the Radical Republicans, Ross soon displayed a disturbing sense of fairness. He faced tremendous pressure, including a telegram that read: "Kansas has heard the evidence and demands the conviction of the president. Signed D. R. Anthony and 1,000 others." Once his "not guilty" vote saved Johnson, Ross was ruined politically. Just how his fellow Kansans felt about him was illustrated by a message from the chief justice of the Kansas Supreme Court suggesting: "…the rope with which Judas Iscariot hanged himself is lost, but Jim Lane's pistol is at your service."

11 A.M.

The story of the pants comes from Captain Palmer. Although he said his charge was mounted, the regiment's Adjutant General's Report later said, "Co. A made a brilliant charge, unmounted, down a narrow lane early in the action, clearing it of rebels…" This may not be a contradiction, if Palmer rode up, then dismounted to fight.

The house behind the apple trees, toward which Palmer ran, was the Lawson Moore home. It is still there today. Abandoned by the family after Order No. 11, it was vacant during this skirmish.

Major Nelson Smith was the highest ranking Union officer to die in the running battle around Westport. For context, three Union generals, including a major-general, were killed at Gettysburg. Two of his colleagues said Smith spoke of a premonition of death. Captain Grover, recalled Nelson told him: "Grover, I had a strange dream last night, and believe I will be killed today about ten o'clock."

3 P.M.

Fort Union was just north of where 10th and Central streets are today. The firing of the 12-pound howitzer that guarded its gate was an emergency signal for the militia to assemble. The horses for the 77th Enrolled Missouri Militia regiment, of which Kersey Coates was the colonel, were stabled next door in the basement foundation of the Broadway hotel that Coates would finish after the war on "Quality Hill." This is the half of the Coates House that survived the 1978 fire. A barracks building served for a while as a cheap tenement. The last vestige of the fort, a guardhouse made of cottonwood logs at what is now 13th and Broadway, was demolished in 1908.

One of those who felt George Todd's wrath was Independence City Marshal Jim Knowles. During the first Battle of Independence in 1862, William Quantrill's band was sent to capture the jail. Todd was smashing open cells when he found Knowles locked in one, having been arrested after shooting to death an old drunken Irishman. Because it was Knowles who supposedly tipped off the Federals about where the guerrillas tended to wade the Little Blue, Todd riddled him on the spot.

Todd had been in charge of the rear guard in the retreat from Lawrence. When the guerrillas charged the Kansans at the cornfield, his horse was killed there, forcing him to hotfoot it after his men. Because his stolen Federal jacket might get him shot by his own side, he left it behind, realizing only later that large wads of U. S. greenbacks had been in its pockets. William Gregg guarded the rear of Quantrill's column for the rest of the day and later remarked that he thought the guerrillas were "doomed," because it seemed "the whole earth behind was blue."

In a display case at the Mine Creek Battlefield museum is a flintlock pistol, or what's left of it. Just its rusted plate and flint-lock hammer were found among the many bullets and other relics left from the fight.

Cook's Store was on the stage line between Sedalia and Lexington and served as the post office for the Germans who had been in the area since 1838. The place is now the town of Concordia, so named on May 17, 1865, by the Lutheran pastor/postmaster, Franz Julius Biltz, who prayed for new concord between the northerners and southerners. The guerrillas hated the Germans, who were not only opposed to slavery and pro-Union but also talked foreign to boot.

Fletcher Taylor survived to prosper amid the mining boom that hit Joplin and became a member of the Missouri Legislature. He died in the San Francisco area in 1912.

Todd was another said to have told friends he would not survive the fight this day. Later, fanciful accounts had him and Major Smith killing each other, with Todd getting off the last shot. Richard Hinton wrote after the war that Lieutenant Colonel Hoyt, the former Red Leg chief, shot him. Hinton's accounts generally are fairly reliable, but this seems far-fetched. If Hoyt actually slew a leader of the Lawrence raid, much more would have been made of the action. Similarly, Captain Grover many years later said Hoyt (who likely carried only a pistol), a trooper of the 15th and one of his own Warrensburg provisionals all fired nearly at once from their line near the Independence Square. He believed the bullet of the unnamed Kansan, who may have had a highly accurate Sharps carbine, probably hit Todd. Most versions stick with the Second Colorado. General Cabell said Todd was hit on the rebels' last charge into Independence, although other accounts say it was on a ridge more east of town. His men dragged their chief off to a nearby house to die — "as a Roman," according to Major Edwards — and then buried him that night. His stone, with an incorrect date of his death, can be found in Woodlawn Cemetery a rifle shot away from the graves of his Colorado foes. Price's response was an epitaph of sorts: Although brave, Todd was a "great scoundrel."

Notes for Chapter XII — Respite

OCTOBER 21 — 5:30 P.M. — GLASGOW, *HOWARD COUNTY*

The burning in Dayton was done not by Colonel Jennison but by his second-in-command Daniel Anthony. Forty-six buildings in the little burg turned to ashes, leaving only the dwelling of a Unionist still standing.

Frank James apparently did get wounded because his scar came up during his murder trial in Gallatin long after the war. Newspaper accounts of the trial indicated it was delivered by a Union saber. Some believe he was hit in the face at the Crooked River shootout just a few days before this. Major John Edwards' *Noted Guerrillas* said he was painfully grazed in the face by an errant shot by one of his own men, Will Gaw, in Camden, where they were attacking some Federals holed up in a hotel. Whatever, the scar is not evident in post-war photographs of the elder James brother.

One example of William Quantrill "cleaning house" in an orderly way occurred about this time. According to Earl Owen in a 1990 article, "Gray Ghost of South Howard County," Quantrill had received so many complaints about the "renegade guerrilla" Richard Kimsey that he went looking for him. Meeting on a Howard County road, he ordered "his troublesome follower" to hand over his weapon. Kimsey made for his gun, and Quantrill shot him off his horse.

The account of the attempted rescue of Lane's piano comes from Leslie's *The Devil Knows How to Ride*, leading one to wonder whether this was the same piano Lane was alleged to have stolen when Osceola was sacked. Lane biographer Bryce Benedict dismissed the looted piano story as "ludicrous" and without contemporary documentation.

It was hard year for steamboat owners. On July 15, rebel saboteurs on the St. Louis waterfront burned the *Cherokee, Northerner, Glasgow, Welcome, Edward F. Dix* and *Sunshine*.

The Union foes, who had withdrawn into the defensive works in the town, surrendered about 1:30 p.m. Colonel Chester Harding believed that the Confederates would move up their artillery and his men would die needlessly. The October 15 battle appears to have cost the Confederates more dearly. They suffered perhaps 50 casualties, including several officers. Eight Federals, including two officers were killed, with 28 wounded. One of the dead was Second Lieutenant George F. Simmonds, of the 62nd U. S. Colored Infantry, a contingent of which may have accompanied him down river. If so, very little notice is made of these black soldiers, which is good news, since after other fights in the West, Confederates often gunned down their black captives.

Some accused Harding of a poor showing, but it was a hot fight. A Union private, John Henry Frick from Clay County, recalled ducking into a yard: "I ran thru the front gate and around behind the house. Several bullets struck the gate post as I ran thru. As I passed a window…every glass seemed to fall out." Jesse Harrold, who was in one of the Federal rifle pits, recalled, "a Rebel in a two story building across the street of where I was and he was breaking the window with his gun and I raised up to shoot him and he fired at me first. There was a two by eight inch plank sit up on edge on the ridge of the bank of the ditch and his ball went in it. He dodged back and I shot through the side of the window and we shot four shots apiece. Three of his went in the bank and the fourth cut my hat rim off." Not long after the surrender, according to Frick, "we saw a Confederate officer with a plume on his hat, followed by his staff coming up the street from the river. This proved to be General Joe Shelby. I heard him ask, 'Are there any western troops among you fellows?' Several of us answered, 'We're all western troops.' 'I knowed it.! I knowed it.! By ___! We always know when we are fighting our kind!'"

Those Confederates seriously wounded at Glasgow were left behind to be captured and shipped to St. Louis stockades. Once healed, they were shipped east, exchanged and sent to Richmond, where they were ordered to join the battered remnant of the First Missouri Brigade at Mobile. About 60 of the former prisoners left the capital by rail in late March 1865, but after only 50 miles the trains ceased running, and they found themselves proceeding on foot. They had reached Eufaula, Alabama, when news of Robert E. Lee's surrender reached them. At that point, they began trudging home.

Various tellings set the ransom offered by Benjamin Lewis at $5,000, $6,000 or $7,000. Whatever the amount, Mrs. Lewis was able to collect it, and her husband was helped home. Bill Anderson surely would have killed Lewis the next day, but his family spirited him away, and pursuit was foiled when neighbors lied about directions. Accounts of the time said Anderson's men forced black servant women to cook breakfast before raping them. Some versions also say Anderson raped a black servant the night before. Never recovering from the savagery, Benjamin Lewis died in 1866.

Nancy Harris McCorkle and Charity McCorkle Kerr, who were in the Kansas City jail when it collapsed.
Jackson County Historical Society

Dick Yager, guerrilla

15th Kansas Cavalry with Orren Curtis at left and George Hoyt in center
Kansas State Historical Society

George Caleb Bingham
Kansas City Public Library

William Penick
St. Joseph Museum Archives

Order No. 11 by George Caleb Bingham
State Historical Society of Missouri

James Lane
Courtesy of Wilson's Creek National Battlefield,
National Park Service

Thomas Moonlight
State Historical Society of Missouri

Henry Palmer
Nebraska Historical Society

Thomas Carney
Kansas State Historical Society

John Newman Edwards
State Historical Society of Missouri

Thomas Reynolds
Missouri Department of Natural Resources, Division of State Parks

Notes for Chapter XIII — Clash of Arms

OCTOBER 22 — 3:30 P.M. — HICKMAN'S MILL CROSSING, BIG BLUE RIVER

The Mockbee house was on the west side of what is now Holmes Road about 78th Street.

The fight at Mockbee farm would lead to accusations of cowardice against other Kansas units. Colonel George Veale bitterly complained that "the battalion of the Douglas County Third" had fled. Veale also condemned Colonel Sandy Lowe's 21st Kansas Militia and Major John M. Laing and his four companies of Jennison's 15th. General M. S. Grant of the militia bluntly said, "Major Laing is responsible for most of my loss, and showed cowardice in the face of the enemy." A December report by Lieutenant Cyrus Roberts said the 21st at least skirmished with the rebels, but Laing turned away from the fight: "I have heard that the officers and men with Major Laing did not wish to turn back, but were eager to assist and thought it very strange that he did not help the militia." Major General Curtis had Laing arrested, but released him because of his alleged bravery on other fields. The charge of cowardice was raised again when Laing was court-martialed the next year, but he was acquitted.

Wounds to the gut produced a 90 percent fatality rate in the Civil War.

Sergeant P. I. Bonebrake later wrote that "little damage" occurred until this last charge, but several other survivors noted that the second charge rocked the militia line, in part breaking it and causing men to desert. Lieutenant Colonel Henry Greene recalled trying to steady the wavering line when "an Enfield rifle ball clipped the end of my chin whiskers and sung its shrill song as it sped past."

Up to this point, the Second Kansas was dealing with one Confederate regiment, Colonel Frank Gordon's, which had been detached from Jeff Thompson's brigade. Then, Shelby's other brigade, that of Colonel Sidney Jackman, came up and joined the next attack.

Captain Sterling Miles lived to give a fascinating account of being wounded. "I was hit in the groin by a rebel bullet. A black cloud seemed to pass before my eyes. I felt it was a darkness of approaching death. I felt a shock of comotion (sic) in the breast, and believed I was wounded there. I clapped my hand on it and cried out to those around me."

Because of the relatively heavy Confederate casualties, reportedly 46 dead and wounded, the rebels believed more than one Union cannon had to be at the Mockbee fight. Supposedly, the rebels so admired Captain Ross Burns' fighting ability that they cried out not to kill him, and so he was clubbed down. Private G. G. Gage later wrote that the cool-headed Burns had removed the gun's sight and hid it in his clothes. His family was said to have the relic after the war.

Veale's 250-man battalion suffered 24 killed, 20 wounded and 68 taken prisoner. Historian Howard Monnett agreed with those numbers but also said, "more than 100 Kansas farmers lay dead in line." Although parts of three other Kansas militia regiments may have skirmished nearby, this number does not seem possible.

Chased by rebel horsemen, Bonebrake survived by abandoning his mare and diving into heavy weeds. He found his way west around Confederate lines and watched the battle near Brush Creek the next day. He then got to Kansas City where he was offered crackers and raw bacon, which after 30 hours without rations "seemed to me the best meal I ever ate." Bonebrake went on to become a prominent banker in Topeka, serving in several public offices, including the state legislature, and promoting utilities and railroads. As chairman of the board of police commissioners, he took pride in driving every saloon out of the city.

3:45 P.M. — MAIN CROSSING, BIG BLUE RIVER, *JACKSON COUNTY*

Lieutenant Patrick Henry Minor was one of 2,080 black soldiers that records show came from Kansas, although, unlike him, nearly all had originated from slave conditions in Missouri and Arkansas. Not enough is known about Minor, whose white father may have owned a Louisiana plantation in Ascension Parish. Minor and four siblings were raised in New Orleans, and some got the equivalent of a high school education at the Preparatory Department at Oberlin College in Ohio. Minor may have gotten further education in France; he taught school in Leavenworth.

Like Doc Jennison, the more disciplined James Montgomery started with the Mound City Sharps Rifle Guards and had graduated to Lane's Brigade for its 1861 romp through western Missouri. Transferring out east, he had raised the Second South Carolina Colored Infantry from the captured islands off South Carolina, where his "praying, shooting, burning, and hanging" — basically jayhawking — shocked Federal comrades. Montgomery teamed up with Harriet Tubman in the Combahee Ferry raid to free 800 South Carolina slaves, who gratefully sang "There is a White Robe for Thee." The white residents of Darien, Georgia, however, were pretty sure Montgomery would end up with the heated end of a fork, having burned that undefended and unresisting town to the ground. "The Southerners must be made to feel that this was a real war, and that they were to be swept away by the hand of God, like the Jews of old." Montgomery said, "We are outlawed, and therefore not bound by the rules of regular warfare."

The Parrott was a combination wrought and cast-iron rifled gun, manufactured mostly as 10-pounders and 20-pounders, although a 300-pounder was produced. A West Point man, Robert Parker Parrott, invented them just in time for the Civil War. They can be distinguished by the wrought-iron band around the breech. Civil War artillerists often could not see what they were shooting at for the smoke. They simply looked at the ruts caused by the recoil of the gun and fired again in the direction they had before.

Actually, a number of Confederates were quite eager to fight. As the militias pulled back toward Kansas City, several rebels suddenly crossed the Blue and attacked the Federals' rear. They were beaten off in a sharp fight that reportedly left a dozen dead and ten prisoners. One of the captured was Confederate Captain Garet S. Von Valkenberg of New York. His brother was Robert Von Valkenberg, a Republican congressman who had commanded the 107th New York Infantry at Antietam.

The action on the Independence-Kansas City road was to draw attention away from General Shelby's probing farther south. His Iron Brigade under General Thompson ran into Colonel Jennison's Kansans guarding Byram's Ford and made no headway. By 3 p.m., more Confederates under Colonel Gordon and Colonel Jackman found shallow spots to cross both upstream and downsteam. Colonel Moonlight's 11th Kansas, stationed at Simmon's Ford to the north, went to help but was too late. Both Federal regiments fell back toward Westport to try to keep the rebels out of Kansas.

4:15 P.M. — MOCKBEE FARM, *JACKSON COUNTY*

Captain Horace E. Bush of G Company told his story to Union doctor Joshua Thorne, who wrote an angry article for the Kansas City *Journal* after treating Bush and others similarly gunned down. According to Thorne, Bush suffered three head wounds, including the left eye, an arm broken by one bullet and a nonfatal chest wound. The 1883 List of Pensioners of Shawnee County, Kansas, shows Bush alive and being compensated for his lost eye. While his survival seems incredible, it should be noted that pistol rounds were smaller caliber and that guerrillas were said to use lighter gunpowder loads to reduce kick and improve accuracy. Southern soldiers, always short of everything, also may have tried to conserve on powder.

Some Westport histories skip over the murder of the surrendering men at this fight. There nearly were many more: Captured members of the Second Kansas were lined up on foot with would-be executioners mounted across from each. "Then occurred a scene out of an old fashioned novel, which no one is ever expected to actually believe," later wrote Private Guilford G. Gage, one of the prisoners. General Jo Shelby rode up and using "several striking and vivid descriptive epithets" stopped any more killings. Skipping over the murders in his own book, Major John Edwards later wrote that "Two hundred and seven prisoners were sent to the rear, though they deserved instant death."

Lieutenant Colonel H. M. Greene also surrendered and survived being shot in the head. His captor made him take off his coat and pants, then shot him twice, shouting, "There, damn you, go off and die!" That night, a dazed Greene wandered across a dead teamster, stripped his pants off and then fell into a low spot to sleep. There he was spotted the next day by Major General Marmaduke's retreating men. Thinking him a southern comrade, they offered Greene water and whiskey until realizing he was a Kansan. "Although displeasure was manifested, no threats were made or violence exhibited," Hinton later recorded.

The scattered members of the unlucky Second Kansas were gunned down not only by trigger-happy rebels. Colonel Veale's report noted how two of his militiamen, Robert Rolls and David Fults, were "killed by Jennison's men." Later, a member of the 15th Kansas Cavalry objected to this "stigma of indiscriminate murders," contending that Fults actually was shot by order of another brigade commander, Colonel Moonlight, who thought him to be a rebel by his lack of uniform.

5:30 P.M. — KANSAS CITY

A pontoon bridge did bob across the Kaw — or Kansas — River, erected not by the military but by civilian entrepreneurs. Colonel Charles Blair, who had responsibility for regiments of nervous and balky militiamen, noted that "the bridge was guarded so none could return" to Kansas.

Samuel Pomeroy would be caught in 1873 trying to buy with $7,000 cash a vote in the Kansas legislature to win re-election. Two years before his ouster, however, he had introduced the bill to establish Yellowstone National Park. He was not too corrupt to become president of the Atchison, Topeka & Santa Fe Railroad.

Reconciling the few vague reports of the commanders' actions on the evening of October 22 is tricky. Some histories indicate a war council was conducted at midnight, although it would seem odd to wait more than five hours after Major General Curtis said he got word that Major General Pleasonton's cavalry was in Independence. Colonel Samuel Crawford's recollection, questionable on many points, said the debate over whether to make a stand before Westport lasted until 2 a.m. It is fairly unanimous, however, that orders were issued around then to start troops moving south at 3 a.m.

Crawford would be elected governor of Kansas the next month. Ingalls would be defeated. Little known now, Ingalls later became a highly regarded writer and U. S. senator. It is his statue at the U. S. Capitol that many Kansans want to replace with one of Amelia Earhart.

Curtis was not the only one wondering where the Federal forces from St. Louis were. The White House secretary, John Nicolay, was in St. Louis dealing with political matters the night before when he received a telegram asking: "While Curtis is fighting Price, have you any idea where the force under Rosecrans is, or what it is doing? A. Lincoln" Major General Rosecrans was around Lexington at this point, grudgingly allowing his cavalry chief, Pleasonton, to move the infantry divisions of Major General A. J. Smith from Pleasant Hill north to Independence as reinforcements. Ulysses S. Grant, the general-in-chief, also was impatient: "Has Rosecrans come upon Price?" he wrote the War Office on the 21st. "If he has not, he should be removed at once. Anybody ... would be better than Rosecrans."Once this campaign was over, Rosecrans returned to St. Louis for a new assignment that never came; he was replaced by General Grenville Dodge. Moving back to California, he became a congressman. He died in 1898.

The Six-Mile House was an old tavern/stage stop between Wyandotte and Leavenworth. Curtis was greatly discouraged by the events of the day, contended William E. Connelley, in his 1918 *A Standard History of Kansas and Kansans*: "In the hope that he might secure better results by fighting on Kansas soil Curtis decided in the afternoon of the 22nd to retire across the Kansas River at night; and he then sent his ammunition and supply trains to Wyandotte. Later he crossed the line himself and was found in camp six miles west of Wyandotte." The story seems to stem from Charles Waring's 1910 account and Crawford's book, *Kansas in the Sixties*, written the year after. Jay Monaghan used it in his *Civil War on the Western Border, 1854-1865*. What is not in dispute is that someone ordered the wagons over the Kaw into Wyandotte City, today part of Kansas City, Kansas. In any event, Curtis was a tiger the next morning, most agree.

Was there a near mutiny at the Gillis House? Crawford said so. Connelley agreed, writing that Curtis consented to return late at night to Kansas City where he dispiritedly agreed not to retreat — but not "until it had been decided by the officers to arrest General Curtis and put General Blunt in command of the army." Monaghan repeated the story. Wiley Britton's post-war history gave poor marks to Curtis's performance that day, but mentioned no officer discontent. In *Action Before Westport*, Howard Monnett judged the story "doubtful" for lack of credible sources, apparently discounting Crawford for old grudges. Monnett sagely suggested that the egotistical Blunt would have put it in his 1866 account of his military exploits. But would he? Crawford's tale had Blunt asking whether the army would stand by him in mutiny. For his part, Curtis said in his report months later that he directed generals Blunt and Deitzler to personally supervise the movement of troops at 3 a.m. "The officers all heartily united and labored most of the night."

10:30 P.M. — SOUTHWEST OF INDEPENDENCE, *JACKSON COUNTY*

General William Cabell, a West-Point trained Virginian, had a hand in designing the Confederate battle flag while he was organizing the Quartermaster Department in Richmond. After the war, he became mayor of Dallas, Texas.

The house from which Mrs. Robert Smith watched the action would soon be the home of artist George Caleb Bingham, who was about to resign as state treasurer. The Smith home would be expanded greatly with the help of the Waggoner milling fortune and is a museum today.

A newly found letter by Third Iowa Private Henry Townsend told of the night fight: "It being dark, they had the advantage of us. They would lay in line untill we got within 30 or 40 Feet of them then fire and raise and run. Sometimes they would stand for 15 or 20 minutes then we would shoot and talk to them at the same time.... they said they did not want to fight us that they wanted to get at the Militia."

Cabell's guns were overrun by Colonel Edwin Catherwood's 13th Missouri State Militia Cavalry in McNeil's command. Cabell also lost his sword, which was being carried by an aide who was captured by men of Phelps' Arkansas regiment. Until a few weeks before, Catherwood had commanded the Sixth Missouri State Militia. In Jesse James myth, he loomed as the Yankee commander who supposedly led the successful sneak attack on Anderson's camp.

The captain was John C. Moore, who before the war was the first mayor of Denver, where he started a newspaper. In later years, he was co-editor of *The Kansas City Times* with Major Edwards, Shelby's adjutant and a similarly unreconstructed rebel. In 1875, he established an evening publication, the *Mail*, absorbed a few years later by *The Kansas City Star*, which eventually ended up buying the *Times*. He had served as Marmaduke's second in the duel with General Walker. A duelist himself in his St. Louis youth, Moore said before his death — of natural causes — at 84 in Excelsior Springs, "I have always been a firm believer in the duel and I believe in it yet."

About 8 p.m., General Pleasonton became too boastful or confused about the geography, sending a telegram that: "The enemy are now out of Missouri." The regiments of Moonlight and Jennison had done everything they could to make sure all of the Confederates had stayed in Missouri.

OCTOBER 23 — 4:30 A.M. — KANSAS CITY

Lieutenant Minor was getting $105.50 a month, his commanders, Major General Curtis, $457 and Lieutenant General U. S. Grant $758. Regulations called for paying soldiers every two months, but according to former Sergeant William Forse Scott of the Fourth Iowa Cavalry, "The troop in the field were seldom paid at intervals of less than four months; and the cavalry, often campaigning beyond the reach of paymasters, were occasionally compelled to wait six, and even eight, months for their money.

Three pairs of horses, lead, swing and wheel, pulled the limber, a two-wheel carriage and ammunition box, to which the Parrott was hooked. Another six-horse team pulled the caisson with more ammunition. A soldier rode the left horse of each pair to guide the gun.

"It is true that the topographical view of our city, at first sight, is any thing but inviting to the vision. Bluffs, ridges and ravines, seem to be a poor and costly place to build a city — and to do business or reside upon the hillside grounds, thus broken and uneven, pre-supposes an outlay of too much money, and also too many unpleasant and tiresome walks." — This from city booster C. C. Spaulding, writing in 1858. He went on to say it would all be worth it for people moving in.

What the soldiers called "bacon" was more likely salt pork, often blue-looking with skin, hair and whatever on it. Yet, it was far better than the commissary's salt beef, what the troops called "salt horse," which had to be soaked for hours, gave off a stench and was eaten only in extreme conditions. One army ditty about the bacon went:

A few may bless, and many curse,
And dream, ere they awaken,
Of Home, where hogs are made with hams,
And not all "rusty bacon!"

At the October 29, 1862, Island Mound fight near Butler, Missouri, Minor was likely the first commissioned African-American officer in our history to lead people of his own race into battle. That involved the First Kansas Colored, later redesignated the 79th U. S. A second infantry regiment, the Second Kansas Colored, became the 83rd U. S. In the colored battery, Minor, Matthews and Captain H. Ford Douglas would be the U. S. Army's first black artillery officers.

The famous quote from a July 1863 speech by Frederick Douglass was: "Once let the black man get upon his person the brass letters, U. S., let him get an eagle on his button, and a musket on his shoulder and bullets in his pocket, there is no power on earth that can deny that he has earned the right to citizenship."

Some bushwhackers were in the southern ranks assembling south of Westport. George Todd's men, now commanded by Dave Pool, would fight this day on Brush Creek on the right of the Iron Brigade.

Notes for Chapter XIV — The battle joined

OCTOBER 23 — 7:15 A.M. — SOUTH OF WESTPORT, *JACKSON COUNTY*

The Fort Scott Road went south out of Westport, then bent east where it briefly joined the Harrisonville Road, then below the Big Blue River turned back west to New Santa Fe. From there it ran 80 miles more or less due south to the fort just inside Kansas. In Kansas City, it became known as Wornall's Lane, then was designated as Wornall Road, after the family who lived in the home at what is now 61st Terrace.

The Iron Brigade originally was known as the Missouri Brigade. The oft-demonstrated toughness of Shelby's men in battle earned them the proud name. "I never had to make a speech to get them into a fight, and most of my 'cuss words' were to make them go slow," said General Thompson.

It is hard to imagine now, looking at the hundreds of stately homes and thousands of trees south of 51st Street, that much of this was bare prairie, with several fields and pastures marked by fences.

Major General Price had stayed in the Boston Adams farmhouse, which was near today's Swope Parkway south of 63rd Street. One old tale has Price dressed in a tattered coat and slouch hat to fool Federal sharpshooters. Although paintings always show Price in resplendent Confederate uniform, he sometimes wore a multi-colored plaid hunting shirt, his "war coat," into battle. Some said Jo Shelby always rode a sorrel, believing his life was charmed on such a horse, having had three of them shot out from under him at the Battle of Cane Hill in Arkansas.

Once his brigade moved west after mauling the Second Kansas militia, Colonel DeWitt Hunter's cavalry and Colonel W. O. Coleman's mounted Arkansas infantry soon were "pressed by a considerable number of Federals, who appeared from the direction of Westport," Colonel Sidney Jackman reported later. "Notwithstanding the superiority of this force we succeeded in holding our ground until night." In the Yankee version, Captain Hinton, who would fill a book with the details, although occasionally not the correct ones, wrote, "... we continued to drive them steadily for nearly four miles and until dark, back to the Big Blue." His source may have been Colonel "Doc" Jennison, who claimed: "I captured 150 stands of small arms from his dead left in the field, and charged him beautifully for four miles." This was an empty boast. Jackman later would report losing only 25 killed and 80 wounded in the two days' fighting south of Westport. The Federals, however, weren't the only ones to exaggerate Confederate losses. Major Edwards later wrote that his hero, Shelby, bore the heaviest fighting in the campaign (excepting Fort Davidson) and had "over 800 in killed." This, too, was wildly overstated. Thompson reported in November that the Iron Brigade lost 239 men, 36 killed, 130 wounded and 73 missing.

Histories disagree on Shelby's mood for this fight. Shelby Foote, a major historian of the war, said the little general's blood was up, and he saw a situation that "though not without obvious dangers, fairly glittered with Napoleonic possibilities." For what it's worth, Edwards later wrote that Shelby was so worried the previous night that he sent a major to Price to suggest "that immediate retreat is almost necessary to the salvation of his army."

Other than when charging into canister or grapeshot, veteran soldiers did not much fear artillery. Ninety-five times out of a hundred, it was a bullet that brought down the Civil War soldier.

Thompson could not forget this moment in his memoirs. Another casualty of Federal artillery was noted by a wounded member of the Second Kansas militia regiment still behind Confederate lines. "Past my feet was borne the body of a man, probably an officer, which had almost severed by a cannon shot, and was carried in a blanket held by two horsemen."

8 A.M. — BYRAM'S FORD, BIG BLUE RIVER, *JACKSON COUNTY*

Colonel Philips' diary for October 20 reads: "Up at 12:30 a.m. Raining and cold…. Marched all afternoon toward Lexington…. Turned awful cold—raining—like to froze. Camped in the night in a hazel brush near Moore's place. Sick. Expect to fight tomorrow."

Four 10-pounder Parrotts of Captain Henry Hynson's Texas Battery waited on the ridge, as well as one or two smaller pieces. The memorial cannon that stands today at the site at 4800 E. 63rd Street is not a Parrott, but a type of Napoleon.

Philips would be fighting General John Clark, of Marmaduke's division. Philips had read law in the Fayette law office of Clark's father, who became a Confederate congressman. The younger Clark had gone to Harvard law school. After the war, the two men would serve in Congress together.

Many of the soldiers on both sides this day woke famished. The diary of Iowa Sergeant Samuel O. Bereman noted: "I slept within ten feet of a dead rebel."

Major General Pleasonton was a West Point graduate in large part because of the War of 1812 action of his father, Stephen Pleasonton. As the British burned Washington, the State Department clerk grabbed the Declaration of Independence, the Constitution and other founding documents and carried them to safety. Congress rewarded him with a plot in the Congressional Cemetery and a promise to educate his children.

Eric Wittenberg, an authority on Federal cavalry in the east, called Pleasonton "a lead from the rear kind of a guy who was a masterful schemer and political intriguer." John H. Monnett, who revised his father's seminal *Action Before Westport*, is less critical, saying: "Pleasonton had run afoul of the Lincoln administration in February 1864 for opposing the so-called Kilpatrick-Dahlgren Raid against Richmond, an abortive maneuver that accomplished nothing except for the compilation of a long casualty list."

A few days later, General Egbert Brown calmly refuted Pleasonton's reasons for his sacking. The thing that rankled most was the order to him on October 23 that stated: "As your brigade has yet done no fighting, the general expects you to push them vigorously to-day… as the other brigades have done so well." Brown replied that his outfit had been in the saddle since before Jefferson City and in its pursuit of Price "had done more fighting, had more casualties (fortunately by few), and killed and wounded more rebels than any other brigade…." The Missouri general noted that on the night of the 22nd in the clashes west of Independence, two of his three regiments had expended their cartridges. And the slowness of the ammo train to come up to his troops had contributed to his delay on the morning in question. Once their cartridge boxes were replenished, he put his men on the road to the front, but said he found that "no preparation had been made by Colonel Winslow for me to pass, nor could he have well done so, as the road led over a broken country, hedged in by dense brush and timber… I pushed on, woke his sleeping men, crowded them forward or to one side…." Despite his treatment by Pleasonton, he received command of the District of Rolla. The United States pension agent in St. Louis from 1866 to 1868, Brown resigned to operate an Illinois farm. He died in 1902 in Missouri.

The "old" troops of the Fourth Iowa, that is, regular, hardened veterans that had come from

Tennessee through Arkansas, told this story differently. As Bereman wrote of it: "Some of the Militia were ordered to charge the rebels but they refused. Col. Winslow of my regt. commanding the Brig. sent for the '4th Iowa.'"

The Federal rifled guns used in this fight often were called, incorrectly, Rodman guns. Their shells had the habit of burying themselves in the ground before exploding, greatly reducing their lethality, but the guns were extremely accurate at ranges under a mile. As one opposing Confederate artillerist in Atlanta rued, "They could hit the end of a flour barrel more often than miss, unless the gunner got rattled."

8:25 A.M. — SOUTH OF WESTPORT

Now known as Wornall Road, "Bloody Lane" was where George Todd pulled off his ambush of the Ninth Kansas the year before. During this battle, several batteries supposedly fired from the lane, withdrawing and being replaced as they ran low on ammunition: McClain's, Eayres's, Minor's and Birdsall's.

The accounts of Privates Iker and Ross are taken from Ellen Williams' 1885 history of the Second Colorado and may represent fighting either before or after the regiment's counter charge.

Historians have had trouble with the Arkansas colonel shot by Captain Curtis Johnson in their duel on horseback. First, the dead man's name usually is written James H. McGhee. Robert D. Norris Jr. noted that the name "seems to have been correctly spelled 'McGehee' only by the good Colonel himself." Second, he wasn't dead. On May 2, 1865, having recovered from his wound, he signed the roll of prisoners paroled at Wittsburg, Arkansas. The error, which is found in many places, including the historical marker near the Loose Park duck pond, may stem from the Kansas City *Journal*, which wrote of "seven dead rebels lying side by side, and near them an officer, said to have been Col. McGhee, around the latter the rebels had built a little pen of rail" near the Wornall house. One clue to the mystery of the deceased officer: One observer spoke of crudely carved Masonic emblems on the enclosing rails.

Colonel Jennison's after-action report would make famous the duel of Johnson and McGehee, but not everyone recalled it. William S. Shepherd, considered to be the Kansas City area's last survivor of the battle, was a member of Johnson's Company E of the 15th Kansas, and he, too, said it was Johnson who shot the rebel colonel. Yet Hinton made no mention of Johnson in his 1865 history, instead praising Captain William H. Greene of the Second Colorado, and especially Lieutenant Colonel Sam Walker, 16th Kansas Cavalry, who "saber in hand, dashed into the midst of the rebels" and was wounded in the foot. Colonel Ford agreed it was his regiment, the Second, and the 16th in the fight, making no mention of the 15th Kansas. General Jeff Thompson did not remark on any Federal countercharge on McGehee's Arkansas regiment. Neither did Colonel John C. Wright, who had watched, appalled. "The battery opened up with grape and canister and cut the men down by the scores, but still they went on until the few who had escaped death were within fifty yards of the battery, when the infantry from behind the stone fence raised and opened up on then with small arms and almost demolished the regiment...."

Another aspect of the battle south of Brush Creek that is hard to square up is the timing. Jennison's report said McGehee's charge came after Major General James Blunt's third assault regained the prairie, to which Richard Hinton agreed in his book. That would seem to make it a little before 1 p.m. Howard Monnett indicated it was after noon. Thompson, however, said the Arkansans' attack occurred hours earlier, perhaps around 8 a.m., just before Blunt was pushed back north of the creek. Britton's early history agreed with him, as did Deryl Sellmeyer's 2007 biography of Shelby. Company E trooper Shepherd, many years later, more or less split the difference at 11:30 a.m. At the risk of cherry-picking, the author notes that some Westport battle accounts are demonstrably off by as much as four hours, and this may be one more. The author tends to follow Thompson, whose after-action report seems more consistently correct and less inflated than that of Jennison. Hinton did say Confederate Colonel Dobbin was repulsed in the first hour of fighting, and McGehee was in Dobbin's brigade. For what it is worth, Edwards also said the charge came early. Another factor: General James Fagan, whose command included Dobbin and McGehee, likely had already shifted southeast earlier to face the threat to the train by the time the Federals drove back south over the creek.

Major Edwards later said: "Shelby advised strongly against (McGehee's charge), and warned him of the concentrated infantry behind the walls. But the rush was made." Here he borrowed from French Marshal Pierre Bosquet's observation from the fatal charge of the British light brigade. "'It was magnificent, but it was not war.'" Wright, who did not admire Fagan, his commander, had much the same opinion: "Never was a more criminally foolish order given, nor was one more gallantly and recklessly obeyed."

8:45 A.M.

One of those Union soldiers pushed back over Brush Creek was John Johnson, although he was born with the name John Garrison. On the frontier, he supposedly became known as "Liver-Eating Johnson," for the tale that he devoured the livers of Indian enemies. That legend became the basis for the movie "Jeremiah Johnson," starring Robert Redford. Johnson survived a bullet and the following infection in his left shoulder at Westport or the Newtonia fight a few days later. This service allowed him to spend his last years in a Santa Monica, California, veterans hospital, where he died in 1900.

The three-story Harris House hotel, at Main and Main Cross, now known as Pennsylvania Street and Westport Road, was demolished in 1922. Across the street was the grocery — read, "saloon" — of Uncle Albert Boone, Daniel's grandson. It's again a place well known for wetting whistles, known as Kelly's. Boone, who had been a pro-slavery Border Ruffian present at the 1856 sacking of Lawrence, had sold out and moved to Colorado by 1860. Union soldiers stationed at Westport usually bunked at Smith's Hotel, which was where Broadway runs today.

The Bent House is the smaller brick building behind the much more expansive home facing 55th Street. The larger house, like the nearby parkway, is now named for its later owner, Seth Ward. William Bent had two Indian wives over the years, Owl Woman and Yellow Woman. One of his sons, George, was causing trouble for Federal soldiers farther west. "…At the time of the breaking out of the war (he) was engaged in farming in Missouri, but left there and is now foremost in leading those wild tribes in the depredations. He is a noted rebel and ought to have been killed long ago," said one commander. After the war, authorities would consider George Bent a dangerous thorn in their efforts to push the Union Pacific Railroad across the prairie.

As one Federal gunner remarked: "If anything could justify desertion by a cannoneer, it would be an assignment to a Parrott battery." General Henry Hunt, chief of Union artillery in the east, had tried to try to pull the Parrotts out of the Federal army two years before but was overruled. Richard Hinton and other writers with Federal leanings would claim elaborately and incorrectly how "a shell from the section under Lieutenant Eayres had struck the muzzle of this gun while the charge was being inserted. The gunner's hand was taken off, the gun burst, as our shell exploded, and six men were killed and wounded, as also several horses."

Were some wounded or captured Confederates executed after McGehee's charge? In his memoirs, Jeff Thompson recalled that some were "brutally murdered before the battery fell back" and that his men were so incensed that they wanted to take Westport then and there. Major Edwards would write that McGehee's men wounded in the melee "were horribly mutilated." John McCorkle, one of the guerrillas fighting the Second Colorado on Shelby's right flank, recalled that Major General Price sent a request that they leave his ranks on Sunday. The reason was to discourage the Federals from executing Confederate captives, perhaps in retaliation for some Kansans gunned down around Byram's Ford by the guerrillas the day before. McCorkle wrote that the Federals executed seven of Shelby's men. Another clue comes from the Leavenworth *Times*, which reported on October 27 that, "Nearly all the rebels killed at the Brush Creek fight were shot through the head. Our wounded were principally shot through the limbs. This is conclusive evidence that the arms used by the Union troops carry farther than those of the rebels, and consequently (are) more effective at long range." Or perhaps evidence of murder.

9 A.M.

Nearly everything in this section comes from Captain Henry Palmer's "The Soldiers of Kansas: Company A, Eleventh Kansas Regiment, in the Price Raid." In it, he said he got permission to return to Westport Saturday to reassure his wife, only to arrive at a madhouse, women and children shrieking and crying on the porch outside. Governor Carney and his staff supposedly were inside, using the place as a headquarters. He said he directed his hysterical in-laws into the cellar under the house and literally put his pregnant wife on ice — actually a pile of sawdust in the ice pit — to keep her safe. Another great tale, but frankly, the more Palmer's stories are studied, the more a great raconteur emerges. Simeon Fox, the historian for the Seventh Kansas, which was denigrated by Palmer, called Palmer "loose-minded." But Palmer's skirmish on the Dover Road and charge at the Little Blue are roughly documented. Records show Private George W. Edwards was killed at the Little Blue as he said, and Private Leander Hull also was part of Company A.

Palmer's pessimism found echoes in some of the Kansas towns. "Two of our citizen-neighbors (militiamen at the battle) thought that 'all was lost' and broke from the ranks, putting spurs to horse, and thought of nothing but saving their families by flight. Their return, almost speechless with fright, created a panic such as we have seldom witnessed, even in Kansas, causing a general stampede to the forests for concealment, and the clearing of almost every house of valuables," wrote Julia Lovejoy from Baldwin City. The understandably jumpy residents of Lawrence also panicked and were two miles outside of town before the rumor of invasion was discredited.

Despite the exaggerations that seem to lurk in Palmer's writings, the story of his trying to get himself shot in the arm rings true amid so much patriotic and formal Civil War storytelling by others. He was not the only man to think of ways to get what later generations would call the "million-dollar wound" that would get you out of the war, but he was one the few to confess it. In the memoir, he said Major General Curtis sent him with 20 scouts to find Major General Pleasanton, who kept Palmer with him on the march south in coming days.

10:20 A.M. — BYRAM'S FORD, BIG BLUE RIVER

Byram's Ford is just north of where 63rd Street crosses the Blue River today. Where a memorial cannon sits today on the north side of the street is roughly where the Confederates' main line stood. The high ground was known locally as "Potato Hill" before the fight; afterward, it was "Bloody Hill."

In his report, Confederate General Cabell would say the deciding factor in this fight was the "rapid and scathing fire into our commands" from the 16-shot Henry rifles. More likely, it was coming from the Iowans' Spencers. Cabell was hardly a good observer, being miles to the south guarding the wagon train.

Lieutenant Colonel Frederick Benteen, commander of the 10th Missouri Volunteer Cavalry, had fought at Wilson's Creek, Pea Ridge and Vicksburg. He was a fierce Union loyalist in a St. Louis family of secession supporters, including his father, Theodore Benteen, who supposedly expressed the wish that his son be killed by the war's first bullet. Another story is that Benteen's company helped captured a steamship, on which his father was an engineer, and that he arranged for his father to be imprisoned after the rest of the crew was released.

History author Phil Gottschalk explains that the importance of regimental colors "was no romantic fancy because the flag was the soldier's rallying point, his guide regardless of the confusion of battle. If the flag went forward, the men would go forward. If the flag stopped, the men stopped. If the flag went to the rear, the men could go to the rear with honor."

Captain Benjamin Johnson of the Confederate Third Missouri described how his men were driven away from the Big Blue "one mile and a half in good order to a skirt of timber at the edge of a small prairie, and we were ordered to form to support Pratt's artillery. The enemy appeared in sight and opened heavily on us. We replied, compelling them to fall back to the shelter of some houses on the prairie. They again advanced at a charge to take our battery. We opened fire on them while Company G, under the command of First Sergeant Woolsey, dashed gallantly forward and hauled the guns off by hand, the balance of the regiment keeping a steady fire upon the enemy. We remained in our position until every gun was discharged and every cartridge expended. Ordered by General Clark to fall back to our horses, which we did in good order." After all that, he reported, "Our loss was 3 killed and 7 wounded."

Major General Marmaduke was not able to write his after-action report, he died without publishing memoirs and his papers apparently were lost in a fire at the Marmaduke Military Academy. All of that lends to the vagueness of who was where after his division retreated from the Big Blue. His adjutant who was on the field, Colonel John Moore, wrote a Confederate history of the war, but simply added fresh confusion. He said Price ordered Clark — the division's strongest brigade — to leave Marmaduke behind at Byram's Ford and head south to protect the train; that Marmaduke at one point was opposing Pleasonton's cavalry "with only members of his staff" — which no one else remembered — and that "Cabell, though hotly engaged himself, sent Marmaduke two regiments when his need was the greatest." No other reference to this northward deployment is found; Price indicated his priority for Cabell, who also did not get to write a report, was protection of the wagon train at Russell's Ford on the Big Blue.

Colonel Philips' diary indicated his ego was somewhat restored after the day's hard fight: "Pleasonton thinks better of myself and the M. S. M. since the fight."

11:45 A.M. — SOUTH OF WESTPORT

Captain G. L. "Lew" Gove was 23 and would die of "brain fever" November 7 in Olathe. Gove County, Kansas, is named in his honor.

A battle marker at Sunset Drive and Rockwell says it marks the "defile" pointed out by the German farmer, but this seems unlikely. If the guns started at Rockwell and then deployed west around the curve of the hill the way Sunset does, it would have been nearly a mile of very rough, heavily sloping terrain to their eventual firing positions just southwest of the Bent House, about 55th Street and Ward Parkway today. The author believes Major General Curtis actually took his guns farther up the creek west to where the divided lanes of Ward Parkway today swing south near the Carriage Club. Kansas City historian William S. Worley wrote that George Kessler "decided that Ward Parkway should follow the bed of Brush Creek ... almost to the point where the streambed crossed the Kansas-Missouri state line. The landscape architect noted that a ravine cut into the bluffs overlooking the Brush Creek Valley just east of the state line. He quickly saw that this natural incline provided a more accessible grade for an approach to the more southerly reaches of the Ward lands...." Such a ravine also seems more likely to be the place Curtis called "Swan Creek," which does not show up on old maps of Westport.

It wasn't until years after the battle that the family of George Thoman identified the unnamed "Missouri patriot of seventy-five years" who Curtis said led the way up the ravine. Paul B. Jenkins, in his 1906 *Battle of Westport*, expanded on the geriatric theme of the "very old and feeble man ... with tottering steps." Thoman actually was 45, considerably younger than Curtis.

Historian Howard Monnett said Lieutenant Gill's howitzers and Captain Dodge's Parrotts were with Curtis, but how many guns made it up the ravine is not clear. Hinton mentioned two howitzers. Not every historian includes this action. Wiley Britton wrote that Curtis took Dodge to his right, "but the thick brush and a rough road made it impossible to get the battery into position...."

After coming from Kansas City Sunday morning, Curtis went to the roof of the Harris House in Westport to observe the rebel lines. Also on the roof was Judge W. R. Bernard, a Westport resident, who later recalled: "Every once in a while Colonel Cloud (Curtis's adjutant) would go down into the street and send a regiment against Shelby. The men would cross Brush Creek, climb the hill, fire a volley, and come scampering back. Then Colonel Cloud would come up to take another look.... It was not very exciting, and I asked the colonel if that was the way battles were fought.... I did not see many men killed and it looked as if a lot of lead was being wasted." If Bernard's boredom may be excused, his lack of veracity cannot be. He is quoted in *Battles and Biographies of Missourians*, William L. Webb's 1900 volume, which leans distinctly Confederate on the bookshelf, as saying: "Along in the middle of the afternoon, a shell from Shelby's battery fell almost within the town... At that General Curtis ordered a retreat." All, of course, is untrue. Colonel Thomas Moonlight wrote later that "As soon as Gen. Curtis heard the roaring of Pleasonton's guns about 10 o'clock a.m., new life seemed to be infused into him...."

11:50 A.M. — RUSSELL'S FORD, BIG BLUE RIVER

The New Santa Fe settlement, often called Little Santa Fe, had begun as a popular stop on the trails west because of its good grass and water. By 1860, it was a hamlet of more than 600 population, but it suffered from being right on the border during the war. About all that is left today is its cemetery.

Much is made of Sterling Price's folly of his long, slow train, which may have begun at about 400 wagons and grown to perhaps 600. But such supply columns were not unusual when armies moved. By this time, the most efficient standard for the well-equipped Army of Potomac was 30 wagons for every 1,000 men, while far-ranging Union General Sherman had 40. By those calculations, Price's 12,000 men might have needed between 360 and 480 wagons, so his train hardly seemed extravagant at the beginning. What was in the wagons seems open to debate. Many have said it was loot collected on the march. But on October 10, after Price had passed Jefferson City, Major General Pleasonton passed on to his commander that: "Gen. Sanborn reports the rebel train as empty. The plunder is carried by the men on their horses and what goods they cannot carry off in this way they destroy..." As we have seen, General Fagan was complaining to Price about the "want of breadstuffs for my division" and how, "Hundreds of my men are without the necessary clothing to be at all comfortable, even in the mildest weather at this season in this climate."

Most histories refer to the ruse of lining up unarmed men at the Blue River. Oddly, the report by Colonel Charles Tyler, commander of the Confederate recruits, does not, although it details a similar, although bloodier bluff two days later on the Marmaton River. The best book on the Seventh Kansas Cavalry, by Stephen Z. Starr, does not remark on it, either.

Based on a statement by A. S. Kelly, the skull surely was Allman's. Kelly, one of the guards assigned by Colonel Joe Porter to guard the Union informant, was later asked by a cousin about what happened, according to Scott E. Sallee's 2000 article in *Blue & Gray* magazine. "Ah honey," the old rebel replied, "those days are to be regretted and forgotten. We left Andy up on Troublesome Creek, and memory of him has been troublesome afterward."

"It seems hard that ten men should die for one. Under ordinary circumstances it would hardly be justified; but severe diseases demand severe remedies," rationalized the *Palmyra Courier*, but *The New York Times* disagreed: "There can be no possible justifications for such a butchery." Colonel William Strachan fired back that in killing guerrillas, "we think we are fighting a battle for the world, for humanity, for civilization, for religion, for the honor of our forefathers, for republics." While Strachan was convicted, Major General Rosecrans voided the verdict. Much was covered up by the Union authorities. Sallee noted that General McNeil's pension records showed he carried a pistol bullet in his hip, put there by Strachan in April 1863. The records revealed only the old "discharged while cleaning" story, but it's more likely the two officers got into an argument. McNeil would have wanted to keep it quiet because the publicity from Palmyra was still raging. This occurred after they had been transferred to Southeast Missouri and McNeil declared: "Where a Union man cannot live in peace, a secessionist shall not live at all." Strachan eventually got an appointment to the customs house in New Orleans, where he died of consumption in 1866.

Thousands of Union infantry had, indeed, marched all that way only to do nothing. General Joseph Mower's infantry had caught up with Major General A. J. "Whiskey" Smith's long column and they were all at Chapel Hill in Lafayette County on October 22, poised to march just a little farther west to cut off any retreat by Sterling Price. After the hard fighting of the day, however, Major General Pleasonton asked for them to come north to Independence to support his push toward Westport the next morning. Major General Rosecrans grudgingly accepted this change in plan, and as the 119th Illinois Infantry adjutant's report noted: "We well remember going into camp late one night, about October 22 and after enjoying a cup of coffee we were ordered to fall in, and we marched all night...." The infantry passed through Independence about daybreak and headed for the Big Blue. "This point we reached too late for usefulness," said the adjutants' report. "We could hear the fight going on, but the enemy were routed before our arrival. We found Price in full retreat. Pursuing no further, we soon after began our movement back towards St. Louis. We had marched a distance of about 700 miles; a weary and uncomfortable march; exposure to the elements more than to the enemy, but truly, a trip that had tried the mettle of the soldier."

McNeil's lack of aggressiveness at Russell's Ford got him before a court martial in St. Louis. Unlike General Egbert Brown and Colonel James McFerran, who also faced Pleasonton's wrath but were acquitted, McNeil was suspended from rank and pay for three months. The Judge Advocate General reversed the finding, however, and any blot on his record did not seem to matter. He got a promotion to brevet (temporary) major-general before the war was over, and as a civilian once more, received a prime Republican patronage plum, postmaster for St. Louis.

12:15 P.M. — WORNALL FARM, SOUTH OF WESTPORT

At Loose Park, not far from where Captain Collins fought, a lonely Parrott gun symbolically points north. A close look, however, shows a Union gun, without the beveled edge the

Confederate foundries put on the reinforcing band on the breech. Many years after the battle, H. H. Crittenden, a son of Governor Thomas Crittenden, led a campaign for federal funding of a Gettysburg-style battlefield memorial park south of Brush Creek. The former corn fields had become the Kansas City Country Club golf links, but the country club was about to move to a new location, and development threatened. In his appeal, Crittenden noted: "This battlefield as a memorial would stand as a constant reminder to the Reds and the foreign element within our borders, that the country is ever ready to defend and protect our principles of government, and our institutions to the fullest extent of the law, even to the shedding the blood of countrymen." Mrs. Jacob Loose, wealthy from the estate of her late husband, founder of the Loose-Wiles Biscuit Co. that produced Sunshine Biscuits, swooped in and bought it in 1926 for the park it is today. She wasn't interested in the battlefield park idea. Decades later, battlefield markers and the Parrott were installed.

Shortages limited Confederate batteries to four guns usually, compared to their Union foes, who enjoyed six.

Lieutenant Colonel George Hoyt's "terrible shout, carrying the heights and the stone fences," called for the charge with sabers, recalled Samuel Curtis. It was the second for the 15th Kansas commander — he was in charge of the regiment because Jennsion had been bumped up to command the brigade — in three days. The "cool daring" of Hoyt at the Little Blue was mentioned in the official reports. Writing about the jayhawkers, Stephen Z. Starr describes Hoyt as "a strange assortment of contradictory qualities. A sincere idealist on the subject of slavery, he was also a braggart, a toady, a shameless liar, and an utterly unscrupulous self-seeker." Apparently, Hoyt also was brave and would be promoted to brevet brigadier general in 1865 for his actions against Price. After the war, he served as Kansas attorney general from 1867 to 1869 as a Republican, but apparently was not renominated. Working as a newspaper editor, he showed up on the Workingman's Party ticket, which was trounced at the polls. By 1871, he was back in his hometown of Athol, Massachusetts, practicing law. He spent two years in the state legislature and bought a stake in the local newspaper, the Athol *Transcript*, to which he gave "a strong political tinge." He died in 1877 at age 40.

Major H. J. Vivian's 1912 recollection was that he'd stayed at the ford until 4:30, but that's far too late for the conditions on the battlefield. The fog of war lies fairly thick on the Battle of Westport. Many reports are contradictory about parts of the battle, and large gaps exist at other points. One chronological measure comes from the telegrams being sent by the Union officers, although not all have times denoted in the *Official Records*. A message from Major General Pleasonton marked 10:30 a.m. said the enemy, probably Marmaduke, was already moving south. One by Major General Curtis at 1:05 p.m. said, "the enemy has been driven seven or eight miles south of Westport," surely an exaggeration of distance. By Curtis's next telegram at 3 p.m., the enemy is on the run at a gallop, and Pleasonton has linked up with Major General Blunt's forces.

The guerrillas riding under Dave Pool were on Shelby's flank, "with the understanding that General Marmaduke was to our right," guerrilla John McCorkle would recall. Riding as a courier, he saw a Federal command approaching from the east. When he reported this to Pool and Colonel Benjamin Elliott, they scoffed and insisted it was Marmaduke's men. "I told them that Marmaduke's men did not wear blue clothes," said McCorkle, but he was sent back to check again. Pistol fire in his direction confirmed his hunch. "I wheeled my horse and dashed back and told Colonel Elliott and Pool that I was going to General Shelby, that maybe he could tell a Yankee from a Confederate." Pool, like McCorkle, would survive the war; he surrendered with 65 men in May 1865 to Colonel Chester Harding at Lexington and went on to help persuade other guerrillas hiding in the Sni Hills to give up as well. He settled into ranching around Sherman, Texas.

12:30 P.M. — SOUTH OF WESTPORT

This chapter is largely constructed from Richard J. Hinton's *Rebel Invasion of Missouri and Kansas*, published the year after the battle. Captain Hinton, originally attached to the Kansas colored militia, had become Major General Blunt's aide-de-camp and apparently was with him at this point. A London-born stonecutter, Hinton had immigrated to New York, where he picked up newspaper work and an abolitionist attitude. With James Montgomery, he had plotted to spring John Brown from jail after Harpers Ferry, only to learn the old man embraced his coming martyrdom. The farmhouse where he said the howitzer nearly was captured probably was the Ben Simpson house, which sat roughly at what today would be a little north of the northeast corner of 55th Street and Wornall (Fort Scott) Road. Earlier in the fight, Westport historian Monnett said, General Fagan had two guns of Blocher's Arkansas Battery here.

The Wornall home, classic Missouri antebellum, still reigns at Wornall Road and 61st Terrace as a museum. Eliza was the daughter of Reverend Thomas Johnson, for whom Johnson County, Kansas, is named. Before the war, the Methodist minister left the Shawnee Mission for a home in Westport near today's 35th Street and Agnes Avenue. It is not clear whether he brought any of the slaves who worked at the mission; the 1860 census does not show them. Johnson died January 2, 1865, when gunmen sent a bullet through his door into his stomach. His assailants are unidentified, but a manuscript found in the papers of Kansas historian William E. Connelley indicated the motive was robbery of $1,000 that Johnson was believed to have at his home.

Major Hunt's wound was minor, and he would get back on his horse. Later, the Irish immigrant would be elected Kansas City mayor. The rebels' guns here probably were those of Captain William Blocher's Arkansas battery.

Hinton's account indicates at least five Union mounted charges here before the day was over. The last general attack, ordered by Major General Curtis, hit General Shelby's rear guard on the north front about the time Major General Pleasonton began mauling the Iron Brigade from the east. As Federal Captain George Grover recalled the moment on the Fort Scott Road: "Just then, the head of a column of cavalry deployed from the timber, about a mile to the left, and advanced upon the rebel right flank, and as they swung into action, the smoke lifted, and we saw their guidons, and blue uniforms, and with wild shouts, 'Pleasonton has come,' again we rode on the rebel line, doubling it up like a jack-knife...."

Notes for Chapter XV — Running south

OCTOBER 23 — 1 P.M. — PRAIRIE EAST OF STATE LINE, *JACKSON COUNTY*

At this point, the fog of war — or the retelling of it — pretty much covers the field. Again, the reports and diaries of the two sides, this time on the east front, refuse to square up. As a result, previous histories tend to mash two different events together. Pulled out of the Westport line, Colonel Jackman's report says he was told to "fall back across the prairie to the point where the gun was captured the evening before." This indicates that his distinct, dismounted fight in support of General Fagan occurred in the vicinity of the Mockbee farm. Yet nearly all recollections by Union officers speak only of a single moment of resistance to Major General Pleasonton's advance — General Thompson's breaking of General Sanborn's line. The exception is the apparently overlooked or ignored report of little-known Colonel J. J. Gravely of the Eighth Missouri State Militia cavalry. Gravely said he was ordered to take his regiment as well as the Sixth regiment and "charge the enemy's line near a house on a prairie ridge, which was done under a most terrific (fire) from a section of the enemy's artillery in position near the above named house" (the Mockbee place?).

He did not mention whether his foe was afoot, but reported that captured rebel officers had been worried about being cut off from the Harrisonville Road and that his action in driving away the artillery (Collins' single gun?) prevented it from being used "against the main force of our army on our right," that is, Sanborn, Benteen and Philips to the north. Gravely said this action occurred about 2 p.m., which does not agree with Shelby, Jackman and Thompson all saying Jackman left the Westport front about noon, but times recalled by soldiers often are off by hours. Was this the Jackman fight? It may be that other Federal officers' reports did not mention Jackman's stand because they didn't experience it or even see it well to the south of the bulk of their force.

Geography is another aspect of this phase of the battle that leaves room for interpretation because of the dearth of landmarks. Period maps show the Harrisonville Road, which was taken by the Price wagon train, ran due south along what is now Prospect Avenue. The Fort Scott (Wornall) Road, after going straight south to about what is now 63rd Street, assumed a southwest course zigzagging to a juncture with the Harrisonville Road. This was the road that ran by Mockbee farm and then merged with the Harrisonville pike north of Russell's Ford at the Big Blue River. Once Price's train crossed the Blue here, it turned immediately to the west and then after fording the Blue yet again turned south once more to Fort Scott on a track that today would be fairly close to the State Line Road. Gravely said his fight was on the Harrisonville Road. Shelby refers in his report to sending Jackman "back to the road taken by the train," but Jackman said he was sent to where the big howitzer had been taken the day before, that is the Fort Scott Road. Captain Hinton, who was not on this front, said Pleasonton drove the rebels beyond the Harrisonville Road, all the way to the State Line Road. But probably only Thompson and a few hundred of the Iron Brigade went as far west. As they turned south on the State Line, yet another Federal force, Colonel Moonlight's 11th Kansas, struck at their rear. In his memoirs, Thompson humorously said he'd blundered onto the wrong road, but ended up doing right by unintentionally decoying the pursuing Yanks away from Price.

Colonel John Philips' First Brigade joined in with Colonel Benteen's Fourth here. A dramatic painting, "Battle of Westport," done by N. C. Wyeth in 1920 for the Missouri Capitol, may more or less depict this moment. Philips, sword upraised, is shown leading a charge toward a terrible collision with onrushing Confederate horsemen. Dr. Paul Jenkins, who produced a rather loose history of the Westport battle in 1906, said this took place on the high ground south of Brush Creek. If that were the case, the painting is highly inaccurate as it does not show the many fences, including the ones that hemmed in the McGehee charge up the Fort Scott Road. Far worse: Philips was nowhere near that part of the battlefield. Another nit: The depicted rebels brandish sabers, which they did not. Still, it's more accurate than the companion Wyeth painting, "Battle of Wilson's Creek." That beautiful work shows the two sides slugging it out across an Ozark stream, although none of the fighting took place on the creek.

A question can be raised about what Pleasonton had been doing with his time. By 10:30 a.m., he sent a telegram saying the fight at the bluffs of the Blue had been won, Winslow had been wounded and the rebels were Running southward, apparently on the Harrisonville Road. Yet, it is not until about 1 p.m. that Shelby came into view on the Fort Scott Road and a new round of fierce fighting erupted. Only about three miles of prairie separated the two locations.

2:15 P.M.

It figures large in local Confederate lore, but almost no Federal report mentions General Shelby's stand at the fence. Most indicate Shelby's condition as an uninterrupted rout. Sergeant Scott, the Iowa cavalryman, did recall how after four miles, the fleeing "rebels gained the cover of a range of wooded hills behind a rocky creek," perhaps Indian Creek. Only Colonel John E. Phelps reported that his Second Arkansas hit a double line of Confederates at a fence and eventually forced them to abandon it. Phelps reported another rebel stand after that: "In three divisions of regiments the enemy stood in the brushwood on both sides of the piece enfilading the road, the other division on open ground in advance and to the right of the artillery (that) well served and well aimed, planted the shells in the (Federal) column with an unerring accuracy...."

The artillery mentioned by Phelps probably were two tubes directed by Lieutenant J. D. Connor of Collin's battery. Confusing historians, Colonel Sidney Jackman's report said Collins came to his assistance earlier in the fight "with his only remaining gun." But Connor surely still had been up on the line facing Westport with the other section. Shelby's report on the campaign would reflect his pride at getting his surviving three guns out of Missouri. The pet bear made it out, too. After the war, Collins returned to Missouri to practice law in Higginsville. "Captain Dick" also served in the state Legislature. He died in 1902 and is buried in the cemetery of the Confederate Soldiers Home in his town. His stone says it all: "One of Shelby's Men."

According to John Edwards' post-war *Shelby and his Men or The War in the West*, they held the wall until dusk or around 6 'clock. That seems unlikely because they would have been cut off by the swarming blue brigades. Shelby did take the time, however, to burn some ammunition wagons behind the fence. A historical marker at the entrance to Forest Hills Cemetery off Troost Avenue says Shelby's fence supposedly ran close to where another line of stones runs today, along Gregory Boulevard (71st Street) and the south edge of the cemetery. But this appears too far north and certainly too far east considering how hard Shelby was pressed. The story of the cemetery fence may be a romantic tale, stemming from the presence of Shelby's grave only a stone's throw from it.

Most call the Battle of Westport the largest west of the Mississippi. Certainly more were gathered in the area for the fight than any other, perhaps 40,000, although Major General A. J. Smith's 9,000 hard-marching infantry never played a part. How many thousands of Kansas militia were gathered are vague, and some units probably never left Kansas City or Olathe on the 23rd. Many of Price's recruits — for whom estimates run from two thousand to ten thousand — largely were unarmed, although, as we have seen, they were placed in a minor role. The manpower of some regular fighting units, likewise, probably is exaggerated. The author suspects that if the number of actual combatants actually exceed the number at Pea Ridge, Arkansas, where nearly all of the 27,000 assembled were involved in bloody fighting, it wasn't by a great deal.

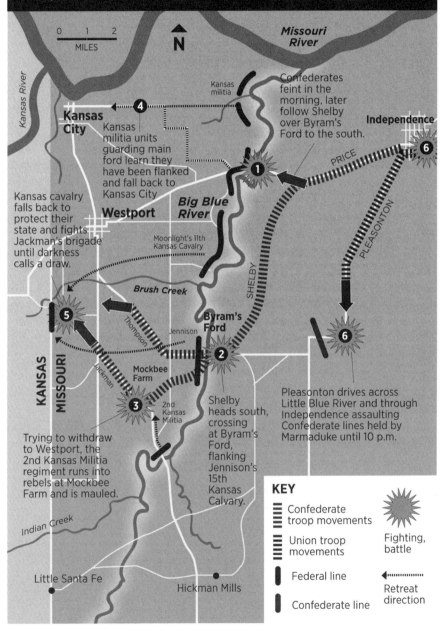

OCT. 22 BATTLE OF THE BIG BLUE

Blunt's cavalry, pushed off the Little Blue River east of Independence the day before, takes new positions with Kansas militia regiments on the "Curtis Line" on the Big Blue River. But the line does not hold. Shelby feints at a main crossing (about 27th Street) then pours his men across at Byram's Ford (near 63rd Street). Just behind the Confederates, however, are Pleasonton's four Federal brig es that swarm across the Little Blue, sweep Fagan's division out of Independence and batter the rear guard of Marmaduke until late in the night.

0   1   2
MILES

N

Missouri River

Kansas River

Kansas militia

Kansas City

Kansas militia units guarding main ford learn they have been flanked and fall back to Kansas City

Confederates feint in the morning, later follow Shelby over Byram's Ford to the south.

Independence

PRICE

①

⑥

Kansas cavalry falls back to protect their state and fights Jackman's brigade until darkness calls a draw.

Westport

Big Blue River

Moonlight's 11th Kansas Cavalry

PLEASONTON

SHELBY

Brush Creek

Thompson

Byram's Ford

Jennison

②

⑥

⑤

KANSAS **MISSOURI**

Jackman

Mockbee Farm

③

2nd Kansas Militia

Trying to withdraw to Westport, the 2nd Kansas Militia regiment runs into rebels at Mockbee Farm and is mauled.

Shelby heads south, crossing at Byram's Ford, flanking Jennison's 15th Kansas Calvary.

Pleasonton drives across Little Blue River and through Independence assaulting Confederate lines held by Marmaduke until 10 p.m.

Indian Creek

Little Santa Fe

Hickman Mills

KEY

≡ Confederate troop movements

≡ Union troop movements

▮ Federal line

▮ Confederate line

Fighting, battle

◀┈┈┈┈ Retreat direction

Dave Eames, Kansas City Star

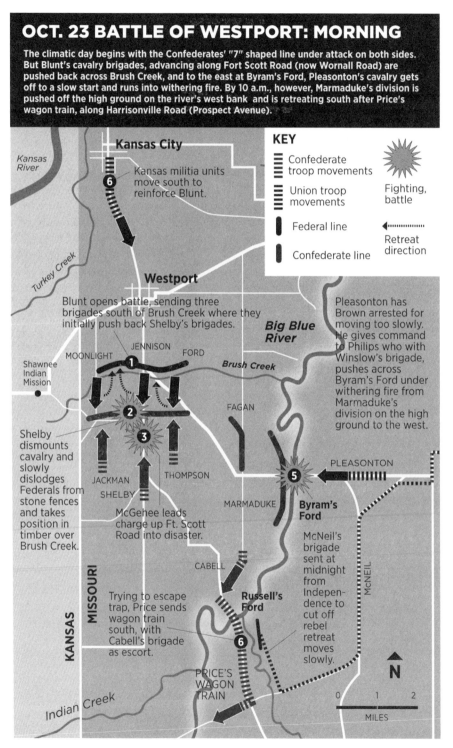

OCT. 23 BATTLE OF WESTPORT: MORNING

The climatic day begins with the Confederates' "7" shaped line under attack on both sides. But Blunt's cavalry brigades, advancing along Fort Scott Road (now Wornall Road) are pushed back across Brush Creek, and to the east at Byram's Ford, Pleasonton's cavalry gets off to a slow start and runs into withering fire. By 10 a.m., however, Marmaduke's division is pushed off the high ground on the river's west bank and is retreating south after Price's wagon train, along Harrisonville Road (Prospect Avenue).

Kansas River

Kansas City

6 Kansas militia units move south to reinforce Blunt.

KEY

Confederate troop movements

Union troop movements

Federal line

Confederate line

Fighting, battle

Retreat direction

Turkey Creek

Westport

Blunt opens battle, sending three brigades south of Brush Creek where they initially push back Shelby's brigades.

Big Blue River

Pleasonton has Brown arrested for moving too slowly. He gives command to Philips who with Winslow's brigade, pushes across Byram's Ford under withering fire from Marmaduke's division on the high ground to the west.

JENNISON   FORD

MOONLIGHT

Shawnee Indian Mission

Brush Creek

1

FAGAN

2

Shelby dismounts cavalry and slowly dislodges Federals from stone fences and takes position in timber over Brush Creek.

3

JACKMAN

SHELBY

THOMPSON

MARMADUKE

McGehee leads charge up Ft. Scott Road into disaster.

PLEASONTON

5

PLEASONTON

Byram's Ford

McNeil's brigade sent at midnight from Independence to cut off rebel retreat moves slowly.

CABELL

MISSOURI

KANSAS

Trying to escape trap, Price sends wagon train south, with Cabell's brigade as escort.

Russell's Ford

6

McNEIL

PRICE'S WAGON TRAIN

Indian Creek

N

0   1   2

MILES

Dave Eames, Kansas City Star

OCT. 23 BATTLE OF WESTPORT: MID-DAY

Sensing the vaccum on his right as Fagan joins the retreat south, Shelby bleeds regiments off the Brush Creek line, just as Curtis and Blunt launch a decisive attack. About to be cut off from Price's column, Shelby throws Thompson's leading regiments against Pleasonton. Thompson, hit by a counter-charge and artillery fire, retreats. Shelby gathers some of his scattered men for desperate stands to slow the Union pursuit. Price's army escapes the trap when McNeil fails to block the southern ford.

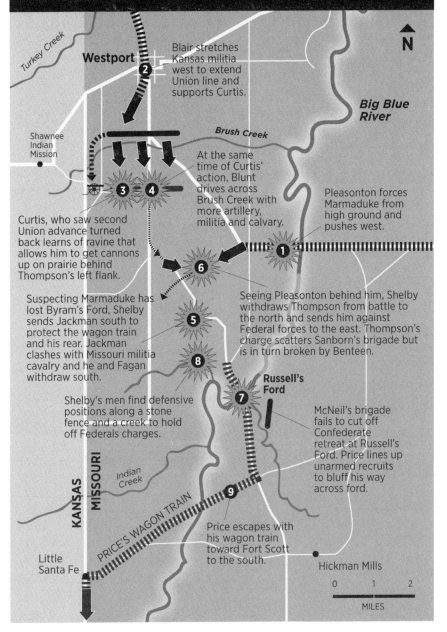

Turkey Creek

Westport

Blair stretches Kansas militia west to extend Union line and supports Curtis.

2

Shawnee Indian Mission

Brush Creek

Big Blue River

At the same time of Curtis' action, Blunt drives across Brush Creek with more artillery, militia and calvary.

3 **4**

Pleasonton forces Marmaduke from high ground and pushes west.

Curtis, who saw second Union advance turned back learns of ravine that allows him to get cannons up on prairie behind Thompson's left flank.

6

1

Suspecting Marmaduke has lost Byram's Ford, Shelby sends Jackman south to protect the wagon train and his rear. Jackman clashes with Missouri militia cavalry and he and Fagan withdraw south.

5

Seeing Pleasonton behind him, Shelby withdraws Thompson from battle to the north and sends him against Federal forces to the east. Thompson's charge scatters Sanborn's brigade but is in turn broken by Benteen.

8

Shelby's men find defensive positions along a stone fence and a creek to hold off Federals charges.

7

Russell's Ford

McNeil's brigade fails to cut off Confederate retreat at Russell's Ford. Price lines up unarmed recruits to bluff his way across ford.

KANSAS

MISSOURI

Indian Creek

PRICE'S WAGON TRAIN

9

Little Santa Fe

Price escapes with his wagon train toward Fort Scott to the south.

Hickman Mills

| 0 | 1 | 2 |

MILES

N

Dave Eames, Kansas City Star

Samuel Pomeroy
Kansas State Historical Society

John McNeil
Courtesy of Wilson's Creek National Battlefield,
National Park Service

Alfred Pleasonton
Courtesy of Wilson's Creek National Battlefield,
National Park Service

Richard Collins
State Historical Society of Missouri

"Shelby and his Men at Westport"
Andy Thomas, artist, Carthage, Missouri www.andythomas.com

African-American artillery battery, Fort Leavenworth
Kansas State Historical Society

"Battle of the Blue," action at Mockbee Farm, by Benjamin Mileham
Kansas Museum of History, Topeka

N. C. Wyeth's Battle of Westport
Missouri Capitol, Jefferson City

Notes for Chapter XVI — Dead and dying

OCTOBER 23 — 9 P.M. — KANSAS CITY

There is no indication of when Mrs. H. S. Millett submitted this memory, which is included in H. H. Crittenden's *The Battle of Westport*, published in 1938. The next day, she said, the women gathered quilts for the wounded, who convalesced in the church and the Lockridge ballroom just east on Fifth Street. After a week, the wounded were dispersed.

Joshua Thorne had been Chief Surgeon for the Union forces in Kansas City, setting up in McGee's hotel at 16th and Grand known variously as the Planters', the Farmers or the Southern. A professional biography indicates Thorne had resigned this position months before this battle. Apparently, he volunteered his services in the crisis. English-born, Thorne specialized in homeopathic medicine.

Robert Van Horn, Kansas City's mayor in the critical first year of the war, was an energetic Union man. In 1861, he got Federal soldiers from Fort Leavenworth to quickly protect his western town, then organized Van Horn's Battalion, in which George Caleb Bingham served as captain of the Irishmen who made up Company C. In the 1861 Lexington battle, Van Horn was wounded, captured and exchanged. As colonel of the 25th Missouri Infantry, he went on to fight at Shiloh in Tennessee and Corinth in Mississippi. When he returned to the border he became General Ewing's provost marshal, which meant it fell to him to enforce Order No. 11 — with forbearance and sympathy, some later said. A few days after the Battle of Westport, he was elected to Congress, where he would prove instrumental in securing the first Missouri River railroad crossing for Kansas City. Before and after the war, he owned the city's most important newspaper, the *Western Journal of Commerce*. After Van Horn sold it in 1896, the nameplate was changed to *The Kansas City Journal*. It finally ceased publication in 1942.

The remains of 15 Confederates, some of whom may have given up the ghost in this church, are in Union Cemetery under a monument today, although originally buried elsewhere. Thorne, who treated them, ended up there as well. Another mass grave of rebels was said to be a little south of the Bent House. "Union" Cemetery does not denote a side in the war, but a place where the dead of both Westport and Kansas City were united. This burying place also holds the grave of Medal of Honor winner Nathaniel Gwynne, who at age 15 charged across a field at Petersburg, Virginia, to recapture some Union colors. Having enlisted just the day before, he lost an arm and took two bullets in the leg. He ended up a lawyer and real estate agent in Kansas City and served in the Missouri House, where he sponsored veterans' benefits legislation. He died at age 33.

Elizabeth Millett faded back into obscurity, although her husband was a partner in the prominent printing firm, Ramsey, Millet & Hudson. The baby, Van, grew up to be a well-known artist and president of the Paint club, which evolved into the Kansas City Art Institute.

No one ever came to claim the lock of hair.

OCTOBER 24 — 9:35 A.M. — RAY COUNTY

"Lyon" and "Reno" were the code established by General Egbert Brown in July to prevent disguised guerrillas from getting too close. In January, troops were ordered to hail one another by shouting "America" and to respond with "Dodge" as the countersign. That the bushwhackers had their ways of finding out the secrets was shown by the report of Major L. C. Matlock at Glasgow: "Anderson used our signals August 20 when approaching our men; that spoils them for my use."

This killing of a courier is fiction, but two months earlier Major Henry Suess noted that "Anderson's gang killed Private James Warren, Company M, Seventh Missouri State Militia Cavalry at Mills Landing, on his return from Carrollton, where he had been sent." Eisenhour's beheading may have taken place on the 25th.

Guerrilla forces may have tied down one out of three soldiers in the occupying Union armies at times. "In no other way does the enemy give us so much trouble, at so little expense to himself," wrote President Lincoln.

The luck of Council Grove in May 1863 has other versions. One was that a friend from Santa Fe trading days, Malcolm Conn, lived there and talked Yager out of plundering the place; another says a Federal unit not far away intimidated the raiders.

Reports of Yager still on the prowl were being circulated as late as June 1865 by Captain Curtis Johnson, 15th Kansas Cavalry. In his book about the guerrillas after the war, Edwards unsurprisingly puffed up Yager's last moments: "Poor Yager! He fell there, propped against a tree that he might face his foes, but as he fell he avenged himself. Three (Federals) died with him and two were wounded. It might be said of him that he died literally with his revolver belt buckled." Union troops knew Yager was badly wounded and spent time looking for him, but the official records do not indicate they knew whom they had stumbled across. Yager probably was in no shape to lift a revolver when the Federals finished him off.

The James brothers and others were soon to rejoin William Quantrill and leave Missouri two months after the Westport battle. They slipped away disguised as — what else? — Union soldiers. Most doubt the story that Quantrill had decided to go east to assassinate Lincoln. Likely, he hoped to eventually surrender outside Missouri, where he might not be noticed. In Kentucky, prime guerrilla country, he continued raiding, however, and took a bullet in the spine after being surprised by a squad of hired guerrilla hunters. He died June 6, 1865.

This man burned in Lawrence was Daniel W. Palmer, but there were several others. Rev. H. D. Fisher barely escaped this fate when his wife tugged him out of their burning home wrapped in a rug. "With demoniac yells the scoundrels flew hither and yon, wherever a man was to be seen, shooting him down like a dog," Fisher would write. "Men were called from their beds and murdered before the eyes of wives and children on their doorsteps. Tears, entreaties, prayers availed nothing. The fiends of hell were among us...."

Larkin Skaggs, a preacher, was too drunk to notice that his fellow bushwhackers had withdrawn. He was killed, scalped and his body hung from a tree, where it was pelted with stones and riddled with bullets. The next day it was dragged behind a horse until the skin was gone, then thrown in a ravine and burned. Leslie noted also the fate of Tom Corlew, accused of being a guerrilla spy who had moved his family out of town the day before the raid. He was put on trial immediately, but the jury turned the decision over to the crowd of angry townsmen. Thrashing at the end of the rope in a barn, he, too, was pumped full of bullets by the mob.

The author chose to look upon Riley Crawford more sympathetically than most. In *Gray Ghosts of the Confederacy*, Richard Brownlee wrote: "Little Riley Crawford was to kill every Union soldier that fell into his hands...." Quantrill biographer Paul Petersen called him "as efficient at killing as 'Bloody Bill' Anderson." In his brilliant novel, *Woe to Live On*, Daniel Woodrell's protagonist is fond of Crawford, who "had grown into a killer young." Yet, the Baxter Springs possum player is the only death specifically attributed to our Riley (and he was drunk at the time) anywhere in historical accounts. All this makes Crawford a very blank canvas. The author suspects he was not idle at Lawrence, but finds no record placing him at any other 1863 or 1864 guerrilla depredations.

7:30 P.M. — KANSAS CITY

Combs' letter actually was written on October 28, 1864. It was published as "The Story Behind the Letter," in October 2000 *Blue & Gray Chronicle*. George Combs, 23, served as a sergeant in C Company, which was commanded by his brother, James, just a year older. Lieutenant Combs had been noted for gallant action at Lone Jack, Missouri, in 1862. A baby boy would be named James, after his father.

The Thompson farm where the generals gathered was at what is now Wornall Road and 96th Terrace.

Notes for Chapter XVII — Backs against a wall

OCTOBER 25 — 10:45 A.M. — MINE CREEK, *LINN COUNTY, EASTERN KANSAS*

Colonel John C. Wright, who commanded a regiment under General James F. Fagan, was scathing: "I never saw Fagan under fire but once during the whole war, and it was seldom that he was near enough the front to see what was doing." That "once" was the fight below Westport when Colonel Jackman came to his aid. Fagan left no record of his whereabouts when the Mine Creek fighting occurred.

The woman Major General Marmaduke could see was Mrs. Barbara Dolson, who left a sharp mental image of Sterling Price's men:"The advance of the rebel army reached our house just as breakfast was ready. The few who came in first sat down to the table and went to helping themselves. The house was then soon full of rebels. I went to the door and looked out; the whole valley seemed full of men. The first that passed seemed to be marching in some order. At the head of the column was an old rebel flag all torn in strips, fluttering in the wind. But as they came on they seemed to be in more and worse confusion, and traveling faster, until as the last wagon train passed they … were going at a dead run."

The Confederate retreat had followed the road that had been just inside Missouri but now swung gently into Kansas and went between two large mounds just north of Trading Post. The rebels' rear guard set up a defensive line on these hills, which was attacked at daylight and given up without much of a fight. The Confederates lost a pair of 2-pounder skirmish guns at the Marais des Cygnes River crossing that they probably had captured at Fort Davidson. In the hamlet itself, the Federals found abandoned wagons, half-eaten cattle carcasses and, reportedly, terrified and half-clothed women residents.

11:35 A.M.

After the war, Lieutenant Colonel Benteen stayed in the regular army as a captain and survived the 1876 battle of Little Big Horn. There, he displayed his leadership and coolness under fire, although some questioned his decision to stay with Major Marcus Reno in a defensive position rather than riding on north to find the doomed and possibly already dead Colonel George Armstrong Custer. Most agree now that could have been fatal to the entire command. He was promoted to major, but then faced dismissal for drunken conduct at a fort in Utah. President Cleveland reduced his sentence to a year's suspension. Benteen died in 1898.

According to a story heard at the Mine Creek battlefield site, a New Jersey cavalryman waiting for the call to charge nearly a three-quarter long line of Confederates recalled hearing two of his comrades. One noted: "We're in for a hell of a fight today." To which the other spat a stream of tobacco juice and replied: "Hell, you're dressed for it, ain't you?"

Often, every cavalry company started with two buglers, so the sounds from Benteen's brigade alone would have come from more than 50 horns.

While Sergeant Bereman's diary entry tells this story well, he was a little weak on his numbers. Perhaps 2,500 Federal troopers were in the charge against nearly 5,000 Confederates massed on the north side of Mine Creek, according to Lumir F. Buresh in his *Oct. 25 and the Battle of Mine Creek*. It was the largest cavalry battle west of the Mississippi. Bereman called it a "glorious fight" and said Major Abial Pierce "covered himself with glory & his saber with blood." Buresh's exhaustive book notes that many were killed by Fourth Iowa sabers, but those would be the officers' blades only. Bereman said the enlisted men had left their blades in Memphis. The loss in the Fourth Iowa, he said, was, "A Lieut. in co F. killed, & perhaps twenty in the regt. killed & wounded." Pierce reported that his "regiment captured over 200 prisoners with two stand of colors."

Bereman returned to Mount Pleasant, Iowa, where he married and became a druggist. He later moved his family and business to Atchison, Kansas, where he died in 1904.

12:30 P.M.

After the fight, Colonel Philips spent a night in agony at Fort Scott, then decided to continue the pursuit of the Confederate army by riding in an ambulance. Major General Pleasonton, however, gave Philips' brigade the duty of escorting the Confederate prisoners back north. In another one of his letters to his wife, Lieutenant Colonel Bazel Lazear, the First Missouri commander, would write that he reached Warrensburg with 600 prisoners, who would be shipped on to St. Louis. Having won Pleasonton's respect for his Missouri State Militia on the battlefield, Philips and his troopers returned to their kind of war, running down guerrillas and their supporters and "mustering" them out.

Despite the Federals' disdain for Confederates who wore Union blue, reports show that Philips and other commanders also sent out men dressed in the garb of the enemy. In Missouri, hundreds died for fatally mistaking an identity. "Guerrillas could be dressed as Union troops, and Union militia often went around dressed as civilians, which made many … assume they were guerrillas. Uniformed Union troops could pretend to be guerrillas dressed in Union uniforms and behave precisely as did guerrillas," wrote Michael Fellman in *Inside War*. "In a guerrilla war where both sides wandered in small bands rather than marching in large columns, part of the terror for civilians was that they could never know for certain to whom they were talking and therefore could not trust anyone."

Federals were still killing prisoners a week later. On November 3, a Private Abram Kirby was dragged from a train carrying prisoners to St. Louis. At Hermann, he was tied to a stake and shot for wearing a Federal uniform.

Philips reported flatly that "A number of prisoners taken … were dressed in our uniform… and in obedience to existing orders from the Department Headquarters … they were executed." It was probably not only the Confederates in Union overcoats who were massacred at Mine Creek; some Kansas units arrived on the scene with revenge in mind. The number of victims executed/murdered is vague, but the comparison of how many were reported killed — between 200 and 400 — in the action offers a clue. The usual ratio of wounded to killed in a battle is 3:1. Mine Creek historian Lumir Buresh noted, however, that the rebel dead on this field at least equaled and may have doubled that of the wounded. And once again, the newspaper correspondent for the Leavenworth *Times* was clueless — or complicit. "One remarkable fact is worthy of mention. Nine of every ten rebels killed and wounded, are shot in the head—showing the accuracy of the aim of our boys." Another measure that many must have been executed was that the Federals suffered only eight fatalities, although 56 seriously wounded.

1 P.M.

_____

After the campaign, Confederate Governor Thomas Reynolds wrote a long, excoriating article in the *Texas Republican*: "Hearing of reports industriously circulated, charging Generals Marmaduke and Cabell with drunkenness in the battles last October, near Independence and the Osage River (Mine Creek), and putting on them the responsibility for disgraces and disasters which the almost unanimous opinion of the army at the time justly attributed to the glaring mismanagement and distressing mental and physical military incapacity of Major General Sterling Price." Price retorted that he had heard of no rumors of drunkenness and called Reynolds' charges a "tissue of falsehoods." After the war, Reynolds came up with a new story that Marmaduke had not wanted to join the invasion, because "He had a very low opinion of Gen. Price's military capacity, and believed him and his staff, so malignantly hostile to him … that should he go, a regular plan would be formed and carried out by them to ruin his military reputation, throw on him the blame of any disaster that might occur, and perhaps even have him killed or captured."

Much of this chapter comes from Lumir Buresh's book on the Mine Creek fight. He told the story of Colonel Jeffers differently, saying that Jeffers was trying to help the Harris battery across the creek when forced to surrender to Second Kansas Colonel William Cloud, who was acting as an aide to Curtis.

Normally, Colonel Charles Blair was commander of Fort Scott, but he had taken most of his units north to play a major role in the Brush Creek fight two days before. As he marched south with major generals Curtis and Pleasonton, he fretted that the nearly defenseless fort would be wiped out.

In his autobiography, William Cody would claim he was part of a scouting party that captured a small detachment of Confederates. "…While we were rounding them up I heard one of them say we Yanks had captured a bigger prize than we suspected. When he was asked what this prize consisted of, the soldier said: 'That big man over yonder is General Marmaduke….'" Cody went on to say he was chosen to escort the general to Fort Leavenworth, becoming fast friends on the way. More nonsense.

Buresh noted that Mine Creek also might be called the Battle of the Future Governors: Marmaduke and Lieutenant Colonel Thomas Crittenden of Missouri; Colonel Samuel Crawford of Kansas; Colonel Thomas Moonlight of Wyoming, and Illinois Cavalry Colonel John Beveridge of that state. Price also had been a governor, as had, briefly, one of his aides-de-camp, Trusten Polk, who more recently was expelled from the U. S. Senate in 1862.

6 P.M. — NORTH OF DRY WOOD CREEK, *VERNON COUNTY*
_____

What happened to the big gun captured with George Gage? Clearly it did not make it to Arkansas. On December 24, 1910, *The Kansas City Times* reported it found but not yet retrieved from the muddy bottom of "Blue Hole in Flat Creek" four miles north of Cassville in southwest Missouri. There was confident talk of a ceremony involving both state governors, but apparently the hunt was a bust. "Everybody keeps looking for it, but it's never been found," said Blair Tarr of the Kansas Museum of History. The last clipping on the search is dated 2005.

While the distances often were exaggerated in contemporary reports, many of the prisoners were driven about 140 miles before being released on Saturday, October 29, seven days after their capture.

Before the 15th cavalry found their mistreated fellow Kansans, Colonel Doc Jennison said, "our scouts caught somewhere in the woods a lanky specimen of a greyback who could give no satisfactory or proper account of himself, but from papers in his possession it was evident that he belonged to the engineer corps of the ragged rebs ahead. I ordered him to be securely guarded during the night, intending to send him to headquarters in the morning; but in some inexplicable manner the fellow managed to hang himself to an apple tree before sunrise, or somebody else hung him there." The Kansans' treatment of the rebel probably stemmed in part because of the path of death and destruction left by Price's column in east-central Kansas before it crossed the line back into Missouri. But then, too, the jayhawkers were always handy with a rope.

Andrew Huntoon later wrote that General Shelby rode back to tell them: "Gentlemen, I am doing the best that I can; you are getting just as good a fare as my men are." That seemed to be true. Between Carthage and Newtonia, Missouri, some cattle were killed, and the prisoners received their share to cook on sticks. At Newtonia, about 90 prisoners finally were paroled, something that could have been done much earlier. Shelby had to leave their oath-taking, Huntoon said, "when the screech of shells over our heads caused us to be moved about two miles farther."

Gage became a brick manufacturer, home builder and real estate dealer. In 1895, at his own expense, he erected the Soldiers' Monument in Topeka Cemetery dedicated to the men who died at Mockbee farm. After his death in 1899, his widow presented the 80-acre Gage Park to the city.

OCTOBER 26, 2 A.M. — SHILOH CREEK, *VERNON COUNTY*

At some point on this campaign, Captain Levi Utt became ill from "extreme exposure" and was sent back to St. Louis for treatment of typhoid fever. The regiment's historian, Simeon M. Fox, called him "the most fearless man that I ever saw, when in the greatest hazard he seemed entirely unconscious of danger."

Colonel Thomas Moonlight was given general's stars and command of the District of Colorado and ended his military career battling Indians. In 1888, he was elected Kansas secretary of state. During President Cleveland's first term he was appointed governor of Wyoming and in 1893 became minister to Bolivia. He returned to farming four years later and died in 1899 in Leavenworth.

Senator Lane had stayed with the troops since Westport and was at hand when General McNeil asked him to go to the rear and hurry up reinforcements and artillery. According to Buresh's history of the battle, "… the frenzied Lane galloped back at full speed. With his coat flying, his angular frame like Ichabod Crane's going to the rescue, he raced up to Pleasonton and pointing a bony finger screamed his favorite expression, 'Good God, man!! We need more troops at the front or all is lost.'"

After daybreak, Colonel Benteen took his brigade to Fort Scott as well. The supply wagons finally showed up, however, and McNeil's men gorged on the three pieces of tack distributed to each, and their bedraggled horses got unshucked corn found in a nearby field. Only Benteen's brigade of Major General Pleasonton's command stayed with the pursuit into Arkansas. By their return north, a good many of his cavalry horses had given out, leaving troopers to drag saddles, weapons and gear on foot. The same happened to the 11th Kansas, who lost 250 horses when the starved animals got into a cane brake and ate the hard stalks.

Remounts were always a cause for night sweats for the Civil War quartermaster, but more so for the Confederacy, which started the war with less than 2 million horses, while the North had more than double that. Mules were another matter; the South had about 800,000, more than twice the Union. Trying to bring as many men to a fight as possible, cavalry commanders usually had little choice but to keep their suffering horses on the line until they completely broke down. On average, a Federal cavalry mount might last only a few months. After the 1863 chase of Colonel Shelby through central Missouri, Colonel Philips reported that his Seventh Missouri had ridden down and abandoned 54 horses and that eight more were shot.

In spring 1863, Captain Charles Adams, First Massachusetts Cavalry, characterized himself a slave to his company's horses, "yet with every care the marching of the last four weeks disabled ten of my horses, and put ten more on the high road to disability, and this out of sixty — one horse in three." He wrote how "dashing cavalry raids" often were executed on weak, gaunt, rough-looking animals. "To estimate the wear and tear on horseflesh you must bear in mind that … a cavalry horse when loaded carries an average of 225 lbs. on his back… The horse is, in active campaign, saddled on an average about fifteen hours out of twenty four. His feed is nominally ten pounds of grain a day and, in reality, he averages about eight pounds. He has no hay and only such other feed as he can pick up during halts." It is estimated that more than 1.5 million horses died in the Civil War. An artillery officer wrote of watching all but four of the 57 horses in his company take bullet after bullet in an 1864 action and finally die in their traces.

Despite it all, Utt must have loved the army life. He and other officers tried to keep the Seventh in service until the troopers' last three-year enlistment expired in 1867, according to Starr's book on the jayhawkers. The enlisted men were not interested in staying in the army any longer than they had to, and Private Webster Moses wrote to his new wife: "If the officers succeed as they hope to they cannot remain with the Regiment as they would soon be shot down like dogs and not even get a decent burial. Our officers are a very low set of fellows who do not like the prospect of going to work for a living."

Notes for Chapter XVIII — Final shots

OCTOBER 26 — 2:20 A.M. — SOUTH OF THE MARMATON RIVER

Exactly a month earlier, Major General Rosecrans had telegraphed some intelligence and some wisdom about Price's train to the Kansas commander, Major General Sam Curtis. "He has 300 wagons in his train, which he will hardly be able to keep."

Offering one of his two wagons to the bonfire, Dr. William McPheeters consolidated material to a single vehicle — which also would end up abandoned a day later after it "ran into a ravine and in the hurry and stampede … by which I lost all my medicines and instruments, most of my clothes, and all my papers and personal effects…." Lieutenant Colonel Jesse Ellison recalled his loss in the burning train that night, "our commissions from Mr. (Jefferson) Davis. Beautiful documents."

Apparently in their rush south, the Confederates abandoned their cattle herd, said to have been about 5,000 head, despite being guarded by a hungry army. Some beef, without salt, had been shared with the famished Kansas prisoners on the 24th. After that, the cows more or less vanished. Colonel Philips would comment that many loose cattle, horses and mules were wandering the prairie and should be rounded up.

General Jeff Thompson was in such a poor state that a sympathetic soldier stole a spare pair of pants from another officer to give to the unsuspecting Thompson.

Rather than surrender, Colonel Alonzo Slayback went to Mexico, where family lore has it, he gave English lessons to the emperor and was made a duke. After his mother ventured to Cuba to send a demand for his return to Missouri, Slayback became a prominent lawyer in St. Louis. He was active in political and social life, helping form the Veiled Prophet Ball. Insulted by an 1882 item published in the *Post-Dispatch* that belittled his military record — "the colonel once marshalled a female sewing society" — he went to the office of editor John Cockerill to demand an apology. As Slayback was taking off his coat, apparently to give the editor a sound slap, Cockerill, a Union veteran, pulled a pistol from a drawer and put a bullet into Slayback's armpit. Cockerill was not indicted, because a gun was found in Slayback's pocket — placed there before the police arrived, according to a years-later deathbed confession by a newspaper employee.

9:30 A.M. — OLD ALBANY, *RAY COUNTY*

This is not the Albany in Gentry County, Missouri, but an old river hamlet later absorbed by Orrick. A few accounts say these happenings occurred on the next day, the 27th, based probably on a report by General Fisk. But that day Cox sent his own report, saying "our expedition on yesterday…."

General Rains had been dismissed two years before for repeated episodes of drunkenness but was still in the Missouri State Guard. He appears to have lobbied for the invasion and may have been in south Missouri well into October. A rebel force identified as his was reported near Licking before returning to Arkansas.

McCelland "Clell" B. Miller was captured and would have been lynched if the Union commander had not prevented it. It may have helped that Miller could have been just 14 or 15, with some stories saying he had joined the band only days before. He would meet his fate a dozen years later, gunned down in the streets of Northfield, Minnesota, during the James and Younger brothers' botched bank robbery.

Just about the only thing certain about this charge was its deadliness for Anderson. Brownlee says he went alone, but most reports said Rains rode beside him to his death. Cox initially reported that Rains escaped, but another officer reported finding his body the next day. Later, Cox offered another version, saying three men burst through his line, the third being Archie Clement, who supposedly panicked the teamsters and scattered the Union wagons in the rear. Adding slightly to the confusion is a list of 10 names of dead guerrillas from this action supposedly buried at an old cemetery outside of Orrick. Rains' name is not among them.

Anderson's body was taken to Richmond, where the dead man was propped in a chair for the local "photographist." Family lore says the Union soldiers cut off the head (and perhaps more) and put it atop a telegraph pole. His corpse was dragged through the streets before it was buried in an unmarked grave outside of town. Some accounts have the local militiamen gathering to urinate on it. None of this appears in official reports, of course. After the war, in Richmond with his wild west show, Cole Younger held a funeral for Anderson at the grave site. Many years later, a grave marker was installed.

Cox would take two of the revolvers and Anderson's mare but divide the gold among the militiamen who had risked their lives. Legend has it that Anderson also carried a silken cord with 53 knots, one for every man he killed. Cox did not mention it, although perhaps he did not recognize what it was.

During the December 1869 bank robbery in Gallatin, Missouri, Jesse James blew out the brains of the cashier, John W. Sheets, who had done nothing to provoke the action. It was a case of mistaken identity, supposedly. The story goes that James had whispered something to Cole Younger just before the pistol blast about how the man looked like Sam Cox, who did live in Gallatin.

OCTOBER 28 — NEWTONIA, *NEWTON COUNTY, SOUTHWEST MISSOURI*

This part is taken from *The Civil War Reminiscences of General M. Jeff Thompson*. He added that "On the 10th of June (1865) I signed my parole and took off my uniform at Memphis and took an old-fashioned drink." General Jo Shelby was gracious to Thompson in his report, saying he "needs nothing here to establish a reputation already known over the United States. He was always with his brigade, and that was always where the firing was heaviest."

One aside to the tale of Lieutenant Christian: He allegedly sliced the ears from his victims. Hill lore was he showed his handiwork to his wife, who was so shocked that she bore him a son without one or more of his ears.

Colonel Moses Smith, wounded three times, died, one of 630,000 to perish in our Civil War. "While only 5 percent of all Federal soldiers were killed or mortally wounded in combat, almost 12 percent of the Confederates suffered a similar fate. The death rate from all causes, including accidents and sickness, was much higher.... As many as 25 percent of all Southern soldiers may have died. The North actually suffered more war deaths, almost three men for every two lost by the South," said Dorothy Denneen Volo and James M. Volo in their *Daily Life in Civil War America*.

A 1918 edition of the *History of Colorado* noted, with a bit of a sneer, that, "Until the autumn of 1864, Ford's troops engaged in combating the fierce guerrilla through Missouri, a form of warfare much disliked by all northern soldiers, but popular among certain classes of Confederates." One must be careful about what one asks for. In this stand-up fight, the Second Colorado got knocked about the worst, losing 42 "killed outright," according to a regimental history.

Although the 15th Kansas was in Blunt's line, its colonel, Doc Jennison, was not. "Two evenings previous I had been rather severely kicked by a mule, and not supposing a battle imminent, had accepted a seat in an ambulance with Gen. Curtis, neither of us being aware of the fight until it was over," he wrote.

The soldier's diary of Private Taylor Bray, who was in General Sanborn's brigade, reads somewhat differently from the supercharged newspaper prose of the day. "Oct. 28 - We marched at 6 a.m. to wards Newtony (Newtonia). Passed Bowers Mill at 1 p.m., fell in with General Blunt's rear gard, crossed Shoal Creek and through Granby. Blunt had a considerable fight at Newtony. Our Brigade ordered up. The Rebs fired 3 shots at our Regiment. 2 of the boys run. We then dismounted and marched of a mile in line of battle. The Rebs fell back. We then went back to our horses and marched round east of town. Sent Companys C, M, and H on picket. We camped for the night. All quiet during the night."

"All that men could do had been done," summed up Shelby's report on the 1864 campaign.

OCTOBER 29 — ST. LOUIS

Ten forts and two redoubts defended St. Louis. No. 4 was a little south of where Lafayette Park is today.

The *Daily Democrat* of St. Louis noted, "We have heard many express regrets in view of the retaliation inflicted, but measures must be taken to prevent barbarities upon our people by giving the enemy a lesson in their own tactics. If the rebels find that for every man they murder in cold blood one of their own number will suffer death, they will see that they are playing at a losing game, and be induced (to) practice more honorable warfare."

The major who had not appeared was Enoch Wolf, captured at Mine Creek. He was selected to die for the murder of Major Wilson, but lived to be 92 years old because the president intervened. One story is that Wolf made it known that he was a member of the Masonic fraternity. One wonders how many Masons escaped death in the Civil War because of their fraternity. In his memoirs, *Confederate Guerrilla*, Joseph Bailey notes how he rescued one of six doomed Federals in Arkansas because he knew the captive to be a Master Mason.

The captain who made the point about retribution to his firing squad was William C. Jones. He was given charge of the remnants of the 10th Kansas, many of whom had mustered out in August after their colonel, William Weer, was court-martialed for drunkenness and misappropriating funds while in command at the Alton prison.

Sterling Price's men had committed another atrocity in Carroll County that got little notice. A month before the invasion, Lieutenant Monroe Williams and four other Confederates were recruiting north of the river. All wearing Union uniforms, they were surprised while sleeping in some woods and killed by Captain William Beaty and a squad of the 65th Enrolled Militia. As Price's army moved west across Missouri, Lieutenant Colonel David A. Williams, the brother of Monroe, crossed the river at Boonville with 150 Confederates with recruiting and revenge on his mind. On October 17 at Carrollton, this force captured 160 militiamen, all but seven of whom were paroled. Beaty and six others were marched to a ravine and executed.

PRICE FLEES BACK TO THE SOUTH

After escaping the trap below Westport on Oct. 23, 1864, Price swung into Kansas for pillaging outside the "Burnt District" emptied by Order No. 11. Two days later, fleeing from Mine Creek, the Confederates took another stand at the Marmaton River, where the exhausted armies called a draw. Price then burned much of his wagon train and continued the retreat. Blunt caught up with the rebels at Newtonia, the last battle of the campaign, another draw.

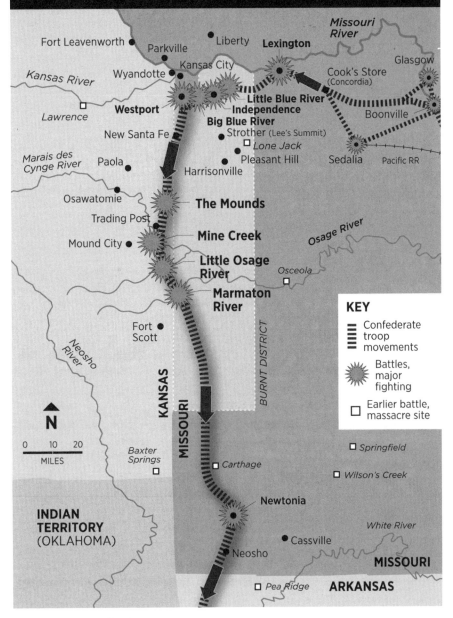

Dave Eames, Kansas City Star

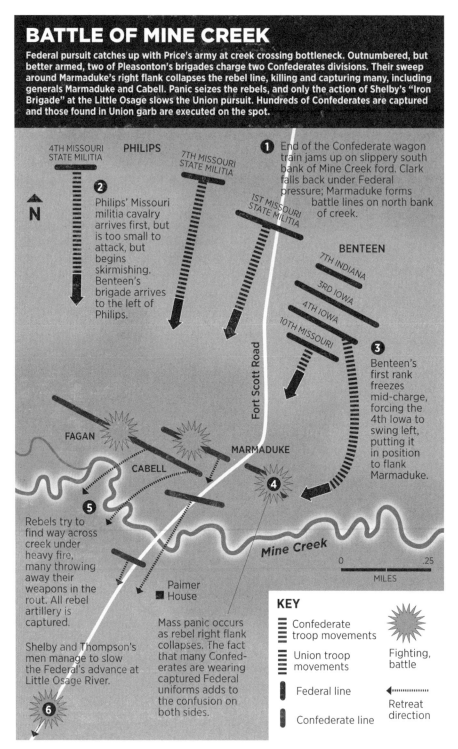

BATTLE OF MINE CREEK

Federal pursuit catches up with Price's army at creek crossing bottleneck. Outnumbered, but better armed, two of Pleasonton's brigades charge two Confederates divisions. Their sweep around Marmaduke's right flank collapses the rebel line, killing and capturing many, including generals Marmaduke and Cabell. Panic seizes the rebels, and only the action of Shelby's "Iron Brigade" at the Little Osage slows the Union pursuit. Hundreds of Confederates are captured and those found in Union garb are executed on the spot.

4TH MISSOURI STATE MILITIA

PHILIPS

7TH MISSOURI STATE MILITIA

1ST MISSOURI STATE MILITIA

N

❶ End of the Confederate wagon train jams up on slippery south bank of Mine Creek ford. Clark falls back under Federal pressure; Marmaduke forms battle lines on north bank of creek.

❷ Philips' Missouri militia cavalry arrives first, but is too small to attack, but begins skirmishing. Benteen's brigade arrives to the left of Philips.

BENTEEN

7TH INDIANA

3RD IOWA

4TH IOWA

10TH MISSOURI

Fort Scott Road

❸ Benteen's first rank freezes mid-charge, forcing the 4th Iowa to swing left, putting it in position to flank Marmaduke.

FAGAN

CABELL

MARMADUKE

❹

❺ Rebels try to find way across creek under heavy fire, many throwing away their weapons in the rout. All rebel artillery is captured.

Shelby and Thompson's men manage to slow the Federal's advance at Little Osage River.

Mine Creek

0   .25

MILES

Palmer House

Mass panic occurs as rebel right flank collapses. The fact that many Confederates are wearing captured Federal uniforms adds to the confusion on both sides.

❻

KEY

Confederate troop movements

Union troop movements

Federal line

Confederate line

Fighting, battle

◀·············· Retreat direction

Dave Eames, Kansas City Star

Bill Anderson in death, Ray County, Missouri
Courtesy of Wilson's Creek National Battlefield,
National Park Service

Fredrick Benteen
Massachusetts Commandery Military Order of the
Loyal Legion and the U.S. Army Military History
Institute

William Cabell
State Historical Society of Missouri

William Jeffers
State Historical Society of Missouri

Federal prisoners of Price's retreating force
Kansas State Historical Society

Riley Crawford
Courtesy of collection of Emory A. Cantey, Jr.,
quantrillsguerrillas.com

Troopers at Fort Scott, Kansas
Kansas State Historical Society

Gratiot Prison, St. Louis
State Historical Society of Missouri

Notes for Chapter XIX — Closure

NOVEMBER 2 — BOONSBOROUGH, *WASHINGTON COUNTY*

The rains were only the beginning of the bad weather in Arkansas. It would turn very cold and then snow. One soldier's diary noted that wagon mules froze to death in Boonsborough.

At Fayetteville, General Fagan's men indeed did not capture much. They peppered the town during a snowstorm, but most could not be induced to attack.

The fictional exchange in this chapter is used to introduce Major General Sterling Price's official report of his campaign. Probably it was not prepared until the column reached Texas. How Lieutenant Colonel Lauchlan MacLean actually felt about the campaign is unknown.

Price's report, which noted 43 battles and skirmishes, said 16 stands of colors were captured, which seems a clear exaggeration.

For gilding the lily, Captain T. J. Mackey took top prize. As he later testified: "On the 23rd (we) engaged the enemy in force in (the) vicinity of Westport and defeated him…." Mackey was an engineer, but had a future in public relations.

Price would cross the Arkansas River on November 8, "carrying away with him the murderers, marauders and bushwhackers that infested Missouri, Arkansas and Kansas. He entered Missouri, feasting and furnishing his troops on the rich products and abundant spoils of the Missouri Valley, but crossed the Arkansas destitute, disarmed, disorganized, and avoiding starvation by eating raw corn and slippery elm bark." This was not Federal exaggeration. The Confederates' own Major John Edwards told how "Toil, agony, privation, sickness, death and starvation commenced." Wolves were hunted for meat, and there is a story of soldiers fighting over a dead skunk.

NOVEMBER 3 — ODESSA, *LAFAYETTE COUNTY, WESTERN MISSOURI*

The year before, when bushwhackers burned the courthouse in Marshall, some women were accused of displaying rebel flags or colors. One "Miss Bryant was accused of waving the skirt of a dress used in calisthenic exercises in the Boonville ladies seminary of which she was a member," noted the *History of Saline County, Missouri.* "It was made of strips of red and white muslin. She was taken to the female prison at St. Louis where she stayed for some months until released on filing a $3,000 bond."

This chapter is built in part on "Can Forgive, But Never Forget," written by Mrs. W. H. Gregg for *Reminiscences of the Women of Missouri During the Sixties.*

The rude description of the guerrilla bride was from the Leavenworth *Times*, which "reported that Coon Thornton, the guerrilla chieftain, was married a short time ago to a Miss Archer, of Platte county, a sister to one of Cy. Gordon's Lieutenants."

The woman that Lizzie Gregg heard entering the house was Martha Sanders, who supposedly rode with her bushwhacker husband, Dick Maddox. He adopted the name Matt Sanders. Legend has it that Martha Sanders did some spying, too. Shortly after the war, Dick Maddox was killed by a Cherokee in a brawl at Fort Smith, Arkansas. Martha then married George Shepherd, another former guerrilla, who had the distinction of having cut the throat of James Anderson, Bloody Bill's brother, on the lawn of the Texas Capitol in Austin. When Shepherd ended up in the Kentucky penitentiary after an 1868 bank job, she married again, making it a little troublesome when Shepherd got out. Had she ever been sweet on Cole Younger? On a snowy day during the war when his winter dugout was betrayed, Federals found Younger's gloves left behind. The pair was marked, saying they had been presented by a Miss M. E. Sanders.

Dick Maddox's brother, George, was the only guerrilla to be tried for the Lawrence outrage. After being granted a change of venue to Ottawa in 1866, he was acquitted of killing a Union man by a jury that stayed out only 10 minutes. In his Quantrill biography, Edward Leslie called it "either a stirring testament to the essential fairness of the American system of jurisprudence or an indication of the wholesale bribery of the jurors." Maddox wisely made an unobserved exit out the back of the courthouse and raced away with his wife while the Lawrence crowd in the courtroom howled their disbelief.

Without provisions, the newlywed Greggs and the rest of the party would have starved. The Burnt District was so desolate and picked over that the only food was apples in abandoned orchards. At a cabin in Indian Territory the party would share a stew of dog meat, which the women pronounced excellent. Following the path of the Price retreat, they would see dead horses and mules from which the hungry rebels had cut out steaks. The ambulance broke down, but the band attacked a militia unit and gained a wagon. Two days into the Indian lands, they fought Federal soldiers and later a combination of black troops and pro-Union tribesmen. Lizzie Gregg would recall bullets whizzing about her head on her bridal tour, but said the band only lost a horse, while killing dozens of their foes. When they got to Texas, Gregg would rejoin Shelby and his wife would stay with a transplanted aunt.

NOVEMBER 4 — COOPER COUNTY, *CENTRAL MISSOURI*

Cole Younger returned home to an uneasy existence under Radical Republican rule, helping their mother on the farm until banditry lured him away.

Everyone agrees where Riley Crawford died, Cooper County, but versions conflict on when. Some bushwhacker rolls say November, and the author chose that month to carry this tale. A memoir by Warren Welch placed Crawford's end in summer 1864. John Edwards indicated it was after George Todd's raid on Tipton on September 1. Others say it was after Centralia late that month. Whenever, his death was "lamented by his comrades," especially by Pool. Riley "had become to be regarded as something nearer than a member of his company. Boy as he was, none had ever gone further in battle, nor stood to his place longer in extremity." All seem to agree he was in the saddle when hit in the bowels with "buck and ball," a round consisting of a heavy .65-caliber ball and three buckshot pellets, "fired by a militiaman in ambush from a fence corner." This story veers from historical fact in placing Riley alone on the road as well as letting him die quickly. In truth, he lingered for hours in agony.

BIBLIOGRAPHY

T. Lindsay Baker (ed.) *Confederate Guerrilla: The Civil War Memoir of Joseph Bailey.* Fayetteville: University of Arkansas Press, 2007.

Michael E. Banasik (ed.) *Cavaliers of the Brush.* Iowa City, Iowa: Press of the Camp Pope Bookshop, 2003.

Michael E. Banasik (ed.) *Missouri in 1861: The Civil War Letters of Franc B. Wilkie.* Iowa City, Iowa: Press of the Camp Pope Bookshop, 2001.

Carolyn Bartels (ed.) *The Civil War in Missouri Day by Day, 1861 to 1865.* Independence, Missouri: Two Trails Publishing, 1992.

Carolyn Bartels (ed.) *The Last Long Mile, Westport to Arkansas, October 1864.* Independence, Missouri: Two Trails Publishing, 1999.

O. S. Barton. *Three Years With Quantrill, A True Story Told by His Scout John McCorkle.* Norman: University of Oklahoma Press, 1914, 1992.

Bryce Benedict. *Jayhawkers: The Civil War Brigade of James Henry Lane.* Norman: University of Oklahoma Press, 2009.

Ira Berlin, Barbara Fields, Steven Miller, Joseph Reidy and Leslie Rowland (eds.) *Free At Last: A Documentary History of Slavery, Freedom, and the Civil War.* New York: The New Press, 1992.

Roy Bird. *Civil War in Kansas.* Gretna, Louisiana: Pelican Publishing Co., 2004.

Wiley Britton. *Civil War on the Border, Vol. II.* New York: G. P. Putnam & Sons, 1895.

Richard S. Brownlee. *Gray Ghosts of the Confederacy: Guerrilla Warfare in the West 1861-1865.* Baton Rouge: Louisiana State University Press, 1958.

Lumir F. Buresh. *October 25th and the Battle of Mine Creek.* Kansas City: Lowell Press, 1977.

Seymour D. Carpenter. *Autobiography, and Personal Reminiscences, of*

Dr. Seymour D. Carpenter, Lieutenant Colonel, in the War for the Union.

New York: The New York Public Library, Astor, Lenox and Tilden Foundations, 1914.

Albert Castel. *Civil War Kansas: Reaping the Whirlwind.* Lawrence: University Press of Kansas, 1958, revised 1997.

Albert Castel. *General Sterling Price and the Civil War in the West.* Baton Rouge: Louisiana State University Press, 1996.

Albert Castel and Thomas Goodrich. *Bloody Bill Anderson: The Short, Savage Life of a Civil War Guerrilla.* Mechanicsburg, Pennsylvania: Stackpole Books, 1998.

Jack Coggins. *Arms and Equipment of the Civil War.* Garden City, New York: Doubleday & Co., 1962.

Richard Collins. *General James G. Blunt: Tarnished Glory.* Gretna, Louisiana: Pelican Publishing Co., 2005.

William E. Connelley. *A Standard History of Kansas and Kansans.* Chicago: Lewis Publishing Co., 1918.

William E. Connelley. *Quantrill and the Border Wars.* White Fish, Montana: Kessinger Publishing, 2004. (First published in 1910: Cedar Rapids, Iowa: Torch Press, and in 1956: New York, Pageant Book Co.)

Richard Cordley. *A History of Lawrence.* Lawrence, Kansas: E. F. Cordwell, Lawrence Journal Press, 1895.

Samuel John Crawford. *Kansas in the Sixties.* Chicago: M. F. Hall Printing Co., 1911.

H. H. Crittenden. *The Battle of Westport.* Kansas City: Lowell Press, 1935.

Roger D. Cunningham. *The Black citizen-soldiers of Kansas, 1864-1901.* Columbia: University of Missouri Press, 2008.

William A. Davis. *Diary of a Confederate Soldier: John S. Jackson of the Orphan Brigade.* Columbia: University of South Carolina Press, 1990.

Joanne Chiles Eakin (ed.) *Recollections of Quantrill's Guerrillas, as Told by A. J. Walker.* Independence, Missouri: Two Trails Publishing, 1996.

Joanne Chiles Eakin and Annette Curtis (eds.) *Terror on the Border.* Independence, Missouri, 2007.

Joanne Chiles Eakin and Donald R. Hale (eds.) *Branded as Rebels.* Independence, Missouri: Print America, 1993.

John N. Edwards. *Noted Guerrillas, or the Warfare of the Border.* St. Louis: Bryan, Brand & Co., 1877.

John N. Edwards. *Shelby and His Men; or, The War in the West.* Cincinnati: Miami Printing and Publishing, 1867.

Michael Fellman. *Inside War: The Guerrilla Conflict in Missouri During the American Civil War.* New York: Oxford University Press, 1989.

Harriet C. Frazier. *Runaway and Freed Missouri Slaves and Those Who Helped Them, 1763-1875.* Jefferson, North Carolina: McFarland & Co., 2004.

Griffin Frost. *Camp and Prison Journal embracing scenes in camp on the march and in prisons.* Quincy, Illinois: Quincy Herald Book and Job, 1867.

Henry Louis Gates, Jr. (ed.) *Lincoln on Race & Slavery.* Princeton, New Jersey: Princeton University Press, 2009.

Donald L. Gilmore. *Civil War on the Missouri-Kansas Border.* Gretna, Louisiana: Pelican Publishing Co., 2006.

Thomas Goodman. *A Thrilling Record: Founded on Facts and Observations obtained during ten days' experience with Colonel William T. Anderson.* Des Moines, Iowa: Mills & Co., 1868.

Thomas Goodrich. *Black Flag: Guerrilla Warfare on the Western Border, 1861-1865.* Bloomington: Indiana University Press, 1995.

Phil Gottschalk. *In Deadly Earnest: The Missouri Brigade.* Columbia, Missouri: Missouri River Press, 1991.

Richard J. Hinton. *Rebel Invasion of Missouri and Kansas and the Campaign of the Army of the Border Against General Sterling Price, in October and November, 1864.* Ottawa, Kansas: Kansas Heritage Press, 1994. (First published in 1865: Chicago, Church and Goodman.)

Louis O. Honig. *Westport: Gateway To The Early West.* It Happened in America Series, c. 1950.

Paul B. Jenkins. *The Battle of Westport.* Kansas City: Franklin Hudson Publishing Co., 1906.

Philip Katcher. *American Civil War Commanders: Confederate Leaders in the West.* Oxford, United Kingdom: Osprey Publishing, 2003.

Fred L. Lee (ed.) *The Battle of Westport.* Kansas City: Westport Historical Society, 1982.

Fred L. Lee. *Gettysburg of the West, the Battle of Westport, Oct. 21-23, 1864.* Independence, Missouri: Two Trails Publishing, 1996.

Edward E. Leslie. *The Devil Knows How to Ride: The True Story of William Clarke Quantrill and his Confederate Raiders.* New York: Random House, 1996.

James E. McGhee. *Campaigning with Marmaduke: Narrative and Roster of the 8th Missouri Cavalry Regiment CSA.* Independence, Missouri: Two Trails Publishing, 2002.

William M. McPheeters. *I Acted from Principle: The Civil War diary of Dr. Will M. McPheeters, Confederate surgeon in the Trans-Mississippi.* Edited by Cynthia DeHaven Pitcock and Bill J. Gurley. Fayetteville: University of Arkansas Press,2002.

Jay Monaghan. *Civil War on the Western Border, 1854-1865.* Lincoln: University of Nebraska Press, 1955.

Howard N. Monnett. *Action Before Westport, 1864.* Niwot, Colorado: University Press of Colorado, 1964, revised 1995.

Col. John C. Moore. *Confederate Military History, Extended Version.* Wilmington, North Carolina: Broadfoot Publishing Co., 1988. (First published in 1898: Atlanta, Confederate Publishing Co.)

Joseph A. Mudd. *With Porter in North Missouri.* Washington: National Publishing Co., 1909.

Doris Land Mueller. *M. Jeff Thompson, Missouri's Swamp Fox of the Confederacy.* Columbia: University of Missouri Press, 2007.

William Barclay Napton. *Past and Present of Saline County Missouri.* Indianapolis: B. F. Bowen & Co., 1910.

Jeremy Neely. *The Border Between Them, Violence and Reconciliation on the Kansas-Missouri Line.* Columbia: University of Missouri Press, 2007.

Bruce Nichols. *Guerrilla Warfare in Civil War Missouri, Vol. I, 1863.* Jefferson, North Carolina: McFarland & Co., 2004.

Bruce Nichols. *Guerrilla Warfare in Civil War Missouri, Vol. II, 1863.* Jefferson, North Carolina: McFarland & Co., 2007.

Daniel O'Flaherty. *General Jo Shelby: Undefeated Rebel.* Chapel Hill: University of North Carolina Press, 1954.

William E. Parish. *Frank Blair, Lincoln's Conservative.* Columbia: University of Missouri Press, 1998.

William E. Parish. *Missouri Under Radical Rule – 1865-1870.* Columbia: University of Missouri Press, 1965.

W. M. Paxton. *Annals of Platte County.* Kansas City: Hudson-Kimberly Publishing Co., 1897.

Cyrus Peterson and Joseph Hanson. *Pilot Knob: the Thermopylae of the West.* New York: Neale Publishing Co., 1914.

Paul R. Petersen. *Quantrill of Missouri: The Making of a Guerrilla Warrior.* Nashville, Tennessee: Cumberland House, 2003.

Christopher Phillips. *Missouri's Confederate.* Columbia: University of Missouri Press, 2000.

William Garret Piston and Thomas P. Sweeny. *Portraits of Conflict: A Photographic History of Missouri in the Civil War.* Fayetteville: University of Arkansas Press, 2009.

Jerry Ponder. *Major General John S. Marmaduke CSA.* Mason, Texas: Ponder Books, 1999.

Thomas C. Reynolds. *General Sterling Price and the Confederacy.* Edited by Robert G. Schultz. St. Louis: Missouri History Museum, distributed by University of Missouri Press, 2009.

William Forse Scott. *The Story of a Cavalry Regiment, The Career of the Fourth Iowa Veteran Volunteers, From Kansas to Georgia 1861-1865.* New York: G. P. Putnam's Sons, 1893.

Deryl Sellmeyer. *Jo Shelby's Iron Brigade.* Gretna, Louisiana: Pelican Publishing, 2007.

William A. Settle, Jr. *Jesse James Was His Name.* Columbia: University of Missouri Press, 1966.

Robert E. Shalope. *Sterling Price: Portrait of a Southerner.* Columbia: University of Missouri Press, 1971.

Ronald D. Smith. *Thomas Ewing Jr.; Frontier Lawyer and Civil War General.* Columbia: University of Missouri Press, 2008.

Leverett Wilson Spring. *Kansas: The Prelude to the War for the Union.* Boston: Houghton, Mifflin and Company, 1885.

Ian Michael Spurgeon. *Man of Douglass, Man of Lincoln: The Political Odyssey of James Henry Lane.* Columbia: University of Missouri Press, 2008.

Stephen Z. Starr. *Jennison's Jayhawkers: A Civil War Cavalry Regiment and its Commander.* Baton Rouge: Louisiana State University Press, 1973.

James W. Steel. *The Battle of the Blue of the Second Regiment, K. S. M, Oct. 22, 1864.* Chicago, 1896.

T. J. Stiles. *Jesse James: Last Rebel of the Civil War.* New York: Alfred A. Knopf, 2002.

Donal Stanton, Goodwin Berquist and Paul Bowers (eds.) *The Civil War Reminiscences of General M. Jeff Thompson.* Dayton, Ohio: Morningside House Inc., 1998.

Jason Schwartz. *Fighting Words: Pistol Packin' Dan Anthony and Frontier Journalism.* Philadelphia: University of Pennsylvania, 2007.

Union Historical Company. *The History of Jackson County.* Kansas City: Birdsall, Williams & Co., 1881.

Dorothy Denneen Volo and James M. Volo. *Daily Life in the Civil War America.* Westport, Connecticut: Greenwood Press, 1998.

Hamp B. Watts. *The Babe of the Company.* Springfield, Missouri: Oak Hills Publishing, 1996. (First published in 1913: Fayette, Missouri, Democrat-Leader Press.)

W. L. Webb. *Battles and Biographies of Missourians or the Civil War Period of our State.* Kansas City: Hudson-Kimberly Pub. Co., 1900.

Franc B. Wilkie. *Pen and Powder.* Boston: Ticknor and Company, 1888.

Ellen Williams. *Three Years and a Half in the Army: A History of the Second Colorado.* New York: Fowler & Wells Co., 1885.

Larry Wood. *Other Noted Guerrillas of the Civil War in Missouri.* Joplin, Missouri: Hickory Press, 2007.

Larry Wood. *The Civil War Story of Bloody Bill Anderson.* Austin, Texas: Eakin Press, 2003.

Ted P. Yeatman. *Frank and Jesse James: The Story Behind the Legend.* Nashville, Tennessee: Cumberland House, 2000.

Cole Younger. *The Story of Cole Younger, By Himself.* Chicago: Henneberry Company, 1903.

History of Boone County, Missouri. St. Louis: Western Historical Co., 1882.

The War of the Rebellion: A Compilation of the Official Records of the Union and Confederate Armies, Series I, Vol. 22, Part I, and Vol. 41, Part I, II, III, IV, Washington, D. C.: Government Printing Office, 1880-1901.

ARTICLES AND REPORTS

Samuel O. Bereman. "Diary of Sergeant of 4th Iowa Cavalry." Internet published.

Michael E. Carter, Maj., USAF. "First Kansas Colored Volunteers: Contributions of Black Union Soldiers in the Trans-Mississippi West. 'Master's thesis, Webster University, Kansas City, Missouri, 2000, Fort Leavenworth, Kansas, 2004.

Roger D. Cunningham. "Douglas's Battery at Fort Leavenworth: The Issue of Black Officers During the Civil War," *Kansas History,* Winter 2000-2001.

Roger D. Cunningham. "Welcoming 'Pa' on the Kaw: Kansas's 'Colored' Militia and the 1864 Price Raid," *Kansas History,* Summer 2002.

James M. Denny. "The Battle of Marshall: The Greatest Little Battle That was Never Fought," Remarks prepared by the Missouri Natural Resources historian for the Mid-America Civil War Round Table, 2001.

Joanne Chiles Eakin (ed.) "The Story Behind the Letter," *The Blue & Gray Chronicle,* Vol. 4, No. 1, Independence, Missouri, October 2000.

Joanne Chiles Eakin (ed.) "Anderson Girls" and "Murderous Scoundrels: Some of Quantrill's Men at Lawrence," *The Blue & Gray Chronicle,* Vol. 2, No. 4, Independence, Missouri, April 2008.

Thomas J. Fleming. "Verdicts of History, III: The Trial of John Brown," *American Heritage,* August 1967.

Simeon M. Fox. "The Story of the Seventh Kansas," *Kansas State Historical Society Collections,* Vol. 8, 1903-1904.

Marian Franklin (ed.) "The Watts Hays Letters," first published online in 2006.

Albert R. Greene. "What I Saw of the Quantrill Raid," *Kansas Historical Society Collections,* Vol. 13, 1913-1914.

Mrs. W. H. Gregg. "Can Forgive, But Never Forget," *Reminiscences of the Women of Missouri During the Sixties,* Missouri Division, United Daughters of the Confederacy, reprinting by Morningside House, Inc., Dayton, Ohio, 1988.

George S. Grover. "The Price Campaign of 1864," *Missouri Historical Review,* Vol. 6, April 1912.

Erich Langsdorf. "Jim Lane and the Frontier Guard," *Collections of the Kansas Historical Quarterly*, Vol. 6, No. 3, February 1940.

William Lay and Bob Dyer. "Civil War Incidents in Howard County," *Boone's Lick Heritage*, Vol. 6, No. 1, March 1998.

Vivian Kirkpatrick (ed.) "The Civil War Letters of Colonel Bazel F. Lazear," *Missouri Historical Review*, Vol. 44 & 45, April, July, October 1950.

Kip Lindberg. "Chaos Itself: The Battle of Mine Creek," *North & South*, Vol. 1, No. 6, August 1998.

Kip Lindberg and Matt Matthews. "The Baxter Springs Massacre," *North & South*, Vol. 4, No. 5, June 2001.

David D. March. "Charles D. Drake and the Constitutional Convention of 1865," *Missouri Historical Review*, Vol. 47, January 1953.

Matt Matthews and Kip Lindberg. "'Better Off In Hell' The Evolution of the Kansas Red Legs," *North & South*, Vol. 5, No. 4, May 2002.

George T. Ness, Jr. "Missouri at West Point: Graduates Through the Civil War Years," *Missouri Historical Review*, Vol. 38, October 1943.

Henry E. Palmer. "The Soldiers of Kansas: Company A, Eleventh Kansas Regiment, in the Price Raid," *Kansas State Historical Society Collections*, Vol. 9, 1906.

Henry E. Palmer. "The Soldiers of Kansas: The Black-Flag Character of War on the Border," *Kansas State Historical Society Collections*, Vol. 9, 1906.

J. David Petruzzi. "The Fleeting Fame of Alfred Pleasonton," *America's Civil War*, March 2005.

Fletcher Pomeroy war diary. "The 7th Kansas Cavalry in the Civil War." Topeka: Kansas Historical Society.

Scott A. Porter. "'Bashi-Bazouks' and Rebels Too: Action at Camden Point, July 13, 1864," *Missouri Historical Review*, Vol. 101, January 2007.

Marguerite Potter. "Hamilton R. Gamble, Missouri's War Governor," *Missouri Historical Review*, Vol. 35, October 1940.

Scott E. Sallee. "Missouri! One Last Time," *Blue & Gray*, June 1991.

Scott E. Sallee. "Porter's Campaign in Northeast Missouri, 1862," *Blue & Gray*, February 2000.

Kyle S. Sinisi. "Adapting to Maneuver Warfare in a Civil War Campaign: Union Reactions to Sterling Price's Missouri Expedition of 1864." Fort Leavenworth, Kansas: Combat Studies Institute Press, August 2005.

Walter B. Stevens. "Lincoln and Missouri," *Missouri Historical Review*, Vol. 10, January 1916.

Mary B. Townsend, "The Third Iowa Cavalry in Sterling Price's 1864 Missouri Raid." *Missouri Historical Review*, Vol. 105, October 2010.

"The Battle of Mine Creek and The Capture of Marmaduke," *St. Louis Globe Democrat*, September 13, 1884.

NEWSPAPERS

Daily Missouri Democrat of St. Louis

The Missouri Republican of St. Louis

Kansas City Western Journal of Commerce

The Daily Times of Leavenworth

The Commercial of Leavenworth

ACKNOWLEDGEMENTS

I would like to acknowlege the many friends and long-suffering family members who supported me through the writing and polishing of these old tales. I also wish to thank *The Kansas City Star* for the opportunity to recount the war in the border region and to let many Civil War historians, archivists, authors and enthusiasts know how much I appreciate their assistance in my reconstructions of this fateful fall in 1864. Last, I would wish to remember my late parents who would have loved this book even if it were not written by their son. My father could not pass a single Gettysburg monument without hopping out of the car; my mother was a history lover in her own way, a voracious reader of biographies. One of the greatest of their many gifts was the life-enriching appreciation of the world's narrative.